True Love and Bartholomew

Rebels on the
Burmese border

For Eh Doh and Zenobe

Contents

List of illustrations   viii

Foreword   xi

Preface   xv

Acknowledgements   xxii

1   A bronze drum   1

2   Boar Tusk's children   11

3   White collar Flowerland   31

4   True Love at home   52

5   Water child, land child   65

6   A simple man   82

7   Fighting mean, fighting clean   102

8   Great Lake and the Elephant Man   118

9   Bartholomew's boarders   141

10   The three seasons   161

Interlude: from the Kok river   183

11   Last of the longhouses   196

12   A delicate bamboo tongue   220

13   True Love in love   243

14   Fermented monkey faeces   263

15   Perfect hosts   282

16   Old guard, young Turks   296

17   True Love and White Rock   320

18   Insurgents in a landscape   338

19   True Love and sudden death   359

20   Portraits   372

Notes   379

Bibliography   387

Index   391

Illustrations

1 The bamboo dance: 'They had to skip through a
moving grid of poles.'   8
2 'They keep away from the markets and the beaten
track, fully occupied with the thousand tasks that weigh
upon them.'   19
3 Riverside: 'Army and militia families lived beyond the
jail.'   33
4 True Love and Silver's house '. . . became usable bit
by bit'.   56
5 'Barterville has a harbour, an inlet from the main
stream where boats are safe from the current.'   74
6 '. . . calling at every home in the name of the Revolution:
"It's Thera Bartholomew. Anyone sick?"'   100
7 'A garment to gladden the hearts of *Soldier of Fortune*
readers.'   104
8 'To own elephants is the dream of every family.'   129
9 A trainee nurse making rice ration sacks. 'Their desires
were impossible to gauge, but they could be seen to
dream.'   158
10 'Everyone is waiting. When the rain stops, the harvest
and the fighting will commence together.'   162
11 Militia at Maw Daung. 'I thought they looked a sad
and feeble bunch. They proved me wrong later.'   213
12 Pastor Moses reading from the Sgaw Karen New
Testament at an evening prayer meeting.   225
13 'Moses performs the ceremony . . . just as at any Baptist
wedding anywhere in the world.'   251
14 'The need for positive solidarity being greater than ever,
pork feasts are central to any National Day.'   274
15 'These are just church people who have never been
outside Australia before.'   283
16 Colonel Marvel instructs a young militiaman. 'I was
young and vigorous then. Today I am a much older

Published by the Press Syndicate of the University of Cambridge
The Pitt Building, Trumpington Street, Cambridge CB2 1RP
40 West 20th Street, New York, NY 10011, USA
10 Stamford Road, Oakleigh, Melbourne 3166, Australia

First published 1991

Printed in Great Britain at The Bath Press, Avon

British Library cataloguing in publication data

Falla, Jonathan
True love and Bartholomew: rebels on the Burmese border.
1. Burma. Karen. Social conditions
I. Title
305.895

Library of Congress cataloguing in publication data

Falla, Jonathan
True love and Bartholomew: rebels on the Burmese border/Jonathan Falla.
     p.   cm.
Includes bibliographical references.
1. Karen (Southeast Asian people)–Politics and government.
2. Burma–Politics and government–1948–   I. Title.
DS528.2.K35F35   1990
959.1′00495–dc20

ISBN 0 521 39019 2 hard covers

BS

True Love
and Bartholomew

Rebels on the Burmese border

JONATHAN FALLA

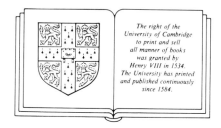

The right of the
University of Cambridge
to print and sell
all manner of books
was granted by
Henry VIII in 1534.
The University has printed
and published continuously
since 1584.

CAMBRIDGE UNIVERSITY PRESS
Cambridge
New York   Port Chester
Melbourne   Sydney

man. But my belief in our future has not dimmed one
bit.'   305
17 'These were the most contented afternoons that we had
together.'   335
18 The church at Betelwood, with school classes
underneath.   345
19 'The KNLA began to show its desperation, recruiting
women and young boys.'   369
20 My neighbours posing: 'Now they want all the portraits
that they can get.'   377

MAP

Map of Burma (Myanmar)   xxiii

Foreword

by Nigel Barley

The names of most areas of the world elicit a simple but powerful response in the minds of anthropologists. Each bears the burden of a particular specialisation. Australia 'means' art and kinship, Africa lineages, witchcraft and magic, India castes and religion. Largely this is because classic texts of the past have burned these associations into the heads of generations of students.

It is the misfortune of Burma to 'mean' politics. Students of anthropology cut their teeth on the politics of Burma, but a politics reduced to abstract systems that permit a sort of detached overview. There are no people in such systems, just a faceless interplay of forces and models that swing back and forth suspended in a sort of idealised time.

In *True Love and Bartholomew*, Jonathan Falla offers us the *human* face of political change in contemporary Burma, a behind-the-lines view of the Karen Free State. It is a place at once very real yet almost imaginary, a place unrecognised or rather wilfully forgotten by the outside world, a mountain enclave continuing a struggle with lowland Burma that is older than any of its people know. Used against the Burmese and Japanese then swiftly abandoned by the colonial British, 'won' for Christ by missionaries, the Karen are currently fighting for their identity and their very lives. This is not an adventure story, for the bloody battles with the Burmese, the rapes and tortures suffered at their hands are off-scene and merely rumble in the distance like stage thunder. We encounter them as memories or consequences. Nor are these Karen noble, uncorrupted hill tribesmen whose austere lives are an example of simple integrity to the spoiled children of the West. Like ourselves they are trying to find a way to make sense of their lives.

Riverside, where the book takes place, is a village of functionaries, of more or less displaced persons, where the seriousness of events is judged by their ability to disrupt administrative regularity. In a country of sarongs, it alternates between the white collars of modernism and the striped shirts of traditional identity. This adds

to the unreality of the place for there is always something unreal
about empires of paper and the way they can be used to create
a substitute world, sustained by illocutionary force alone. Indeed,
it is only the individuals here who seem real at all, since events
impinge not with a bang but a dull reverberation of official responsibilities. Even the collective identity of the Karen seems mysterious
and unfocussed with groups moving in and out of 'Karen-ness'
according to shifting circumstance. Much of everyday life becomes
a protracted attempt to define just what 'real' Karen means.

Time comes in here again, for Jonathan Falla's text somehow
conveys that difference in the speed of time that marks off remote
places, even if that remoteness consists of only a few hours' walk
from the frenetic rush of urban life. People seem to move at a slower
pace. Outlines are less sharp. The air is thicker and has a colour
and resistance of its own. It is here that Bartholomew, True Love
and the others with their fragrant names lead their lives and combine
the political public rites of a national state with the family warmth
of an Asian village. Their trials and triumphs speak to us in a
way that is both earthy and deeply moving.

This is not a book of political polemic that pleads the Karen
cause. Jonathan Falla, indeed, finds many aspects of the Karen
revolution unpalatable. It is pervaded by a sense of sadness at the
suffering and hopelessness of an unwinable war and the bleak future
of refugee Karen in an increasingly unfriendly Thailand. Yet it
is not political argument that wins our sympathy but the representation of an appealing humanity in the round.

One of the conventional tests of an account of an alien culture
is how much it all clicks and fits with no loose ends, its inevitability
engineered in from the start. But we all know that life outside con-
structed ethnographies is not like that and *True Love and Bartholomew*
has a rich sense of the incongruities and absurdities of the human
lot. History, politics, arcana from the meaning of tattooing to the
technology of vernacular architecture – all pass before us almost
incidentally as in everyday experience. There is all the erudition
that we find in more formal texts but with none of the pretension.
What we are finally offered is a fresh and sharp view that is anthropological in the truest sense. It conveys to us the 'feel' of another
way of life.

Jonathan Falla went to the Karen as a Western-trained nurse
to assess their medical needs yet he has a number of cultures on
which to draw, the Jamaica of his birth, Indonesia where he studied

traditional music and Uganda where he worked for OXFAM. He has previously published poetry and translations of Malay fiction as well as written on topics as diverse as travel, ethnomusicology, developmental politics and tropical health. Perhaps it is this that gives him that ability to move sympathetically and easily between worlds that readers will find in these pages.

Preface

Down the long spine of hills that divides Thailand from Burma lies a string of independent states unrecognised by any government except each other's – and most certainly not by the government in Rangoon, against whom they are rebelling. These are the enclaves of Burma's insurgent ethnic minorities, the Kachin, Karen, Wa, Shan and others, together with the outlawed Burma Communist Party and, over on the western border with India, the Arakanese and Chin. The Burmese government says that it is currently facing thirty-three separate rebellions; some of these, notably those of the Communists and the Karen, have dragged on since the late 1940s – four decades of forest warfare.

Of all these insurgent peoples, the Karen have long held a special place in European and North American affections, since well before the present troubles began. This is partly because of dramatic successes by American Baptist Missionaries in the nineteenth century, giving rise to the idea of the Karen as a chosen people waiting to be liberated by the 'white younger brother' of their own prophecies. But there were other factors. The Karen have on several occasions fought and died in support of the British, most remarkably in the Second World War, when their suffering and resilience impressed their colonial masters. Besides which, visitors have rarely failed to be delighted by their generosity and openness, and to be surprised by their sheer numbers. Possibly 4 million people may be regarded as Karen (the estimates, and the criteria, vary widely).

Prior to 1986, I had never heard of them; among my friends and relations, only my anthropologist brother had. Britain soon forgot her wartime allies and the Karen could hardly believe the speed with which they were 'sold out' to their old enemies the Burmese, and the lack of interest in their fate since. Bemused by this neglect and betrayal, the Karen from time to time send off letters to the Queen and to Mrs Thatcher recalling past loyalty and requesting support. They receive no reply.

Meanwhile, the missionary fad has long since waned. As early as 1907 a report prepared for the University of Chicago thankfully noted 'a very marked decline in the cult of the Karen'.[1] The most recent general description of Karen society in Burma, by Harry Marshall, dates from 1922. Almost all the early descriptions were either by missionaries or by colonial civil servants. When post-war, independent Burma closed her doors to foreign researchers, most work on the Karen there ceased.

There are Karen in Thailand also; a flow of migrants and refugees from successive wars has built up their numbers over the last two centuries. Modern accounts have looked only at these Thai-Karen, who live as quietly and as unobtrusively as they can, hoping only to be accepted by Thai society and officials. But a major aspect of Karen life since the first records of them in the eighth century AD has been the almost constant, and frequently violent, confrontation with more powerful lowland peoples in Burma. Life is different in Burma, and it is the Burmese that they fight today. Their rebel state, which they call Kawthoolei, is entirely within the borders of Burma. Normally able to stay and work with Karen only in Thailand, contemporary writers can at best give only an embarrassed nod towards that crucial feature of Karen consciousness, the rebellion in Burma, while most journalists who cross the border have only a passing interest in the war as a cultural phenomenon. The Karen have been resisting and fighting the lowland states for a millennium or more. Oppressed they may be, but rebellion is a deeply embedded part of their very identity.

Kawthoolei is often translated as 'Flowerland', but the precise etymology of the name is debatable,[2] and flowers, at least in the usual colourful English sense of the word, are few and far between in the hill forests.

Although very dense, this is tropical rainforest only by the broadest classification. In fact, for several months of the year it is tinder dry. It is more accurately designated as Mixed Deciduous Forest, crowned by hardwood trees of spectacular height with, growing between and draped among them, ferns, low scrubby bushes, clumps of bamboo, vines and creepers, orchids and lianas. During the rains (May to October) there are a thousand shades of green but, as the forest dries out around Christmas, these begin to turn to olive greys, yellow and ochre. Every year, fires burn off much of the undergrowth, leaving the great hardwoods standing in blackened debris which does something to enrich the sand and muddy laterites of the topsoil. 'Teak forest', it is often called, but in our district, if there ever had been many *tectona grandis* to be seen, they were long since felled.

At some 1,500 kilometres north of the Equator, the seasons are well marked. In pre-monsoon April and May the heat is oppressive, but dry season nights can be bitter; Karen occasionally experience near-freezing temperatures in the northern hills. These hills rise to peaks of around 2,000 metres. The border landscape is marked on small-scale maps as a spine of an even, pale brown. The larger the scale, however, the more confused and broken are the ridges and river valleys. The jumble of near-identical green-clad slopes drives cartographers to a despairing confession: 'Contours impossible to reconcile'. Man-made landmarks are often easier to grasp; the villages, the little pockets of farmed colluvial flatland in the bends of the rivers, the slash-and-burn ricefields on the steep hillsides, the scars of deforestation and of open-cast tin mining. But these are all very transient.

Prior to the Second World War, writers such as Reginald Le May, Maurice Collis and Reginald Campbell described these Thai-Burmese forests as infested with tigers, white rhinoceros and other perils. Little of that particular excitement survives. I never heard or saw anything of the tigers that patrolled the perimeters of the nineteenth- and early twentieth-century travellers' camps, snatching away their porters and their ponies. Nor had any Karen I met there. The villagers once sheltered from carnivores (and from each other) in longhouses enclosed in thick stockades – but no longer. Only the elderly Justice of our district, Harvest Moon, claimed to have met a black panther on a forest path in his youth: 'I pointed my umbrella at it like a rifle – then we both ran away.'

Dangers there still are, smaller-scale but unpleasant enough. Leeches and ticks gorge on you, but at least the resulting infections are merely local. The mosquitoes kill. This is one of the most malarial – and drug-resistant – areas of the world. Everyone has malaria. Even small children have abdomens packed with grotesquely distended spleens, the result of innumerable attacks.

But the forest has many pleasures also – the slow, magnificent hornbills beating high over the river, or the dozen species of kingfisher skimming across below. The wild parliaments of monkeys and the glimpsed mountain bears, the elegant green tree snakes and gabbling button-tailed drongo birds. They all provide wonderful company on forest walks, and fine eating afterwards. There is the strange explosive crack of bamboos splitting in the dry heat, and the sinister and spectacular forest fires that explode in high columns by day and creep in slow ranks across the hills by night. 'Flowerland' is no Arcady, but only to those who hate the livestock and the enclosure is it 'jungle'.

It is certainly not impenetrable. At the village of Riverside, where I mostly stayed, I was an easy fifteen km walk from the Thai border. Except in heavy rain, cars could get in and out readily. A Thai city was just three hours drive away. This was not a fearful wilderness in the back of beyond.

I spent most of the year from October 1986/7 in the Karen Free State of Kawthoolei. I had a variety of research interests, into music, into language and 'culture', and into public health, supported in this last by a small London-based charitable agency called Health Unlimited. This organisation offers 'care amidst conflict': that is, they try and assist civilian populations in areas cut off from government services by war or similar disruption. Our project was to survey the demography and disease patterns, the economics and the drug supplies in rebel territory, and then to investigate the viability of a village health-care scheme, working with Kawthoolei's Health and Welfare Department and starting out perhaps by training paramedics. I should stress that the opinions and ideas expressed in this book are my own, and not the responsibility of Health Unlimited.

All my visits were to one district of the rebel state; not the General Headquarters, but an area that had long been regarded as a quiet backwater of the war and was only now beginning to see sustained Burmese pressure. The society that I found here was typical neither of the 'traditional' Karen hilltribes – who may still be found in other areas of Burma and Thailand – nor even of Kawthoolei as a whole. It was, rather, a bizarre forest hybrid of tradition and revolution, with a powerful character of its own.

I lived in a family house and tried to speak the language; this book describes what I saw and learnt. It is not a travelogue, nor an adventure story; I was never involved in any fighting. Nor is it a history – although chapter two does give some account of how the Karen came to be in their present plight. It is, rather, a portrait of what appeared to me to be a very singular thing – a completely illegal and unrecognised nation state defended by only a few thousand armed men, which has yet been the home of thousands of families since well before I was born.

In this state, most of the people have only ever known a condition of war. But the state has provided food for many, and the only health care, education and other services and infrastructure that they've ever known, and all from bamboo or roughsawn timber huts in the midst of a forest. All the machinery of government is there – an executive and an army, a judiciary and a foreign office, tax gatherers and teachers, doctors and nurses, agricultural, mining and forestry officers, Transport and Communications Departments, organisations of Youth and of Women, a prison service, a treasury and an established church. They have had forty years to get organised.

I am not an apologist for Kawthoolei. There are many aspects of the rebellion that I cannot like, and I have persuasive friends who argue that they should have given up this particular fight long ago and sought some political accommodation within the Union of Burma. But, as the Burmese Army closes in, their choices are horribly limited and many of them simply don't know what to do. Like decent people anywhere, most Karen just wish that the war would go away. In the meantime, their villages are being burnt, their men shot and their women raped. Large numbers of them find themselves in that deadest of ends, a Thai refugee camp. The Karen cannot win their war. As the last of their self-determination is whittled away, there is for me a poignant urgency in writing about the brief period when they have actually attempted what historians and archaeologists deny in their past, but their stories claim they once possessed – a state of their own.

A note on language, and proper names: Kawthoolei is a polyglot place. Many Karen rebels are Rangoon-educated, many preserve strong links with the British. Apart from several distinct varieties of the Karen language, English and Burmese are both widely spoken with widely differing degrees of proficiency. The same speaker may, in mixed company, switch rapidly between all these. My own conversations were similarly jumbled. My friend True Love spoke fluent English, so that is what we used together. Bartholomew spoke no English, and with him I spoke Sgaw Karen. Great Lake, William and others came anywhere between the two, and our conversations were a happy macaronic babble. It would be impossible for me to imitate all these variations or to indicate every degree of translation taking place, and so I'm afraid the reader must accept a possibly rather bland uniformity of English rendition of the conversations.

A number of songs and rhymes are quoted. With one or two obvious exceptions, these were all originally in Karen and noted or tape-recorded by me. Any English translations given are my own, as assisted by True Love and other friends. Copies of the recordings are now with the British Institute of Recorded Sound (National Sound Archive) at 29 Exhibition Road, London SW7.

Karen proper names are as linguistically confused as is the language of daily speech. A Karen may carry a whole clutch of names including one Burmese, one English, one formal Karen name and a nickname too. Karen give their children nicknames (wrote Harry Marshall: 1922, p. 170) in order to disguise their love. A name implying parental contempt – Stinkpot, Rottenfish or the like – fools malevolent spirits into thinking that the parents cannot be harmed by an attack on the children.

The English name might have no particular connection with the Karen or Burmese. It is often biblical in character – James, Moses, Ruth – but equally it might be Frank or Daphne. Sometimes the English is a literal translation of a Karen or Burmese name (True Love, for example) but others are just approximations of sound: thus, a man with the Burmese name Lin Naing is also known as Lionel.

There are no rules at all as to which name a person is commonly known by. Thus I might find myself talking with three young men known locally as Kan Gyi (a Burmese name), Wah Paw (Karen) and Wilfred. There are numerous instances of this in the following chapters. I have usually altered names for the sake of privacy, but have not tried to unscramble the characteristic mix. For place names, I have usually given a simple English approximation to the Karen original. As these are people's homes in a dangerous and politically sensitive area, I cannot specify the precise location.

Karen script is based on Burmese, and is quite unlike our own. As a result there are wide variations in spelling when Karen is rendered into English. Kawthoolei, for example, may be spelt Kaw Thu Lay or Kawthule. For the sake of clarity and consistency I have taken one spelling and stuck to it. This has occasionally meant altering the spellings given by other authors in quotations.

Even as I prepared this book for press, one name has been changed by government dictum, that of Burma itself, which in mid 1989 was declared to be now called the Union of Myanmar. This is apparently a revival of a pre-colonial title. It is rather as though Westminster were to announce that Britain is now called Albion.

I fully acknowledge the right of any country to call itself whatever it may wish, and perhaps in some future edition of this book we might change Burma to Myanmar throughout. But, for the present, I'm afraid Myanmar means nothing to me, and I have not used it.

Strathdon, Aberdeenshire
1988

Acknowledgements

I needed a lot of help in writing this book. Expert advice, information and encouragement came from Professors Robert Le Page at York, the late Eugenie Henderson of SOAS and Douglas Sanders in Vancouver, from Elizabeth Lewis and Carol Osborne, Michael Mahda, Martin Smith, Virginia Nicholson, Louise Hayman, Dr Harold Dixson, Simon Hale, Carrie Bell, from Walter Cairns and the Scottish Arts Council, from my three CUP 'readers', Andrew Turton, Nigel Barley and Gustaaf Houtman, and my editors Jessica Kuper and Wendy Guise, from my agent Sebastian Born, my brother Stephen and my sister Deborah. My inimitable mother compiled the index, William Riviere struggled to control the prose even as the author kicked and scratched, and Chris, Helen, Joanne and Ruth gave me a home in which to write. Thank you all, and to the staff of the Indian Institute of the Bodleian Library, the Siam Society in Bangkok and the Tribal Research Institute in Chiang Mai, Northern Thailand. I don't know why they bothered with me, but they did, and my knowledge of Karen history and cultural traditions would have been far poorer without them.

Extracts from R. P. Winter's report on the Karen are quoted with permission from the United States Committee for Refugees. Some of the material in chapter seventeen first appeared in a different form in the *Minnesota Review*.

It goes without saying that I could not have worked without the 'cooperation' of the Karen people. What that word cannot convey is the extraordinary open-house hospitality and helpfulness extended to me by all sorts, from Karen National Liberation Army officers to the humblest of forest farmers and their children. I cannot begin to name them all, but True Love, Great Lake and Bartholomew stand out as generous informants. I hope I have done them some sort of justice.

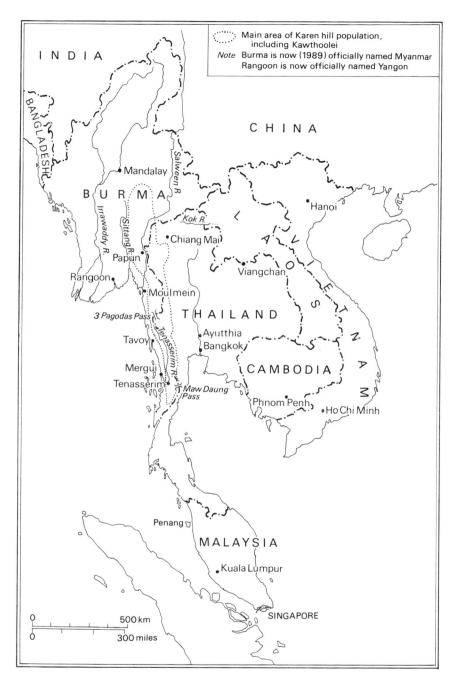

Map of Burma (Myanmar)

A bronze drum 1

White Rock woke us before dawn with martial music from a ghetto-blaster. At 4.30 a.m. he called us in the name of Ba U Gyi, first leader of the Karen rebellion, to honour the flag and the Karen New Year. And so Fragrance got up and crept about the kitchen, blowing up the fire and putting rice on to boil. I watched her from my hammock.

When it grew light, Bartholomew, her father, tied a Karen flag to a long bamboo and lashed it to a post at the front of the house. At six-thirty the drum beats began, rapid and alternating between a dull thud and a hard clack, soft stick and hard stick, accompanied by a battle horn – the Karen type made of a cow horn with a brass reed, capable of two thin, weedy but nonetheless penetrating notes. Bartholomew put on his Karen shirt of thick cotton, with vertical red stripes and long fringes, and we pinned two campaign medals to his chest. The girls put on their long white dresses, and flipflops which the evening before they'd taken to the river and scrubbed clean with old toothbrushes. Then we went to the football field.

At 7 a.m. in December the sun had not yet appeared, and the forest was cold and damp. Mist blurred the kapok trees, palms, bananas and bamboo clumps – ostrich feather fans drawn with a soft pencil. The steep forested hills less than a mile away were hardly visible.

On the far side of the field there was a fenced-off flagpole, and a bamboo frame supporting a large and ancient drum of dull grey-brown bronze. A man in a red striped tunic sat on a piece of sacking, beating the drum with his two sticks, hard and soft. Behind him stood a soldier in camouflage battle-dress, blowing on the black horn, stopping the narrow end with his thumb to change the note. A handful of other soldiers stood about behind him, waiting for the villagers. The ceremony was not compulsory.

Out towards the centre of the field was a white-painted wooden podium; a microphone stood in front of it, a generator in the nearby bushes. A soldier fussed about, tapping the microphone and tweaking leads. A guard of honour in fatigues and flipflops stood to one side with grounded carbines and M16s. A double row of villagers began to assemble watching them, fifty yards off. Most were women and had long Karen dresses of heavy weave, horizontally barred in deep reds, indigo and black, topped with a clean blouse and, if they were lucky, a windproof jacket. It really was cold.

Then, as the drum and the trumpet continued to call, the schoolchildren came, two hundred or more, all in uniform white shirts and dark blue skirts or trousers. They marched from the school compound in a thick column headed by William, their headmaster, who drew them up in a body seventy yards long and five deep, facing the drummer and the flagpole.

In front of the honour guard, another group of fifteen formed a line: the governing élite of this backwater District of the Karen revolution, more elderly than most others present. The Governor, Colonel Marvel, was there at the left of the line, his red tunic over a white cotton shirt with stout black army boots and a beret on his balding head. Next to him, Harvest Moon the Justice, big and portly in a Karen sarong and a beret also. Most of the Departmental heads were there – Roger of Transport, then the propaganda chief whose name translates as 'Devourer of the Country',[1] Bartholomew of Health and Welfare, Pastor Moses of Bethany Baptist Church, and a selection of Lieutenant-Colonels, Majors and Captains of the Karen National Liberation Army, in scarves and woolly hats. Edward the Education Officer stood to one side with Colonel Oliver the Army CO, a pistol on Edward's hip but not on the Colonel's. The mist began to clear, a weak sun lighting the dense green of the hills and the scuffed grass of the football pitch.

When all were assembled, the flag was raised and saluted. Then Colonel Marvel stepped onto the podium and spoke at length while the soldier struggled to keep the public address operating, jiggling the microphone in the Governor's face. He spoke of the Karen year past: had it been a satisfactory one for Kawthoolei? On balance, no. The military situation in this District at least was static, but their community had stagnated. What had been achieved in health, in education, in social welfare and in trade? Not enough. Where were the new initiatives in commerce, where was the discipline they would need if they were to keep their heads above water; if Karen liberties were not to sink beneath Burmese oppression? There could be no shirking the responsibilities that every one of them had to face; the Burmese would close in, would give no chances, would not wait for the Karen to catch up with their tasks before depriving them of the freedom they'd fought nearly forty years to defend. The struggle, the duty was unremitting.

Everyone clapped. The military commander added a few words; William led them in the national anthem. Then everyone turned, shook hands and wished each other a Happy New Year, and we went off for the village breakfast.

Tables had been built by the Justice's house, long bamboo structures topped with split bamboo panels and with integral benches, each seating forty. On them were arranged enamel plates of plain rice and, in the centre, bowls of fermented fish paste, boiled plantain and fat pork. This was, very importantly, a pig feast – like those that had always in the past brought animist Karen villages together to mark the rites of passage or the expiation of sins. Good Karen always had fowl and swine ready for communal consumption, and now the Revolution required to be honoured in the same way. The pork had been cooking slowly in its own fat in giant woks over open fires half the night, stirred by soldiers, and now blubber, bristle and flesh swam lukewarm in bowls of that same fat.

A first sitting set to it: senior men at one table, everyone else scattered amongst the mob of children, in the midst of whom a very old lady squatted uncomfortably on her haunches up on the unfamiliar bench. The schoolgirls served to begin with, carrying plates back and forth between the tables and two vast steaming baskets of rice, where the Justice's nephew Golden Love and Glory his friend doled it out generously. Soon, though, restraint and order surrendered to cheerful gluttony, children screaming with laughter, young soldiers milling, dogs scrapping under the tables over dropped pork fat, the villagers swirling amongst the long tables, feasting and rising and belching and some of them sitting and eating again. I photographed the bigwigs, and out on the football pitch the soldier dismantled the public address system. Venerable and irreplaceable, the bronze drum was detached from its frame and carried away to safe keeping. All that by 9 a.m. and a long day of unity and symbolism still to come.

The drum and the battle-horn together form the insignia of the Karen National Liberation Army (KNLA). Every soldier wears it on his hat, cast in yellow-coated base metal. Of these symbols, the drum is the more potent. A Karen bronze drum is a massive object, about three foot deep and a little less in diameter. 'Like an upturned cooking pot', wrote a French archaeologist, Georges Coedès (1962, pp. 17–18); in fact they are always suspended sideways with a cord through two loops of bronze. The wide, hipped body is decoratively ringed, with a pronounced lengthways seam from the casting. The broad face has so many rings as to resemble the cross-section of a log – except that, in the centre, there is a many-pointed star. I'd seen drums like this before; you can't have a standing interest in South East Asia without meeting them sooner or later. At home in Britain, in a book entitled *The Dawn of Civilisation* (Christie: 1967, p. 284), I have an illustration of a drum almost identical to that which was now hanging from bamboos on the football pitch, but labelled 'Dong Son' – that is, of a culture that flourished in what is now northern Vietnam around 400 BC. These huge bronze drums are regarded by archaeologists as the epitome of Dong Son culture; they are also regarded, in revolutionary Kawthoolei, as the symbol of the Free Karen.

Whether the drums had any nationalistic significance for the Dong Son people – or even whether they were in any sense special to that culture – is another question. Coedès says that the Dyaks of Borneo, Melanesia and Oceania, fourth and third century BC China and even early western European art have all been claimed as design sources. From such disparate origins, the Karen have made the drums their own. In a small stapled booklet called *Karen Bronze Drums*, Pu Taw Oo ('the old man of Toungoo') says that the first drums were made some 3,000 years ago by a 'Chinese Karen' people called the Kemuh, who were skilled in geometric designs. A more resonant shape for the drums was obtained from 'the monkeys' – by which was perhaps meant the Lahu people, who make themselves a black costume with a little tail.

By the time of British rule in Burma (continues Pu Taw Oo), the drums were made only by Karen living up north in the Shan States. A last centre of manufacture was destroyed by the British in a punitive expedition against tax-refusers. The drum-makers heard gunfire, abandoned the village and, each man carrying two drums (no mean feat), they fled south. They never recommenced manufacture.[2]

A drum was worth 'more than seven elephants', and some Karen began to sell them to outsiders. A steady export trade grew up. Even the Kings of Siam bought them; there are several in the palaces and museums of Bangkok, painted black, red and gold and suspended from antlers.

But the leaders of the Karen rebellion put a stop to it. With no more drums being made, the patrimony was being squandered – and that potent symbol diluted. Today the Kawthoolei government prohibits the sale of drums to non-Karen. In fact, they have made it a capital offence.

When not out on the football pitch, the drum at Riverside was normally slung from the rafters in the school office. I asked Ruth the Headmistress where it had come from. 'Oh, I don't know, our ancestors. Every village is supposed to have one. In fact it was once the ambition of every headmen to have a drum made for him. When he died it would be smashed to bits – in our old burying grounds you can see the pieces everywhere.'

The school was obviously the place for it, since the design of the drums is educational and admonitory. 'The old man of Toungoo' describes in his booklet several variants on the theme. In the basic form, the flat, star-patterned face of the drum has four small frogs in cast bronze an inch or so in height, squatting near the outer edge and all facing in an anticlockwise direction. Lt Col MacMahon (1876, p. 279) was baffled by these: 'Whether the instrument is intended to emulate the voice of the frog or not must be left to conjecture for no one can give any reason for the frog being there.' But today, everyone knows the reason. These are the little Karen, unified in purpose. On the side of the drum is a bronze elephant, moving down the flank away from the face. That is the lumbering Enemy, in retreat. Near the elephant there are small lumps on the ground; faced with the solid resolve of the people, it has shat itself in fear.

In drum variants two and three the frogs and elephants are doubled and trebled, the frogs sitting pick-a-back. In variant four, however, there's a disturbing new note. Two of the Karen frogs have turned around, are heading the wrong way round the drum face. Disunity is quickly penalised; the elephant on the side has turned also, and now approaches menacingly. In variant five, two elephants are actually among the frogs on the drum face, while two more close in up the flank. Variant six features elephants only.

The Riverside drum was a type three. It would be a lugubrious soul who commissioned a drum in the later variants to hang in his village. Having a drum was a responsibility; its spirit required annual food and liquor, or disaster would befall the village. Pu Taw Oo insists that the drums could be used on any festive occasion

– a wedding, or a new house – but the drums were also beaten, all night, for funerals; presumably (if Ruth was right) prior to being broken up and scattered. They were also a means of defence, as drums have been the world over, against the dire consequences of lunar and solar eclipses.

In disputes, drums were the best possible indemnity, better than pigs or buffaloes. The deep monotone of the drums propitiated the spirits of the forest whose intoxicated song the echo was. MacMahon wrote that, 'A scene of the wildest revelry ensues', but always with a melancholic undertow: 'the music softens the heart, and women weep for the friends that they have lost'. How sad the drums were! But also, how essential. In Karen thinking, Pride does not ride before a fall: here, 'the proud shall lose their drums'.

The flag of Kawthoolei has a drum on it. The overall design of the flag is not unlike that of the United States – horizontal bars of blue and red with a box in the top left corner. Here, though, instead of stars there is a brilliant rising sun, with the Karen drum silhouetted against it.

In the early days of the insurrection, Karen raiders sometimes left a Union Jack at the scene of an attack; a statement of allegiance that must have been regarded with rather mixed feelings by the departing British. The symbolism of the present flag is conventional. There is, of course, a song about it. A young woman teacher called Ku Wah recorded it for me:

> There's nothing quite so lovely as our flag.
> The white signifies purity,
> the red, boldness.
> The blue is for loyalty,
> and there are nine rays of sunlight
> and a golden Karen drum.

The nine rays, she told me, are the nine traditional 'nations' of the Karen.

Ku Wah was, for her age, an important person. She could activate symbols. She not only knew more of the old songs than anyone else, she knew the traditional dances as well. Which was perhaps not saying very much: a Karen in northern Thailand once told a visiting anthropologist, 'We are the only people in the world who do not dance' – it was said with pride, as an identifying mark. For many Karen, dancing is a rather suspect activity, verging on the immoral. Under the heading, 'High Moral and Ethical Standards', the Karen writer Saw Moo Troo (1981, p. 2) says:

There is no dancing among the Karens. In fact during funeral ceremonies there is a form of dancing with bamboo flute blowing and obstacle jumping displayed between bachelors and spinsters but there is no body-touching even.

In a whole year I was to see Karen people dancing, in any manner, just three times. Yet the glossy calendars put out by the Karen National Union each year always feature the 'national dances'. The changed emphasis is not so difficult to understand. Karen in Thailand now preserve their separateness by negative accommodation to the Thai state they wish to be accepted by, and so they avoid 'national' display. For the rebels in Burma, the opposite need applies – you don't create nationhood out of a negation. And so dance they must, to show themselves and the outside world what they understand by 'Karen'.

On the football field, the flag remained – in the hot, still air curled against the flagpole, guarded by a relay of soldiers sweating it out in the sun for an hour apiece. By ten o'clock the drum was long since back in the school office, and the morning was given over to sports – volleyball, football, wheelbarrow races and tug o'war – 'Very old Karen game, Mr Jo, you'll not have seen this before' – all organised by a jocular young teacher in military uniform called Nixon ('I was born the day that man was elected; my father thought it must be auspicious.')

There was to be a celebratory concert. All afternoon – indeed, for several afternoons beforehand – there were dance rehearsals, a mixed group of young teachers and students stamping it out by the school kitchen. They needed all the practice they could get: none of them knew the steps too well, and there was just Ku Wah to lead and instruct. The moves were complex and tricky. There was the Bamboo Dance, in which they had to skip through a moving grid of twelve long poles upon the ground, picking up their ankles smartly as the bamboos were rhythmically, energetically smacked together by twelve young men. Then there was the Rice Planting Dance, in which files of boys and girls wind in and out while some mime the stabbing of seed holes with bamboo staves and the others dab their feet into the centre daintily, to press the seedlings in. And there was another, elaborate dance in which the lines swung about and permutated to form letters, spelling out whatever you wished. The practices went on hour after hour in the hot afternoon and on into the evening by the light of a neon strip over the door

Plate 1. The bamboo dance: 'They had to skip through a moving grid of poles.'

of the kitchen, the words and the rhythm marred by the noise of the generator, the dust cloud from the stamping feet and clapping bamboos sapping the thin light of the neon.

Thump, thump, thump, clack – the crossed poles pounded on the ground three beats, then cracked together on the fourth, snapping at the dancers' ankles, little puffs of talc-fine dust wisping between their toes as they skipped across the grid. They were not getting it right.

'Do these young people really know the traditional dances at all?' I asked, rather belligerently, of the soldier who was strumming out the accompaniment on a guitar; it was the same man who had been busy with the recalcitrant public address in the morning. He said,
'Here you can see them dancing a traditional dance.'
I pointed out that there was actually only one school teacher who knew how to do it. But he countered,
'That's our Karen way. Our dance troupes always have an

instructor who knows the traditions.'[3]

But, I persisted, most of these were Delta Karen, not forest villagers. Many were city kids for whom these dances might not be part of the heritage at all.

'No, that is not right. In all the towns of Burma where the Karen live we know these dances. We do them!'

'When?'

'At Karen New Year, all in Karen costume.'

'The Burmese Government allows that?'

'We must thank the British colonial administration, which gazetted the Karen New Year as a public holiday. The Burmese would not dare to reverse that now.'

On a bamboo stage behind the church, lit by pale incandescent lights, the evening began as official programmes anywhere do, with speeches. The public address was prone to feed-back, the generator to stalling. The villagers gathered in front of the stage, small children crosslegged in front, their elders on the wooden benches from the church hall. In the background, women sold chicken soup and noodles and rice-flour fritters by the white light of pressure lamps or the smoking flame of naked wicks stuck into tin cans filled with paraffin. Others were selling Burmese cigars:

'You want to be careful with those. Feel them carefully, weigh them in your hand before you light them.'

'Why?'

'Sometimes they pack a .22 bullet inside, facing backwards.'

'Who does that?'

'Rival cigar companies.'

In the darkness I bumped into a figure in camouflage green hugging a carbine. Very occasionally I glimpsed a courting couple sidling off into the shadows.

After the speeches, after the sports prize giving, a special item – Homage to the Elders. There were four of them, three old women and an old man, and to a Karen version of *Silver Threads among the Gold* they were led on stage by Karen girls in maiden's dress – a long white tunic with a pinched waist and delicate scarlet stripes. Each Elder was presented with a rose – red for three of them, white for the oldest lady. Then they were each presented with a cardboard box containing a Thai sponge cake smothered in foaming fake cream. Throughout, the two incandescent lamps at the front of the stage switched on and off by turns, throwing a hard and ghastly light onto one or other side of the old faces.

And then the dancing. The performers were gathered behind the stage, all in their red and white shifts. To the strumming of an electric guitar, they moved out onto the rickety stage which rattled and trembled with every movement. The Bamboo Dance had had to be scaled down to eight poles to fit the platform. For the Planting Dance, the staves had been twined with green crêpe paper. Once again, Ku Wah sang to keep them moving, with a song of tragic and doomed love, performed with gentle and unmorbid charm. Lastly, the dancers spelled out, in English, KAREN NEW YEAR.

That was all the dancing. There came an announcement: after the singing there'd be a church service and then a special treat. I left, to take a New Year's drink with a friend, just as a choir of schoolgirls were coming onstage to sing a call to arms, and then a slow hymn in waltz time:

> The old year has passed away, the new year come.
> Just as light dispels dreams, so your old life
> is now melting away, and a new life dawns.

Walking half a mile through the black forest, flashing my torch only to establish the way and to avoid snakes and centipedes, I could hear the electrified choirs of the Revolution singing in the traditional New Year.

After midnight, returning home, I passed the stage again. The church service was over; it was now the 'treat'. The Education Department video machine was hitched to the generator. An 18-inch television was placed on the front of the bamboo stage. The air had grown cold and the thick, heavy mist was settling down into the valley again, oozing between the ferns and the bamboos and the banana palms. The same crowd was still there but packed tighter now as some 300 Karen rebels, children and Elders pressed towards the little screen. They pulled their jackets tight against the chill, tugged their woollen balaclava helmets over their heads and necks and settled down for a showing of old war epics. As I tied up my hammock, they were watching *The Battle of the Bulge*.

In answer to the question, 'Who is a Karen?' one of the answers should
be (1) one who can claim his ancestry to Toh Meh Pah and (2) one
who possesses, maintains and cultivates the legacies bequeathed to him
by the said forebear and his predecessors. The writer maintains that
anyone who treasures and upholds these inheritances is a Karen though
he may not have a drop of blood from this tribe.

Saw Moo Troo (1981, p. 1)

I knew a 'revolutionary teacher' called Bastion. He was an educated,
intelligent man who took the traditions seriously, and so I asked
him if he'd tell me the story of Toh Meh Pah, the ancestral culture-
hero of the Karen. A few days later we met on his verandah for
a cigar and a recital:

THE STORY OF TOH MEH PAH

Once there were two brothers who lived and farmed together in the far
north. In time, both married and raised large families, but they stayed
living and farming close to one another.

One day a wild boar came and wrecked the rice fields. The elder brother,
although sixty years old, pursued the boar through the forest and found
its lair. The boar was rooting about nearby. The old man raised his spear
and aimed for the pig's head, just where the long and lethally sharp tusks
joined the skull on each cheek. He thrust forward with his spear which
passed through the boar's head and pinned it to a tree. The animal was
so big that the old man couldn't move it by himself, so he returned home
and told his sons to go and fetch the carcase. But when they reached
the place there was no pig – only the spear fixed in the tree, and the
two giant tusks lying on the ground. The young men picked these up
and brought them home, giving the old hunter the name Toh Meh Pah,
or 'Boar Tusk'.

Toh Meh Pah decided to make a comb out of one of the tusks. When
he had done so, he combed his hair with it – and instantly felt quite
young again, not sixty but a mere twenty years old. He realised that
the comb had magical properties, so he kept it safe. In future, whenever
age weighed on him, he'd simply take out his comb and shed a decade
or two.

With his youth and vitality assured for ever, it was not surprising that Toh Meh Pah's family rapidly increased in number. Soon there were too many of them for their land in the hills, so Toh Meh Pah declared that they'd have to go and find a new home where the soil was richer and could support them all. He would go ahead and find the place first – and so he set off.

In every region that he passed through, Toh Meh Pah tried the same experiment. He dug eight holes in the ground, all the same size, and used the earth from the first to try and fill the others. The richer the soil, the more it would spring out and expand. Generally the soil from one hole would fill two or three more but at last he found a place where seven holes could be filled in this way. This was perfect, he concluded, and he returned to fetch his family.

So he and his brother and all their children packed up and moved, following Toh Meh Pah through the forest. After a long march they reached a river where they sat down to rest and eat. In the water they found some snails, and on the bank there was roselle (hibiscus) growing. They'd never tried eating either but they looked good, so fires were lit and snails and roselle put on to boil. After a while someone poked one of the snails with a knife and said, 'It's still hard. And you can see the blood coming from it; can't be cooked yet.' So they waited, but after several hours the snails were still hard and the blood (which was of course the colour from the roselle) was still bright. Toh Meh Pah grew impatient, wanting to move on; after another hour he announced that he was going ahead with his family, and that they'd blaze a trail by cutting down banana trees so that his brother could follow when the snails were cooked and eaten. Off he went.

But, wait as the brother's family might, the snails never cooked – until at last some Chinese travellers came by and laughed at them and showed them how to take the end off the snails and suck out the contents. They ate quickly and set off to follow Toh Meh Pah – but they'd waited so long that the bananas had grown up again and the trail was obscured. And that was the last the Karen ever saw of Toh Meh Pah, or his children, or his magic comb.

'Thank you', I said, 'but isn't there something wrong? The Karen are supposed to be descended from Toh Meh Pah, is that right? But then, he took his family with him so they must have been lost too. And you must be descended from the brother's family.'

Bastion looked crestfallen and muttered that he didn't know, he'd only read the story from the book and didn't understand all the old words. That evening I asked another young soldier-teacher to explain this discrepancy – but he didn't know either, saying 'I'm from Rangoon'. There seemed to be a flaw in the whole foundation myth of the Karen people.

'Perhaps Toh Meh Pah went on alone, without his children?'
'That's it. He left us behind. We're orphans.'
'Well, you'll have been brought up by his brother.'
'Right, we're orphans. We're waiting for Toh Meh Pah.'

The origins of the Karen have been debated ever since the American Baptist missions began to take an interest in the early nineteenth century. After years of fruitless activity among Buddhist Burmans, the Baptists began, almost by accident, to convert Karen in large numbers. So remarkable was their success that a veritable 'cult of the Karen' grew up amongst Christians in the United States.

The usual assumption is that the Karen are of Mongol origin. There is little direct evidence for this other than a vague facial resemblance to a dimly perceived stereotype of the 'Mongoloid', some confused linguistics and a tradition (shared by most peoples) of having come from somewhere else. The Karen speak of *Thibi Kawbi* - which, with disarming ingenuousness, has been understood as 'Tibet and Gobi (Desert)'. Karen stories also mention *htee seh meh wah*, which means 'water pushes sand flows' – or, more elegantly, 'river of flowing sand'. This has also been taken to mean the Gobi Desert. Another popular theory was that the Central Thai word for the Karen, *kariang*, means 'from the Yang River' (the Yangtse).

Some Karen claim that they were the first inhabitants of Burma; most migration theorists give this honour to the Mon, but everyone agrees that the Burmans arrived much later. The Karen say that they came in two waves, the first in 1125 BC, the second in 739 BC; it was this second that finally established them in Burma and consequently the modern Karen calender calculates 1988 as 2727. If they really did set out from somewhere in northern Tibet to come south, they had a most formidable journey ahead of them.

All the migrants had to do was to follow the course of the rivers which have their source in China and on the Tibetan borders, and which flow through valleys that sometimes lie very close together, and then debouch into Indochina as if through the neck of a bottle.

So wrote the French archaeologist Georges Coedès in 1962 (p. 22); certainly the Salween River that is now at the heart of Kawthoolei rises in the Central Tibetan plateau. But, a century before Coedès worked, his compatriot the Lazariste priest Régis-Evariste Huc travelled by the upper reaches of the Salween and considered himself very lucky to survive:

Snow, wind and cold beset us with a fury that increased daily. The Tibetan wilderness is, without any shadow of doubt, the most terrible place imaginable. Since the ground rose steadily, vegetation decreased as we advanced and the cold reached a frightening intensity. From then on, death hovered over the poor caravan ... For several days we had seemed to be passing through a vast graveyard where human bones and animal carcases lay strewn everywhere, telling us that in this land of death and the unleashed forces of nature, the caravans that had preceded us had had no better fate than us.[1]

Men froze to death in the saddle. They came upon a herd of wild oxen fixed in the ice, caught by a freezing wind half way across a river. If Toh Meh Pah saw any of this, the memory is lost. What could have induced him to make such a journey? The only clue, in his story, is the appearance of the Chinese. Perhaps the Karen were, as the writer Saw Moo Troo says, 'persecuted by a cruel king' and driven to flee south. Flight is a recurrent theme in Karen history and culture, as we shall see.

Another tradition, largely ignored, says that the Karen came to Burma from across a sea so wide that hornbills took a week to fly across it – which would suggest India, possibly. But these traditions are very treacherous. I never met any Karen who knew them from any source other than schoolbooks. Admittedly, I lived among relatively urbanised people; still, the stories quoted by foreigners and by the Karen themselves are almost always based on a handful of conversations recorded by a tiny band of nineteenth-century missionaries.

Even as Régis-Evariste Huc wrote, mission rivals to the south were dreaming up more exotic provenances for the Karen. The missions found that there were elements in traditional Karen beliefs which could be seen as the pale ghost of a Christian faith, and that Karen oral literature appeared to prophesy the return of Christianity to their people. Inevitably the speculation came, were they one of the Lost Tribes of Israel? Alternatively, might they not have picked up this quasi-Christianity from the Nestorians, a church of heretics founded in the fifth century and based in Persia, spreading to reach north-western China by the seventh century: perhaps the Karen came from there? Or were they part of a Chinese Imperial Army that twice descended on Burma c. 1400 (a theory reported by Donald Mackenzie Smeaton in 1887)? A more ambitious thesis still, popular in British Burma in the 1870s, was that the Karen were 'a remnant of the ancient Huns, preserved through the lapse of 1788 years uncomminuted with the blood of strangers'.[2]

Who you were determined where it was you wanted the Karen to have come from. In general, the more you liked them, the more western you considered them. The official *Handbook on Burma* (1968, p. 20) from the Directorate of Information (Rangoon), reflecting centuries of animosity, states that the Karen are of 'Thai-Chinese origin' – thus pushing them out to the north-east. The Danish writer Erik Seidenfaden (who, like many Danes before him, served with the Thai Gendarmerie) liked them, and wrote that 'they must be classed as Tibeto-Burmese.' Seidenfaden (1967, p. 117) actually like them even more than that, and noted happily: 'among the lassies real beauties are not rare, which has led some students to call these Karen *Europoid Tibeto-Burmese*'. (This is some advance on Lt Col MacMahon who in 1876 (p. 5) could only report that, 'As far as we could judge there is no prevailing disproportion between different parts of the body.')

Although the traditions speak of the migrations as having occurred nearly a millenium earlier, the first possible sighting of the Karen comes in the eighth century AD when inscriptions mention a people called the 'Cakraw', who are thought to have helped sack the capital of the pre-Burman kingdom of Pyu in Upper Burma. It is at least possible that these people were 'Sgaw' Karen (see below). Thereafter the Karen remain oddly shadowy figures up until the eighteenth century. There are mentions of the *kariang* in Thailand in the fourteenth century and after, but it is not certain that this term applied to the same people as it does now. It is a peculiar and important aspect of Karen identity that the name, or names, given them by the outside world are not the names they use for themselves. 'Karen' is not a Karen word. There is no single term in their language that covers all the people claimed to be 'Karen' which can make it difficult to decide who, precisely, we are talking about – and has led some to call them 'a people without a history'.[3]

The term 'Sgaw' (sometimes spelt 'Skaw', or even 'Chghaw') denotes one of the main subgroups of the Karen. The Sgaw are the largest group of the so-called 'White Karen' and, in certain respects, the dominant one. There are also the Pwo, the Pa-O, the Bwe and others, and then a large group known as Kayah, or Karenni. The terms Red and White Karen were once used. The labels are confused and confusing. In certain circumstances, depending on who they are wanting to associate themselves with, the Kayah may or may not admit to being Karen at all, and each group has its own distinct language.

From the outset there was rivalry between the groups. The Pwo became known as the 'mother' group, the Sgaw as the 'father'. The Pwo regard themselves as the guardians of Karen tradition; the Sgaw dispute this. In the solidarity atmosphere of the Free Karen State of Kawthoolei, such matters are in abeyance; it was often difficult for me to establish whether friends considered themselves to be Sgaw or Pwo or something else.

The traditions say that the Pwo Karen were the first to migrate and that they settled by the rivers in the hills but that, shortly afterwards, the Sgaw arrived and drove the Pwo downstream, 'to drink brackish water'. Today the Pwo tend to be cast as the lowland or coastal people, the Sgaw as the highlanders – although in fact all the Karen are widely distributed throughout large areas of Burma.

The hills were by no means a secure stronghold, and the highlanders were soon caught up in the recurrent and bitter disputes between Burma and Siam. Incursions and raids across the dividing mountain chain persisted for centuries. Then, in 1752, a new king called Alaungpaya raised his standard at Shwebo in Upper Burma, and for the next half-century there was almost constant warfare in, and between, Ava (Burma) and Siam. Armies crossed and recrossed the hills. The Burmese sacked the Siamese capital at Ayutthia and the Siamese took their revenge. Caught between the two, the Karen and other tribes played a dangerous game, acting (not often voluntarily) as spies or border guards, or occasionally as spearhead troops for one or other army, while having to provision both as they passed through the Karen hills. Already they tended to take sides against the Burmese; the Siamese and their allies took more trouble to cultivate Karen sympathies, and to recruit them as mercenaries rather than simply impress them as slaves. Both countries, however, had problems of underpopulation, and both from time to time casually rounded up hill tribe villagers and took them home as demographic makeweights.

The wars across the mountains petered out in the early 1800s, partly through mutual exhaustion, partly because the old rivals now had more pressing problems. Siam was never completely subjugated by any colonial regime, although European influence at times came close to that. But the French were rapidly taking over 'Cochin China' and 'Annam' (now Vietnam, Cambodia and Laos), and the British East India Company, having seized an island off Burma in 1753, followed by a more courteous embassy to the

Burmese Court of Ava in 1795, were getting itchy trigger-fingers at the thought that the French might grab Burma before they did. The Burmese foolishly allowed their own internal conflicts to impinge on the borders of British India: a first war began in 1824 and the British took over Lower Burma. Petty quarrels with the Burmese crown (over, for instance, the wearing of shoes in the Royal Presence by ambassadors) led to a Second Burma War in 1852, and then final annexation which, in 1885, saw the abdication of King Thibaw, his departure from the capital at Mandalay and the end of Burmese sovereignty.

There had been missionaries – French, Italian and Portuguese Catholics – in Burma long before the British came. In 1740 Father Nerini had noted the 'wild populations styled Cariani living separately from others and in full liberty'. Captain Michael Symes of His Majesty's 76th Regiment of Foot (India), the envoy who arrived at the Court of Ava in 1795, went to these missionaries for much of his information about the country; thus, from the outset, the British were aware that, besides the Burmans with whom they were treating, there were other peoples both in the Delta villages and tucked away out of sight in the forests. The Burmans hardly encouraged contact with the Karen, dismissing them as 'wild cattle of the hills'. Still, the newcomers were intrigued and Captain Symes investigated the 'Carianers' further. A modern American evangelist, Don Richardson, concerned once again with tribal prophecies of the return of the Book, gives an account of a meeting between Symes' embassy and the Karen:

The year is 1795, and deep in the jungles of Burma hundreds of native tribesmen rush out to a clearing to greet a white-skinned stranger . . .

'This is most interesting', the guide said. 'These people think you may be a certain "white brother" whom they as a people have been expecting since time immemorial.'

'How curious', replied the diplomat.

'He's supposed to bring them a book', the guide said. 'A book just like the one their forefathers lost long ago. They are asking – with bated breath – hasn't he brought it?'

'Ho! Ho!' the Englishman guffawed.[4]

Sadly, he didn't have any books with him at the time, and it was another thirty years before the American Baptists converted their first Karen.

As soon as the British had established themselves in Lower Burma they began to explore their new domain and encounters with the

Karen continued. Most reports struck a similar note: 'The Karens are a simple, timid race with a spirit broken by centuries of oppression', wrote Dr David Richardson who, in the 1820s, made research tours of the country. Turning up late at one village, Richardson was embarrassed at the seeming servility of the Karen who got out of bed to clean and cook rice for him at midnight.[5]

For the next hundred years, travellers on both sides of the border remarked the hill Karen, or Karieng or Carianers, as shy, cowed and retiring:

In a gorge of the mountain, and on almost inaccessible heights, I found a small tribe of Karians ... who, for the sake of their independence, live here in seclusion ... (Henri Mouhot (1864, vol. 2, p. 110))

They keep away from the markets and the beaten track, fully occupied with the thousand tasks that weigh upon them. (Lunet de Lajonquière (1904, p. 226))

My father was Commissioner of Tenasserim ... (*his papers*) went to show that they were much oppressed and exceedingly humble, calling themselves 'the insects of the hills'. (Sir Mortimer Durand, (in Scott: 1916, chairman's response))

A people capable of being afraid. (Rev Harry Marshall (1945, p. 22))

The American Baptist missionaries, who arrived at much the same time as the British conquerors, thought the Karen 'a meek and peaceful race'.[6] As they developed their stereotype of the Karen, so satisfying as converts and so saleable by fundraisers at home, the missionaries persistently overlooked the cross-border slave-trading forays and the internecine village raiding that made the Karen many enemies in the hills. An important part of the mission stereotype was that a high percentage of Karen quickly converted to Christianity, with only the recalcitrant dregs clinging to animism and Buddhism. It's an image that even George Orwell reflects and it is quite untrue. No more than one quarter of the Karen have ever been converted. But stereotypes are the stuff of Imperial literature, even with writers who were genuinely interested in their subject:

The White Karen is of a heavier, squarer build than a Burman, and much more solid. He is, in fact, a sort of picture-poster representation of the comic paper's view of the German professor ... The White Karen are credited with truthfulness and chastity, but they are very dirty and

Plate 2. 'They keep away from the markets and the beaten track, fully occupied with the thousand tasks that weigh upon them.'

drink heavily. In disposition they are heavy, suspicious, and absolutely devoid of humour, like the German professor. (J. G. Scott (1916, p. 30))

Throughout the colonial period the Karen sided more and more closely with the Christian British against the Buddhist Burmese. In the First Burma War they provided the invaders with scouts, receiving a commendation for their work in Major J. J. Snodgrass' *Narrative* (1827, p. 141) of the war.

These people seemed heartily glad to see us ... they willingly undertook to carry letters and communications from one corps of the army to another ... They seemed most anxious for the expulsion of [the Burmese enemy] ... and gave much useful information regarding his strength and situation ... It certainly reflected no small honour on the good faith of our Carian friends that our movements, known to so many, should have been inviolably kept secret.

When the Karen and Mon rebelled against the Burmese in 1838, however, the British did nothing to help them, declining to be drawn into Burma's internal affairs. In the Second Burma War of 1852, Karen guides led the British into Rangoon to seize the Shwedagon Pagoda; they were none too popular with the Burmans at the time, and large numbers fled to British-controlled territory to avoid reprisals, causing problems of crowding in Rangoon.

The British always administered the hill tribes separately from the rest of Burma, under direct rule of the Governor. This was simple expediency: there was little point in establishing elaborate protocols to control isolated villages about which the British were the first to admit they knew very little, and which gave no trouble anyway. Besides which, it kept the feuding peoples apart. For the Karen there was more to it, and the orphans of Toh Meh Pah were keen to make the most of British protection. For many, rapid conversion to Christianity brought them into the 'home church' confronting Burmese Buddhism and gave them a patron. In return the British often entrusted their own children to Karen nannies, saying that they made better nurses than Burmans. Even today there are Karen women in Britain who originally came with returning expatriate families.

Smeaton spoke for British opinion in Burma when he described the 'loyal Karen' as 'at heart true to the British government'. But this loyalty was by no means automatic, and in the late 1850s the reputation for placid obedience took a nasty knock, as reported half a century later by ICS surveyor R. C. Rogers:

After the Second Burmese War ... a Karen who called himself a *minlaung* (the incarnation of a prince), collected around him a number of adventurers and evilly disposed persons and . . . reduced these tracts to complete subjection. They were driven out by a mixed British force of military and police aided by friendly natives.[7]

Meanwhile, Red Karen slave trading was being used by Burmese local officials to needle the British; they encouraged the Karen to seize Burman and Shan villagers from territory under British protection for sale across the border in Siam – a source of drawn-out problems that it took a special diplomatic mission to solve.

But most Karen settled very comfortably under the wing of the whites. They worked well and hard and, as trusted employees and sometimes co-religionists, the 'wild cattle of the hills' could become more sophisticated. When they accepted Christ (says the *Karen Baptist History*) they brushed their hair, cleaned their faces, became teetotallers and kept the Sabbath.[8] The French traveller Lunet de Lajonquière, crossing from Siam in 1904 and descending the hills into Burma, described his pleasure at arriving at an official 'bungalow' at Kowkareit where he was received by a most courteous native manager:

He was a tubby, dark-complexioned little man of the Karieng race; converted very young by the American Baptist missions, he'd been brought up by them and they had found him this position – of which his parents, left far behind in their squalid little hut on some wooded mountaintop, could never have dreamed. He was dressed in a long silk *sarong* and white shirt, impeccably starched and fastened with gold buttons. He spoke fluent English, and placed himself at our disposal with all the grace in the world. (1904, pp. 228–9, my translation)

It was the Baptist missions, as much as British officialdom, who nurtured the Karen; at times the relationship is reminiscent of Indians and Jesuits in seventeenth-century Paraguay. When a wave of serious Burman unrest began in 1886 the missions organised their Karen converts into levies to hunt down the Burman 'dacoits'. The colonial authorities were less enthusiastic about promoting racial conflict – to the angry frustration of the missionaries. As fighting spread throughout the country, with Buddhist monks reported to be accompanying Burmese insurgents, a prominent Baptist, Dr Vinton, wrote a long series of letters describing the Karen response:

My Karens universally interpret this as God's sign that Buddhism is to be destroyed for ever . . . Every mission has promised a levy *en masse* of all the able bodied men. They all agree to refuse all pay and to fight from pure loyalty to the Queen.

What more could a colonial power ask for? Dr Vinton certainly knew what to ask for in return:

To make our Karen districts safe we want at least one thousand guns more ... so far from being daunted, I never saw the Karen so anxious for a fight ... The heathen Karens are to a man brigading themselves under the Christians. This whole thing is doing good for the Karen. This will put virility into our Christianity.[9]

The authorities were less impressed and insisted that the Karen be disarmed like everyone else.

This rebellion persuaded the British that there might be some value in employing Karen to suppress Burman, but not all the experiments that followed were entirely happy:

It seemed a mistake to show a mistrust of the Burman, to set one race against another ... In March 1888 ten parties of Karen were enrolled to pursue dacoit bands but they were so unsatisfactory that they had to be disbanded ... Without proper European supervision the Karen were rowdy and disorderly and inclined to display race animosity towards the Burmans. *Burma Gazetteer*[10]

Still, the British knew that the Karen could be useful to them. There was no one else to watch the long border with Siam that was not even properly demarcated until 1890. Both British and Siamese employed the Karen as border patrols. In 1930 the Karen were used to suppress the rebellion of a Burman, Saya San. Then came their finest hour, with the collapse of the British Burma Corps at the hands of the Japanese in 1942.

The war between the British and the Japanese in Burma began across those same hill passes through which Siamese and Burmese had plagued each other, with the Karen caught in the middle once more. As inclined to stereotyping as anyone else, the Karen called the Japanese 'Shortlegs' and the British 'Longlegs', and threw in their lot with the Longlegs. In the pathetically ill-prepared Burma Rifles, Karen, Kachin and other tribesmen served in some numbers. About 3,000 Karen were recruited, but far too late, as General Slim (1956, p. 73) acknowledged: 'The British-led Karen levies, newly raised and partially trained ... were swept away.'

My older Karen friends put it rather differently, saying, 'The British ran away and left us to fight the Japanese.' They usually managed to laugh at the memory.

The Burmese did much as the Malays and other colonised

peoples: that is, scenting the collapse of imperial power, they tried to gauge where their best chance of post-war independence lay; as the British and Japanese faltered by turns, the Burmese tacked about accordingly. For the tribes, however, the issue was very different. Karen leaders must have known that full independence for them was a nonsense; their territorial base in the hills was in no way a viable entity as a state, while half their people lived in the towns and villages of the Delta anyway, jumbled in with Burmans, Mon and the rest. Antipathy between Karen and Burman had steadily deepened over the years and, with the Japanese occupation, it hit new depths. In 1942 the Burma Independence Army (Burmese nationalists backed by the Japanese) massacred seventeen Karen elders at Papun – an event well remembered in Kawthoolei today. In inciting the Burmans to rise against the British, the Japanese gave them a free hand against the Karen also, and the atrocities increased. In reply the Karen formed self-defence bands – one of which was named Toh Meh Pah, after Boar Tusk himself.

After the British retreat into India in 1942, the hilltribe recruits were discharged: 'Each man was given his rifle, fifty rounds, and three months pay, told to go to his village, wait for our return ...'[11]

'Stay-behind' groups operated in the hills, trying to harass the Japanese and to keep up morale and resistance of the tribes. The most famous of these was an English major called Hugh Seagrim – 'Grandfather Longlegs'. As Seagrim sat tight in the hills, the Karen went to extraordinary lengths to protect and supply him – and the Japanese went to comparable lengths to find him. It is not recorded how many Karen were tortured and killed in the process. Finally, the responsibility for the suffering that he was causing was too much for Seagrim; he surrendered and was executed.

The stubborn loyalty of the tribes left British soldiers abashed. Richard Rhodes James was one of the Chindits, the airborne force under Orde Wingate who made extensive use of the tribes:

We trusted these villagers absolutely, and never found our trust misplaced. The whole country was covered by an intelligence system which guaranteed our safety. Day after day they looked after us, guiding, warning, advising. Their food had been pillaged by the Japs but they gave generously of their scarcity ... What had these men to gain? We gave them money and parachute cloth but from the Japs they got death. As we passed through the villages they implored us to stop. 'Stay with us, or if you can't do that, come back soon. The Japs will kill us for this.' And they did.[12]

The parachute cloth did come in useful. Major Seagrim's biographer, Ian Morrison, says that in 1945 many of the Karen were dressed in silk.

At last the Allies reinvaded Burma – 'Like crunching a porcupine quill by quill', said Churchill – and the Japanese gave way, their retreat rapidly becoming a rout. General Slim (1956, p. 499) decided that the moment had come to allow the tribes to act, with proper European supervision:

Their [the Japanese] way led them through the country of the Karen, a race which had remained staunchly loyal to us even in the blackest days of Japanese occupation, and had suffered accordingly. Over a long period, in preparation for this day, we had organised a secret force, the Karen Guerrillas, based on ex-soldiers of the Burma Army, for whom British officers and arms had been parachuted into the hills. It was not at all difficult to get the Karen to rise against the hated Japanese; the problem was to restrain them from rising too soon. But now the moment had come, and I gave the word, 'Up the Karens!'

As the Japanese attempted to cross the rivers on their way east, swimming or clinging to bamboo rafts or logs, looking for a safe landing, they were slaughtered. It is estimated that the Karen killed 12,500 Japanese. Slim was the author of a much-quoted tribute: 'The Karen are no fair-weather friends.'

They were rewarded, of course. The British gave a 'large sum of money' to the hill peoples, founded three Karen scholarships at Rangoon University, built a forty-bed hospital (named after Seagrim) and a model farm. The money was later thought to have been excessive; having flooded the cash economy, the British found it difficult to recruit Karen labourers.[13]

Post-war, the question was 'Who will be independent of whom?' Karen nationalism has been dated to the aftermath of the Second Burma War (1852), and a Karen National Association was founded in 1881 – the first modern political organisation in Burma. Sir San Crombie Po, a Karen doctor, had published his *Burma and the Karens* arguing for a Karen state in 1928. Even before that, the British had decided that the Karen would be better off in a separate state or province, 'Kawthoolei'; they might be less troublesome that way. J. G. Scott told the Central Asian Society in London in 1916 that the reasons for an 'independent' Karen State were pragmatic:

there had been persistent Karen slave raids into Shan territory, which might be contained by redrawn boundaries, while arguments over the ownership of teak forest had been settled with promises of independence. Teak was one of the main reasons the British had wanted Burma: the Karen lived in the teak forests, and the Karen were the expert elephant drivers, without whom teak extraction would be very difficult. It is not difficult to imagine what sort of 'independence' the British were thinking of. But there were other precedents. The Shan people to the north had, at various times, constituted free states, even while nominally under Burmese rule. San C. Po in 1928 hoped for no more than similar regional autonomy within a federation. Meanwhile, the British approved an anthem for the Karen:

> The Lord's chosen children,
> people expecting God,
> Blessed you are.
> You've been persecuted
> and enslaved as well.
> The white brother liberators,
> God sent them back.[14]

At the end of the war the British prepared to shed this turbulent colony as fast as possible. Should the various 'nations' of Burma be kept together as a unitary whole? Four Karen representatives travelled to London and repeated their case for autonomy to the Frontier Areas Committee of Inquiry – stressing always that they had never desired to secede completely, only that they wished to manage their own affairs, and to have their rights respected. A champion of the Karen, Michael Lonsdale, wrote of the Commission of Inquiry: 'Not a single political, economic, cultural or other reason was advanced by any Karen witness for desiring a Karen State. The motives that guided the Karen were suspicion and fear.'[15]

To promote their cause, a Karen Central Organisation was formed in 1945, which became the Karen National Union in 1947. The agreement reached between Attlee's ministers and the Burmese leader Aung San, in which the Karen and other tribes were lumped together into the Union of Burma, has always been regarded by the Karen as a British betrayal. Aung San was, it seemed, reasonably well-disposed towards them, and held a conference of the leaders of all the tribal groups. The official *Handbook on Burma* (1968, p. 35) describes the proceedings:

Scepticism was voiced in some interested, including foreign, quarters, on the willingness of frontier areas to become merged in a single independent state ... However, thanks to the fraternal spirit prevailing among the frontier peoples and the statemanship displayed by General Aung San ... representatives spoke with one voice in opting for a merger of their areas with Burma proper.

On 14 July 1947, Aung San was assassinated by Burmese rivals together with most of his cabinet, an event which the Karen still puzzle over, write about and can barely refrain from considering as a blow aimed at themselves. Sterner Burman spirits took over.

The atmosphere deteriorated rapidly, but the British were by now only interested in getting out, fearful that they might be caught up in the same partition nightmares that had overtaken India. The Independence of the Union of Burma was declared on 4 January 1948:

To the Karens the fanfare of trumpets sounded like the last trump ... the notes of jubilation like weeping and the gnashing of teeth. (Lonsdale (no date, p. 8))

The following day the KNU declared Karen Independence as 'a statement of feeling'. But although a Communist rebellion broke out almost immediately, for the moment the Karen and the other hill tribes submitted to the new government. Indeed, Karen troops saved the Government from an army mutiny. However grateful the ministers may have been, by the summer of 1948 Burman and Karen were murdering each other out in the villages. The Karen began to form armed defence associations, preparing for the worst, and in August, they took over two towns, Thaton and Moulmein, without any bloodshed. Their leader, a London-trained lawyer called Ba U Gyi, persuaded them to surrender both towns: an act, say Karen historians, of unparalleled honesty compared to Burmese deceits. On Christmas Eve 1948 Burmese soldiers threw hand-grenades into a Karen church and bayoneted the fleeing congregation.

On 31 January 1949, at the town of Insein a few miles north of Rangoon, the rebellion of the new Karen National Defence Organisation began in earnest.

Some histories say that it was attempts to disarm the Karen battalions of the army that led to the trouble.[16] Others suggest that the well-organised Karen were by now only awaiting an excuse to strike back. Pastor Moses of Riverside, who was at Insein as a young Baptist seminary student, remembers a further provocation:

The final spark was money. There had been a lot of tension but then payday came and the Burmese refused to pay any of the Karen teachers or public servants. Street fighting began, but there were a great many Karen there and the Burmese were driven out of the town. Barricades were put up but we had almost no guns, just very old weapons, shotguns and so on. Day after day there was fighting and shooting over the barricades but by some miracle of God few Karen were ever hurt. The Burmese aircraft used to fly over every day and drop bombs but I never heard of anyone being killed. I have no fear of Burmese planes.

Moses was at Insein for three months, finally leaving in order to take a sick friend home to his village. The Karen attempted to capture Rangoon but failed, and it could be argued that they've been losing the war ever since. The Karen fighters, about 1,000 of them, dug in at Insein to meet the counter attack. In the following stalemate, trippers from Rangoon went to the front and took pot-shots at the Karen for one rupee. After 112 days of siege a truce was called and Ba U Gyi went to Rangoon to negotiate. Under cover of the truce the Burmese troops moved forward to new pos-itions, making the Karen position untenable – another instance, the Karen say, of Burmese duplicity: 'We are too honest. We were tricked at Insein, we are always tricked.'

Those were heroic days; an old grandmother at Riverside taped a song for me in honour of one of the early Karen commanders that gives some feel of the atmosphere:

> Moulmein, Tavoy, Mergui, Palaw –
> here many Karen were tortured by the Burmese.
> Villages were burnt, there was starvation.
> Hey, though, we mustn't fear the Burmese!
> Let's go to the battlefield, we're KNU soldiers.
> Life or death, we're never afraid.
> Bo Jakay will lead us into battle.
> Death and life are in God's hands.
> Hey! Why should we fear the Burmese?

I don't wish to present a detailed history of the rebellion; that has been done elsewhere.[17] The next three decades may be sketched in brief. For a while the Karen did well, holding large areas of the country and outfighting the Burmese. Certain ex-British army officers were caught assisting them and were thrown out of Burma. In 1954 a government Boundary Commission announced a Karen State of Kawthoolei – but as it consisted only of poor hill tracts around the Salween River, which could never support an influx of 2 million Delta farmers, the Karen turned it down scornfully.

Faction and recklessness took a heavy toll, and by the 1960s they had lost most of the early gains. A coup in 1962 brought the Army to power in Burma under a General, Ne Win, who for Baptist Karen became the socialist Antichrist. Ne Win made an initial attempt at negotiation which failed. By now half the country was in revolt: in addition to the Karen and the Communists, there were Mon, Kachin, Karenni and Arakanese revolutionary movements. Today there are even more.

Losing ground, the Karen forces regrouped in the eastern Dawina and Tenasserim Hills, towards the Thai border, as the new Karen National Liberation Army (KNLA) under General Bo Mya. He had converted from Buddhism to the Seventh Day Adventists, and he now repudiated all the Karen's former Communist leanings. The right-wing Karen National Union (KNU) assumed political control. For a while the pressure was on the Burmese Communist forces, but in the mid seventies Ne Win turned his attention back to the Karen. He announced his *Four Cuts* policy that would bring them to their knees: cut them off from their own people, cut off access to the outside world, cut the KNLA supply lines, and cut off their heads. Burmese battalions launched offensives into Karen territory. In 1974, in a pitched battle at Myawaddy that lasted six days, Karen and other rebels fought so fiercely that the Burmese Army was only saved by its airforce. The Karen struck a medal for participants in the battle, hailing it as a great victory because, for the first time, they and other groups had fought side by side. Bo Mya, the rebel leader, became President of Kawthoolei.

But Ne Win hadn't given up. In 1979 *Four Cuts* was extended to the southern districts of Kawthoolei. In the Karen account of this assault, more than a hundred homes were burned, eighty Karen villagers killed and twenty-eight women raped by Burmese troops. The Karen fell back towards the border once more, thousands crossing over to safety in Thailand. In 1984 the pressure was increased yet again, and the KNLA began losing ground and population fast.

Today the situation of the Free Karen State of Kawthoolei is one of dreadful simplicity: there's not much of it left. Until the early seventies, for the hill Karen at least, the war was far away and they continued quietly farming their steep fields and shooting monkeys, while the leadership fell into factions and put tolls on the Thai-Burma smuggling. Now the war has come to the hills. Since 1984 the fighting has not let up, and no dry season passes without foreign journalists shaking their heads and pronouncing the Karen finished: 'They cannot last another offensive.' They do last, year by year, losing some firefights and winning others, losing territory and regaining some of it later. But the Burmese have succeeded in closing almost all the toll-gates on the border passes, thus depriving Kawthoolei of much of its revenue. Today, although the KNU have claimed that 2–3 million Karen live in Kawthoolei, the reality is a fraction of that and the territory that the Karen National Liberation Army can to any degree defend consists of little more than a strip of forested hill country stretching for hundreds of miles down the border. There is no 'Front Line' as such – the 5,000 KNLA soldiers would have to be spaced one every hundred yards to achieve that. Instead, there is a game of cat-and-mouse (with the roles alternating), and points of contact on the main routes through the forest. And these the Karen defend ferociously. Although outnumbered twenty-to-one by Burmese conscripts, the KNLA retain certain advantages: many of them are hillsmen, at home in the forest and motivated to outfight the Burmese boys from the Delta. They are readily supplied with food by their own people, whereas the Burmese must carry everything through the forest with them. Even if the Burmese capture and destroy a Karen base, the Karen can always slip across the Thai border to sanctuary until time and logistics oblige the Burmese to withdraw. Short of some bungle by the KNLA, it is therefore difficult for the 100,000 or so Burmese regulars to defeat them, even though they may temporarily overrun the territory. Nor do the Burmese seem able to prevent KNLA detachments from roaming about the coastal plains.

It is a truism of guerrilla warfare that if the big conventional army is not winning, then it is losing – and if the guerrillas are not losing, they are winning. The truism does not apply to Kawthoolei. However erratic the fighting, the economic stranglehold draws tighter daily. The end will come either with the economic annihilation of Kathoolei, such that they can no longer buy rice and bullets, or with a change in Burmese policy following Ne Win's death. Neither option is very far in the future.

The events of these long years – the factions, the tremendous territorial gains and their equally spectacular losses, the shifts of political complexion – are little discussed in most Karen homes now; the wasted opportunities are too painful to contemplate, perhaps. What they do remember are the service and suffering they experienced during the Second World War, the promises betrayed by the Attlee government, the fights at Insein and Myawaddy, and their first leader Ba U Gyi, who was killed in an ambush in 1950 and proceeded directly to the Karen pantheon to join Toh Meh Pah.

Boar Tusk is remembered in a variety of ways. You can now fortify yourself with a patent blood tonic named after him. There are also faint traces of colonial rule still to be seen, even in our quiet backwater. Sometime after the First World War the British established a telegraph line to Siam out through these hills, and at the village of White Elephant, a couple of hours away by boat, there was a relay station. The wire is still in use – cut into a thousand small pieces it does for all kinds of tasks in Karen homes. Old men, ex-Burma Rifles, may be seen from time to time with an Enfield .303; where they find ammunition for these I can't imagine.

Pastor Moses regarded British Burma with the deepest nostalgia:

I knew a good many soldiers of the Royal Berkshire Regiment, when they returned after the defeat of the Japanese. The Christian soldiers made good friends with the Baptist Karens. If they were transferred to some other base they would always take with them letters of introduction to the local Karen church, and they would come and sing every week – very beautiful quartets sometimes. They were nice men. One friend of mine told me that he helped to give out rice rations to the British soldiers and that he had to inspect ration cards; he was amazed because some of the soldiers could not read or write. Can that be true of Englishmen? They taught me some lovely songs which were new in England then. Do you know this one?

> I'm going to buy myself a paper doll
> That I can call my own . . .

Moses' attitude to Britain was a little ingenuous, as he well knew: 'If only the British were back in Burma, we would not have our present troubles.'

Bartholomew, in whose house I was living, would turn these nostalgic sentiments around, if for some reason he wished to get at me. He would say, without comment but sure that I knew what he meant,

'You sold us out.'

White collar Flowerland   3

The houses of these strange people are of the most miserable description – mere pigeon houses perched in the air on poles, with a notched stick as the sole means of egress and ingress to the dwelling. They are, however, well adapted for protecting their inmates from the ravages of the periodical deluge, and the still more destructive inroads of prowling tigers, in which the woods abound.   Major J. J. Snodgrass (1827, p. 141)

I wrote home that I'd reached Riverside by elephant – but it was only my rucksack, my oil lamps and the tin of paraffin that rode down to the village. Elephants are slow and uncomfortable transport; walking is pleasanter. Unfortunately, between Headquarters up at the border and the lower village, where the tributary debouches into the great river, we had to wade the stream thirty-seven times. I was accompanied by Timothy, the Army medical officer, who wore wellington boots – but the water reached our waists.

Half way down the valley there was a hamlet where we stopped at the store, and a rotund little gentleman with a jaw abscess called on his wife to serve us tea, giggling as he recounted his days in the Burma Rifles: 'Ordinary soldier, sixteen shillings a month, no pension! Hee hee!'

There were no villages here ten years back. Headquarters had been at Barterville, on the banks of the main river at the next tributary to the south. In many respects it made more sense there; that was where not only the trade but also much of the population was, in Barterville itself or the villages nearby. But at that time there was no motor road from Barterville to the Thai border. Strategy came first. Now Headquarters was on the hill with ready access to Thailand, and 'government family lines' on the banks at Riverside, with only a few other Karen settlements nearby. It was a sad shift of priority which was reflected in a change in Riverside's Karen name; previously it had been called after a stream that descended from the Burmese hills, on the eastern side of the big river, but now we knew it by the stream that came from the Thai side.

I arrived in the rains, driven down the first section of track in a four-wheel-drive pickup – *fowehka* – continuing by foot along what Timothy called the 'Karen Super-Highway to Burma'. The *fowehka* stuck in the mud; the elephant had other troubles. We met her, very distressed, cowering in the bushes and bleeding from a head wound, with her baby at her side. 'Oh, elephant broken down', said Timothy. The elephant had fallen foul of a swarm of bees; maddened, she had careered through the forest until she smacked her head on a tree.

Three hours later, cresting a rise, suddenly there was the river below us, and then the village on a broad half-circle of land between the line of hills and a bend in the stream. I tried, as we entered, to work out the topography, but it was smothered in vegetation.

We walked in, and passed a high fence of woven bamboo prettily draped with flowering vines, where a lackadaisical gate flopped open on a compound of scattered buildings and a few men milling. Outside the gate, spelt out in English in small red flowers, was the single word, JAIL. We passed a flagpole and a football field and, visible above a screen of trees, a new tin roof and a blue painted tower with fretworked grilles at one end – Bethany Church. Opposite, an unmistakable school – a row of cement-floored class-rooms under more corrugated roofing painted in flaking camouflage mottle. There were teachers' and students' hostels, middle and senior school blocks, school kitchens and a church hall with decaying hardboard walls. Half a mile further on was a hospital and a house built to advance order for a French medical team who had never come, medicine stores and rice stores, a hostel for army nurses and – by far the largest structures in the place – two Thai sawmills. Between these public fixtures were small clusters of half-concealed houses. All this was scattered across a square mile of colluvial plain, with broad dirt tracks running through it and a Thai-built logging road dividing the village from the ridge of hills. On the main road, a sign by the school and another by the jail requested, in Karen and English, that drivers proceed with caution.

The village fell into 'quarters' – informal, but clear. Along the track that followed the bend in the river, army families had their houses. At the northern end, the hospital was flanked by medical staff hostels and by the small homes of the waifs and strays who had come in under the shelter of the Health and Welfare Depart-ment. Round the sawmills clustered the shacks of the Thai work-force. Edward of the Education Department, his staff and many

Plate 3. Riverside: 'Army and militia families lived beyond the jail.'

of his students were all within one hundred yards of the school compound, while more Army and militia families lived beyond the jail. Along a lane between the main track and the river, delicately screened by kapok trees, was what I came to call Millionaires Row, the substantial hardwood houses of Bartholomew, of Harvest Moon the Justice, Moses the Pastor and Morning Star the Colonel's son, and senior officials from the Forestry, Transport and Information Departments. Each had its compound well-stocked with bananas, white and richly-scented *mali* flowers, kapok and acacia trees and perennial shrubs and roses. Millionaires Row had its own shops.

Houses throughout the village had plenty in common, of course, especially the clutter of baskets and tools underneath, the dogs and chickens resting in the shade, fishnets draped over poles and babies sleeping in hammocks. In other respects, the architecture in each quarter reflected the status of the inhabitants. The misfits in Health and Welfare care showed their poverty by building houses like those of the forest Karen described by Major Snodgrass – small, all-bamboo, thatched and ephemeral. At the other extreme, Millionaires Row bulked large with solidity and permanence. Between the two, the teachers lived in trim little boxes, modern, cramped and characterless. The sorriest were the shacks of the poor Thais, who lived stuffed like culinary rabbits into rows of tiny wooden hutches, one barely head-height room apiece and a porch where they cooked and chatted in celibacy and linguistic isolation, their bizarre great logging lorries, with square-cut cabs and massive timber frame-works on the back, drawn up by the porch.

The solid homes of the revolutionary hierarchs spurned the shifting impermanence of Karen farms; these modern nationalists stayed put. But forest tradition had been rejigged, not rejected. The tale of Golden Horn and Harvest Moon's houses illustrated the delicacies of adjustment. Harvest Moon the District Justice was a massively built man. He was kindly, with a keen sense of humour, but he personified authority. His position was of recent date. 'People think of him as a very stern and moral man,' I was told, 'but he was a drunken sailor not so long ago.' Harvest Moon had put his wild youth behind him and was now a figure of integrity, the law, the family, and had a big solid house to go with it.

He had two daughters. The eldest girl, Laura, was a rare and precious thing in Kawthoolei, a qualified nurse. It was no surprise that she married Golden Horn, one of the fastest-rising stars in the District, a shrewd and efficient young administrator who had become a Township Secretary. When I first met Golden Horn at an army camp in the forest, he was wearing a Hawaiian floral shirt, a gold watch, several rings and smart little gold-rimmed glasses. Behind these, his eyes were acute. He was no traditionalist. Instead of moving to his in-laws' house at marriage in the old Karen manner, he built a new and grander house next door to Harvest Moon. The couple soon had a first baby.

One evening shortly afterwards, Laura was sitting by the lamp with her child talking to her cousin Shelley, himself a nurse in the Health Department. The lamp was getting low and Shelley went to fetch a can of paraffin. It's not absolutely necessary to extinguish a paraffin lamp while you refill it, as long as what you are pouring in really is paraffin, but by the time Shelley had realised his mistake, all three of them had horrible petrol burns. They were taken in a pickup truck, three hours on dirt roads out to hospital in Thailand and Shelley survived, although badly scarred. Laura and the baby died.

They were buried in a peculiar little cemetery by Golden Horn's house, with tombstones of cement blocks painted blue. The local children hated the tombs but there was no avoiding them. When Golden Horn had recovered from the double loss of his child and his wife, he married her younger sister.

Karen have – or used to have – firm ideas of taboo and transgression. It is very unusual for a widower to remarry, for fear of *chai* – terrible events consequent on flouting the rules. Perhaps Golden Horn felt that, with his child dead too, everything of that former marriage had been obliterated and there was no risk of *chai*. Perhaps he now felt that he had nothing to lose, or perhaps he simply didn't care for such old-fashioned nonsense.

But it was not to be shaken off. When the second daughter moved across from Harvest Moon's house to her husband's home next door, she felt most uncomfortable. Not only were the two garish tombs of her sister and the baby always in front of her: she found that all her sister's belongings had been carefully preserved by Golden Horn and were still there in the bedroom.

Something had to change. Traditional Karen housing also observes strict rules, so that the family spirits are not offended at being forced into conjunction with related spirits with whom they are incompatible. To ignore such strictures would again be *chai* and something ghastly would result. Which is what people now began to say that Golden Horn had done, his new house being both grander and (worse) higher then his respected father-in-law's. Surrounded by relics of her dead sister, the young wife believed

herself doomed. Modernist reform and Christianity notwithstanding, Golden Horn was obliged to exchange houses, dropping below
the level of the old Justice. The family was very cagey about the
matter, saying only, 'it is more convenient'.

For all the pretensions of the better quarters, there were effective
social equalisers in the village, chief of which was the river. We
all washed ourselves and our clothes in the same waters, and every
few houses had a small gravel beach with a slab of heavy timber
chained up where you could preen, and pound your skirts and
underpants. From 4 p.m. until dark, the banks were busy. Small
children thrashed and splashed, mothers and soldiers alike stood
waist-deep washing their hair, or soaping their shirts on the slab.
Elderly gentlemen waded out in sarongs while matrons delicately
tipped bowlfuls of the brown river over their breasts. Teenage girls
pushed fifty yards upstream against the strong current, filled their
long skirts with air so that they billowed behind them like patterned
flotation sacs and then came bobbing and giggling back down to
the beach.

When the rain was torrential, contrivances of split bamboo and
plastic pipe quickly filled the storage jars by our kitchens; at other
times we all had to go to the river. But now progress and wealth
were beginning to divide the village. The Education Department
had a small petrol pump that lifted water up the thirty-foot bluff
to a tank by the school, but the smart new teachers' houses, built
after the riverbank had already been fully colonised, were inconven-
iently far from the water. Every afternoon saw teachers in their
bathing sarongs with towels and clean underwear on their arms
trailing through the village pushing a cartload of plastic drums.
The hospital too had a pump which filled a big galvanised tank
– but with everything from pus-thickened bandages to tubercular
patients washed on the same muddy spot under the tap, it was
to be avoided. In Millionaires Row smarter houses such as Harvest
Moon's had water for their kitchens petrol-pumped to a cistern,
but to bathe they still went to the water. Except for Edward. He
built himself a bathroom with cement walls and a tin roof. When
his jars had been filled by the school pump, Ruth and he could
bathe in private behind a closed door. The rest of us, pastors, nurses,
forestry officers, soldiers and prisoners too, all went down to the
beach.

I wondered, do adult Karen ever take all their clothes off? They bathe clothed, they sleep clothed, and in the absence of privacy in their houses I suspected that they usually made love three-quarters clothed. Never once undressed in half a century! Except, of course, the modernists with cement bathrooms.

King Chulalongkorn of Siam (r. 1868–1910) had a particular fondness for the Karen. He liked to visit their settlements and even wrote poems about them, in one of which he comments on inadequate toilette:

> Girls, girls; these Karen are lovely,
> hair bunned with pins comely, so fair,
> decked with pins richly, at great cost.
> Their faces talced, they're so, so demure.
>
> Frisky dances; the girls' glad steps whirr.
> But, if you approach, bad odour –
> robed in homespun smocks.[1]

'At first sight', wrote Lunet de Lajonquière in 1904 (p. 200), 'they seemed to me very dirty, and I have never altered this impression.' J. G. Scott (1916, p. 35), considered that, 'many of the women are distinctly comely; they would also be fair-skinned if they ever washed themselves'. I heard that hill Karen have just one new homespun shirt or smock a year, which in that time never gets washed. I asked a friend about it and he shuddered: 'Even if they do go down to the river, some of them never get their clothes wet. I've seen girls walking very slowly into the water, rolling their smocks higher and higher up their necks as they go in until it's all sitting on their heads.'

But in our District bathing has become an elaborate and decorous process of wet and dry sarongs, of nylon trunks and sachets of shampoo. Fish nibble at your legs as you stand in the river; if you have any open sores, the fish bites can be exceedingly painful. In the Second World War 'Burma Railway' museum at Kanchanaburi, Thailand, there is a painting of a soldier, covered in tropical ulcers, deposited in the river to have these sores cleaned by the fish; I cannot understand how he bore the pain. In one respect at least, Karen custom holds firm. The sick are never bathed in the river. They are too vulnerable to malignant forces as it is, without immersing them in that powerful ambience to be nibbled by fish and spirits.

In traditional Karen society, roles such as that of Justice, Nurse and Secretary had no place. *Real* Karen are swiddeners (that is, farmers who use forest land in rotation by slash-and-burn clearing), animist or Buddhist by religion, leading simple lives cultivating rice on steep hillsides, the men trapping and training elephants, the women raising pigs and weaving the heavy red, white and black Karen cloths on backstrap looms. Most people in Riverside possessed Karen costume, but few could have woven it. The cloth was now produced on half a dozen large treadle looms tucked under the official guesthouse up at Headquarters, and people wore the costume on special days – weddings, Karen New Year, Kawthoolei Martyrs' Day. Hill Karen to the north do still wear the old stuffs, but in our region harsh economics long ago got the better of weaving. As far back as 1880 southern Karen men were reportedly in cheap ready-mades from Thailand. A village of red and white is a dim memory in these parts.

Few people in Riverside had any experience of traditional Karen life, and that alone set it apart from other villages on the river. These were soldiers and government staff. The former had little time for swiddening; the latter were Delta Karen pushed or pulled here by the war. They were Rangoon or small town educated, with a wider experience of the world but less skill in the forest. They had little in common with the forest people – sometimes not even language, since the newcomers were predominantly Sgaw Karen and the residents often Pwo. In a people famous for their individualism and self-sufficiency, the inhabitants of Riverside were, almost without exception, attached to large institutions, to Departments or the church or school.

Around which social life revolved. We would meet for a game of volleyball at *Boys Boarders*, or to watch a football match between teams from Riverside and from Headquarters. The school organised end-of-term picnics; I watched boatloads of children being ferried over the river in highly unstable canoes to carry their food off into the forest for a few daylight hours. The rock band rehearsed in the kindergarten, and videos were shown on the steps of the church hall.

Everyone had a role, a job to do. Such were the demands of organising the State that many people had two. An independent state administration requires personnel; without functionaries the people may be no worse off but they will hardly recognise authority. And those functionaries must have certain basic skills in literacy, numeracy and related activities. The smaller your population, the higher the ratio of bureaucrats to citizens will tend to be – if you can find the staff at all. The population of Kawthoolei, especially the 'skilled' population, is tiny, and a further result is the ever-greater concentration of those skills; if everyone is doing several jobs, the only answer is to have all the jobs in the same place. Thus Riverside became a typical 'new town', with white-collar housing billowing in all directions.

But with virtually no labour force. With everyone so busy about their Departments, it was remarkably difficult to get anything new done, as Janice found.

Janice was a Karen woman who had left the forest far behind. Her grandfather had, like many other Karen foresters, been a valued employee of the Bombay-Burmah Trading Company (which dominated the teak trade in the British period), and had been taken by them to work in Borneo. As a result, Janice had been brought up in Singapore and Malaysia and the woman I met was now a Bangkok sophisticate with a Thai boyfriend called Two Shoes. He was always introduced as her 'husband' with a chorus of knowing smiles. I liked them; a friendly, talkative young pair, smartly dressed and cheerful, always ready to give me a lift or to show me their latest project. They were energetic entrepreneurs and Colonel Marvel had invited them to stimulate income generation in the District. They tried to establish a basket-weaving concern. They installed two bamboo-splitting machines under Morning Star's house, brought in half a dozen Thai basket-makers to show the Karen how to do it, and looked about for Karen to train. But they couldn't find any. In this impoverished, besieged society of rebels, so desperately in need of foreign currency, no one had the time or inclination to earn a living making baskets to sell to Thailand. I met Janice and Two Shoes driving despondently about the village in their pickup looking for a workforce: 'It would be easier', said Two Shoes, 'to find diamonds.' The basket-weaving project was abandoned two weeks later.

> 'What is it with my people?' said Thomas the Thai-Karen missionary. 'They are desperately poor here, but they grow almost nothing. In any other poor country those school-children would be digging the fields every afternoon, but here every grain of rice they eat is imported!'
> 'That', said (of all people) Arthur the Agricultural Officer, 'is not what childhood is for. They will have to work hard soon enough.' Which is one reason why the air-raid shelters at the

school were such half-hearted and forever unfinished construc-
tions.

The only labourers available were the malefactors in the prison,
of whom there were some two dozen. They could be seen setting
off each day carrying heavy iron *parangs* and guarded by a small
boy with a red neckerchief and an AK47 on his arm. They would
cut bamboo for school fencing, repair the roads or assist with some
civic building. They could be called upon for almost any task, but
their services were so much in demand that applications for their
use had to reach the Colonel weeks in advance. Their lives did
not seem especially unpleasant, their yoke appeared quite light.
I asked Morning Star, medical officer to the jail, why they didn't
run away. He replied, 'Where would they go? They cannot stay
hiding in the forest for long and when they are recaptured they
are sent to the jail at GHQ, which is much harder for them and
where they wear irons on their legs.'

Departmental heads held sway in Riverside. Edward was an empire
builder, an indefatigable organiser rushing up and down between
Riverside and Headquarters on a yellow motorbike, a zealot of the
Education Department and, with Finance also in his charge, an
awkward antagonist for anyone whose work he considered less than
essential. Pastor Moses was the rock of the Baptist Church, elderly
and slow, but a man of considerable physical presence and a conservative moralist. He observed the tribulations and intrigues of
the revolutionary leadership without participating directly – but
his nod of approval counted. He was one of my best informants,
both as to the undercurrents of Karen politics and also on the culture
of the past; but when he mentioned that he had a 'Karen coat'
of a sort I'd never seen before, and after I'd badgered him repeatedly
to show me, it was not some traditional wrap but an old sports
blazer in white Karen homespun, with pink piping.

Then there was Bartholomew of Health and Welfare, constantly
struggling for funds and to maintain the civilian independence of
health care against an army take-over. There was Roger of Transport, a man with a moustache and small pointed beard (most
unusual in a Karen), who always drove sitting on a loaded pistol
and who could bring other Departments to a halt by not making
the *fowehka* or the one official boat available. There was 'Devourer
of the Country' of the Information Department, which strove to

keep up interest and commitment to the cause out in the villages, and the officers of the Agriculture and Forestry Departments who bravely confronted the task of nurturing the Revolution's natural resources. Each had their staff and their supporters in the village.

Faction was quietly rife, though many did their best to put self-interest aside. William, the Deputy Headmaster of the school, represented a union of the most powerful strands in village life, church and school. He stood on the steps at eight o'clock each morning leading 250 children in prayer, oaths of allegiance and the Anthem.

He also personified another link, the (literal) marriage of educated urban sophistication to simple country ways. He brought his young wife some status and financial advantage, but in the event, it was not Bella who had to adapt to professional life in town, but William who had to learn to live in the hills.

Coping had more than immediate practical significance. William saw a need for a new 'universal Karen', at once traditionalist and modernist. He was himself a teacher, administrator and modernist leader, and also a cultural conservationist of old ways of which he really knew very little. Embarking on some carpentry, I mentioned to him that my borrowed saw was blunt, and he offered to sharpen it. As we crouched over the jig and produced appalling noises with a file across the saw's teeth, he said quietly, 'If you come here to Kawthoolei you must be a craftsman and a teacher, and a doctor and a soldier and a religious man; you must be prepared to be everything.' It was to William's house that I went for Karen folk-tales. Not that he knew these himself, but he was very keen that I should hear them, and so he would go and ask someone, or look them up in books and learn them for me. Then we would sit on his balcony at night with one small paraffin lamp (even as schoolmasters go, William was poor), light the Burmese cheroots that I'd brought, dandle his small children and have a recitation.

William had been a schoolmaster in Burma. Other school staff – if not simply former pupils put up in front of the class – were graduates (or perhaps drop-outs) from Burmese colleges. A handful of professional teachers stiffened the school. Of these the most formidable was Dierdre, known to many just as Pipi (Grandmother). Now in her sixties, she'd been a teacher all her working life and was regarded with awed affection by the village. She was a Delta woman and, in a small and kindly way, an élitist snob. She'd been used to better things than this untidy forest, and to higher educational and intellectual standards. She had an acute idea of what it meant to be a Karen, and felt that moral standards in this heterogeneous community of displaced persons were not up to scratch. Behind her bespectacled smile, this slight little figure disapproved of a good deal.

My closest friends – True Love, Bartholomew and Great Lake – will have more than their share of attention in this book. But there were many who welcomed me often to their houses, gave me meals and cigars and plenty of their time. Their generosity in this respect lead me to one of the most fertile fields in Riverside – the gossip.

Riverside was famous for its gossip. People came 'to hear the news', and at Headquarters up the hill, which would have preferred to have regarded Riverside as just a safe dormitory annex, they knew that to hear the dirt they'd have to come too. There were even one or two people in the village, of rather vague official standing, who were widely considered to be 'ears' – not of the Burmese, but of Colonel Marvel the Governor.

The village was no mere hotbed of malicious prattle. Although a dormitory of recent history, where few major decisions were ever taken and which bore little resemblance to the lives and villages of most Karen, Riverside was the point of contact where the Revolution met the people. Neither party – nor villagers nor revolutionary hierarchy – quite trusted the place. The Colonel would sweep through unannounced, dropping into half a dozen leading homes in an effort to feel the popular pulse but never more than half-satisfied with the answers he received – as well as wasting much time in tying and untying his army boots before entering each home. Forest villagers avoided Riverside if they could, but might have need of the hospital, or trade or education or some official duty to bring them there. Officials undertaking tours of inspection all embarked at Riverside, finding boats and crews there and leaving their world of cars and generators, videos and fluorescent light behind. Beyond Riverside, they must do as real Karen.

For other villagers it must have been a bewildering place, where young men rode motorbikes but had no more subtle method of catching a monitor lizard than blowing it apart with an assault rifle. Schooling here was far more advanced than anything older villagers had ever known, but what little farming they did in Riverside was frequently inept – vegetable gardens insufficiently watered or weeded, and inadequately protected from marauding pigs. Or rice fields made too little and too late, because everyone relied on the rice ration given to 'members of the Revolution'. Few of the inhabitants knew how to thatch a house, but many could give injections. Few of them knew the old songs, but when occasion demanded that they learnt one for some public ceremony, most of them could handle a microphone with confidence.

The Delta revolutionaries have taken on an exceedingly difficult task; they must project two images of the Karen neither of which are altogether true, and which are potentially contradictory. They must be seen to run an efficient modern state; otherwise, neither the Burmese nor the outside world will take them seriously. And they must uphold a strong sense of common cultural identity, or the Revolution will soon falter. But this large and heterogeneous grouping known so imprecisely to outsiders as the Karen has in fact very few common features running right through it. Language, customs, dress, laws, daily life – all these vary widely. Above all, the disparate groups of Karen recognise no common sovereign.

This is another sense in which Riverside marks the conjunction of the Revolution and of forest life. One of the few common features in traditional Karen society is the autonomy of the villages, and these villages have an egalitarian power structure. The 'elected headman' is a bureaucratic imposition by British, Burmese, Thai and now Kawthoolei authorities needing someone to deal with. His power was always very limited; he is only the mouthpiece of consensus. It is not a prestigious job. If there is any traditional 'head' of the village it is (at least in animist areas) the priest. While important as an arbiter and spiritual leader, he has no final authority either since, if villagers don't like the way he does things, they simply split off and build anew elsewhere.

That is not how you run an orderly Revolution. The Free Karen State of Kawthoolei is divided into Districts, Townships and Tracts – roughly equivalent to British Regions, Counties and Parishes. The State claims to be democratic, and there is a system of four-yearly election of village representatives to make up the Township Standing Committee of secretaries, Departmental officers and the like. This committee nominates a Township Chairman, and a representative from the Township goes up to the District Committee which in turn sends delegates to the Supreme National Congress. This pyramid of democracy looks a great deal better on paper than on the ground. The man (and it is a man) sent from the village may well not be the elected headman, but someone he asks to go in his place. When the Township nominates a chairman, the District may disapprove, overrule it and appoint someone else. The District Standing Committee is formed by co-opting and appointment. No one elected the District Chairman, Colonel Marvel; he was sent from GHQ. And, while in theory the President of Kawthoolei is elected by the Supreme National Congress, in practice they have not been able to hold a full Congress since 1974. The following year the Burmese turned their attentions from the Communists to the Karen, the battle of Myawaddy was fought, and the KNLA General Bo Mya took over from his elderly Marxist predecessor Mahn Ba Zan. No one has seriously challenged Bo Mya since.

'So, no Congress for fourteen years now', said Highlander, of the Information Department, who was telling me all this. 'It's very difficult, with the war and Burmese pressure and so on.'

But Kawthoolei is no military tyranny. No one was shy of telling me what they thought, and no one ever complained in my hearing. At least, not at Riverside, where most people are government workers anyway. What they think and say to each other out in the villages, I cannot claim to know. I was almost always in the company of revolutionary officials – and even if not, that is how I was associated.

Thus Riverside is the interface between a revolutionary hierarchy with a General on top, claiming to fight for the people, and the traditional liberties of those normally acephalous people. Highlander said, 'We've been looking at constitutions; what do you think of Yugoslavia?'

Highlander was himself part of another, parallel system of power: the family. Highlander's father had had two wives and fourteen children. Of these, an elder brother was a Department Secretary; another brother (Golden Horn) was a Township Secretary, as was a third brother. One sister was the wife of Harvest Moon the Justice; a second had been the District's other properly trained nurse (like Laura, now dead, but of malaria). A third sister was the one trained midwife, who ran her own clinic downriver at Barterville – though, as she made a profit out of it, she was not regarded as being 'in our revolution'. Everyone of importance in Kawthoolei seemed to be closely related. This made the search for a proper constitution essential – or, to the more cynical, an irrelevance.

There was a community of outsiders at Riverside for whom the place was a dreadful jungle backwater – the Thai sawmill workers. They were very isolated. I sometimes heard them call cheerfully explicit propositions to the KNLA nurses who lived nearby, but in spite of centuries of contact, they spoke almost no Karen and almost no Karen spoke Thai. Very rarely does a Karen who has gone to Thailand and learnt the language return to live in Kaw-thoolei.

The Thais were friendly and civil to the Karen, but certain little incidents can't have helped them to feel at home. Late one night there was a burst of gunfire from the riverbank near the sawmill. Some Thais had borrowed a small boat to go night fishing. A Karen soldier had spotted something on the water; it was a moonless night and he could see little. Fearing it to be a sneak Burmese attack he had yelled a challenge. Unable either to understand the challenge or to reply, the Thais had said nothing until the soldier opened fire and they jumped overboard to swim for their lives.

The Thais had no land to cultivate and, if the mills were working, little free time. There was nothing for them in Riverside but their rows of rabbit hutches. Not surprisingly, they hated it. For them, this was an uncouth wilderness. There were no cinemas, no bars, no restaurants, nothing that they would dignify with the name of 'shop'. They just wanted to go home – and, after only a fortnight, that is what Janice and Two Shoes' basket-making instructors did. If the sawmill workers weren't paid they too would soon leave, on one occasion removing and selling some of the mill machinery in lieu of wages. Riverside had just one redeeming feature: those ingenuous jungle Karen would bring in the most extraordinary forest exotics to sell for a song; the Thai workers bought them up, took them home and made all the profit. There were bizarre items like mountain bear's gallbladder, which Bangkok Chinese would turn into medicines. Or Karen 'elks', big placid deer with grey velvet hides and resigned expressions, worth a small fortune over the border. Or – oddest of all – the six-footed tortoise that I was once shown, with extra feet half-way up its back legs. The sawmill foreman had bought it off a Karen for B.30 but he could resell it for many times that in Bangkok.

There were plenty of other Thais to be seen in Riverside – I often wished I'd been a little more sure who they were. The group of three 'teachers', for example, who appeared one day and engaged me in conversation while one tried very hard to take my photograph, so that I spent several minutes in a ludicrous dance trying to keep my back to the camera. There were businessmen who came with Landcruisers, chainsaws and sometimes the mail too, and traders in pickup trucks who kept the shops supplied with sacks of prawn crackers and crates of Fanta, even blocks of ice for Millionaires Row. How did they regard the rebel state? As a captive market, presumably.

Hard daily news was elusive. A full company of troops could pass through the village without anyone being able (or prepared) to tell me where they were going. The gossips kept me informed as to the minutiae of life. For commentary and analysis I went to breakfast with Pastor Moses.

They were leisurely exchanges, our breakfasts. We seldom ate before ten, and we ate well – duck curries, grilled fish, eggs and plenty of vegetables, well spiced. Moses cooked these invitation meals himself. We gave each other language lessons. He spoke English with ponderous care, and taught me to pronounce Karen as though he was schooling me in the Psalms. He tried to have me compose his international correspondence for him, to Baptists in Malaysia, Australia and Japan, but this was nerves and laziness on his part; he could write decent English if he chose. And we would pump each other. Moses asked, what did I think of Russia? Was I a socialist? Or a communist? If so, why? What was my church? Would I please explain, what is a Quaker? Ah, I see, a sort of communist . . . and so on.

For all his air of timelessness, Moses too was a newcomer. He'd been a pastor near Rangoon, but his eldest son had come to Kawthoolei to join the KNLA. This son had also been a prominent Karen Christian and the Burmese had known all about his new career. They had started making threatening noises towards the family in Burma.

'It's not easy to be a Christian in Burma anyway. There are restrictions on importing and printing Bibles, every pastor must be registered and is supposed to inform the authorities of the names of his whole congregation.'

Moses, his wife and daughter Fair Flower had come by bus and by foot to Kawthoolei and then Riverside. The congregation built him a house and paid him a stipend of c. £150 p.a. to cover his expenses, more if he had travelling to do.

Consensus has it that some 20 per cent of Karen are Christian, with perhaps 30 per cent Buddhist and the rest animist. In our District, Christianity had a stronger hold. The indigenous population here had been relatively thin before the reversals of the war pushed lowland Karen this way, besides which the missions had begun their work out of Tavoy in the south more than half a century before they were free to work in Upper Burma. Perhaps half the river villagers were Christian. It was not exclusively Baptist; there were a few Catholics too. Converts to Seventh Day Adventism like General Bo Mya were rare here, but traces of their influence could be found. I received an official invitation to a function that was entirely in Karen script but which specified the day with the English word Thursday. In the old Karen system, Monday is simply 'the first day', Tuesday 'the second day' and so on. But, in that way, Saturday would come out as the sixth day. As Adventists regard Saturday as the Seventh Day and Sabbath, the General wouldn't have liked that – so, Thursday it became.

At the full moon, lying in my hammock in Bartholomew's house, I could hear drumming from the old Buddhist and animist village of Lama, half an hour downriver. Just occasionally Buddhists came to Riverside; one might hear them chanting prayers in the evening. But the Baptists had no serious rivals.

Soon after I arrived they consecrated the new, blue Bethany Church and hung it about with crêpe streamers and balloons. Scores of elders of the Kawthoolei Karen Baptist Convention were invited from GHQ and elsewhere for the celebrations. Of the 100-plus expected, only two dozen arrived; the Thais were being difficult on the border. Even so, we felt suitably awed by the authority of those who attended, and by the rich display of red-and-white Karen tunics they brought to the village. They radiated confidence, this educated élite from the plains now seated on the uncouth hillsides. Kawthoolei's Information Department struggles to counter the impression of a purely Christian rebellion, claiming in its 1986 birthday tribute to Bo Mya that, although he became a Christian at the same time as becoming leader of the Revolution, he has since then risen above the sectarian divide to unify the people. Dr Vinton's letters of 1886 can still describe the view from Riverside: 'The heathen Karen are to a man brigading themselves under the Christians.' Whether the daily life of animist and Buddhist families in other villages is really much disturbed by the dictates of the Christian KNU is another matter.

In this hegemony, the Church's staunch ally is the Education Department. Riverside has the mother school. With between 250 and 300 pupils from up and down the river, it is by far the largest in the District. The buildings are well scattered. At eight each morning they line up by class in front of the junior block for prayers, but the kindergarten and middle-school children then have to walk 100 yards to reach their buildings.

'We had an air raid four years ago', said Edward. 'There was just one old propeller-driven plane. It didn't drop any bombs but it did machine-gun the village. There were three casualties – two ducks and a tin of cooking oil; we ate them all. But the boys' hostel was also hit. After that we decided to disperse the school.' They painted camouflage mottling on the roof, and now from time to time they set the children to re-dig the air raid shelters, which the next hard rain washes in again.

The Karens . . . look on Christianity and education as inseparable factors in their civilisation. A school must always have a church, and a church can never be without a school.

So Smeaton asserted in 1887 (p. 226). Christmas 1986 illustrated the union.

In December I was staying at the house built for the French medical team that never came. It had a high balcony where I would sit reading and writing by lamplight, nervous of leaning back against the wall for fear of scorpions. At that time of year Karen crept about at nights in coats and mufflers through thick, cold mists. One evening I heard carol singing coming from houses nearby. It approached – a choir of schoolchildren and their teacher. They sang 'Have a Christmas to You' (to the tune of 'Happy Birthday') and then 'Every Day with Jesus'. Sam, Bartholomew's stepson, thoughtful as ever, came ahead to prepare the way with me and to suggest a sum for the collection.

> 'Where are they from?' I asked.
> 'From Lama village.'
> 'But I thought most families at Lama were animists.'
> 'Yes. They do not mind.'

On Christmas Eve, Ruth and Edward extended a cordial invitation to dinner. On the road I was headed off by a messenger:

> 'Edward asks that you do not come yet. He has a visitor.'

Edward usually liked his visitors to look at each other. I went to a nearby teacher's house to be consoled with a glass of country spirits. When I was summoned again half an hour later Edward said, 'Two men that I did not know came to see me. They said they were Thai officials and were asking if they could help us. But I think they were Burmese spies.'

We dismissed them, and sat down to duck and pork with banana cake and coffee, while militiamen set off fireworks in front of Bethany Church. More carol singers arrived. They'd walked three days through the forest from Betewood in the Western Valley, and their voices were strange.

'They are Pwo', said Edward. 'You can hear, their voices are much higher in tone than the people here.' But they were singing in Burmese.

At 9.30 p.m. there was a performance that would have graced any British church or school hall – a Nativity pageant. Edward had written the script; the dialogue and incidental music (Rossini to reggae) were all pre-recorded. It took place on a stage behind the church, with clusters of balloons, a Christmas tree of bamboo and wire covered in green and red crêpe, and red and gold *Merry Christmas* banners. The Nativity was retold in full, the cast of schoolchildren, teachers, soldiers and revolutionary functionaries dressed in the manner of Christmas pageants anywhere. Herod wore silky green polyester trews, a yellow T-shirt richly trimmed with sticky gold paper, a long woollen overcoat, a crown of metallic ruby-red card and a painted moustache and beard. He sipped tea from a blue plastic beaker, brooding. His infanticidal cronies wore balaclavas, Burmese Army berets or cotton headdresses in Hollywood Arab fashion. The angels, with star-tipped paper crowns, were all in white except for Gabriel who achieved a sinister touch with black gloves. Two white seraphim with rouged cheeks spotted my camera and demanded 'play photo! play photo!', framing themselves against a stand of dripping ferns. The shepherds, with crooks and nylon bomber jackets, carolled from the bamboo wings. Joseph was in a green checked tablecloth, Mary in a skull-tight white coif. She carried a cardboard box trimmed with red crêpe and containing straw and a bundle of cloth.

In my photographs of the evening, everyone is grinning delightedly. The fun was also educational; this was a school, not a church production. After the pageant the children sat a quiz on Bible knowledge. After that, a midnight service, and then communal chicken porridge at one in the morning.

Christmas Day; I gave some friends a clock that I'd bought them in Bangkok. The husband formally shook my hand in thanks. I asked him what he was giving his wife and he said quietly, 'My love.'

There were plenty of church services, and lots of sport. Teams fought out a volley-ball tournament and then battled in the heat on the rough football pitch, while Moses and I watched from folding chairs on the touchline.

But Boxing Day was most memorable. The Education Department, with nothing to give the children, decided that they would at least have a festive meal together. But at the last moment there were gifts. A European charity decided that it would donate £2,000-worth of school supplies for the coming year, the fruits of Edward's skilful negotiating in Bangkok. A visiting Englishwoman gave money to buy sweets and biscuits, and we spent half the night on Edward's verandah putting toffees and custard creams into paper bags labelled 'Jesus Loves You' and the like, done in felt-tip colours by children in the United States – another donation.

In the morning the school benches were brought out in front of the classroom block and formed into a wide semi-circle, with the Christmas tree at its centre and the gifts stacked on tables. The children assembled and sang a Creed of Youth, the Lord's Prayer and a Psalm under William's direction. They then recited the Four Principles of Ba U Gyi, Kawthoolei's founder:

> For us, surrender is out of the question.
> Recognition of the Karen State must be completed.
> We shall retain our arms.
> We shall determine our own destiny.

After which, class by class in blue and white uniforms, they stepped smartly forward and received their six exercise books, three ballpoint pens, three pencils, a box of coloured crayons and a Bible Story colouring book, all in a plastic bag, together with their sweets and custard creams. There were packets for the teachers too, of soap and toothbrushes. A soldier took class photos, and the jovial sergeant Nixon asked me to take one of a group of boys about to go with him to the front line for the first time. They'd all joined the KNLA very young but had been sent for schooling first. Now their turn had come. It was a solemn moment.

Not so the feast; this was inspired gaiety. Each class had planned and cooked its own menu, scrounging a chicken here, some noodles there, even putting a few *baht* together to send out to Thailand for jelly puddings in plastic tubs. The teachers were not supposed to help. When the hour came the tables, scattered among the trees, were heaped with food. On some tacit signal, teachers and guests descended like the Tudor court on Progress, moving from one class table to another to feed with all their pupils in turn. With shrieks, hoots and giggles the children scuttled about to see what each other had cooked, the little jellies were passed out, there was singing, warmheartedness, broad grins and delight. I've seldom enjoyed a Christmas dinner quite like that.

Nor, it seemed, had Nixon. Beaming upon the scene, he invoked with happy contempt the name of the Burmese general who, with his *Four Cuts*, proposed the economic strangulation of Kawthoolei: 'If Ne Win could see us now, he would cry! He would cry!'

4 True Love at home

After two weeks at Riverside, I thought it was time that I began to move about. Edward of Education lent me his boat and found a boatman and an escort. The latter was that soldier-teacher who had played a large part at the New Year ceremonies. Introducing him, Edward said, 'You can call this funny man True Love', and of course I thought that he was joking.

True Love was a Delta Karen. At thirty-two he was very handsome, verging on the prettyboy. Slim but muscular, with graceful and well-groomed features, he could not have looked less like an unsophisticated tribesman – though when public occasion demanded, he tried, in Karen red-striped shirt and sarong. The result, quite devoid of wear and tear, was unconvincing. There was also a quiet confidence in his movements that suggested refinement, not the timidity of a 'people capable of being afraid'. He gave an impression of discreet competence – though I soon realised that the sometimes coweringly shy village people were far more adept at negotiating the forest than True Love. He had a polite ease in his manner with strangers and superiors; it suggested his agreement with the destiny that had placed him where he was on the Karen ladder – a sergeant-clerk in the KNLA, and occasional secondary school teacher. I was later to see the depth of his frustrations, but he accommodated them so well as to be, in terms of revolutionary thrust, emasculated. Well equipped to be a Karen yuppie, he was, rather, a model non-commissioned officer. He was also Edward's protégé.

Little of this, apart from his good looks and quietly cheerful good manners, was apparent on that first boat trip: only the excellent guide and humorous travelling companion. He was, however, quite ready to tell me how he had come to be a forest-dwelling insurgent:

My grandfather was a teacher and politician who worked for the Karen people. When the British fled to India he was murdered by the Burmese. But I still have a lot of family. My father is a retired postmaster, my mother was headmistress of a school near Mergui; Karen have always been willing to work for their country, you see. Then there were eight children, but my brother who was a doctor died of malaria. I'm the oldest. I went to high school, I got good grades and I wanted to read Natural Sciences at Rangoon, but my father said all the other children needed an education too, and in Burma that costs money. So he asked me to go to work. Well, I obey my father.

I worked as a fisherman. In Burma we have foreign trawlers that have been confiscated for fishing in Burmese waters, and I was on one of these, no. 502. It was big; we had maybe forty people on board to sort and gut the fish, with big freezer holds where we had to work dressed up in special clothes and thick gloves, at minus forty degrees! You had to keep moving and when you came out into the hot tropical air your lips didn't work and you couldn't talk.

We had all the latest navigation equipment on that boat. It had come from Thailand, it was new. We sailed the length of Malaysia and sometimes into ports, but we were never allowed to land. I have seen other countries only from the sea.

So, I worked a year for the People's Pearl and Fisheries Corporation. This way I really found out what it meant to be a Karen in Burma. There was never anything serious, but day after day there were little insults, or people not doing things you asked them, or promotion always going to the Burmese. Even travelling to see my mother at Mergui could be difficult: the Burmese make endless problems for the Karen – they often won't sell us plane or boat tickets; even on the buses they can be difficult. So I began to study history and the story of the Karen people. In Rangoon I met a Karen who told me about Kawthoolei and asked me to join the Revolution, and so I made up my mind. I resigned my job and my friend put me in touch with the KNU underground. They had found others wanting to go as well, and a group of us travelled together, walking through the forest.

I didn't teach here straight away: I was up north at GHQ for a while, and a soldier at the Front Line for six years. But nothing was happening for me there at GHQ. I'd come all that way but I had no real place in the Revolution.

Then Edward came to visit GHQ in 1981: he was looking for teachers for the Education Department down here and he recruited me, Dan, Wilf, Nixon and White Rock. And here we all are.

You can't imagine how difficult it is when you first come to Kawthoolei. I didn't know anyone here, and I suddenly realised that I had left all my family behind. I had never lived in the jungle before. I wanted to do everything I could for the Revolution, but it was only with Edward and his wife Ruth's help that I could settle here. So, now I am a soldier and a teacher.

It was to become a familiar story. Desperate for skilled manpower, the KNU recruiters in Burma often go for students – with at least half a skill, and with youth and activist enthusiasm, without as yet the survivalist caution born of adult married life, they are an obvious target. There is a song that True Love and Ku Wah (the singer and dance teacher) recorded for me that describes the calls to duty. 'A traditional song', said True Love. It describes a mountain called Kwe Ke Baw:

> Kwe Ke Baw! When I came there, what sights I saw!
> To the west, the Salween River gliding smoothly by.
> All round the mountain, rich rice fields
> and below, the lovely town of Pa-an.
> To the east, Taw Naw mountain looks enchanting.
> This is our heritage from our ancestors,
> This hill is Karen country, these are Karen villages.
> But the people are poor, and they wait
> in hope that educated Karen will come,
> to teach them how to escape from poverty.
> Hear me, all Karen! This is your responsibility.
> We call you to join us!

The call to *educated* Karen is revealing: 'We do not want all the Karen people to move to Kawthoolei', said a gentleman from the Foreign Office. 'If they all came here we would lose our hold on the Delta, which is our country too.' The KNU wants a strong central cohort of skilled revolutionaries. Semi-skilled will do. White Rock had been a botany student at Rangoon but had dropped out. He'd known True Love there; they'd been politicised at the same time. White Rock had been trying to organise Karen students into groups to come to Kawthoolei but the police had discovered what he was at; he'd narrowly avoided arrest.

Each university generation has sent its recruits. Highlander, of the Information Department, arrived earlier: 'I came in 1968. I was a student reading economics at Rangoon. I had wanted to be an airforce pilot but my father told me not to be stupid and to try to work in finance or banking. Then I heard about my people's troubles and I left college . . .'

Others had purposefully completed their education, like the surgeon who ran the Health Department at GHQ. He said he'd always known that he would come to Kawthoolei, but he'd also known that he would be more use fully trained, so he'd worked his way through the Rangoon hospital system first – 'to gain experience'. And then he had left his wife and family behind, and had not seen them since.

When I first met True Love he had no home. He'd been married nearly a year before I came, he and his wife Silver moving into a friend's house while he did something about his own. The Education Department – that is, Edward and Ruth – provided the timber, the nails and the tin for the roof, because Silver taught the senior kindergarten (KGB) and True Love was a part-time teacher also. But he had to construct it. 'I once helped a friend to build his house, so I know what to do. The students help me sometimes.'

He'd been given a month off his Army duties to build – which our river jaunt interrupted but he didn't argue. When we returned I helped him as far as I could. It was a simple structure raised on stilts as usual. The procedure was to erect the timber posts, tie them together with the major floor supports some four feet off the ground, put in roof joists and cap it with a simple ridge roof of tin – and then, having laid a rudimentary bamboo floor, many Karen would immediately move in. True Love felt that Silver might like some walls also, so we put up a few of those.

He was no expert; he probably knew more about gutting fish than building houses. But the only tools required were a hammer, a saw and a sharp *parang* (machete), and these he could handle. He made the wall panels by taking a six-foot piece of green bamboo, chopping it lengthwise with dozens of incomplete cuts, making one full-length split, then opening it out and stamping it flat. Then he'd take another bamboo, make a short cut at one end and pull hard, so that with a most satisfying *crack* it split neatly in two and could be subdivided again. These were the fixing laths. I held the panels up while he drove nails through them. We could wall off a whole room in an hour, or half the house in a day. Similar panels of split bamboo made the floor; Silver came, and the cooking pots were installed.

But there were flaws in the work. The floor supports were too far apart, the bamboo sections were sagging and a carelessly heavy tread might go straight through them. And the walls were only a single panel thick – the best houses always had double walls – and when the wind was blowing the rain would come straight through and saturate everything.

The floor really was no good, and there were points of status and professional pride to be considered also. It is the mark of a modern, settled Karen of standing to have a planed wooden floor. The Colonel, for example, thought it wrong that Pastor Moses should sit on bamboo, and had donated a stack of hardwood planks

Plate 4. True Love and Silver's house '. . . became usable bit by bit.'

for his house. Traditionalists and forest dwellers, Bartholomew and the Front Line troops might make do with split bamboo, but the teachers at Riverside were not that sort. So the Education Department found timber for Silver and True Love. The Department also possessed an electric planer which could be run off the school generator. The new floor was laid. I regretted it; bamboo was a pleasure, split and trimmed, rounded by nature and worn to a high polish by passing feet, with any dirt simply falling off through the gaps. The timber put splinters into you, always felt dusty and, in the cracks between the boards, harboured scorpions.

   There were now two bedrooms at one side of the house, a long public room running the length of the other side, with a kitchen area at the back and a small balcony and table at the front. All these only became usable bit by bit. Quite apart from the time that I'd taken up, True Love's duties up the hill at Headquarters kept recalling him. Besides which, the nails kept running out and there was no cash in the Army kitty to buy another kilo; or the Thai workers at the sawmill, unpaid for months, had given up and gone. So the work crept on, never finished. One week some torn piece of green plastic would be replaced with bamboo walling. The next, a few more joists for the kitchen roof might be added, and eventually the last tin sheets arrived so that at least Silver could cook out of the rain.

As the essentials neared completion, True Love began to add refinements. The built-in table on the verandah was shaped like the body of a guitar. There was a hutch for a baby squirrel in one corner, small shelves for a little mirror and an untidy handful of broken combs and Burmese cheroots. By the front steps, inspirational dicta, precisely quoted and neatly lettered onto card, were pinned to a main post: 'I know not what course others may take, but as for me, give me liberty or give me death!'

As personal effects began to emerge from cardboard boxes in the bedroom, different aspects of the householders' characters emerged also: beat-up cassettes of pop music (but no cassette player). Bibles and hymn books, political primers and histories. There was also a surprising quantity of household goods – surprising because, as revolutionary workers, both Silver and True Love received a rice ration but no cash salary at all. So how did they acquire the plates, the glasses, the pans?

> 'Many of these were presents – some from Edward and Ruth, some from Thomas the missionary. But we do have a little cash sometimes. My mother-in-law bakes cakes which we can sell, or we can raise pigs. Enough for a few things.'

Pigs, ducks and chickens lived under the house. True Love swore that he hated pigs, which was convenient as traditionally they are the property and responsibility of Karen women. The chickens passed their days in planning assaults on the kitchen; a characteristic noise in Karen homes is a metallic *clack*, *clack* as beaks go for cold rice in aluminium pots. When, on frequent occasions, I came with Ku Wah and my cassette machine to record songs, the livestock joined in and were immortalised.

The inhabitants of the house were always changing. Anthropologically, Karen society is sometimes described as matrilinear and uxorilocal – which means that inheritance passes through the female line and that newlyweds go to the wife's parents' house. Under the Revolution, tradition was adapting to modern expediency.

Silver's parental home upriver was of no use to her and True Love; they both had official jobs and had to be where duty took them. But the family could come to them, and Silver's mother, grandmother or sister were usually there, sometimes her father too. Custom once dictated who could live with whom in a Karen house – adolescent boys shouldn't sleep in the same house as unmarried sisters, etc. – but in Riverside such things were being quietly discarded.

True Love would say that he was pleased to be rid of many of the old customs; he was no iconoclast, but some things were inappropriate now, even harmful and unfair. Anyway, he and Silver had little say in the matter; as servants of the Revolution, calls could be made upon them from many quarters, and their little wooden house (its upright, four-square, stark new timber frame topped with brilliant tin about as traditional as the video-recorder in the school) was always full. The Army could require them to billet officers, or the Education Department might ask them to put up a teacher who had come from another village for an upgrading course. Or the Colonel might decide to send primary school children from Headquarters down to the river and expect True Love and Silver to make room for one or two. Edward, involved in endless small deals with gentlemen from Bangkok, required him to accommodate three Thai workers who were there in secret to find, cut and polish fine cross-cuts of timber for luxury table tops, to be smuggled out before rivals got wind of the operation – and so these men camped for a while on the verandah before building themselves a separate bamboo shelter. True Love couldn't refuse anyone; the various Departments, after all, were not only providing his rice, but all the building materials as well. There was even a suggestion, shortly after my arrival, that True Love should build an extension onto his house for me.

As a man about the village, True Love wore the standard sarong of dark red. But on our many journeys on the river or through the forest he always dressed his best as a soldier, neatly turned out and clean, his sleeves rolled, his green beret finished with a KNLA badge. Only his feet were less than parade-perfect, but there practicality ruled: plastic flipflops are not only cheap – they are a lot easier if you are constantly in and out of houses and kicking them off; also, when climbing in and out of the boat to negotiate rapids. He would carry his M16, or a .22 and a box of shells borrowed from Edward, and he'd represent the Revolution.

Just which branch of the Revolution was, however, difficult to pin down. What, I frequently asked him, is your job this week? 'I'm a teacher', or 'I am called to do the accounts for the Army', or 'Edward has asked me to do all the illustrations for the new English course', or 'I am to assist with your surveys'. In a small rebel enclave attempting to be a fully fledged state, anyone with education mattered and a fluent speaker of English with even just the beginnings of a science education was worth his weight in gold, and the Departments were fighting over him. At first I thought it flattering to him, to be regarded as the facilitator of so much. Then I saw the frustration: to be the universal tool of the People's Revolution is a glorious and servile role.

On our early journeys he was ever the courteous official guide; he would interpret my conversations with the village headman or teacher, and then explain to me the election of Township representatives. As often as not he was seeing villages for the first time himself; we would explore and interview, sling our hammocks and tell each other stories or find the nearest rough guitar and teach each other songs, and a partnership was established.

To begin with, sending notes to the Colonel or the Adjutant Officer requesting True Love's services for a trip to new territory, I feared that I might be disrupting routines and wearing thin their patience. But I then realised that there were no routines to his life. For very short spells he would become more predictable, working a regular office week at Headquarters. He would set off at eight on a Monday morning to walk three hours uphill, and reappear at Riverside late afternoon on Fridays. Such weeks were the exception.

> 'What are you doing next week? Will you be a soldier, or a teacher, or what?'
> 'I don't know.'
> 'Well, will you be here or up the hill? I wanted to ask your help translating some songs . . .'
> 'I don't know. Have a *Duck Brand* cigar. Silver is baking us a cake.'
> 'When will they tell you?'
> 'I'm not sure. I don't know who I work for just now.'

In fact for much of the time he seemed to do very little but wait for the next Departmental secondment, or sit on Edward's verandah, or tinker with Edward's motorcycle. He pointed to a series of small scars that afflicted his lower leg.

> 'You see those?'

'War wounds?'
'Motorcycle. I keep burning myself on the exhaust pipe.'

In a village new to both of us he'd be efficient, brisk, caring – the Revolution made flesh with a line to sell. At other times he was just a boy of thirty-two; maybe I had something to do with it. We gossiped in the dark, we pretended to hold cigarette lighters under each other's hammocks. Often we simply giggled half the night, making up absurd Karen nicknames for our acquaintances.

Within Riverside he tried to be more dignified. He was always referred to as *Thera* – 'master' or 'teacher'. It was a status he owed partly to his high-school graduation, partly to his manner, and partly to Edward. He was Edward's creature, and Edward had made of him a factotum.

If there was any ceremony being held, whether a wedding or the opening of a Health or Education or Army training course, there'd always be a solemn minute of homage to the flag, and it was True Love in uniform who directed. If there was a video to be shown to the public, True Love was called to switch it on. If there was a concert to be arranged, in aid of the Women's Organisation or Karen New Year, True Love took charge of the construction of the stage, the provision of a generator. At every state function – KNU Day, Kawthoolei Martyrs' Day, Karen New Year – he'd be the one to attend to the PA. On Martyrs' Day, a most solemn commemoration at the wooden obelisk on the parade ground, True Love led the procession of wreath-laying Departmental representatives. He was a man who seemed to matter, but who was very rarely consulted. Only on Edward's verandah, where he would pass long afternoons reading the *National Geographic*, did I hear him in discussion, asking questions of Edward, from whom he was learning a sort of political theory.

I would ask him, 'What would you *like* to be doing?'
'I love to teach sciences here. My pupils love me, I think.'

And, from the few lessons I watched, I think they did – there was constant laughter but he drove them hard and they were learning. At other times, especially if there was news, any news from the Front Line, he would be restless.

'I am bored with teaching. I am stuck in this village which is not a real Karen village; I want to be out and seeing my people.'
'What does that mean, then?'
'I want to be a soldier again!'

But he made no move to further his aims. He never asked for transfers. He cultivated none but Edward, his patron; when he was working at Headquarters he avoided the houses of the various Colonels and Majors. He had no one's ear, he offered few opinions. Each Monday evening at Headquarters there was a 'free discussion' to which anyone was welcome who wanted to hear what policies were being made, or to voice an opinion. Many people, of different ranks and Departments went, but never True Love, though he was asked to. He'd find an excuse.

'Why don't you take part in Monday discussions?'
'I don't want anything to do with it. So much talking.'
'But you could influence decisions, take a role . . .'
'I know what I am good at. And if I cooperate with everyone, they let me do as I want.'

There was one department that he declined to cooperate with: the 'Organisation Department', whose true remit was propaganda. Their work consisted mainly of travelling about the villages, deep into Burmese territory, talking to Karen everywhere about the Revolution. One might have thought it tailor-made for True Love, but he turned them down flat.

He had an addiction, and that was music. Although he possessed no instrument of his own, he was recognised as one of the leading guitarists of the village – which meant that he was likely to feature at any public function in that capacity as well as half a dozen others. He never sang in public, but in private he had a fine voice. 'Country and Western' was what he liked but he would accompany, tirelessly, the schoolgirls and young teachers who performed the 'traditional' songs and the endless hymns of Kawthoolei:

O blessed land, beautiful Kawthoolei,
I love your beauties, will give my life for you.

Our ancestors loved liberty, but other nations oppressed them,
so with their children they fled.
Then our country was looted by the oppressor.
O God, bless us, your children . . .

Many of our conversations took place on Sundays; little else was allowed. That was when you really knew this to be a Baptist community and, in the new blue Bethany Church, there would be a programme of services from early morning on – services for youth, for women, for the Revolution's many special days.

But True Love never went if he could help it. Silver sometimes wished to, but she hated to go alone. She would work on him for days, and he would protest, 'God is with me everywhere', and look bored. Yet he was without question devout. He'd composed gospel songs himself once. He carried a prayer book on our travels and read it in his hammock at night.

Not that he did anything else on Sundays; if he was bored in church, he was far more bored at home. Unwritten laws weighed upon him. 'I can't build my house, I can't start the new latrine we need. People would talk, there would be complaints.'

Work was out. Games were definitely frowned upon. Travel was not encouraged; I once arranged an expedition with True Love and Bartholomew, starting on a Sunday, and neither seemed to think twice about it until the day before, when both Great Lake the boatman and Pastor Moses raised doubts as to its propriety. We went anyway, for the protocol of Sunday *was* unwritten and there were many, Christians included, who flouted it. Even Great Lake himself, whose shopcupboard had the words 'No Shopping Sunday' painted (in English) on the slats, was forced to recognise this and did a reluctant trade with people who, had he refused, would not have been moved to piety but would simply have shopped elsewhere.

True Love's regard for the Kawthoolei Revolution was that of an infatuated lover frightened of marriage. He was caught, but in his own way would sulk and freeze in the embrace. He took two paces back from the Establishment. He lived *near* the church – his house was only a minute's walk away, and the blue belltower could be seen; the bell's ringing filled the verandah. At the rear of the building, Silver patiently baked cakes in a sandbox over a charcoal stove, deprived but uncomplaining and far too intelligent to drag him there under duress. True Love on the front balcony read over his English language textbooks or, since I had no desire to sit through long church services either, he'd talk to me. It was one of several ways in which he worked, tantalised, upon his fragmentary world view. It was he who listened to the radio, and to news and rumour from Burma and Bangkok.

'We have heard of an agreement between Burma and the United States to give the Americans a naval base on a small Burmese island in return for a lot of money. Why should the Americans support a socialist dictator like Ne Win? Because the Indians are letting Russian ships in the Indian Ocean use their ports. And the Burmese receive assistance from the Russians too; more Burmese trickery, you see?'

Right or not in detail, he knew how the world wagged. I gave him Alfred McCoy's *Politics of Heroin in S.E. Asia*, which was just to his taste – history, war, political intrigue, the exploitation of the hilltribes exposed. Salman Rushdie's Nicaragua pamphlet *The Jaguar Smile* delighted him: another oppressed people fighting its way out from under. He managed to conclude that the Nicaraguans had gained their freedom in spite of the socialist Sandinistas.

Thus we sat on Sundays, smoking cheroots and drinking sweet coffee from a Thermos flask I'd bought them. In front of the house, the usual students were tinkering with a motorbike. Others strummed guitars or went out to tea with their lovers. If they'd had motorcars they'd have been washing them – which, at Headquarters up the hill, was precisely what they were doing.

Week by week I recorded more songs. In True Love's compositions, the simply devotional had given way to soldierly sentiment. On my tape of *Love and Duty*, there are church bells in the background:

> I love you, Karen girl, your sweet voice
> singing to your man and to your country.
> But I'm a soldier for my land and my people;
> it's my duty to be brave and loyal.
> I hope to see you one day soon,
> our life will be wonderful then.
> But now duty calls. Someday,
> when I come back from the Front Line,
> I hope to see your welcoming smile.

'I wrote that for the soldiers', he said, 'and you can hear, they all sing it.'

On occasion the lethargy of Sunday would get the better of both his humour and his singing. Once he stopped in mid-song, looked vacant a moment and then apologised:

> 'It's my own song, but I can't remember the words. It's about remembering my family and my home in Burma. Sometimes I write to my mother, but I'm afraid to do so often in case the Burmese intercept the letters and make trouble for her – she might lose her school pension. It is six years now since I saw any of my family. One year ago my parents wrote to me asking me to come to a village downriver to meet them. But it was Christmas and we were very busy – I couldn't go, but I learned later that they had come there to wait. Then my brother wrote to me, mentioning our former life together, and made me think a lot about that time and what is happening

to them now. I know my parents have problems with some of my brothers and sisters at college, and no money. Of course I think about this, but there is nothing I can do.'

I told him that I was thinking of writing about his situation; would it make problems for anyone if I used a photograph?

'No, I look quite different anyway. When I came I was young. But I have been ill. I now look much ... rougher. They'd not recognise a photo.'

But they might recognise him in the flesh.

'I've had a letter from my brother again. He says that, if I was thinking of going to visit them, I should forget it. he thinks that there have been people looking for me.'

Silver serves sponge cake, True Love digs more cheroots from his haversack. The church bell announces yet another service and coloured parasols can be seen moving towards it. We consume quietly as visitors drift in and out.

'No, no going back now.'

'If it come by land, weep; if by water, laugh!'[1]

It is sometimes said that the mark of a true mariner is that he cannot swim: he knows the sea far too well to expect to elude it. On this count, the riverine Karen of Kawthoolei are naturals, since few of them can manage a decent dog-paddle. It's only city slickers like True Love who show off in the water, freestyle. It was also True Love who told me the Karen phrase meaning 'citizen' – *Htee po kaw po*, or 'water child land child'.

On 1 November, True Love took me downstream in Edward's boat – like most of them a dugout with a single plank raising each gunwale clear of the water by eight or nine inches; the bow a small platform shaped like an old-fashioned pen nib, very solid to withstand ramming of rocks, trees, the riverbank. At the stern, there was a platform where the pilot squatted, steering by hauling on the 'longtail' motor, a two-stroke Rotax that shook the boat, with two metres of drive shaft trailing in the water behind it, the propeller made of cast alloy, light and friable and called 'the boat's leaves'. In the bow, the *klee koh* (boat head) stood with a pole watching for rocks. Down the boat's five-metre length, were thwarts that made hard sitting after an hour or two, but kept the log-hull from collapsing and curling up like a dry leaf. Baggage was heaped on duckboards, with anything up to a dozen passengers tucked in. I had True Love, and Timothy the Army medical officer carrying an M16 assault rifle – the two of them side by side, in uniform, scanning the banks for something to loose off at. But travelling companions in a Karen boat do little other than restrict your feet: the loud insistent noise of the motor defeats conversation; you can barely hear yourself think, so you pass the time in looking about.

It's a substantial river. A month before, flying in off the Andaman Sea towards Bangkok, it was quite recognisable from the air. Often fifty metres wide, it slips and chops its way south between chains of high forested hills – dozens of them, dark dense green without relief. Small areas of flatland lie in the bends, mostly farmed, though you can see little through the fringe of waterside bamboos and acacias, squat shrubs and mango trees. Tributaries debouch off the steep banks, coming out of the forest laden with sand that builds up high-piled fans at each mouth. In the dry months they are like flat-topped slag heaps bulldozed high above the river level. In places the mud banks rise to pink-purple bluffs of a hundred feet or more. In the gorges, rock spurs clatter down to awkward scatterings of boulders in the water. True Love shouted to me:

You see that cliff? It's called Naw Loh Kaw. Near here used to live a man called Po Ghweh (orphan). He went out courting one day and while he was gone an elephant crashed into his fields and wrecked all his rice. Po Ghweh when he returned was furious; he chased the elephant to the river and killed it with a spear thrust through the neck. Then he dragged the elephant over the mountain to this place where he cut the carcase up and left the bits of meat out in the sun to dry – you see the big blocks on the bank there? Then Po Ghweh climbed that hill there and sat scaring the birds off with his slingshot. You can see all the stones he fired scattered in the water.

The place is known as Risky Rapids. On the US Airforce maps I had brought with me, rapids are marked with a jagged break in the line of the river – which is appropriate because your ride is interrupted; you get out and walk, True Love leading you one, maybe two hundred yards over shingle or through dense forest, while your boatman takes on the rapids – on the way down, the *klee koh* stands poised to fend off rocks with his pole, or, on the ascent, to push like crazy to get the boat up the narrow channels of fast water.

There are rapids and rapids, of course. Some are cascades, with heaps of water falling between big boulders, and from a rock the passengers watch the attempt, biting their nails and praying that their bags don't all go in. Other rapids are long passages of wide, shallow water, all broken and racing abreast, rocky beneath but you can't see where. Such stretches you ride down in the boat very fast, with True Love laughing and gripping the sides, and with a waterproof over your front because it is a lot wetter going down rapids than it is labouring slowly up, when the Rotax roars but you make a very slow pace hard by the bank, examining each shrub as you pass.

Elsewhere there are complex channels, elaborate slaloms, con-voluted and very difficult and here even the experienced boatman will get out a minute, stand on a rock and plan his approach and his course with the *klee koh*. These long, fast runs usually leave the walkers well behind; the boat picks you up from some bay or beach beyond. These are the rapids that smash the brittle propellers, as the boatman heaving the longtail over for a tight turn clips a boulder. You know when that has happened because the engine suddenly races highpitched and then dies, and if they are coming upstream they'll not appear for a long time and if you go back fifty yards you see them, the *klee koh* hanging on branches or midstream rocks to hold them there while the boatman quickly swings the engine round and the longtail inboard, unbolting and replacing the remains of the propeller as fast as possible – you always carry three or four spares. If it happens coming down, the boat will be washed past you out of control, the *klee koh* poling wildly to keep up some steerage way, the longtail now nothing but a rudder.

Rapids are always exciting, but rocks in slow water are worse, for there are places where the riverbed is littered not with rounded boulders but with sharp snags like stone sharks' fins or giant knapped flints, that can smash a hole in the thickest hull. In the rains they are no bother, you ride above them, but around February in the dry season, when the water level falls, you creep down these reaches with your *klee koh* standing and peering anxiously at the smallest eddy on the surface, the only benefit being that, with no rain, the water is clear and he has a chance of seeing rocks and signalling a change of course before the impact, or before the grating slither of a sandbank, with Great Lake telling you all to get out in midstream and drag the boat over it. When the first rain clouds the water with silt, without yet raising you safely up, you have little more than instinct to save your hull from the jags.

But most of the time on the river there is nothing to do but sit and watch the steady rearrangement of the mountains as you move between them, or to look up at the steep swidden fields in the forest on rounded hill flanks high above the river, like a partly shaven skull after a brain operation, fire-blackened or newly green, True Love pointing – 'Look, Karen!' – at the weeders making their way across.

You watch the birds: we made out five species of kingfisher on the first day, and there were ten more to come. Or the great hornbills, huge, crossing way up with a big wing beat you can hear. Karen don't shoot hornbills, saying that they mate for life, fly in pairs and are symbolic of faithful love.

Crested hawk-eagles and little dun-coloured fish-eagles sit in the high branches (until True Love prods Timothy and the latter fires at them.) The fish are high-spirited, much given to jumping, and one leapt right over the boat between us – but mostly they run along the surface of the water up on their tails for ten or fifteen feet before dropping back in abruptly. Plenty of snakes too, slipping from bank to bank and often not seeing the boat until we were almost upon them. One somersaulted to turn back from us. Another dived under us, so long that I could see head one side, tail the other. Another left all evasion far too late and the *klee koh* swung his paddle high over his head and chopped down very hard, snapping the snake's back.

Once, coming down a rapid, a black turtle going the same way put its head out of the water to look at us. In a quieter reach such good meat would have been in trouble. The lads watch for anything edible; we slewed into the bank in pursuit of a larger turtle lying on the sand. They jumped out and chased down the beach after it but turtles move faster than you'd think. Monkeys are plentiful, as is the ammunition thrown at them, but no one ever hit a monkey from my boat. There are wild chickens, stupid and slow to fly. True Love spotted a flock of them and we beached. He adjusted his beret and crept back through the scrub with a .22; we heard five slow, careful shots and thought we'd have a bird each for dinner but he'd only got two.

There are big monitor lizards to be shot: they make good curry and are very saleable. There are bears, valued for their gallbladders (medicine for the Thai-Chinese) as well as their meat, but they stay well out of range, glimpsed on hillsides. And once, there was what looked like a deer lying down and drinking at the waterside; a passenger with a Kalashnikov took aim and was about to drill its head when someone pointed out that it was actually a buffalo, a calf, and dead already.

There are other people on the river. We'd pass deeply laden boatloads, whole families on the move, or traders with boxes of tinned pilchards, pomade, torch batteries and less-than-fresh Thai cakes for the downriver villages. We'd recognise a pastor, or a Kaw-thoolei government officer in transit, or a teacher moving from her home village to her posting with her small tin trunk of clothes and books. The men wore palm-leaf bowler hats, the women kept the sun off with umbrellas wider than the boats. True Love would wave or nod if he knew them, but as often as not the undemonstrative Karen pass with no more than a stare.

Other boats are from a poorer, more remote world. There are plenty of Karen who have never had B.8,000 (£200) for an outboard, and whose small dugouts – often with no gunwale and only an inch of freeboard – creep up the sheltered sides of the stream, a ragged woman paddling as her husband casts nets. These we never spoke to, and I realised that there was a sub-stratum of Karen society living away from the villages in small huts scattered through the forest, whom I never got to know but then nor did True Love, for he could tell me next to nothing about them and was uneasy as we passed, rocking their tiny, waterline boats with our wake.

Karen reserve in no way implies indifference. Just as, in the Golden Age, British motorcyclists would stop to help each other fix their Norton singles at the roadside, so Karen boatmen's spanners and expertise are at each other's disposal. I spent almost as much time in watching the running repairs as in travelling; the substitute Thai-made parts on the engines give poor service.

'What if we can't get it fixed?' I asked True Love, two days downriver and surveying my motor in pieces all over the back of the boat, half of it in peril of dropping out of sight into the turbid water. 'What if there's some large part broken? What'll we do? How will we get home?'

'We'll stop worrying, we'll borrow someone else's motor from a village and we'll return it when we can. No problem. Anyway, we can make parts here.'

And they could, then and there by the riverside, out of a tin can and a bent nail cut with a sheath-knife and hammered with a wrench. For the passengers it was a pleasant excuse for a swim, a snooze and a foraging party after edibles in the forest.

Between villages there are men with animals. The cattle smugglers, bringing their fatstock from the coastal plains of Burma, swim them across the river to reach the tracks to Thailand. There are elephants in the water, their *mahouts* perched behind their ears and urging them in to bathe. Once they'd have been used for logging; now they are trapped and trained to carry ammunition and rice for the army. We gave elephants in the water a wide berth; the noise of the engine sent them wild.

After two or three hours the noise was too much for us also, the hard thwarts and the immobility were too much; you had to stop. True Love would shout to Great Lake the name of a village – Black Turtle, White Sand, Durianville or Barterville – and we'd head there.

Villages are barely noticeable from the water, but there will be signs that you've arrived. As you near habitation, fishnets in the river have to be negotiated, their bamboo or plastic bottle floats telling you when to raise the longtail. At the water's edge, boats are tethered with their motors swung inboard and wrapped in plastic, moored alongside large bamboo bathing rafts. Buffalo might be wallowing in the shallows, making the approach a problem, edging through them. Small vegetable gardens, fenced against pigs, fill any half-worthwhile waterside patch. Dogs let rip. Bathers look up and small children run.

We'd land, tie up the boat, hide the petrol and heave ourselves up the steep bank to sprawl on the verandah of the nearest house where the betel and areca-nut bowl would be pushed deferentially to *Thera* True Love by the householders. If we were in luck, a boy would be sent up a coconut palm and we'd have fresh milk. We might be here to talk with the villagers about the selection of village paramedics, or to assist some of Bartholomew's Health Department trainees with a clinic. Children would be quietly sent out with the word.

They are small villages for the most part, averaging some forty houses; with five to a house, a population of about 200 is common. The missionary Harry Marshall wrote in 1945 (p. 5), 'Their villages are small for they do not have the power to form a large society', which is a negative description of a preference for knowing all your neighbours. But you can hardly estimate the size of a Karen village without a guide, for you can't see more than two or three of the houses scattered among the trees. The effect can be exceptionally attractive, a forest variant of the garden-city principle, every house in its own areca-glade, its neighbours glimpsed between the slim ringed, uncluttered trunks of palms – near enough to be reassuring, far enough to be unobtrusive.

Most houses are low, long and thatched in the enveloping way thatch has, the interiors dark and smoky. Kicking your flipflops off at the ladder's base, climbing (and hurting your feet on the thin rungs) brings you to the reception area, the sections of floor at subtly different levels, a few inches only, a gentle division of space and function. At the front, where the betel-and-areca bowl is always waiting, the smooth split bamboo floor, worn and dark and red stained, is promptly covered with a large mat of woven plastic with a design of purple cockerels and green roses. Pillows are brought out for you, homemade and stuffed with wild kapok, their cases embroidered (in Christian houses) with Victorian pieties: *God is Love, Home Sweet Home, Jesus With Me Now*. The pot of cool tea and two smeared glasses are pushed towards the visitors. You recline, half-listen as True Love applies small iron shears to an areca-nut and relates the news to the head of the house, while small children in vests crawl about and pee through the bamboo slats. In the background, daughters put on the evening's rice and curry. Sunlight, already chopped about in its passage through the trees, is sliced neatly as it comes in through the vertical slats of the kitchen walls. The smoke from the fire, rising in curlicues, is cut by the hatched light into short blue-grey twists like Van Gogh brush-strokes. You can lie supine watching the smoke creep across the art-deco patterns of fan-palm thatching, turning it brown–black. You can fall asleep if you like. Cats, dogs, chickens and pigs are doing just that beneath the house, shifting only to dodge True Love's betel-spit coming through the slats.

There was a boom in the timber trade some years back, and in many villages there are one or two far grander houses from the period. There the whole atmosphere is different. High – both stilts and ceiling – and reached by real stairs with gates at the top, spacious and solidly divided by hardwood walls, these houses are never so welcoming or attractive as their poor bamboo cousins. There is a dark dustiness about them, a heartless cool. One sits up on benches at a refectory table to eat. The floor has no spring to it.

If we were staying, I'd be looking at once for a corner with stout posts from which to sling my small camouflage hammock, and True Love would do the same. He was almost as soft as me, and as little inclined to sleep on a mat on hard boards. Only in this respect do big timber houses have any advantage – their posts take the weight of hammocks easily, whereas in bamboo structures there were occasions when I almost demolished someone's home in the act of going to bed. Just once, in a huge house with flush timber panelling, we were pushed to find places to tie ourselves up and so slept two-tier in the only available corner, one hammock over the other. Climbing into the top I nearly put my foot in his face; when I was asleep he prodded my buttocks with a ballpoint.

In the morning, after weak tea and bananas, I'd walk about while breakfast was being cooked. Any village that figures in the Kawthoolei government scheme of things will have certain civic features: a football field, a school with its roof of thatch or tin depending on village resources, and the teacher's house nearby. There will be a shop in a locked side-room off someone's house, stocked with prawn crackers and vitamin pills, fishnets and flipflops. The grandest structure in a Christian village (they are generally more prosperous) will be the church, sometimes with the schoolroom tucked in underneath it. If the congregation is flourishing, this can be magnificent – painted timber with shutters, a portico and a bell tower, the bell a substantial piece of scrap metal – in one village, the top half of an unexploded British bomb.

I'd be called to breakfast, *Thera* True Love saying grace for us. And then hurriedly back down to the boat and the river again.

On, past the waterside hints of other villages. On these early trips I was trying to draw both a topographical and a sociological map of the river and its communities, to talk (through True Love) to 'representatives', to try and establish the size of the population, its religious, economic and cultural make-up, its state of health and its languages – and, first of all, the village names. In this respect, communities have certain unhelpful habits, like moving. In Karen swidden (slash-and-burn) agriculture, villagers follow the fields as the farmers turn their attention each season to new hillsides. Elsewhere, in the high Dawina Hills, the small bamboo and thatch villages remain for very few years before the fields give out, the houses rot and the whole moves on. Here on the river there are strategic sites – near tin mines, or good routes to Burma or Thailand – on which the villages are more settled, as the big timber houses indicate. But permanence is a questionable good. Age is almost a vice in a village. One, with a high proportion of animists and Buddhists, was persistently referred to as 'our oldest, laziest and dirtiest village'; it was actually one of my favourites, stocked with mature custard-apple trees.

Bamboo house-posts rot away in a couple of seasons. Hardwoods might last a decade or two. In more settled villages, the houses – decaying from the moment they're built – perform a slow dance about the static hardwood core of church and school. Other communities shift in their entirety. Arriving at a familiar bluff and climbing to the headman's house, we found nothing but ruins and the headman – a curious, dotty old fool – perched on the shattered remnants shelling nuts and saying, yes, they'd all moved down below the rapids and he'd be joining them in a day or two. We found the population now comfortably camped in quick-built huts on sand and shingle banks, enjoying the cool proximity of the river while the summer lasted, before the rains filled it and pushed them back to higher ground.

Home for the foresters is not a solid point of reference, but simply where you happen to be. True Love, the city boy, was only a little more used to this than I. There are other factors. The war restricts the area in which the Karen can move – although, with no clearly defined Front Line, it is a case of *tending* to Burma or Kawthoolei. But the fighting also promotes movement. With each season, each Burmese push, certain forward villages retreat to the river and encamp there. When the rains come, when the mud is deep and the undergrowth thick again, movement along the riverbanks is difficult and dangerous, and the upstream villages are safe enough. But from October to May there are fewer obstacles to the Burmese soldiers and they bring their camp downstream until they meet Karen resistance; they put villagers to flight (many are refugees already), they disrupt schools and farming.

And they plant landmines on the forest tracks, to rip the feet off farmers and blow shrapnel into their eyes. When the Burmese soldiers have gone, the small Front Line villages return cautiously upstream and the people, going to their fields, walk along mined paths.

As the rains end and the Karen prepare for the work of the harvest, villages empty as people move out to the fields and build temporary huts. Captain James Low, sent from Madras 150 years ago to assist with early survey work in the new colony, observed them doing this: 'The Karen are fond of changing their ground ... Temporary huts were noted in one instance to have been built connected with each other and forming a line of about one hundred yards.'[2]

'Karen picnic!' shouted True Love over the Rotax, pointing; it was in fact a village school in a fragile shelter on the beach. There were scores of casual waterside settlements, one sheet of red-and-yellow striped plastic sufficient shelter for many families, their washing draped on bushes in the middle of nowhere, their fishnets festooning the small trees, their boats the only solid things in view. Even the affluent headman of Sesame went to the fields for three months. We stayed with him in his summer hut, a large, springy structure by a stream in an open-sided valley. It had few walls; it was just a high roofed platform housing necessities – his gun, lizard traps, spare propellers and dark bottles of homemade medicines. As a place to rest out of the dry, direct April sun, freshened by a steady breeze, it was delightful.

Plate 5. 'Barterville has a harbour, an inlet from the main stream where boats are safe from the current.'

As the seasons change, so do the patterns of trade, and the village that I think of as 'Barterville'[3] shifts its footing at the waterside. Barterville is, in our District, unique: a village almost entirely made up of shops, a dozen at least, mostly bamboo but with one or two more solid buildings, lining the main street. One of the most important settlements on the river, it has no school and no church. Behind the village lie two direct routes to Thailand which pass up small valleys where the soil is rich in tin ore and the forests still worth Thai efforts in extracting timber. This is the way the cattle smugglers leave Burma and, in return, powerful six-wheel-drive trucks bring paraffin and petrol, foodstuffs, cheap cloth and motor spares, their Thai drivers buying up any forest specialities the Karen have brought to Barterville – monitor lizards, anteaters, live songbirds and wild honey.

Barterville has a harbour, an inlet from the main stream where boats are safe from the current. There are always plenty of boats

here. Up on the high bluff the locals and the visitors sit together
eating fritters and listening for motors, watching them swing into
the bay or departing – I once saw a longtail motor shake itself
off the back of a boat and drop into deep water. With heavy rain
the river can rise so dramatically as to wash out the stores nearest
the bank, reducing them to filthy heaps of wet bamboo and thatch
on an expanse of rapidly cracking mud; but such is the advantage
of this position that the floods have barely subsided when the traders
are back and rebuilding – even though, with another good storm,
it could all be gone again tomorrow.

I came to Barterville with True Love to buy a boat. Clearly
I couldn't expect to monopolise Edward's and, at B.3–4,000 (less
than £100), it was an obvious purchase. But in this society of boatmen, buying one proved a problem. Boats appeared to come in
only two sorts – the unsuitable and the unavailable. True Love
said:

> 'I have a friend who knows about boats. He is the pastor of Black
> Turtle. We'll go and ask him tomorrow.'

I found True Love again that afternoon at one of the riverside
shops. There was a fisheagle sitting on the arm of the bench. It
was tethered but hardly needed to be, since it had a bullet wound
in the base of one wing.

> 'A good shot', said True Love.
> 'What are they going to do – eat it?'
> 'I think they will keep it as a pet.'

The eagle blinked at me slowly: it wasn't long for this world.
True Love was leaning over a home-made draughts board of warped
plywood with pieces of roughly torn dark and light scrap paper.
His opponent was a villain in a filthy but once smart checked shirt,
his hair slicked back with oil – probably a knife-fighter.

> 'This is the pastor', said True Love. 'He says there is only one
> boat for sale here, and it's a year old and they want B.4,000
> for it, which is too much.'
> 'I think I'll have one made.'
> 'That will be difficult. It's the harvest now; no one will have
> the time. We must keep looking. The pastor says there are
> a couple of boats upstream.'

I must have looked rather dubiously at the pastor; True Love
said,

> 'He's a good man – very conscientious and not proud. There

are some pastors that I cannot approve of, who care only for
... other things.'

I taught him the word 'venal'.

Ten days later we found a boat, four hours upstream at White
Ponds, the last village of any substance before the Burmese camp.
It was new, of the best wood, a pale pinky-yellow in colour. Everyone
agreed that it was ideal – sound, the right size and a snip at B.3,000
(£75). There was, however, a problem. The owner wanted not Thai
Baht but Burmese *Kyat* – more use among traders and smugglers
on the Burma run. Finally he capitulated in the face of the greater
purchasing power that he'd have with the Thai currency.

We towed the boat home, and I spent much of the coming year
maintaining it. The engine had to be mounted, floorboards made,
the hull painted inside and out with black bitumastic seal. Bartholomew stood in it, rocked about speculatively and pronounced it a
bad and overpriced boat. It was, he said, unstable – and so, like
many others, it had bamboo tubes tied to the hull by a system of
my devising – stitched on at intervals with yellow nylon cord. Lastly,
the join between the dugout hull and the gunwale boards had to
be filled. This was done by mixing powdered *pwenyet* (a tree resin,
better known as *dammar*) with diesel oil, the resulting compound
being pressed into place and then scorched with a red-hot metal
rod. G. P. Andrews of the Indian Civil Service listed *pwenyet* amongst
the most valuable forest products of Mergui District when he sur-
veyed it in 1912, praising its qualities as a caulking material. He
can never have used it. Once set, it has no flexibility at all and I
passed futile hours over the months plugging the gaps with shredded
coconut fibre dipped in bitumen paint. I never met a Karen boat
that didn't leak like a sieve. Given the rocks and the rot, they only
last three or four years anyway, so nobody bothers much.

No one believed that I could be any better than helpless when
it came to looking after the boat. I'm not a bad carpenter but,
when I made the first set of floorboards, Bartholomew's son Sam
simply took them apart – then reassembled them almost identically.
I hated not being able to do anything for myself. When the oar
broke, I set myself to turn a plank of wood into a new one. It
was, I freely admit, a rotten oar, too cumbersome, too heavy, all
wrong – but the degree of incredulous scorn it aroused still took
me aback. A new house was being built at the time and Bartholomew
said there was no need to look for new and expensive main posts:
could we have half a dozen of Mr Jo's oars, please? His own boat-

building skills were not infallible; he fastened the stabiliser tubes with a cord passing under the boat, which cut loose on the first rock we grazed.

The fact of a white man claiming to 'own' a Karen boat at all, with the basic rights of determining its usage that I assumed this to entail, was not one that all villagers accepted. In a world of river transport where there are too few boats to go round, it is agreed that boat-owners gave lifts to anyone in need. This seemed an admirable ruling to me and, in time, priests, colonels, teachers, traders and plain Karen farmers all had rides in my boat. Still, I did like to be asked. No one, not even True Love, saw my point of view; my own plans for where and what I might be carrying counted for little. At the slightest hint of a journey, I would find passengers waiting by the boat with no more thought of asking than the average commuter has of sending a written request to British Rail before boarding the 8.05 at Godalming. Having bought the Rotax motor, I decided to obey the handbook and run it in carefully for twenty hours: thus I would limit passengers to six, about half the possible loading. Coming down to the boat one morning to set off on a long journey downstream, I found a young man and his tin box already installed. I had more than a full load of companions booked already so I apologised and asked him to get out. He looked blank. True Love repeated, 'The white man says sorry, he can't take you', but still there was no response. Five minutes later an observer would have been puzzled to see a Karen repeatedly place a trunk in a boat which a white man would as persistently lift out and place on the bank. After three or four of these exchanges I was not so much angry as fascinated. I tried imagining the scene played out between two complete strangers around a private car in an Aberdeen street. Frequent appeals to True Love only made him look shifty. He offered no explanation.

At last the other man gave up and sat on his box sadly. My own prearranged passengers got in and we departed. Once more I asked True Love to explain: 'He was a soldier, that man, a good soldier. But last year he received a head wound and nearly died. When he recovered he began to act very strangely. He knew he was ill and he asked the Colonel to release him from the army; it was granted on compassionate grounds. He's trying to get home now. He's been waiting two weeks for someone to give him a lift.'

'For Heaven's sake, why didn't you tell me? I'd have taken him!'

'I didn't know what to say . . .'

Circumventing rapids, following True Love through the scrub bushes on a shingle beach, I saw him freeze and crouch, waving me to do the same and bringing the M16 off his shoulder. I knelt and looked past him, dismayed. There were some two dozen strange-looking soldiers approaching us along the riverbank, clearly not Karen. So much for our quiet backwater. They were taller, darker, sharper-featured men, and several were wearing red headbands. They carried assault rifles of many types, grenade launchers, crossed bandoliers and long knives. They were moving downriver, about to cross a small tributary stream right in front of us where, I suppose, True Love could have made a mess of them before they made a mess of us. But all at once he relaxed and turned to grin at me:

> 'Muslims.'
> 'Come again?'
> 'They are Muslims who are now fighting with us, the Kawthoolei Muslim Liberation Front. There are not so many of them; they began their revolution just a few years ago.'

He stood up and called a greeting. The leading soldier, in mid-stream, tensed and brought up his Kalashnikov but, seeing True Love walking towards him and waving, called back.

Their great-grandparents had been Bengalis once, perhaps. Approaching us, all smiles, their leader shook my hand and addressed me in that caricature King's English supposedly spoken by educated Indians: 'Good morning, Sir; it is nice to meet you here. May I ask, where have you come from today ... etc.' Two things in particular marked him as being no Karen; he had unshaven stubble on his chin, and wore a crescent moon badge. They were heading for the southern Front. You never knew what you might meet on the river.

The river has always had a central place in the lives of the local Karen. It provides their protein, their hygiene and their freedom of movement for trade and travel. Its nature is that of a motorway, for like motorways it always leads past settlements and rapidly beyond, while to stop at a village you turn off it.

With the coming of the Revolution its position changed some-what. It became crucial to the cohesion of the District as an administrative – and revolutionary – reality. It gives the KNU an overview of its claimed territory, and the District a definition that it would otherwise lack. Officers of the Forestry, Finance, Health and

Education Departments can cover their field of responsibilities in a couple of days, visiting several villages between breakfast and their evening meal. On the other hand, the individual officer's knowledge of the river, its rapids and its villages might well be less than the intimacy enjoyed by the locals – if, as is very likely, he is a Delta newcomer. His overview will have the blandness of travelling bureaucrats anywhere. Even our boatman, Great Lake, was a newcomer brought here by the Revolution. He knew the downstream rapids no better than I did. It was only his skill – his *general* skill – that kept us out of trouble. That, and a sharp-eyed *klee koh* up front.

Motorboats permit rapid movement of things that previous generations might not have thought of moving at all – the sick, books being smuggled into Burma, bulk foodstuffs for the Army, bicycle wheels, also being smuggled into Burma, soldiers – including, potentially, the enemy. This river valley had been quiet enough until the Japanese chased the British upstream and the British chased them back.

In most warfare, rivers are a matter of bridgeheads, lines of defence, opposed crossings. But in the rainforest, where land movement is generally very slow, gaining a river gives you the possibility of dramatic acceleration, eluding or outflanking your enemies or rushing right through their heartland. Movement by both sides concentrates on a narrow strip along each shore. The contrast is sharp, between invisibility on the forested bank and exposure on the glassy killing ground between. The river is, for the defenders, both their strength and their greatest liability. The tiny KNLA, faced with the greatly superior Burmese Army, can redeploy its forces very rapidly if necessary. But it is also essential to keep a check not only on who is crossing the ill-defined 'borders' of Kawthoolei, but on who is moving on the river. There are KNDO checkpoints to do that.

This is an artery that may be severed. To the north, the river valley looks from the air like a shepherd's crook that turns west into Burma and then south again. There, its headwaters rise in a wide and fertile region between two mountain chains. This rich, secluded western valley is Karen heartland. The villages are bigger, more prosperous, more deeply involved with Burma. But the capture by the Burmese of a small town near the top bend in 1984 ended all river access to that area. Sooner or later, boats heading upstream have to stop, and the passengers and freight take to the forest. Leave it too late and you'll be machine-gunned. The safest route to the western valley now is a three-day walk through the forest and over the mountains.

Downstream, the Burmese create other difficulties. Their offensives, coming eastwards through the forest, sometimes reach the river. They burn villages, destroy fields and capture both people and their livestock. Hearing news of an attack, and gauging the line of approach, villagers load their movable property into boats and shift two or three hours to the north, while KNLA detachments take up positions on the bank to prevent the Burmese striking rapidly upstream.

Other developments are also changing the status of the river in Karen lives – by far the most important, the timber trade. The rivers of Burma and Siam were once the key to the timber business. Felled logs would be heaved by Karen-trained elephants into small streams during the dry working season. When the streams bulged with rain, the logs were lifted and carried to the main-stream where, lashed into rafts, they'd be floated down to a sawmill. The whole process, from initial ring-barking (girdling) of teak to its emergence from the forest as sawn logs, could take five years. This was how the British 'teak wallahs' (like George Orwell's character Flory) had to work.[4] But Thai lumbermen today don't have that sort of time: neither Thai politics, nor Thai nor Japanese capital will wait that long. The riverside sawmills are all at half-cock, the river itself is being made redundant by 'roads' – a title little merited by the dirt strips driven through the forest by bulldozers that scatter snapped bamboos like discarded cocktail sticks. The seasons seem to matter very little now, although during the rains the Caterpillars have to pull the logging lorries through the mud, and remake sections of road after virtually every vehicle that passes. I could hear them from my house at Riverside, cutting branch on branch of new extraction road, far off in the forest. And it was happening very fast: by the time I left a year later, the mileage of logging road had perhaps doubled, and I was beginning to wonder whether I shouldn't have bought a motorbike instead of a boat.

Thai traders soon saw the trend. Where once they chartered Karen boats to reach the villages, or sold to Karen middlemen, now they can drive straight to many communities with a pickup, sometimes even a taxi, full of Pepsi and prawn crackers. Kawthoolei allows the roads because Kawthoolei's toll gates are being shut tighter each year by the Burmese. Revenue from timber is virtually the only income the state still has. But it is not merely a selling-off of the patrimony: it is, increasingly, a military risk. Where a Thai bulldozer has cut a road, what is there to stop a Burmese tank from following? The military significance of the river may be under-cut as fast as its economic role.

Waterways the world over are not, of course, what they once were; roads are so much faster. Few Karen will ever be able to afford a pickup: £200 for a Rotax is about their limit. But what if no one can be bothered to supply them with river-ready motors any more? In the Thai provincial capital three hours away, where I did my shopping and would then go to another river to sit and drink cold beers on big floating bars, there propellers were becoming hard to find. A hardware dealer to whom I spoke said yes, he'd sold them once – and motors, and other spares.

'But there are not many boats on the river now, because there are roads everywhere these days, good fast roads. Who in his right mind travels by water?'

6　A simple man

Bartholomew, head of the Health and Welfare Department, was almost a 'traditional' Karen. Before leaving for Burma I had bought a volume of photo-ethnography called *Peoples of the Golden Triangle* by E. and P. Lewis, in which the Karen are present as a nation dressed in red and white-striped homespun with their hair in buns on one side, living a life of illiterate animism and primitive but effective agriculture from thatched huts on the hillside. In the quasi-urban, educated atmosphere of Riverside, Bartholomew stood out as being distantly related to these traditionals.

He was not young – nearly sixty now, he'd thus been about twenty when the rebellion began. Under short, thin hair his face was angular, high-cheeked and simian, usually set in a scowl which I soon realised was a long-running joke. His eyes could change suddenly from shrewd, narrow slits to wide ingenuousness. He was evidently a man who worked hard, tough and grubby about the fingernails, with a deformed right wrist that he'd broken years ago and which now became swollen and painful after manual work. He stumped about, extracting more entertainment from grumpy irony than anyone I've ever met. Shy and retiring, he could also play the buffoon, or let loose a terrible rage – which usually ended with the household helpless with laughter. He was my boss, and in December 1986 I moved into his home.

He was a repository of practical skills. If there was something he couldn't make, he would learn. He joked (like William the teacher) that in Kawthoolei one had to be a *kay ler thera*, an 'everything teacher'. He put a handle on an iron-bladed chopper for me, whittling and trimming a piece of hard, matured cane, then weaving three delicate little bands of basketwork to slip over and grip the haft firmly. It was beautifully done. I watched him thatch houses, lash down bamboo floors and weave bamboo walls, cultivate fruit gardens, repair boats and raise smallstock. I went with him to gather medicinal leaves in the forest, and saw how he ground hard yellow wood into ointment on a stone. These were things that all Karen claimed were simple matters, but not many of the town types at Riverside were actually much good at. Bartholomew also administered a government department, and I was told that he could do an acceptable amputation if need be, should a villager step on a landmine. Bartholomew, insisted True Love, was 'a simple man' – but it was obviously a complex concept.

He was greatly admired for all this. Edward of Education said, even before I'd met Bartholomew, 'He is the revolutionary Karen I admire above all others. He is a model for us.' Not a model that a sophisticate like Edward felt especially bound to emulate, perhaps, but everyone agreed that Bartholomew's devotion to his people, their cause and their traditions was matchless and lifelong.

But Bartholomew was not exactly the 'traditional Karen' that he appeared to be. A schoolteacher who claimed to know him well told me his story: 'He comes from a small village near Moulmein, where his parents were farmers. They weren't Sgaw or Pwo Karen but Pa-O, one of the small tribes, and were animists until recently, then Buddhists. Bartholomew had just a simple Karen village school education, but when he was still in his early teens he became a dresser at a mission hospital. Then, when the Karen Revolution began, he became one of the first KNDO medical staff – he's the only one of the originals left now.'

But other people gave different versions: 'He comes from Thaton which is quite a town now, and not a Karen town, but Burmese. That family were never traditional Karen and if you asked Bartholomew for the old Karen stories, he wouldn't know them. He went to a Buddhist monastery school, all his education was in Burmese – that's why he can't read or write Karen very easily and gets his assistant Shelley to do all the paperwork. He joined the Revolution when it began and trained as a medical orderly with the KNDO. You know why? Because if you're an officer or any sort of professional, you get the pick of the women. It worked, too. One day he was called to a house to see a young woman who was sick. After he had visited very often to care for her, he married her. When she died he married again quite soon. Bartholomew really likes women.'

Well, why not, I thought; they seem to like him, as do I.

Becoming a health worker in Burma in 1948 was an act of multifaceted significance. Pre-war public health had been very poor; this was sometimes blamed on Buddhist reluctance to take life in putting down vermin, and sometimes on Burmese antipathy to the colonial education system. Most doctors were Indian or Chinese, and most nurses were Karen and Christian. With the Japanese invasion, the health services collapsed. The Japanese and Burmese administrators were ineffective, and there were epidemics of smallpox, malaria and dysentery. Post-war, things were little better. Out of this context, Bartholomew had undergone a three-fold conversion, becoming a Christian, a health worker and a Karen revolutionary – a package deal, as it were.

With the Revolution at the start, Bartholomew had known the revered Ba U Gyi. Long service, perserverance and native wit had made up for his lack of higher education, and he'd brushed up his image to suit. From being a hard-drinking Buddhist with an eye for the girls, he'd become a reformed, teetotal Baptist with a large family.

He'd been at the epic six-day battle of Myawaddy, and had the campaign medal to show for it. As the Karen National Union extended its authority in the south, they'd decided to try out a civilian Health and Welfare Department (elsewhere, what health care there was came from the Army) and Bartholomew was made its head. So he was unique in Kawthoolei, and if he found the realities of administration to be a burden, there was no doubting his prestige. At the Karen New Year parade he stood in the front rank with the Colonel. When, in November, he was ill himself, they paid out a large sum of money to hire a car and send him to the American mission hospital at Sangklaburi in Thailand. He was valued, he was deferred to. But still they said, 'Bartholomew is a simple man'.

His first marriage had produced five daughters; I only ever met one, Lili, wife of Great Lake the boatman. One had gone to Thailand. One had died of a fever two years before. Two daughters had gone out in a boat with their mother one day, when the rains were heavy and the river was in spate – and all three had been drowned.

So Bartholomew married again, a schoolteacher called Vermilion, and they had four more children. There was Fragrance, now a teacher herself in her early twenties, a robust and competent young woman, attractive but shy and easily teased by her younger siblings, desperately ticklish and prone to embarrassed giggles. James her brother, still at school, wanted to be a pilot. His father wanted him to be a doctor. His chances of doing either were poor. The next daughter, Welcome, was at thirteen quite capable of running the household if need be, and had that slightly grumpy seriousness of middle daughters who regard their big sisters as frivolous. Monkey was an eight year old tom-boy whose favourite occupation was getting rubber bands very painfully entangled in the hair on my legs as I sat reading.

Vermilion too had been married before, to an Indian mines manager who had been murdered at Barterville. She had a son called Sam, a small and wiry, dauntlessly cheerful and intelligent twenty-three year old. Then there was a grandaughter – child of the daughter dead of fever. There was also an adopted nephew, and there was Bartholomew's own sickly, wasted brother. All these people, any combination of them and indeed not a few others, could be found one night or other in Bartholomew's three-bedroomed, tin-roofed, bamboo-floored house. When he first invited me to stay I laughed, saying that he hadn't got room for his own, but I'd misunderstood; there was plenty of space if you readjusted your concepts of privacy.

It was a tall house, built on high, timber piles. The roof was of corrugated steel, now elderly and dusty grey-brown on top, smoke-stained near-black underneath. Apart from the timber frame almost everything else – floor, walls, internal partitions – was of smooth split bamboo. One end of the house was a cramped muddle of a kitchen – fireplace (made of clay boxed in with timber), a low circular dining table, sacks of rice and untidy heaps of vegetables, a cupboard full of white enamel plates, open tin cans half-full of condensed milk and drowned ants, and whatever was left of yesterday's fried fish jumbled up with stone pestles, pots of fermented fishpaste and handfuls of small bitter berries from the forest. There were battered and blackened pots hanging on the wall, crockery jars of salt and of cool drinking water, and lugubrious unlabelled bottles containing what may or may not have been cooking oil. At that end of the building, everything was dark, smoked and grubby. It was where the spiders and cockroaches lived, enjoying the penumbra. Only by the back steps was there much light, where we washed the dishes in pails of riverwater, and the girls decapitated and curried chickens, with yams and pumpkins. In season, precarious contrivances brought rainwater splashing in to wide aluminium basins, scratched and dented. The bamboo floor, shiny with pumpkin peelings at the best of times, was black and rotten. If I didn't tread carefully, with my feet splayed sideways to cover several slats, I risked going straight through.

Two small bedrooms at the back of the house were occupied by whichever senior child was in residence at the time, the girls taking precedence. Bartholomew and Vermilion had a larger room, but small children piled in with them. Other children slept on, around or under the dining table curled up (with a blanket) on mats on the springy bamboo.

The front half of the house was more open. A raised section of floor did for guest accommodation or snoozing in the afternoon. Here I tied my hammock, and slung my rucksack from a nail amongst the KNU calendars and a poster portrait of the King of Thailand. A large *tokay* lizard lived behind this poster, a speckled monster that did me no harm except deprive me of sleep as, at two or three a.m. it puffed up full of air, cranking itself in spurts of mechanical clucks to announce to its girlfriends on distant trees that something splendid was to follow. Then, after an excruciating pause of a few seconds, it unleashed three or four resonant blasts *to – kay!*, *to – kay!* before subsiding with a nasal *eeer*. With each full-blown, lung-swollen blast from behind the poster, the King of Thailand would sway backwards and forwards in the breeze. If I thrashed at the picture to drive the lizard off (it was only eighteen inches from the head of my hammock), it made such a noise marching across the tin roof to find a new resting place that I'd be wider awake than ever.

The main steps, with a clutter of worn-out plastic flipflops at their foot, rose up to where a good timber table stood on the verandah, fitted with benches jutting out from the side of the house. Here visitors would find the pot of cool tea. Here I sat myself, half-awake at 6 a.m., and quietly drank sweet coffee and ate bananas. Important guests were served formal meals here – the Colonel was none too keen on crouching at the low kitchen table. Each evening the children struggled with homework or Fragrance studied the Bible, Bartholomew and his sons tinkered despondently with Health Department accounts and I sat, legs extended along the bench, back against a housepost, writing my notes for the day and smoking a Burmese cigar, enjoying the breeze. I was very happy in that house.

They cared for me. Any suggestion that I might cook was met with laughter, and only by being ill-mannered did I ever get to do the washing up. I had a pottery mug with a lid, decorated *à la chinoise* that I'd brought back from Penang, and they kept that always full of tea for me. If I was very prompt I'd get to do my own laundry but I couldn't stop them washing and ironing my hammock. Watching Welcome chopping wood one afternoon, I thought, 'That at least I can do for them', having won a ribbon for axemanship at Forest School Camps in the Lake District, aged eleven. I firmly removed the axe from Welcome and set about the logs. After five minutes I was soaked in sweat and removed my shirt. Three minutes later I broke the axe, at which point I also realised that Welcome had taken my shirt to the river and was now washing it for me.

They would take it in turns to run the house, though by and large Vermilion left it to her daughters Fragrance and Welcome, while she reclined upon the bamboo slats with a cigar, or planned a trading trip downriver on a borrowed boat, taking with her bales of striped Karen shirts (from the looms up at Headquarters) and assortments of medicines, lollipops and sherbets bought from the Thai traders.

In Bartholomew's house the traditional costumes were folded and stored carefully in tin trunks in the bedrooms, brought out for solemnities and parades. I have a sweet photograph of two of the youngest children, Pu and Monkey, shyly showing off their new Karen clothes – at the ages of six and eight. In the north, in both Thailand and Burma, there would be no question of them wearing anything else – but not here.

Another tradition was alive and well in Bartholomew's house: pillowcase embroidery. Given the usual run of *God Bless Our Home* texts, it was tempting to think of this as another product of the nineteenth-century missions, but Carl Bock wrote in 1884 (p. 323), of the Buddhist Lao of Northern Thailand that, 'Many of the upper classes are also skilled in embroidering the cushions or pillows which take the place of chairs.' Wherever it came from, Fragrance was an expert. Returning from school teaching in the afternoon, she'd sling a hammock in the cool under the house and snooze and sew there. She made three pillowcases for myself, my mother and father, with texts such as *Love Faithfully*. The crimped borders she trimmed with green lace; she embroidered red and purple roses and then, on mine, a portrait of me as a yellow dinosaur playing a purple guitar, amid green lace bows. Under pressure she confessed that True Love had designed that.

Revolution was kept together with tradition. Folded neatly in the tin trunk alongside the striped shirts was a Karen flag, hand-painted onto thin fabric so that the strong dyes showed clearly

on the reverse. Bartholomew would tie it to a pole and lash it to
the front of the house on national days. In the corner of the parental
bedroom stood a carbine. I never saw Bartholomew use it, but
a Departmental head had to be ready to fight. One long wall was
decorated with almost every KNU calendar since the house had
been built ten years ago. They hung opposite my hammock and
there was one in particular that I liked to stare at. It was a poster-
sized reproduction of a painting that showed the Karen marching
in a solid column through a fecund landscape of woods and rice
fields, winding up a hill to the foreground past a road sign directing
them to liberty and happiness. The people – there are thousands
marching – all wear traditional costume. They are shouting and
they raise their right fists in the air. It looks like an old issue of
China Reconstructs.

Technological materialism had made very little headway in the
house – no Honda pump as at the Justice's, no electric light (off
the school generator) as at Edward's. There was a very poor cassette
player, and a handful of rough tapes of Karen love songs and hymns
from Burma. There was also a large thermos flask, the sort that
you press on top to obtain a squirt of hot water from the nozzle.
It was unused. We tried it one day but it didn't work; the plastic
bellows inside the lid had failed. When we opened it up we found
a nest of cockroaches.

It was not the physical aspect of the house that impressed me
so much as the human. I have never seen so small a structure
accommodate such a vast migrant population with so little fuss.
When I set off on my morning visits, I had no idea who would
be there when I returned in the afternoon. Soldiers, teachers,
pastors, poor relations, rich Thais, sick children or any other livestock might be asleep on the guest floor by my hammock. The
population of children went through daily permutations as some
departed to stay with friends, or friends came. Bartholomew brought
classes of his Department nurses, sat them round his verandah table
and taught them the use of thermometers. Fragrance brought her
class from school for intensive evening revision before exams. There
was always tepid rice and a few crisply fried small fish in the kitchen.
People drifted in, ate, drifted out.

Bartholomew would disappear with Sam for days on end, or
Vermilion might go downriver to return a week later with six goats,
sixty litres of honey and quite possibly six relatives also, all packed
into a boat with a 9hp motor that could barely move on the flat,

let alone up rapids, where everyone had to get out and carry the load. There were cats, kittens and dogs foraging; pigs, ducks and chickens came and went from under the house *via* either Vermilion's purse or the kitchen. The goats escaped into neighbours' gardens or were dragged around the football field by the children. A tiny, week-old black kid arrived, and Bartholomew attempted to rear it on condensed milk and jungle greens selected for nutritional value and tenderness, but it didn't thrive. Amongst its problems was the bamboo floor. Its tiny hooves slipped on the shiny, convex slats and went straight through the wide gaps. Sometimes all four went down together and it would lie with its feet dangling below, looking like St Lawrence on his grid and bleating hysterically until rescued by Monkey or Fragrance. It died quite soon.

In this mêlée, I had no privacy whatever, occupying as I did nothing more than a corner of the verandah. For a time I had a mosquito net draped around a plastic mat on the floor. It gave the faint illusion of a room of my own and at night I would lie writing by the light of a small lamp just outside the net – but Fragrance either didn't realise what I was doing, or didn't approve and would come and firmly blow the lamp out. With the hammock I felt that I intruded less upon the family's space, since children could sleep underneath me at night and I could untie and roll myself away out of sight in the morning.

I found this public life no problem; perhaps because my status was somewhat detached anyway, or perhaps because in such circumstances privacy is not a physical but a mental state.

So far from showing symptoms of crowding and stress, I never saw a saner family. The children hardly ever squabbled. At daybreak, after rolling away their sleeping mats, they set about their tasks without being told. The smallest – Pu, Bi and Monkey – would sweep the leaves and dust from the compound, carrying the debris in saucepans to throw into the bushes. James cut firewood and the elder sisters prepared breakfast. All of them trotted back and forth up the steep riverbank bringing old plastic oil cans full of water. Vermilion sorted trade goods or spent half an hour brushing out her splendid hair, while her husband fed the chicks he was raising under a wicker basket in a shed at the back, then sharpened choppers and made besoms for yard-sweeping from new green switches gathered by Welcome. Fragrance brought me coffee and bananas, and I just sat and watched. Breakfast at 7.30, school at eight, and a sudden calm in the house.

Outside of school hours there were other tasks. Like any established Karen house, this one was delightfully shaded by its garden. There were papaya and coconut palms, banana and kapok trees, fat white frangipani and dense acacias, one of which had a rich purple bougainvillaea ramping through it. There were two tasteful stands of striped bamboo and, lower down, chilli bushes, cacti standing in old paraffin tins and borders of the little sweet-citron scented *mali* flowers. All this had to be kept trim, and the whole family would be mobilised to plant new bananas, or to pick and sort chillis – or to trail off into the forest, hot and unenthusiastic, to fetch green bamboo for new fencing. Bartholomew supervised in grubby T-shirts with his sarong hoiked up and tucked in at the waist, thus exposing his most spectacular claim to be a true and traditional Karen – the intricate tattoos that covered his upper legs from the waist to the knee.

Tattooing was once almost universal among adult Karen males, though Christianity dealt it a heavy blow, objecting both to its spiritual import and to its flag-waving for the libido. But tattooing isn't finished yet.

Among S.E. Asian peoples, tattooing is ancient and widespread. A Chinese chronicle of the third century AD refers to tribes in these parts who tattooed themselves, wore armour of monkey hide and used bows and arrows.[1] Note in passing that tattoos go together with armour. Marco Polo also mentioned tattoos in Burma and Yunnan, in a way that suggests that it was long forgotten in Europe. He adds, 'The man or woman who exhibits the greatest profusion of these figures is esteemed the most handsome.'[2]

Later Europeans described Shan, Lao, Northern Thai, Vietnamese, Burmese and others tattooed in a similar manner, and Carl Bock included in his books illustrations of the elaborate patterns that evolved in different areas.

Why was it done? Bock had seen extensive tattooing in Borneo as well as Siam: 'as a style of manliness, courage and endurance on the part of those who submit to the voluntary infliction of pain. As the Dyak women are tattooed to please their lovers, so the Lao men undergo the ordeal for the sake of the women.'[3]

Of course, another interpretation is possible, as the Karen writer Mika Rolley (1980, p. 16) suggests, describing the Chin people's reaction to Burmese oppression. 'As a measure of self-protecting they adopted the practice of tattooing the faces of their womenfolk to make them less attractive to outsiders.

But most people agreed that tattooing makes you beautiful – and you pay for it accordingly. Carl Bock (1885, p. 171), met a 'professor of tattooing' and described the process in detail:

The pigment is made from the smoke of burning lard, the soot from which is collected in earthenware pots and mixed with the bile of the wild bull, bear or pig ... The operation is necessarily a painful one, especially considering the sensitiveness of the skin in the parts operated upon. The parts tattooed swell up, and become highly inflamed, sometimes causing high fever, but I was informed ... that not more than 2 per cent die from the effects of the irritation so caused.

This was the ordeal that Bartholomew had undergone.

'What do the marks mean?' I asked him.
'They mean that I'm beautiful.'
'Did it hurt?'
'For days.'
'Did your wife think it beautiful?'
'I didn't see that before we were married!' called Vermilion.
'She's lying.'
'How old were you?'
'Thirteen – and out looking for girls.'

It was worth it, for the virility and potency it conferred. In some places, phallic symbols were part of the design. Bartholomew being evasive on the subject, I asked others about the significance of tattoos generally. William the schoolmaster said that you had to be careful: 'A man with tattoos must not pass beneath a woman's sarong [sic], or go under a house in which a woman is sitting, if she is not his wife.'

He did not specify the consequences, but they no doubt involved a spiritual transgression. As if the lasciviousness of tattooing wasn't enough, the Christian missions soon realised that tattooing was especially important to both their animist and Buddhist opponents.[4] In Burma and Thailand, complex charms and religious texts used to be commonly inscribed across the breast and back, where there was lots of space. Bartholomew's sickly brother had three small and rather faint Buddhas on his sternum. On his back there were some curious little tattooed scribbles – as though someone had been totting up a shopping list. In recent years tattooing has developed what one might call an anti-spiritual use. Karen animism is an expensive and time-consuming practice. It requires regular animal sacrifices, and the earmarked chickens, pigs and buffaloes are supposed to be kept separate from those reared as food; this could require a family to almost double its livestock holdings. As economic pressures have mounted, so a means has been found of releasing oneself from this obligation. A ritual tattooing called *cekosi* absolves you from your duties of feeding the spirits. *Cekosi* doesn't claim that you don't believe in the spirits, only that you opt out of supporting them. There's always a nagging suspicion that they'll get you sooner or later; it's a bit like tearing up an income tax return.

In Riverside, among the modernist Christian Karen, tattoos were a relative rarity. I never saw any *cekosi* marks. The young soldiers, brought up in the Revolution, might have markings on their arms, but not the likes of Edward, True Love or Pastor Moses. Indeed, the absence of tattoos was something that set them apart. Moses said: 'Traditional Karen need tattoos in order to get married, but not the educated Christians. Other people still do it. At Insein I used to play football with a team who were mostly Mon, and I was the only one *not* tattooed.'

There were other meanings and uses; the spiritual and political significances of the marks were never far apart. An eighteenth-century chronicle, the *History of Yonaka*,[5] says that in 1770 the King of Ava (Burma) issued an edict that all males in the north of Siam should be tattooed black, the Burmese having seized power in Siam a few years beforehand. Even after the Burmese had gone, the Thais insisted that Karen who wished to become subjects of Siam be tattooed – the Karen were particularly angered at having to pay the 'professors of tattooing' to brand them in this way. Thomas Stern (1968a, p. 320), described Karen leg tattoos as 'a highly popular adornment that is currently being interpreted as constituting a sign of subjection to the Burmese'.

But it was more than just a brand of submission. Nineteenth-century observers soon realised that an outbreak of tattooing in the villages generally meant trouble to follow. Dr. Vinton, that belligerent Baptist who in 1886 was calling on the British to arm the Karen against Burman rebels, repeatedly warned that 'the dacoits are being tattooed and enrolled'. It was a commitment, an oath. Moreover, properly selected markings gave physical protection.[6]

Major J. J. Snodgrass, in his 1827 *Narrative of the Burma War*, describes the Burmese king's crack troops who were tattooed and hence known as 'The Invulnerables'. In 1931 the Burmese rebel Saya San had his followers tattooed to protect them from British bullets: it didn't work then either. But belief in the efficacy of tattoo against modern weapons was undimmed by the Second World War. Shwe Tun Kya was a Karen leader who, after the British retreat from Burma, decided to cooperate with the Japanese if they would guarantee to restrain the anti-Karen excesses of the Burma Independence Army. He was known as the 'Tiger of the Delta'. Mika Rolley (1980, p. 27), wrote of him:

His prowess with women and passion for Buddhist charms and talismans were exceptional. He had been tattooed all over his body by a famous monk called Poo Ya Li, with magic squares, formulae and mystical arrangements of numbers, all to confer invulnerability.

But the Tiger was later arrested and killed:

His body was thrown into the Irrawaddy river so that his spirit would be floated down to the ocean, never to return and thereby to inspire further leadership.

This was the context in which Bartholomew had had himself extensively tattooed. In Riverside today the tattoos are scrappier and perhaps less carefully thought out. I never met anyone who said that their tattoos conferred invulnerability in battle, though I did meet young men with charms and amulets against Burmese bullets. It was difficult to take all the tattoos seriously. One young man had the single English word ELEMENT on his forearm. Others sported snakes or tigers or phrases in Karen script. But in many cases there was no doubt that the markings were a declaration of war. Some had a KNLA insignia permanently in their skin. Others carried the name of Ba U Gyi, or just the word, KAW-THOOLEI. There was no going back to civilian life in Burma for a young man marked like that.

Bartholomew's tattoos were of the traditional type, corresponding closely to the descriptions and engravings in the nineteenth-century travellers' accounts. From his waist down his hips and thighs to just below his knees, his skin was divided and subdivided into neat panels like coffering, elegantly bordered with geometrical and curvilinear designs more familiar to me in Roman grotesques or the painted vaults of medieval Europe than on the legs of tribesmen in Burma. In one respect, though, the designs were unlike those in the nineteenth-century illustrations. The other patterns were clearly zoomorphic. Tigers, fish, birds, bats and other creatures covered Bartholomew's forebears, but his legs were quasi-abstract in decoration. One symbol resembled a three-legged Sanskritic charm, another a cross between a fountain and Aladdin's lamp.

The rest of Bartholomew's family were faintly embarrassed by his legs. They were not really the thing for a modern, Christian Revolutionary. Which begged the question, was that what Bartholomew actually was?

Vermilion didn't like the tattoos at all. They might have been a turn-on for the first wife but when one day the children were tweaking the hair on my legs and I jokingly remarked that I would have to have my thighs shaved and embellished like their father's, Vermilion protested: 'No, not nice at all!'

'If you do it with a medicated needle', said William, 'some tattoo designs protect you against snakebite.' This was one of the array of prophylactics and therapies available in Kawthoolei. Bartholomew would have loved to integrate them all, to rationalise both the traditions and the flood of imported drugs so as to get the best from both. It was an impossible dream.

Karen medicine as described in books is a spiritual matter.[7] If, for whatever reason, one of a person's multiple souls is offended or tempted, it may leave the body which is then exposed to immediate sickness. The patient may have unwittingly insulted an ancestor by, for example, building a house in the wrong place. Or they may have injured a forest spirit who steals the human soul in revenge. Any illness is assumed to have a spiritual cause of this sort, so the first response is to find out what was done to give offence. This is achieved by divination, often using chicken bones. When the cause is known, the offence must be made good – by demolishing the house, perhaps, or by sacrificing animals – and a shaman must recall the soul back to the patient's body, ceremonially tying it back in with strings around the wrist.

The Riverside Christians would not have been seen dead with strings round their wrists, but in other villages the practice continued. For the Karen, religious loyalties are a flexible matter. A change in economic status, or a move to a new community may easily bring about a change in faith – which may be complete or only partial. Equally, Karen attitudes to health and medicine are very syncretic, and the same person might look in many directions for help.

We lived so near the Thai border that there was no hope of controlling the influx of modern medicines. A bizarre selection of drugs could be found in houses deep in the forest, many of them highly sophisticated, very dangerous, very expensive, quite useless or all of these. Weary Karen farmers, drained by the labour of the harvest, could call in at the village shop and buy themselves half a litre of *Stamina Injection*, a Japanese cocktail of water, sugar and vitamins. They'd lie down on a mat at home and have someone – anyone – jab the needle into a vein in their arms and run the fluid in. An old man who'd lost his appetite assured me that he was now better thanks to large helpings of what I heard as 'bubble-and-squeak' – actually, a big bottle of *B-Complex Squibb*. Antibiotics, antimalarials, antihelminthics, immuno-suppressants and non-steroidal anti-inflammatory analgesics – the Karen ate them in handfuls. Or, which is often worse, just one of each. After which they'd down a bottle of Thai or Burmese patent blood tonic, such as *Toh Meh Pah*.

There are in the forest a thousand medicinal plants. Even a city boy like True Love could point out quite a few. Front Line KNLA soldiers knew the ones that would stop diarrhoea, or bleeding or infection in gunshot wounds. Certain trees were said to cure malaria, and almost any leaf you could pick was considered a valuable source of vitamins.

It used to be the case that Karen would take 'western' or Karen cures equally happily but not at the same time. I met patients who, having tried some imported drug unsuccessfully, were now starving themselves as a purge before starting on a course of plant cures. But the barriers are slipping. There are so many half-educated Delta Karen mixed up with the forest people that confusion reigns. Ointments are being compounded of leaves and ground-down antibiotics.

There were virtuoso practitioners to be met in the forest. Saw Salai had a reputation that extended throughout Kawthoolei. He ran a clinic with a few bamboo huts for patients who might stay with him for weeks. He could cure anything that afflicted your blood with infusions of roots and barks. For all his reputation, he eschewed mystique. Indeed, he'd not been practising for long. He was just an old hunter, he said, 'and when you spend a lot of time in the forest you get to know what works'. Bartholomew's wife Vermilion and his Health Department assistant Morning Star both thought Saw Salai a marvel, and walked for days through the forest to consult him. Then there was a man at Four Springs who could set bones by blowing on them (Marshall in 1922 (p. 273) mentioned a Karen 'blowing magic' that could heal wounds and induce tumours). The pastor at Betelwood could treat traumatic shock and blood loss by cutting a fresh coconut, plugging a needle and tube into it and running the milk into the patient's veins instead of plasma or *Stamina Injection*; they swore that it worked very well.

With Bartholomew I visited the headman of Bombshell, on the walls of whose house hung bottles of home-made medicines. There was centipede in petrol, as an antiseptic. There was a tonic made of the entrails of six wild fowl marinaded in rice spirit. Then there was a pain-killer made of millipede ground up in lime juice, which had to be jabbed lightly into the afflicted part with a sharp bamboo sliver previously used for grilling fish. The headman, who had been harvesting rice and whose cutting arm was swollen and aching, was having this treatment from his wife when we arrived, and in the morning his arm felt much better. I asked him if he was teaching anyone else his pharmaceutical knowledge but he said no, he'd not thought of doing that.

As the Kawthoolei authorities contemplated the sums being spent on imported drugs, they saw that they might do well to encourage more self-reliance. The Women's Organisation produced a stencilled booklet called *Cures in Your Kitchen* which describes several dozen home-cures. But no one's heart was in it. White tablets of bitter synthetic alkaloids, red and yellow gelatin capsules of tetracycline were too potent. Even Bartholomew, who knew many of the medicinal herbs and was so proud of Karen traditional skills, would sooner or later back down and prescribe a course of vitamin B injections.

This, after all, was a professional family. The title *thera* – teacher, leader, instructor – was common amongst us. Vermilion called her husband *thera*, he called her the feminine *theramuh*. I was *thera*, and so was their son Sam who had trained as a paramedic and now ran the laboratory. Fragrance was a *chyo theramuh* (schoolmistress) and of an evening if True Love, Moses and Morning Star the Colonel's son were all there for a gossip, the air was so thick with *thera* that one hardly knew who was addressing whom.

Bartholomew ran the Health and Welfare Department from home, out of a plastic carrier bag and a buff-coloured folder. Sam was his factotum, Morning Star his second-in-command and Shelley his clerical assistant. It was a very personal operation. Bartholomew took an avuncular view of his staff and they often stayed in the house also. He would rail at them all in his mock stern manner and they laughed at him, but held him in great respect both for his kindness and for his competence. With people out in the river villages he dealt as a friend. 'You will like travelling with Bartholomew', said Edward to me. 'Everybody knows and loves him.' I never saw him unwelcome, and even when he entered an unfamiliar house he made himself so at home as soon to be rummaging through the pots in the kitchen for a snack. 'Do you know me?' he would say to anyone we met on the road or river. 'I am *thera* Bartholomew', and if they didn't recognise him they had almost certainly heard of him.

For all the personal satisfaction this might have given him, he had one of the least enviable jobs in the District. Health care has a special status in twentieth-century rebellions. It is usually near the top of the list of charges levelled by insurgents against governments, that they have neglected the people's health. It is a priority in their manifestos, and there has hardly been a single popular revolution since the Second World War that has not tried to make popular health a cornerstone of the new order, be it in Nicaragua, Cuba, China, Libya, Namibia – or Burma.

In consequence, wherever revolutions and civil wars are being fought out, health workers are among the first to be found in ditches in the morning with their eyes out. An arm band with a red cross is as much a liability as a safeguard. A feature of modern 'low intensity conflict', designed not for rapid military gain but to exert political pressure, is that civilians and those who care for them are important 'soft' targets. Those who propose to recruit and train such village workers might ask themselves whether they're doing anyone much of a favour.

All sides consider health a key to hearts and minds. The Burmese, who manufacture reasonable and cheap medicines, are particularly hard on anyone caught smuggling drugs to the rebels. When the Burmese attacked, Karen forest hospitals were burnt, Bartholomew's nurses captured. My friend Highlander, of the Information Department, went on a long propaganda tour of outlying villages and it was nurses and medicines that he took with him. Later, I heard him exhorting a group of Bartholomew's trainees: 'Health and clinics are what the Burmese promise the people everywhere. They call that Socialism but they can deliver nothing. But when you, as KNU nurses, come to Karen villages, the people will say, "There, you see? The KNU cares for us!" You nurses are the sign that Kawthoolei remembers its people.'

But in Kawthoolei as anywhere else, health care is never-ending, its provision a bottomless pit into which infinite resources can be poured. Although clinics are often the first thing to be established by new regimes, they are also often the first to be short-funded when the pressure mounts and the leadership needs cash for ammunition.

A civilian Health Department like Batholomew's is especially vulnerable. Not only does it have to survive the stringencies and strains of working under emergency military rule, it may have an ambivalent reception from the populace too. Kawthoolei's mid-wives are a case in point. Karen 'traditional birth attendants' (to use modern jargon) are often men. They have no formal training, they are not appointed or elected, their position is not hereditary nor formal in any other sense. They often pick up the skill and the practice in middle-age. In other words, they exemplify Karen informal social organisation. They are also usually animist or Budd-hist. By contrast, Bartholomew was trying to place in each village a trained, young, female, institutionalised member of a (Christian) hierarchy, to improve 'standards' in birthing. The wretched girl sent out as a village nurse thus represented a threat not only to the traditional midwives themselves but to Karen ideas of social organisation generally. Not surprisingly, little progress had been made.

When, six years ago, the Colonel came from GHQ to take over as Governor (or, strictly speaking, as Chairman) of the District, he brought his family with him. The new District Headquarters was being established with its family lines at Riverside, and Bar-tholomew wanted to build a hospital there. It cost considerable effort. The road had not yet been finished, so materials – cement, breeze blocks, roof sheeting – had to be carried part of the way through the forest and then moved upstream in boats. The staff of the Health Department built it, Bartholomew himself doing the joinery. It was essentially a long, U-shaped shed with a male and a female wing, and a small operating room in the centre. There were twenty-four beds – wooden, and very solid.

The Colonel's son, Morning Star, was put in charge of the new hospital. He was always one of my favourite Karen: gentle, self-deprecating, patient and funny. He was also somewhat eccentric, a hypochondriac who was not happy if not subjecting himself to one or other brand of Thai or Karen therapy. As the Gossips said, this made him the obvious choice for director of the hospital: having all possible diseases himself, he'd have no difficulty in recognising them in others. Having been appointed, he proceeded to give away a rumoured B.20,000 (£500) worth of drugs free to anyone who turned up at the hospital. He was also said to have given away all his own clothes. I liked him enormously for it, but the KNU didn't and ordered him to pay back the money. I suspect his father had to bail him out.

The stress of this period was such that he reputedly didn't sleep for three months. There were other eccentricities. He decided to establish a papaya grove by the hospital – but planted them all upside down. He then held a rock concert in the men's ward. 'Were you anything to do with that?' I asked True Love. 'I sent Dan to look after the musical instruments', he replied.

The inevitable end was that Bartholomew's hospital was taken over by the Army, its nurses put into uniform. 'He's still pretty sore about that', said the gossips. It was inevitable not because of Morning Star's eccentric management, nor because of the undeniable failings of the Health and Welfare Department which, with only a handful of half-trained staff was too small either to work effectively or to generate new skills. No, the takeover was inevitable because, in modern Revolutions, health is too important; the soldiers cannot bear to leave it to the civilians.

Unlike the Army and the Education Department, Bartholomew's Health and Welfare Department had no regular budget. Every time he needed anything at all he had to indent for it to Headquarters, who might well turn him down if there was little cash in the kitty. Thus there was no prospect of any forward planning. He received on balance (he thought) about B.10,000 (£250) a year for drugs, for a local population of 7 or 8,000. He thought of trying a household levy, but when we discussed how much it might be, no one dared suggest more than B.2 per household per month. That would buy one quinine tablet – the adult course for malaria being around fifty tablets. In a situation where almost all transport was still by water, the Department had no boat. Also, it had somehow been established that any 'member of the Revolution' (i.e. a soldier, teacher or other KNU functionary or their family) had the right to call on the Department for 'Family Life Assistance' when, for instance, a baby was born. That meant that one of Bartholomew's dozen nurses could be tied up for two weeks or more.

'With Bartholomew here', said Edward, 'anything is possible.' But for all the respect and devotion he inspired, Bartholomew was

Plate 6. '... calling at every home in the name of the Revolution: "It's Thera Bartholomew. Anyone sick?"'

shamelessly pushed around by the authorities. Once, when we were embarking on a clinical tour of the villages, he was told at the last minute that he'd have to be back days before he'd intended because the Information Department wanted two of his nurses for their Propaganda Tour. When we returned from the trip we found that, rather than wait for Bartholomew to return and allocate two staff to them, the Propaganda circus had already departed taking his two most senior nurses, leaving word that they'd be gone three months. The truth was that Bartholomew had little control over his Department's resources.

The greatest hazard was the Colonel. The Colonel fancied himself as a paramedic, and the bookshelves at his house up at Headquarters groaned under job lots of obsolete US surgical manuals. To do him credit, he was well aware of the importance of village health care. But he couldn't leave anything alone. He would arrive in the village before dawn, summon Bartholomew to a meeting at 5 a.m. and instruct him to redeploy his staff to plug some gap that he, the Colonel, had perceived; invariably, a dozen wider fissures took its place. Meanwhile, there loomed the shadows of the three Rangoon-trained 'real' doctors at GHQ, who couldn't afford to dispense with Bartholomew's services but could not disguise their contempt for his home-baked medical skills. Even I, although firmly on his side, represented another pressure of professional comparison that he was (literally) not qualified to withstand.

Hardly surprisingly, Bartholomew lacked confidence. To organise health care for civilians in the face of a war is a despairing, Sisyphean task. The situation in Kawthoolei changed so often that the best-conceived plans were stillborn. No sooner had he tentatively distributed his paltry establishment to cover the ground as best they could than a Burmese attack elsewhere would have him rushing to see the damage to the local clinic, to try and make it good, try and help the victims by redeploying his small team. Communications were so poor that one rarely knew precisely where anyone else was, and Bartholomew scuttled about sticking fingers into a dozen muddy dykes. Much of the time he was effectively a one-man Department, travelling from village to village with whatever drugs he could scrape together, seeing any patient that asked, calling at every house in the name of the Revolution: 'Is anyone at home? It's *thera* Bartholomew. Anyone sick?'

In the end, his devotion wasn't enough. As the situation of Kawthoolei deteriorated, so the consolidatory instincts of the military authorities began to turn upon the Health Department. I had always assumed that Sam, his efficient and intelligent son, was the heir-apparent in the Department, in the dynastic manner that Kawthoolei has. It didn't happen that way.

But as we bathed *en famille* in the river of an evening, with soft late sunlight, hooting children, the older siblings teasing their parents and the latter smiling benignly upon them, a fragile contentment was palpable.

7 Fighting mean, fighting clean

The quietest and most harmless people in the world.

Major Snodgrass (1827, p. 141)

Karen have an equitable temperament and are not savage or arrogant. They can justly be termed gentle.

Preecha Chaturabhand (1987, p. 180)

When the [Karen] party reach the house, the first rush is made by the two volunteers, and the rest follow. The house is stormed. All the men are killed, whether armed or unarmed. Such women as are thought likely to be useful or profitable as slaves are taken and bound. All the rest are killed. Infants are always killed, and children are often barbarously massacred. Their hands and feet are cut off, and their bodies hacked into small pieces.

D. M. Smeaton (1887, p. 86)

New heroes have come forward since the days of Ba U Gyi and Bo Jakay. I met one of them in a comic-book while I was staying a weekend, with True Love and Bartholomew, at the house of the headman of Barterville – a fine big house on a high bluff overlooking the river.

The title of the comic was *Bright Red Blood*, the Karen phrase implying an immaculate clarity as well as brilliant colour. On the cover, which depicted one of the hero's exploits, the title had originally been printed in Burmese – an offensive blunder. A Karen version had been gummed on top.

The hero's name was Eh Ha. 'You could translate that as "Mr Cool"', said True Love. 'I knew him. I met him down at Pa-an before either of us joined the KNLA. He was a good musician, lead guitarist in a group, and we played together.'

That is not how Mr Cool is portrayed on the cover of the comic. He stands stripped to the waist with his girl clinging to his arm. He has crossed bandoliers on his chest and a hot weapon in his hand. He is the Karen *Rambo*, slayer of Burmese socialists.

The story tells how, at home in the Delta, Mr Cool hears the Karen National Union call. He leaves his lover after an anguished night of talk, walks up into the hills to join the KNLA, and becomes a commando and the leader of a raiding party. After a series of adventures his unit locates a strongly fortified Burmese position which has got to go. The night before the assault, Mr Cool dreams of his girl and of Karen liberation. In the morning he leads the attack, storming five Burmese bunkers more or less single-handed and killing a Burmese captain. But, as he leads his men forward once more, a bullet hits him in the chest and he falls ...

'Actually', said True Love, 'it was a little nastier than that. He was about to throw a grenade and had already pulled the pin when the bullet hit him. He fell on top of the grenade and it blew his side out.'

The lads knew all about the real Rambo, of course. That had been one of the videos screened by the Education Department at Christmas, and they all sat out in the open until the early hours to watch, with the thick clammy mist settling on them. In the morning the military nurses, who were doing a parasitology course, had thick heads and couldn't see down the microscope.

Video shows were a regular occurrence at Riverside. They hardly contributed to a sophisticated examination of the insurgency or its values, nor to a well-informed and balanced world view. Communists in particular came off badly. One night it was Brother Jimmy Swaggart preaching in Atlanta, Georgia, denouncing abortion, Catholics and communists in one breath. The next evening we watched a Liverpool–Juventus match. Then, Thai martial arts heroes destroyed legions of drug peddlers and communists (so we understood – none of us could actually follow the dialogue of that one). *The Killing Fields* came up: 'It's about a journalist fleeing from the communists', said True Love. And then *Rambo* again. The lads loved it. The fact that it was about a white imperialist thug slaughtering Asians who were, after all, fighting for their freedom much as the Karen were – this point was missed. As far as they were concerned, it was about a good guy killing communists. White Rock named his little son Rambo.

I found Pastor Moses reading an old *Reader's Digest* article about the terrible atrocities committed by the communist rebels against their own peasantry in Laos. 'You don't want to believe what you read in that rag', I cautioned him, but I had nothing to offer in counterbalance. *The Voice of America* and *Radio Veritas* choked the airwaves.

On all sides, hatred of Ne Win's pseudo-socialist regime in Burma blurred into a hatred of left-wing politics generally; it made my position decidedly awkward. Moses listened attentively enough

Plate 7. 'A garment to gladden the hearts of *Soldier of Fortune* readers.'

when he invited me to breakfast to explain why I voted socialist, but the 1987 elections in Britain had Colonel Marvel crowing delightedly that his idol, Mrs Thatcher, had triumphed so resoundingly. 'Bad for you, Mr John!' he laughed. It certainly was.

A T-shirt appeared, sold in the village shops and worn by a number of the lads. It was a garment to gladden the hearts of *Soldier of Fortune* readers from Afghanistan to Honduras, especially as all its copy was in English. I bought one. It has the words KAREN

FREEDOM FIGHTER arched over a red KNLA beret and, below that, crossed M16s. Around the guns are the slogans 'Anti-drug, Anti-BSPP (Burma Socialist Progress Party), Anti-Burmese Communist'. At the bottom it says, 'KAWTHOOLEI – Never accept Communism.'

Much of this anti-communism is quite spurious. Not only are the Karen and the Burma Communist Party (who actually began their rebellion before the Karen) fighting the same enemy: much of the Karen leadership was for a long time quite firmly communist in outlook too. In the 1950s, casting around for a theoretical framework for their struggle, they'd looked naturally enough to Mao Zedong's China. One of the senior secretaries at our Headquarters had actually been to China as a link man with the Chinese Communist government.

Things changed with the accession of the Seventh Day Adventist, Bo Mya. Senior Karen with communist leanings tacked about and stayed in place. As the military situation grew more desperate, hatred of all leftists was added to the rallying cries. In 1986/7 negotiations to bring the Burma Communist Party into the National Democratic Front (NDF), the umbrella organisation of Burma's insurgents, were angrily repudiated by Bo Mya.

There have been attempts to portray Karen society and tradition as fundamentally antipathetic to communism, notably in the pamphlet *Karens and Communism* by Saw Moo Troo (1981, p. 8). He claims, for instance, that:

The Karens do not believe in common ownership, for them it cannot be a successful working system. When a certain thing is declared to be communally owned a Karen will ignore its importance and thereby will not bother himself to maintain or take care of it.

This is nonsense. The swidden land farmed by Karen villages is most definitely regarded as common property, which is allocated year by year among the farmers of the village. So are schools and churches and shrines. The KNU's intolerance is not widespread. As news crept down to us of the angry debates at the NDF over Communist Party membership, more than one friend muttered to me that 'We should not hate the communists like this.'

It was Highlander of the Information Department who was most forthright: 'I hate that T-shirt, I do not approve of that at all. We cannot always be anti-communist. Many communists are good people, and right now we need friends. The people who designed that T-shirt had no official authorisation to do it – but someone at the top must have encouraged them. They want us to have the strong-man image, and it's awful.'

And he proceeded to question me closely about Nicaragua and El Salvador, both as to the ideologies and the strategy employed by the insurgents. 'How were the Sandinistas organised? Did they have one central command headquarters or many dispersed bases? I worry that we are too concentrated and vulnerable . . .'

When your back is to the wall in a rebellion and you want foreign support, image would appear to count for a great deal – and the Karen image on offer to outsiders is that of a gentle people, Christian in spirit if not all in name, eschewing from principle the opium trade that funds the Burmese communists, and confronting godless Burmese socialism. And there were plenty of foreigners anxious to help sell this picture. Highlander told me of one of them: 'A few years ago Mr Jimmy the Belgian came from *Soldier of Fortune* magazine. He talked a lot with Edward and others and gave out all those SoF badges you see now.'

True Love had one sewn onto a beret; I wouldn't let him wear it in the boat. I'd seen the fruits of SoF interest in the Karen. In a special issue entitled *Soldiers of Freedom* that was kicking around in Edward's house, they were classed together with other selfless martyrs of the struggle against communism – UNITA, the *Contra*, the Mozambique National Resistance and the Afghan *mujahidin*. The Karen were described as profoundly Christian, and fervently anti-communist.

I tried telling True Love what I thought of *Soldier of Fortune*, suggesting that association with the trade magazine of hired killers might be two-edged when it came to calling for international condemnation of Burmese atrocities. But he riposted heatedly: 'Why should we not welcome SoF? Who else takes an interest in us? These people are on our side!'

Whereas the rest of democracy seemed to be selling out. Even the Thais, even Mrs Thatcher. The world was behaving bizarrely; what had become of ideological solidarity? Could it be that the image, so vigorously polished, had been disregarded? Edward rounded on me with the news that Mrs Thatcher was going to sell the Burmese socialist dictator a number of British 81mm mortars, 'the most accurate in the world. She's even giving him credit! Whose side is she on, is she a socialist now? You write to Mrs Thatcher, Jo, tell her Burmese credit stinks!'

Highlander said: 'For years we have struggled to be decent in the eyes of the world. We have kept clear of the opium trade which all the rebels in the north, the Shan and everyone are involved in. We run a law-abiding state. And what good does it do us? What support do we get? You just sell guns to our enemies. Sometimes I think we would do better to sell opium and fight rougher.'

If they did that, years of moral credit-building would be jettisoned. It is not true that no one except *Soldier of Fortune* takes any interest in the Karen. Others have been watching, certain journalists and periodicals have kept the cause before the public. *The Far Eastern Economic Review* of 2 March 1979 went as far as to call them the 'world's most pleasant and civilised guerrilla group'.

The image of decency is far dearer to Karen hearts than is anti-communism, but it gives them just as much trouble. I called on Highlander one night at the beginning of the rains – which meant that we had to sit close together by the lamp to hear each other talk over the roar on the tin roof. In so doing, I was rapidly coated in creeping termites, just hatched out of the ground by the first moisture, their cumbersome wings able to get them into my hair but not out again. Highlander's daughter had a fever, and we sat bathing and cooling her with damp towels. I asked him about the justice system:

> 'Suppose your cow is stolen and you think you know who did it – maybe you see a man running away. What do you do?'
> 'I go to the KNDO militia and lay a complaint. They arrest him and hold him at the guard house. They interrogate him and make a report to the judge, Harvest Moon, who will sentence him.'
> 'What if he denies it?'
> 'Usually we Karen confess.'
> 'What if you'd suspected the wrong man? He wouldn't confess then.'
> 'We would interrogate him. Softly, you know, but a little like torture.'

I explained what I meant by a trial, and asked if the District ever held such a thing.

> 'Sometimes in a special case we have a meeting, but usually he confesses. Sometimes we have to kill him.'
> 'You what? Why?'
> 'It has happened. About ten years ago we were pressed very hard here and the Burmese were everywhere. If somebody comes to our area that no ones knows, we don't trust him. Why is

he here? Is he a Burmese spy? So, we have to interrogate him. Well, there was a man up at the mines, come from Burma. I was working with the KNDO then. We had information that he was a spy for the Burmese Army. The soldiers beat him, they beat him too badly and he swelled up. But he wouldn't confess, we couldn't get anything from him. At last we had a meeting and we said, "What can we do with this man? If he wasn't our enemy before, he certainly will be now." And so we decided that we had to shoot him; he was taken out into the forest by the soldiers. It was a very hard decision for us to make. And then later we learned that he was innocent, just a simple Burmese man come to work in the mines.'

We continued sponging down his burning, feverish daughter. Highlander himself shivered at another bad memory:

'A few years ago, when I was living up north, my eldest daughter got malaria very badly. I took her out to hospital in Thailand. The young doctor gave her new blood but he said, "I'm afraid it's too late; I can't do any more for her." I watched my daughter die. It was a terrible thing. I chain smoked for a while after that. I do not smoke now.'

A Burmese soldier was brought to the hospital at Riverside. I watched as closely as I could, wondering how he would be treated. There had been persistent rumours of prisoners being tortured, and of a fierce debate within the KNLA and the party; was it ever justified? Did it, or did it not, make the Karen as evil as those who oppressed them?

The young man in the hospital was twenty years old and called Aung Mo. Bartholomew's son Sam was looking after him. Sam took a blood sample and examined it under the microscope. He pronounced Aung Mo to be awash with malaria, and put him on a quinine drip.

'He was captured upriver', said Sam. 'There were three of them; the other two tried to escape and were shot, but this one was already sick and didn't try anything, so the Army nurses brought him here. He's Burmese but he comes from Pa-an which is a very Karen town. He says he likes the Karen. He says he was forcibly conscripted when he was sixteen and made to carry heavy loads for the Burmese Army, and only later given any training. He wants to go home to Pa-an but he knows that if he did that he'd be caught by the Burmese again. So, if he survives, he'll stay here. He's terribly dehydrated, he's been in a coma at times.'

Aung Mo did survive, and was photographed for the KNU

monthly newsletter being tended in hospital. A week later he was up and about and talking very sensibly about how awful life was in the Burmese Army, how they often had no rice so that they either starved or had to pillage some peasants' store. It was proposed that he should be settled in a downriver village and married off to a nice Karen girl who spoke Burmese. Then he vanished. I never found out where he'd gone.

I tried to establish what happened to prisoners. Given a millennium of murderous Karen–Burman antipathy, it seemed unlikely that either side would be humanely disposed. Nor is there, in the region, any tradition of valuing prisoners' lives beyond their worth in ransom or political leverage. In old Burma and Siam, captives had value as slaves but nothing else and were often killed. In 1837 Captain Low (p. 324) reported that, 'The Siamese make it a rule never to give quarter in battle'. The only obvious practical difference today is that, with current communications techniques, they have far more propaganda value.

True Love said, 'We captured a Burmese captain last week', and so I asked him what they did with prisoners. He looked shifty: 'I don't know. We let them go, I think. What would we do with them, where would we keep them? Anyway, there are so many Burmese soldiers that our catching a few makes no difference to them and is only a burden to us. All we're interested in is getting their weapons, so that we can fight back.'

But the Burmese, according to the Karen, fight dirty. 'They kill all their prisoners', said Moses, 'or rather, no, first they torture them and then they kill them. We do not do that.'

Charges of Burmese theft, torture, rape and murder of Karen civilians are commonplace in Kawthoolei and on the whole I believe them, as does Amnesty International. Men, women and children all told the same stories. There was hardly a family that hadn't suffered.

In return, the Burmese accuse the Karen of blowing up trains with the loss of civilian life. The KNU denies this, but does admit to training saboteurs.

There's another accusation that the Karen frequently level against the Burmese – that they force villagers not only to carry rice, water and ammunition for them, but make them walk in front of the soldiers dragging banana palms along the paths to detonate mines. Worse still, says the *KNU Bulletin*: 'For this dangerous work they receive no pay.'

Both sides in this war use landmines. Soldiers have long recognised that smaller mines create bigger problems for the enemy. Dead, he requires only burial. Maimed, he'll need doctors and nurses, transport, blood, drugs, surgery and quite possibly lifelong welfare support. I saw, very often, the characteristic landmine victim, hit in the face and limbs. One former soldier, blinded in both eyes, with a badly damaged left hand and a stiffened leg, earned a miserable supplement to his rice ration by portering. He would collect goods from the Thai traders at Headquarters and then stagger the fifteen kilometres down to Riverside with this load, feeling his way with a stick. I met a KNDO man with damaged eyes stirring the pig stew the night before a village feast. He was in a state of great agitation because he'd dreamt the night before that his sight would be returned to him that day. There was a schoolgirl being cared for by Bartholomew's Health and Welfare Department who had lost one leg. Now getting about painfully on a crutch, she was lonely and depressed, probably unmarriageable and given to bouts of manic giggling. Another former soldier came to stay at Bartholomew's house, one leg and one eye gone. He creaked around the compound at night on his crutch, an alarming sight in the moonlight that, in spite of everyone's best intentions, made the children shriek. There were too many of them, and always legs and faces hurt.

It's difficult to be decent with a landmine. They are not a weapon-concept that is new to the Karen. On one of my walking tours I stayed in a particularly old and dusty house, substantial enough for a large family but now lived in by just the elderly father, who clearly didn't bother much. We were sorting through a heap of ancient sleeping mats – rather nervously: it was just the place for snakes and scorpions – when we came upon a bundle of contraptions, extremely sharp foot-long blades of split bamboo fitted together to make a sort of caltrop, which could be concealed in small hollows on the approach paths to the village. They had all the advantages of a small mine; they would rip up leg muscles and immobilise the victim, leaving him with wounds which (bamboo is notorious for this) would fester and be very slow to heal.

Looking at the blinded, limping victims, I wondered how many had trodden on their own side's traps. It's a problem guerrillas face worldwide; if you protect your territory by mining the approach paths, sooner or later your own people will walk that way.

The better you prepare yourself to hurt others, the sooner you will hurt yourself. In Kawthoolei there are guns everywhere, in every village and most houses. Some families now prefer to shoot the chicken for dinner than to quietly cut its throat. Own goals are inevitable. One teacher threatened to shoot his wife with an AK47 because their child had been scalded with boiling water. Another man came home from a hunting trip and placed his rifle on the table, where his two-year-old daughter reached up and touched the trigger. The shot hit the girl's mother in the stomach, killing her.

At Headquarters there is an armoury. It has its own generator in one shed and, in another, two lathes and a litter of gun parts. There are the corpses of World War Two Enfields and Garands. There's an abandoned attempt to reconstruct a badly damaged Bren gun and a couple of M14s, possibly of Korean War provenance. There are heaps of new wooden stocks for carbines, which seem to shed them rather easily, and a jumble of frustratingly incompatible parts from different Kalashnikov variants. Nearby trees are being shredded by test rounds. They'll get anything firing that they can, and worry about the ammunition later.

I accompanied a visiting photo-journalist called Trevor round the KNLA camp. Trevor was a New Zealander, a regular on the circuit of Asian insurgencies. He was a blend of charm and funny stories with some (to me) thoroughly obnoxious opinions. He must have winded my sentiments promptly. Only a few minutes after we first met he said firmly, 'You're a bit of a lefty, aren't you? Before you say another word, let me tell you that I write for *Soldier of Fortune*.'

Round the camp we went, Trevor exclaiming with delight, horror or amusement: 'Hey, a Browning HMG! And now, that's a 1944 Bren. What ammo do you use? Can you get .303? No, that's not a Bren clip, it's a G3 clip, that's why it doesn't fit. So what bullets do you use? Nato standard? But ... no adaptation? It's too small ... OK, so it wobbles a bit as it comes out. Hey, that AK with the front grip, that's eastern European, that's a collector's piece, you could get $1,000 dollars for that. Maybe I should make him an offer. What's that stock on the back of the Browning? Did you weld that on? It's not supposed to need a stock, it's got handles ... oh, a bit heavy for you little people, eh?'

'This place', he concluded as we moved on, 'is a museum.'

It had been years since I'd read Orwell's *Burmese Days*, but a

small item that stuck in my memory was the description of the
pathetic armoury of the 'rebels' in the story in chapter twenty.
It included: 'Item, six home-made guns with barrels of zinc piping
stolen from the railway. These could be fired, after a fashion, by
thrusting a nail through the touch hole and striking it with a stone.'

So much for the ingenuity of Burmese rebels; the Karen are in
a different class. 'We Karen love guns', said True Love, and everywhere they prove it.

It is an interesting question, how guns first reached Burma and
Thailand in the first place.[1] The *Annals of Ayutthia* and other early
Siamese chronicles mention firearms repeatedly in the mid fourteenth century – that is, very few years after the first record of
the use of cannon in Europe. The Chinese knew about gunpowder
as early as the eighth century, and began its military use in the
tenth century. There's no evidence of its spread to the south then,
but at the time Marco Polo was travelling the region, Kublai Khan
employed firearms against the Javanese. Numerous European
adventurers followed after Polo to China and in 1454 the records
speak of European gunners training the Siamese, forty-three years
before Vasco da Gama rounded the Cape. The Chinese may have
the dubious distinction of having invented gunpowder, but Europeans were there soon enough in roles we now recognise very well
– arms dealers and mercenaries. So, as to the first importers of
firearms to Burma, the field is wide open. Remembering the Victorian theory that the Karen first came to Burma as part of a Chinese
army, there was even the entertaining thought that maybe they
were responsible themselves.

Guns caught on fast. A merchant from Venice, Caesar Frederick,
reached Pegu in 1567 and noted of the King's armies that, 'their
armour and weapons are verie naught and weake ... they have
very bad pikes, their swords are worse made ... [but] his harquebushes are moste excellent, and always in his warres he hath eightie
thousand harquebushes and the number of them increaseth dayly'.[2]

During the eighteenth-century Burma/Siam wars, both sides
must have armed their respective Karen conscripts, who would
have had regular displays of the latest weaponry carried by the
armies marching back and forth through their hills. Karen came
to expect the best, and during the 1886 Burmese uprising were
most offended at being issued with muzzle-loaders instead of state-
of-the-art breech-loading Sniders.

The British of Orwell's day may have been loath to cultivate the native taste for firearms but other foreigners had no such hesitation. The French took charge of the Royal Ordnance factory for King Mindon of Ava in the nineteenth century. More recently, the German firm of Heckler and Koch have been teaching the Burmese to make G3 assault rifles. The Karen needed little prompting: nineteenth-century western accounts regularly noted their skill. Carl Bock met Karen gunsmiths in northern Thailand in 1881, and reported that the other tribes of Thailand obtained their guns from Burma.

Today, Karen manufacture of firearms is flourishing. In any house in our district you could find a gun, and it might just as easily be a home-made musket as an M16. The shops at Barterville sold mild steel tubing for barrels – everything else was home-made. I watched Great Lake the boatman construct a gun for his friend the Elephant Man. It was, as usual, a percussion cap-lock. The paper cap (also sold in the shops) was placed on the touch hole under a small piece of coconut fibre, and the hammer cocked against a sprung trigger. It was complete with sights, trigger guard, a neatly shaped stock, even a ramrod tipped with a spent .22 shell. Apart from the steel tube, Great Lake made it all. 'What do you use for gunpowder?' I asked. He said, 'Bat shit.'

This is another skill of long standing. The soil from the floor of caves in which bats sleep is rich in nitrates which can be extracted by a process formerly called 'lixiviation'.[3] The dirt is placed on a raised bamboo platform and washed with a lye of water mixed with alkaline straw ash. The water, which takes up the nitrate of lime, is then boiled down. From the carbonate of potash in the lye results soluble nitrate of potash and insoluble carbonate of lime. The lime precipitates; white crystals of nitrate of potash remain. Mix that with sulphur and charcoal made from mango wood, and you have gunpowder. How the Karen learnt to do that I've no idea, but they used to be very good at it. Nowadays 'bat shit' – *bla eh* – is just a name; the forest shops sell ready-mix plastic bags with neat cylinders of nitrate and chunks of sulphur. Just add charcoal.

Lt Col MacMahon reveals the secret ingredient that made Karen powder so potent:

> 'The only use we have ever heard of medicine of any kind being put to among the tribes ... [is] *Perry Davis' Pain Killer* as an ingredient in their manufacture of gunpowder.'

Priorities have not changed a great deal since then.

'What about ammunition?' I asked Great Lake.

'Anything that fits. I have a friend who makes bullets by melting down broken boat propellers and pouring the metal into the stubs of broken flashlight bulbs.'

The guns made a glorious bang which sent the wildlife into hiding for hours. But there were risks. I saw men and boys with their brows gone and the skin, very near the eye, tattooed black by bursting muskets.

'Do Karen make anything heavier than these muskets?'

'I have another friend at GHQ', said Great Lake. 'He specialises in making mortars. There was one with a two-inch barrel; the ignition was from an electric spark, with a battery. He used it in battle once and fired three shots. They went in completely different directions which was good because the Burmese were so confused it was twenty minutes before they fired back, by which time he'd got away. Then he showed his mortar to General Bo Mya. Again, he fired three times. The first went very far, right over the fields. The second went not so far, and the third only fifty yards. It was all full of dirt by then. The General did not want his mortar.

'But we make other things that work very well. Have you heard of Eh Ha (Mr Cool)? He led a raid on a Burmese airfield and the Karen shot down two Burmese helicopters using a home-made rocket launcher!'

Others wanted to see a return to traditional Karen ordnance, the crossbow. Karen hunters in some areas still carry them in preference to firearms as they have the advantage of being quiet and not scaring off the quarry. Marshall wrote in 1922 that the Karen used crossbows only for hunting, not for war. During World War Two, however, they were used against the Japanese, the darts poisoned with a bark extract.[4]

Watching Two Shoes the Thai entrepreneur installing his bamboo-splitting machines under Morning Star's house, I asked him why he was doing all this:

'I must help these people make money for their war! They cannot buy their weapons, and I can help them.'

'Are you going to buy them guns?'

'Crossbows are what they need. With cyanide-tipped darts.'

But the Karen can no more fight their Revolution with black powder muskets and crossbows than could Orwell's Burmese rebels in 1932. If the numbers of the KNLA are tiny, at least one reason is that they cannot arm more. The capture of weapons is, as True

Love said, far more important than a body-count of Burmese conscripts. Any firefight in the forest is recounted in the KNU newsletters and monthly battle-reports in terms of rifles and rounds captured. Propaganda videos dwell on neat stacks of Burmese munitions taken in battle. It was a measure of just how quiet our backwater had been until now, how recent the intensification of the fighting, that almost no soldier locally carried a Heckler and Koch G3 rifle – the standard Burmese weapon that would be the usual trophy of a successful skirmish.

What they do carry is a motley assortment ranging from bolt-action rifles and sub-machine guns to grenade launchers. The lucky ones have Kalashnikovs in all their many Russian, Chinese, Czech and other variants – and, of course, US M16s.

Twentieth-century insurrections have glorified and made symbols of their weaponry, as have many wars before. The Empire, wrote Kipling, was won by that 'cross-eyed old bitch', the Martini-Henry, 'as human as you are'. Nicaragua was liberated by the AK47, Ulster is the domain of the Armalite. Forest rebels have their symbols too. The Karen Freedom Fighter wears camouflage and carries an M16.

Aficionados of guerrilla warfare like to say that resistance fighters the world over prefer Russian AK47s to American M16s. Apart from the dubious motives behind this claim, in Burma it is quite untrue. The AK47 has certain advantages. It has a heavier calibre and hits harder. Also, a suspicion lingers (from Vietnam) that M16s jam easily if they are not kept very clean. But the Karen are firearms connoisseurs. They strip and clean their guns with loving care; the precision and ingenuity of the M16 appeals to them. And there are other considerations. M16s come from Thailand, are 'modern' and associated with American sophistication. In the aftermath of Vietnam, and with the US still supplying the Thai Army which has a way of mislaying its rifles, there are plenty of guns and ammunition available. Most importantly, they are light. The block-machined Kalashnikov weighs 9.45lbs, the plastic-and-alloy M16 only 6.35lbs. If you are five foot four and weigh under 100lbs yourself, that matters. Hence the crossed M16s on the T-shirt. They are one of the symbols of the Revolution now, just as the AK47 was a symbol of the Sandinistas. On the verandah of Edward's house, his little son chalked drawings of M16s on the wooden walls.

Which is where I learnt much of this. Edward the Education Officer was widely reputed to know as much about guns as anyone in the Army. Visitors were likely to find him cleaning or re-blueing his Luger as he talked to True Love, or reading *All Warfare* monthly magazine.

It was Edward and True Love, as senior staff of the Education Department, who screened the videos of *Rambo* and *The Killing Fields*. Militarism has been bound into education, together with the church. In the 1880s, Baptist-led Karen sallied forth from the compounds of mission schools to chase Burmese dacoits. Today, for many Karen boys, school leads naturally into the KNLA. They start young. I asked the age of a barely pubescent boy with a Kalashnikov and he said, 'Thirteen; I joined the army last year.' True Love hastened to qualify this.

> 'They don't go to the Front Line so young. They have other duties.'
> 'Don't their parents object?'
> 'If they wish to join the KNLA, Karen parents will not stop them. In fact, you see, maybe they encourage them, because the boys can be sent back here to school, under the Army's protection, and the parents do not have to pay for their rice. Then they go and fight.'
> Trevor was unimpressed.
> 'It's just that they can't be seen sending youngsters to the Front. Bad for their image.'

The school holidays fell due in April, but for the older boys there was no rest. Thirty of them were enrolled for compulsory military training, including Bartholomew's boy James who moved across to sleep in *Boys Boarders* with the other rookies. Instructors came down from Headquarters; the Captain, now seventy-two years old, had joined the British Army in 1937. Every morning the lads could be seen drilling on the football pitch in smart new camouflage shorts and T-shirts, carrying bamboo staves. They were each allowed – on their own request – to fire four rounds at targets. Towards the end of the month they began to play 'tactical games' around the football pitch and its encircling scrub.

For these games they used clappers – a stout piece of bamboo perhaps three feet long, split for most of its length, with which a loud imitation gunfire was possible as you charged your friends. I recognised the clappers; the Pitt-Rivers Museum in Oxford has an old photograph in which they feature in the illustration of a Burmese orchestra.

One of the schoolboy trainees was called Full Moon, an amiable and enthusiastic guitarist who had sometimes recorded songs for me. I asked him what he wanted to do when he left school. He replied simply, 'Kill my enemies.'

I don't like to think of True Love being shot, or of him shooting. After I returned home to Britain in October 1987, I went for a short break to Amsterdam and visited the Tropical Institute there. They showed me videos of the Karen war, including one by a German reporter who had followed a combat unit as it pursued retreating Burmese troops. The Karen soldiers looked like any number of my friends. It came to an engagement; one Karen and one Burmese were shot. The dead Karen was, with loving care, stripped, washed and buried. The young Burmese corpse they kicked in the face. Not much by battlefield standards, perhaps, but it made me feel quite faint.

William the schoolmaster wrote a marching song for the boys:

> Forward Karen soldiers! Filled with power and glory,
> We'll give our blood for our nation,
> Our lives for our people.
> On the battlefield we face many enemies.
> Let's go, Karen!

8 Great Lake and the Elephant Man

Heirs of our black and red costume,
honour your own culture, the drums
we inherited from our ancestors.
If we don't preserve it, it will be lost.
Don't desire other people's houses: ours are fine.
Don't eat others' rice, come back to your mother's!
Water from old wells is coolest.
Flowers from afar will leave you in tears.
                    Song recorded for me by Ku Wah and True Love

Yodoyamai Cordial, my introduction to Great Lake's family, is a patent
medicine, a rich brown liquid much like soy sauce, made in Burma
and widely consumed in Kawthoolei. I bought a bottle because
I wanted a copy of the leaflet that went with it, and because Great
Lake said that he would give the contents to his wife Lili.

On the leaflet there are four illustrations, unfortunately printed
from very old blocks on poor paper, or I'd have had them framed.
In the first scene, desperate persons are drowning in the choppy
seas of Ill Health, only their heads and thrashing hands still above
water. A queenly apparition in the sky, buxom and radiant, is holding up a comforting sight, a glowing bottle of *Yodoyamai Cordial*,
while pointing them towards the good ship *Yodoyamai* which, with
a Red Cross fluttering from its prow, is steaming to the rescue.

In frame two, a wasted figure lies on what threatens very soon
to be her deathbed, dimly lit by a table lamp, her anxious husband
helpless by her side. In the distance, tombstones may be glimpsed
in the penumbra. Useless pills and potions litter the table. The
daughter of the house turns pleading for help to a bespectacled,
capped nurse who holds out for her inspection another shining bottle
of *Yodoyamai Cordial* – which is also observed by the skeletal figure
of Death who, his ghastly countenance clouded with frustration,
mutters the Transtygian-Burmese for 'Drat it!'.

Scene three is lighter. A young mother who for years had failed
to conceive, lies upon her couch with an exhausted smile, surrounded by six adoring infants. At the desk behind her, glancing

up from his papers, is Father. Pipe-smoking, intellectual and smug, he'd known the answer; he too had trusted in *Yodoyamai Cordial*. And the final tableau shows Mother once more, comely and content, seated in the drawing room with a low-cut blouse and flowers in her hair. Father (who has now taken off his spectacles) leans over the arm of the chair and, peering down her cleavage, appears to be about to rip off the blouse while in the doorway the children egg him on and carol hymns to *Yodoyamai Cordial* which has kept mother so sweet and desirable.

I asked Great Lake to translate the Burmese of the contents list. *Yodoyamai*, I was pleased to learn, contains none of the following poisons: opium, marijuana. It does contain honey, dried rhinoceros blood, 'stone blood' (a valued mineral exudate), birds' nests etc., etc. The cordial will cure anything – too little menstrual flow, or too much, malaria, dysentery, thin blood ... It was this latter that had prevented Mother conceiving. Great Lake said, 'My own mother took this medicine. When she was very sick, she drank a whole boxful of *Yodoyamai* – two dozen bottles. And then she died!' (Roars of laughter.)

When he'd calmed down, he said that he'd tell me about his family after breakfast on Sunday.

I often went to Great Lake's house for Sunday breakfast. He liked to tell me that in his house he could cook me 'real Karen food' – though his wife Lili did most of the cooking and I could taste Bengal in hers. They were pleasant, slow mornings. Great Lake took the Sabbath seriously and so, having finished our monkey curry, I'd take cigars from his shop cupboard without asking permission, place two baht in the tin without speaking, so as to save him embarrassment, and we'd recline and smoke them and gossip while his babies crawled between us across the verandah urinating on the chickens below.

Great Lake was much the same age as True Love, a virile and witty thirty-three year old who, when piloting the boat down rapids with an expression of exhilarated concentration on his handsome face, could look very like Errol Flynn playing Captain Blood. He was a man who found everything – myself especially – a source of incredulous amusement. His inquisitive teasing and mockery was so good-natured, and so often turned on himself in equal measure, that his company always entertained and educated me. He even found amusement in his own boredom and irritation.

Both of which he suffered much of. He hated Riverside. It wasn't his home, and it was doing neither him nor his family any good; they were chronically ill with malaria, worms, skin infections and other troubles. 'This place', he said, 'is dangerous for my babies.'

He might have thought the risk worthwhile if he'd had more faith in the local Establishment, but he had little time for them. He never went to church – taking True Love's line that 'God is with me everywhere' – and he would not be seen dead at any official function or parade – extreme behaviour for someone who undoubtedly supported the Revolution in principle. He didn't dislike Bartholomew (his father-in-law) but he never came to his house. In fact he almost never came to that end of the village – the world of bureaucrats and the semi-educated Delta élite. Great Lake stayed upstream by the hospital, near the waifs and strays collected by Bartholomew's Department, and near his friends in the forest.

He would hardly allow that Riverside was a village at all. The ever-changing population of soldiers, schoolteachers, Thais, traders and KNU officials had none of the cohesion and intimacy that he knew as truly Karen. He thought the locals thieves – reasonably enough; someone stole his boat. He made me padlock mine, which made it rather conspicuously the only locked boat on the river. He thought them rootless and maladroit, and would point out that 'real' Karen up north in Papun and the Dawina Hills had no need to buy clothes, shoulder bags and fishpaste, because they could make their own.

> 'All they can make here is babies!' he snorted, 'and just look at them. The women cut their hair; no real Karen woman cuts her hair short. They eat mishmash food which is nothing and no one here can cook Karen soup like I make for you.'

This was not actually true; Bartholomew's family did, but Great Lake never came to see.

> 'I do not like their clothes. Even when they do wear Karen clothes they get it wrong. They wear a nylon shirt underneath, and then only on Sunday. What's wrong with Karen clothes every day?'
>
> 'They're so hot ...' murmured True Love, whenever he had to put his on.

In the stories that relate how the Karen lost their ancestral patrimony, a recurrent theme is the Karen's own stupidity. Thus, for example, they lost contact with Boar Tusk while attempting to soften snail shells by boiling. Great Lake loved to mock his own people. Using the Sgaw term *pwakenyaw* ('the people' – i.e. the

Karen), he evolved the phrase 'Bloody fool *pwakenyaw!*' with which to deride the inept. This could be anything from himself dropping the spanner into the water while trying to change a boat propeller in midstream, to the KNLA being outmanoeuvred by the tricks of the Burmese Army. This self-mockery was a form of pride, a mark of identity: 'We are, at least, our own stupid selves.'

In his house, tucked in the roof, were a number of curious objects consisting of a two-foot long piece of springy cane with an arrangement of string and, at one end, a short, wide section of bamboo. When I asked what they were for, he presented me with one and told me to work it out. I established that it was a trap of some sort (I was doing well – I've seen a French magazine article in which a baffled journalist describes these things as violins)[1]. Great Lake showed me how to operate it.

'For lizards, you see? You put the spike in the ground so that the bamboo ring is over the lizard's hole and then when he comes out he gets this cord round his neck and the spring pulls it tight. Do you know how lizards came to Karen country? I'll tell you. One day a Karen from the Shan States went to visit a Burmese in the Delta. There he saw all the beautiful wet rice fields and he said, "If only we could make fields full of water like that! But in our hills there is never enough rain. How do you do it?"

'Well, just then a *tokay* lizard started to make its noise in the house – *to-kay!* – and the Burmese said, "That's a rain lizard. When they make that noise, rain soon follows. We have lots of them here, which is why it's so wet. Now, I could sell you a pair of rain lizards for just B.25 and you can have all the rain you want." So the Karen paid the money and took the lizards back to the Shan States and kept them and fed them and bred many babies which escaped all over the country. After many months of no rain they had to eat the lizards. Bloody fool *pwakenyaw!*'

We could hear the Bethany church bells ringing a mile away. A group of women passed us, heading for the service. They were dressed in long flower print acrylic skirts and polyester blouses, and sheltered under bright nylon Thai umbrellas. They'd not even opted for traditional dress on Sunday. Great Lake's sister Gratitude set off after them with a Bible under her arm, dressed similarly and falling over her flipflops as she ran. It occurred to me that I'd never seen Great Lake in traditional dress either; he usually wore a sports shirt and a green army beret above a cheap sarong.

In the shadows, Lili attempted to control the children and tidy the clutter of clothes in the house. Lili had a hard life, tending a husband whose vague discontent often turned to lethargy and vitiated his considerable abilities. In his generosity and enthusiasm for conversation, Great Lake was forever inviting people to eat and to stay, and the cramped house became dirtier and less appealing daily as the children grew and people came and Lili had neither the time nor the space to clean and organise. There was gossip about them: why did such a sweet-natured, hard-working woman marry such an indolent character? Do you see how thin and pale she is? Why is he away so much? Why doesn't he work, what is he doing?

Not only was Lili tired and pale and the children sickly; Great Lake himself was unwell. He had a painful chest condition that grew worse after much exertion, and he would need to rest. He would come back from jaunts to the forest looking as though he'd not slept or eaten properly for a week. Half 'spoilt', half 'corrupted' by his own inquisitiveness leading him, fascinated, into modern civilisation and its products, he could not bring himself to trust in western medicine (and, most unusually for a Karen, would never sell it in his shop), but nor could he any longer feel confident in Karen 'jungle cures'. He dithered between therapies and ended up giving Lili the *Yodoyamai Cordial*.

'You were going to tell me about your village and your family', I reminded him; blissful nostalgia flooded his face as he settled his back against the balustrade, ready to describe *real* Karen.

He came from a village south of Toungoo, in rolling hill country looking down from the east of the Sittang River – that is, just inside the boundary of what the Burmese government calls the Karen State. It was a village of one hundred houses, all Sgaw Karen. The British built a road to the village but when the Japanese came they blew up the bridge over the stream. Great Lake's grandfather was headman at the time, and the British gave him a shotgun and a revolver to encourage him to continue supporting them. He sold the revolver – a dangerous thing to be caught with; you can't claim that it's a hunting weapon. The shotgun he passed on to his son, Great Lake's father.

When the Revolution broke out, the village found itself uncomfortably in between the Burmese and the Karen forces. First the Burmese would come looking for rebels, then the Karen would come looking for loyalty and recruits, and the headman had to appease both. No headman ever lasted more than six months because of the strain.

Great Lake was born in 1955. By the time of Ne Win's military coup in Rangoon in 1962, there were three children – all boys – living in the village with their parents and grandparents. Great Lake talked of the village in the present tense – although it was sixteen years since the family had left.

> 'My village is very traditional and people there wear the real clothes. There's a very beautiful sarong, many colours, that a girl wears before her wedding. It has to be made by her mother. When it's finished she puts it on, with a black shirt, but just once to make sure it fits – and then they put it away in mothballs. If she wears it out they are afraid that perhaps her mother will die before her wedding so there'd be no one to make it for her. She only puts it on three days before the wedding; otherwise she always wears the long white maiden's dress for everyday, for work. Which nobody here wears at all except for special parades.
>
> 'We're almost all animist or Christian in my village, – just a very few Buddhists. My father was a Buddhist but he became Christian when he married my mother.'

For a while the village lived in uneasy quiet. The military situation in the area didn't change, and they still suffered visitations. Then, in 1966, General Bo Mya established what is now the Karen National Liberation Army in the hills to the south-east of Toungoo, and not long afterwards the Burmese arrested Great Lake's father as a collaborator. They took him off to jail, leaving his wife pregnant with Gratitude, the only sister. He was in jail for four years.

> 'Then my mother became ill. I never knew what was wrong, but she always had headaches and was feeling sick. She met a Buddhist monk who was a healer and he said, if you come to me I can cure you in two months. She didn't want to go, and so she started to drink this *Yodoyamai*. But she got worse and went to the monk – and two weeks later she was dead. I was twelve at that time and I was very angry with that monk, he has not done my mother any good.'

Great Lake's father was released in 1971. Three months later, his grandfather died and they saw that it was time to move. The area was becoming tense once again as Ne Win began to increase pressure on the insurgents. One day the village got word that the Burmese were advancing and that the KNLA were going to try and stop them. The people decided to evacuate, but they could not agree which way to go. Late at night they abandoned the village;

half of them moved downhill towards the Sittang River into Burmese
territory, hoping that if they behaved themselves they'd be left to
resettle. The other half of the village went east, uphill into the
forest. There was a short battle and both sides withdrew their troops.
Two months later some of the villagers returned to their homes
but Great Lake's father was still in danger. The family stayed in
the forest, buying food from friendly villages – including Burmese
– and they began to cultivate gardens.

Great Lake was seventeen by now. After six months in the forest
his brothers left and joined Bo Mya's KNLA, but their father and
grandmother didn't want to move – they'd made a new home in
the forest. Great Lake didn't know what to do. He drifted. He
went up towards the border, worked with cattle traders for a while,
then found himself in a mining area in the Kachin and Shan States
and passed a year there. Eventually he ended up at Manerplaw,
Kawthoolei's General Headquarters.

> 'I didn't go to join the KNLA, I didn't want to be a soldier;
> I went to find a friend. But they asked me if I would train
> as a boatman. They showed me how to strip and repair the
> big diesel motors they have on the boats there. So, I joined.
> I worked for the Education Department mostly.'
> 'How did you meet Lili?'
> 'She'd been sent up to GHQ to train as an administrator for
> some department; she never finished, anyway. After we were
> married, Bartholomew wanted her back here. He said I could
> have a job as Health Department boatman – only there wasn't
> a boat.'

Perhaps at the time, with a new wife and an enquiring nature,
he'd been happy enough to leave the old hill Karen and have a
look at the south. But having nothing proper to do became just
another reason why he'd never managed to settle. Why had he
not joined the Revolution to begin with, along with his brothers?
The family had, after all, suffered ample aggravation from the
Burmese. But Great Lake wouldn't say why.

The Colonel appeared at my house one morning together with
two Thais, who merely said, 'We are visiting to see your situation.'
They wanted to go half an hour downriver, to Lama. The Colonel
said,

> 'And so, Mr John, why don't I borrow your boat?'

I asked Great Lake if he would take them, and it was agreed

that he would pick them up from the riverbank by the school at ten o'clock. He and I carried the engine down to the boat; shortly afterwards I heard it start and move downstream half an hour early. Great Lake returned that afternoon. He was very angry.

> 'I get to the school early and I wait and wait. Then when this Colonel comes with his Thai people, I cannot start the boat. It starts very easily here; at the school I try for half an hour and it will not start at all. That Colonel gets very angry, he is very rude and calls me things and then he and his Thai people go away.'
> 'What did he call you?'
> 'He called me lazy, stupid, careless Karen!'
> 'Bloody fool *pwakenyaw?*'
> 'Bloody hell! Who am I to be shouted at by him? I am not a soldier, I have no rations, I am a free man. If I help you and I help Bartholomew it is because I like to help you. Any time, I can stop, I can go away!'

But he was not completely free, as he very well knew. In Kawthoolei, service to the Revolutionary State is a matter of subtle but powerful unwritten ties and obligations. When I first came there, I expected to employ paid staff – a boatman at least. But nobody is employed in that sense; nobody receives wages, only support as necessary. However, even for a village farmer who is 'not a member of the Revolution', the obligations are there. If the Colonel had requested transport from Lama on to Barterville, a boat would have been found. Though the cost of the petrol would have been reimbursed by the KNU to the private boatman, no fee would be paid for the work. He would do it because, whatever he thought in his heart about the war and it prospects, he was a Karen. And also, perhaps, as an extension of those rules of hospitality and service that require each village to convey travellers to their next destination.

The Colonel could not impose too far. He could expect the village boatman's services for two days, perhaps, but not two weeks. As long as it stayed within the bounds of the reasonable, Kawthoolei was an offer that couldn't be refused by anyone who came within its orbit. The only alternative, if you really didn't wish to serve at all, was to leave that orbit, to go away to Burma or to Thailand.

While he was here, Great Lake had little choice but to accept some degree of obligation. He also had family ties. He had a wife and small children and, whatever he felt, Lili didn't want to leave her father Bartholomew's village. Great Lake didn't evade his familial duties. The littlest child (the daughter of Lili's dead sister) stayed with them. When Vermilion needed escorting through the forest to visit Saw Salai the healer, Great Lake went with her. Bartholomew's sickly brother, who slept in the laboratory, ate at Great Lake and Lili's table.

Indeed, so many of the waifs and strays seemed to lean on the household, as a surrogate of the Health and Welfare Department, that Great Lake was beginning to think that he might be obliged after all to ask Bartholomew for a rice ration. But he wasn't going to give up their independence easily. When he first came to Riverside he prepared fields and grew millet. His harvest was 2,000 kg. But then he found that the southern Karen didn't like millet, and he couldn't sell any. The weevils started to eat it but still he couldn't find a buyer. He even offered it to the KNLA at a knockdown price but they didn't want it. The Revolution runs on rice. Finally he bought some piglets and fattened them up on the millet, making a small profit.

Next they opened a shop. Great Lake had tried this once before and had been burnt; he'd gone into partnership with a man at GHQ who had run off with B.6,000 worth of stock, leaving Great Lake a brief note and B.200 'share of the profit'. Now he and Lili worked together. He built a slatted cupboard at the corner of the balcony, and Lili made weekly trips up to the border to buy the usual goods – biscuits, soap, ballpoint pens and exercise books, cigars and fishing weights, tinned milk and flipflops. Other Riverside shopkeepers went only monthly, but Great Lake and Lili were determined to corner the market at their end of the village with a high turnover and cut prices. The nearest rival, Brina by the hospital, was quickly disadvantaged. A little packet of *Lion Brand* marie biscuits that sold for B.10 on the border and B.20 at Brina's, Lili would sell for B.15. The possible profits were infinitesimal; Great Lake hoped to make B.300 profit a month, but it was hard going with cigars at B.2 for three, and half a dozen competitors. And there were risks. Lili bought me a dozen boat propellers, but she'd ordered the wrong size and the border traders wouldn't take them back; eventually I carried them out to Thailand myself. She bought what she thought was a jar of coffee – but it was *Coffee Mate*. I relieved her of that also. Transport was precarious and uninsured: things got lost or squashed frequently.

They even tried buying a block of ice from Thailand and burying it packed in sawdust along with a crate of green *Fanta* – but there weren't enough hot, thirsty Karen passing along that path and Gratitude, swinging expectantly in a hammock nearby, grew very despondent at the lack of custom. The experiment wasn't repeated.

In truth, Great Lake was no trader. Lili did the work, while her husband fed the prawn crackers to his offspring. 'Your children are eating your profits', we all told him, but he laughed and smiled handsomely and said, 'I love my babies.'

The shop was better left to Lili while Great Lake went after forest game.

> 'I caught a deer in the river! It was swimming, it's a baby, like a dog, swimming across and I was swimming too and I caught it in my hands!'
> 'Where is it now?'
> 'I've sold it to some Thai people.'

There was a little white monkey that appeared briefly on his balcony, also a baby anteater. They were both reared for a short time and then sold to Thais. Deer that he shot went the same way. He could carry 20 kg of fresh venison over the border and get B.25 (60p) a kilo for it. Cattle, too, he bought and resold. This brought him decent money, but was hard work. There were bigger killings to be made from the more exotic.

Again, the Colonel played a role. He arrived in his pickup one very hot morning bringing his sister, who was on a visit with her wealthy Thai husband, to view the resident Englishman. The Colonel, mopping his brow with the little blue towel that he always carried around his neck, sent his bodyguard up the trees to fetch coconuts.

They lounged on my verandah. Great Lake appeared, hovering deferentially at the foot of the house steps. He had something that might interest the visitors, perhaps? The dried gallbladder of a mountain bear, a flattened circle of leathery brown. Bears' gallbladders are much prized by Thai-Chinese apothecaries, and this one was offered by Great Lake for B.800 (£20). The Colonel's guests took it, saying that they would see if they could find a buyer in Bangkok. And that, I believe, was the last Great Lake ever heard of the bear's gallbladder.

In this haphazard manner the household economy wobbled on. One day Great Lake was flush and offering me B.1,000 for my short-wave radio: the next he said that someone had borrowed

B.3,000 from him and not paid it back, so that they were having to live on Lili's savings.

All that he wanted was independence and a future. Denied both, he dreamed of an Arcadian ideal of traditional Karen life, untrammelled by war, cash economies, nylon shirts or bureaucracy. The nearest he could come to this ideal – in the vicinity of Riverside at least – was at the forest hut of his closest friend, Red Star the Elephant Man.

There is nothing dearer to the Karen than elephants. They are not, as we see them, lumbering mountains of flesh, but celestial. The constellation we call the Great Bear is to them The Elephant, and the Pole Star is a little mouse running up the Elephant's trunk. To own elephants is the dream of every family, far more than a fine house, a television or a pickup truck. In Thailand, where the various 'hill tribes' live cheek by jowl, the successful Lua, Yao or Lisu farmer invests surplus capital in constructing irrigated rice terraces, but the Karen prefer to buy elephants. They love them and pamper them, and Lt Col MacMahon describes them decorating the head and trunk of their favourites with beautiful arabesques done in coloured chalk. Karen consider that they know the ways of elephants better than anyone, and it is a widely agreed reputation. For centuries the Karen have been famous as elephant trappers, trainers and drivers, and as elephant thieves.

Throughout much of S.E. Asia, elephants represent power, majesty, justice. Moghul emperors of India used white elephants to trample convicted felons, and one of the Karen surgeons at GHQ told me a remarkable story: his grandfather had, before World War Two, captured and trained an especially fine white elephant with which he had toured as far as the United States and Europe, being photographed together with crowned heads *en route*. When he reached India, a rajah offered him a large sum of money for his white elephant but, like any Karen, he loved elephants more than money, and he refused. The rajah said nothing – but the next day the animal was found dead, of poison.

The 1685 French Ambassador to Ayutthia was shown the royal white elephant of Siam dwelling in a gilded pavilion and dining from massive golden bowls with mandarins in attendance.[2] No traveller could resist describing the trapping and breaking of wild elephants – an elaborate procedure using tame females to lure bulls into vast kraals. Held in pens alongside trained animals for several

Plate 8. 'To own elephants is the dream of every family.'

days, the new captives would gradually become resigned to their fate.

Europeans have never been quite so enthusiastic. Lunet de Lajonquière complained bitterly about his 'deplorable' Karen elephant transport:

The elephants arrived very late and as usual gave us endless headaches. Some were sick. Others, that had not been carrying loads, found that state of affairs preferable and refused to allow anything at all on their backs. Our boys and the escorting gendarmes thought they'd mount astride, seated in a row, [but] the malicious brutes began to shiver their backbones until our impromptu cavaliers were either thrown or jumped to the ground of their own accord.[3]

British teak-wallahs, while expressing admiration for, and total reliance on the animals' strength for shifting logs into the rivers, were nevertheless wary of them. A logging elephant on the rampage was a formidable problem, the more so because a creature so valuable could not simply be shot but must somehow be trapped and calmed. In general the teak-wallahs were happiest leaving all that to the natives. Lt Col MacMahon (1876, p. 377), thought Karen elephants a dubious asset at the best of times:

The commissariat elephants, when not employed by other departments, seemed to have nothing to do but carry their own food, wag their tails and trunks in their stables, die of *ennui* and form subjects for inquests.

None of this would make any impression on a Karen. Quite apart from the prestige, elephants are a good investment, and are still of some economic importance. The historian D. G. E. Hall (1981, p. 940), looking for an illustration of the disruption of the Burmese economy caused by the insurgents, picked on the fact that as late as 1957, of the 3,000 elephants owned by the Department of Forests, the rebels controlled 1,500. In the 1960s Thai-Karen had a near-monopoly on logging elephants and contracted their services to timber companies for good money.

Perhaps some still do. The Thai foresters that I met had little time for Karen elephants: 'Caterpillars' are less temperamental. But the animals have other work. From Hannibal's day at least, and right up to the present, their military career has been almost unbroken, and that is their contemporary role in Kawthoolei.

The French ambassadors of 1685 remarked of the white elephants that are 'so highly esteemed in the Indies', that they had a warlike role – but not as combatants; rather, white elephants 'hath been the *cause* of so many wars', as envious potentates tried to capture (or poison) their rivals' prestige symbols.[4] The KNLA employ elephants which have been described as an élite cavalry used for long-range patrols deep into Burma on sabotage and intelligence-gathering missions.[5] Their real value is more symbolic. The days of the armoured war elephants that failed to crush Clive at Plassey are long gone. The last recorded frontline use of war elephants in Siam was against Yunnan Chinese in the 1880s while in Burma they had to wait for the Japanese to bring them back into military logistical use. There were good reasons for their decline. Even in 1693, Simon de la Loubère remarked that elephants are 'not proper for war':

They very much rely upon the Elephants in Combats, though this animal for want of Bitt or Bridle, cannot be securely governed, and he frequently returns upon his own Masters when he is wounded. Moreover he so exceedingly dreads the fire, that he is never almost accustomed thereunto.[6]

In the forest, an elephant is sure-footed but slow and, with wooden clappers hanging from its neck, far from silent. It is (obviously) difficult to conceal and very vulnerable. An elephant patrol would be seen long before they saw the enemy and, blundering into even a small force of Burmese, would be cut to pieces. What matters to the Karen is the mere existence of these patrols; the supreme power-symbol of South Asia is seen to be mustered for Kawthoolei.[7]

While of limited fighting value, the elephants do have logistical importance. Although their load capacity is small, they can carry a lot more, and further, than a man. And they can go almost anywhere. The French ambassadors witnessed a royal elephant hunt, a grand affair in which thousands of Siamese soldiers trapped a herd of elephants against a steep mountain wall:

but that being looked upon to be inaccessible to those creatures, they had ... neglected to secure it by fires, guards and artillery: however ten or twelve of them escaped that way, and for that purpose made use of a very surprising expedient; fastening themselves by their trunks to one of the trees that were upon the side of that very steep mountain, they made a skip to the root of the next, and in the same manner clambered from tree to tree with incredible efforts, until they got to the top of the mountain, from whence they saved themselves in the woods.[8]

Riding an elephant through thick forest, I was alarmed to see the Karen *mahout* turn the animal to our left to descend what appeared to be an impossibly steep mud slope. To my delight, the elephant lay down and tobogganed.

Elephants can scale mountains and swim deep rivers, but there is one thing they cannot do, which is jump. An elephant cannot take all four feet off the ground together and thus cannot get across even quite a small ditch. But there are not many ditches in the forest, and for supplying rice and ammunition to an army dug into positions on steep wooded hills, elephants are incomparable.

Red Star is a freelance elephant trapper contracting to the KNLA. When we met he was in his thirties, quietly spoken, the gentlest of men. Karen love to say of themselves that they desire only a life of peace and seclusion in the forest; of Red Star it was true. He had no family, only his elephants. He had a home near Moulmein, in Burma proper, and would return there from time to time. But what he liked best was trapping, training and caring for elephants, and the KNLA paid him to do it.

Great Lake introduced us. Red Star had come into Riverside looking for help. He had a she-elephant which had recently given birth, and the umbilical stump of the baby had become infected. Red Star wanted something to kill the maggots. In my house there were various antiseptics and sprays, so we carried a selection to Red Star's camp to see what could be done.

He lived a short distance upstream from Great Lake. We took a tiny fishing canoe, no more than a scraped-out half log and very unstable. Into this climbed three adults, Great Lake's two small children and a dog which clambered in and out of the boat threatening to upset it. We poled slowly upstream for half an hour and reached the camp.

Red Star had brought the she-elephant here to give birth in tranquillity, away from human disturbance. At a point where a large shingle bank pushed the river out sideways, forming a small bay, he and one of his assistants had built a shelter for themselves, a low, thatched platform just large enough for two blanket rolls and the lightweight clutter of any Karen hut – a gun, a shoulder bag, spare clothes and odd bits of string tucked into the bamboo frame, a toothbrush and a betel-box. Twenty yards away the mother elephant was chained to a tree. Her baby, now a week old, was not secured but never went far from its mother's feet. Its eyes were bright and pink-rimmed while its mother's were tired and grey, tucked back in folds of skin. Its trunk was an encumbrance which it had not mastered, and which now flopped about like a massive worm pinned to its face, getting in the way when the baby tried to reach its mother's dugs between her forelegs. The mother shifted backwards and forwards, uneasy at the intrusion of unfamiliar people, occasionally throwing a trunkful of soil and leaf-mould in a wide arc about her. But she showed no concern when Red Star knelt by her infant and sprayed insecticide on its wound. The baby would scarcely leave its mother's side for the next seven years; they would then begin to break it in and train it.

In front of the hut was a small fireplace, smouldering low. Suspended over it were two dark and shrivelled objects. One was the stomach of a porcupine that Red Star had shot two days before. The other was the elephant's umbilicus. They were both being smoked, ready to be sold to Thai apothecaries.

> 'What will happen to the elephants?' I asked Great Lake, Red Star being rather taciturn.
>
> 'The Army will use them for transport. There are four working here, but they want more up at GHQ. My friend will be taking them there soon. They have to walk all the way up through the forest. It's a long way – it takes maybe two months. Then he will come back and look for more elephants.'

Which is not as easy as it once was. Captain James Low wrote in 1836 (p. 43):

Elephants are so numerous throughout the provinces that it would not be an easy matter to affect any very sensible diminution of them ... They are not much dreaded and generally walk quietly away if not molested.

Now Red Star was having trouble finding them. At any news of wild elephants, he would travel the length of the District for a chance of trapping them.

> 'How does he do it?' I asked.
>
> 'He makes a camouflaged pit on the forest path, and the elephant falls in. Once it is in the pit, they put ropes round it and light fires to stop the elephant sleeping for three days. After that it will not fight you. But you must teach it elephant-Burmese so that it will know what you wish it to do.'
>
> 'You speak Burmese to elephants?'
>
> 'Most of it is like Burmese. But if you want to work in the teak forests on the Thai side the elephant should know Thai also.'

Any Karen boy of twelve can drive an elephant, say the anthropologists. Not at Riverside, but there were only two or three animals there. One in particular I saw a lot of, since it was often hobbled and left to browse amongst the undergrowth in a peaceful corner by the main track. They were not always well controlled. When I first came to Kawthoolei, a she-elephant carried my bags down from the border. She had an infant with her, two years old, which had a reputation for trouble. As I followed perhaps half an hour behind, walking with Timothy, we passed a house where a woman wept and ranted; the young elephant had casually uprooted her only papaya tree in passing. A few days later the same mother delivered boxes to the hospital laboratory building where I had been temporarily lodged, and while they unloaded her, the child put its trunk in through the laboratory window and started playing with the microscopes.

There are greater dangers. One of the four animals working in the Township was killed when a tree being cut down fell across its back. If nothing else, this meant enormous financial loss. At Barterville, an elephant with a Karen mother and four small children riding was startled by something and reared up; the harness snapped, throwing the passengers out and seriously injuring them. I was thankful that the amateurs of Riverside usually left elephants to Red Star and his professionals.

Great Lake was devoted to Red Star, both for himself and because he represented everything that was just beyond Great Lake's grasp. As often as he could, perhaps several nights a week, Great Lake would take his small fishing canoe upstream to the elephant camp. Sometimes there would be an ostensible reason – a hunting expedition, or some artefact that they were constructing between them. At other times there was no such pretence.

They loved to go hunting together, taking the small carbine that the KNLA had issued to Red Star, and also the splendid black-powder musket that Great Lake had made for him. If not sold to the Thais, the game would be cooked by Lili and a portion carried over to my house by Gratitude in a small glass bowl. Often this was venison:

'We know where we can find deer, and at this time of year they are calling to their lady friends so we pick some grass and put it on our mouths and make a kissing noise to them, so they come very close to be kissed and we shoot them. Today I hit one deer through the throat but it ran away.'

Sometimes Red Star would accompany us in my boat, riding *klee koh* while Great Lake steered. I never felt safer; Bartholomew knew the river better but no one had sharper eyes than Red Star. For him it was a way of gathering intelligence reports of wild elephants, and a way of seeing the world. Just as Great Lake went to Red Star for tranquillity and a link with tradition, so Red Star looked to Great Lake for a link with society. They met half way.

I found both of them on Great Lake's verandah one morning.

Great Lake was toying with a white plastic descant recorder that some mission visitor had left behind. I played them a tune on the recorder, but they were not greatly impressed; clearly I needed real Karen music.

> 'If I could find such a thing', I said. 'I've read about Karen harps and the like but no one here plays them. True Love is the best musician in the village and all he can play is John Denver.'
> 'Red Star can do it.' I looked hopefully at the Elephant Man and he nodded.
> 'He can make what you want. You want a Karen harp? A *ghwey* too? He can make them, no one else!'
> 'What's a *ghwey*?'
> 'A little stick with a piece in the middle that shakes. You hold it in front of your mouth and pull it and it goes *bong bong*, very loud. Karen get this idea from the cricket which shakes its legs over a hole in a tree to make a very loud noise.'
> A Jew's harp, in other words. I said to Red Star,
> 'If you can make those things, you can name your price.'

They talked to each other out of the corners of their mouths for a moment. Then Red Star asked if I would fetch him a radio next time I went to Penang. Also, I would have to supply some guitar strings for the harp. Neither of us could believe our luck.

Some weeks later I went to collect the instruments. The rains had begun and the river had risen up over the shaded beach where the baby elephant had been born. Red Star now lived up on the bluff, out of reach of flooding. It was a tiny house, the size of Bartholomew's kitchen. In it, five elephant trappers lived together. It was the archetypal Karen forest dwelling. No hardwood was involved: it was bamboo throughout and would last them one or two seasons only. Even the main supports were bamboo and, although there were rags soaked in diesel oil tied round them to deter ants from climbing the outside, nothing would stop the mites that would devour the soft, sweet fibres from within. Too springy to hold a high hut stable on their own, the main bamboos needed props and buttresses at each corner, giving the structure the precarious look of the timber-propped end wall of a half-demolished British terrace. The floor was made of *pudah* – flattened bamboo panels that gave you a light, rough and noisy floor that was quick to make and adequate if you weren't staying long. It was also nice to sleep on.

The roof was bamboo, long split halves laid with the opening alternately up and down, to form corrugated tiling. The walls were single layers of *pudah* panelling, done with no great refinement. In this high and flexible house of glossy new bamboo, light streamed in through all the chopped walls, the floor and ceiling, as though the single room was enclosed entirely by delicate golden slats of softened sunlight, crossing and hatching each other at many angles as it fell across the herringbone of the rolled sleeping mats. The only breaks in this seductive effect were the towels and T-shirts, the catapults and choppers, hats, nets and firearms hanging on every wall.

The standard Karen fireplace, an oblong of baked mud in a bamboo frame, was topped by a rack on which stood a cardboard box big enough to hold a washing machine but labelled *Ajino-Moto* (MSG food seasoning). That was the only private storage, and for the five men who slept in this single room there was no privacy whatever. Their only escape from each other was either the front balcony where they could sit with the big bamboo tubes used for fetching water, or swinging beneath the house in a hammock of old sacking. That, or going off into the forest. It was a proximity I could imagine five Englishmen enjoying for no more than a few hours.

The elephant men were not always there together. Some would be at their family homes, or trading some forest trophy, or away scouting for elephants. Still, they had to spend long periods in the forest. The KNLA gave them a rice ration, a lump sum for each elephant caught and handed over, and a fee for training and caring for the others. By Kawthoolei standards it could, if the trapping went well, be very good money – so good that Red Star, with no family of his own, had more ready cash than he knew what to do with. And that was the other bond between him and Great Lake. When the latter needed B.3,000 to buy the initial stock for his shop, he went to Red Star for an interest-free loan. When he finally bought my radio, it was actually Red Star who paid. In return, Great Lake had made him the musket. It hung on the wall of the hut.

Musical instruments were beyond Great Lake's range, but the elephant men were all involved in making mine. They'd done two harps; the first had cracked. The second had a sound box made from a single section of giant bamboo, sixteen inches long and eight across, carefully dried to a pale beige colour. A long curved neck rose up from one end and the six guitar strings stretched down to a soundboard made from an old gilt biscuit tin, beaten to shape. The harp, apart from some adjustment to the fit of the tuning pegs, was finished, but the Jew's harps were to be made there and then. Red Star had, a month before, placed a piece of bamboo over the fire to dry out thoroughly. He now took this down, quartered it lengthwise and handed the pieces round to his assistants. It took an hour to make three Jew's harps. Each was made at speed but with minute care, the vibrating tongues shaved infinitesimally for the fine tuning, the finished items rubbed with a thick layer of beeswax and then toasted over the fire. To their surprise, I could play the Jew's harp as well as any of them. But while the Karen strung harp is also of a type that can be found on several continents, its literature is exclusive and exclusiveness its subject. Red Star and the elephant men began to play and sing a succession of jaunty, pithy couplets on a repetitive theme – the perils of abandoning your own culture. This, of a Karen family gone from their home country:

> *Pwa ter moh, law mah ler Yuh,*
> *Klee ta thaw bah, hsaw ta uh.*
> A Karen woman lost in Thailand -
> no sound of rice husking, no cock crow.

The woman is so disorientated that she cannot set up a proper home, and they now buy all their food – just what happens, as more and more Karen drift into semi-urbanised wage labour in and around Thai towns. The absent sounds are the spirit of Karen village life that she's left behind.

'These are very old and difficult songs', said Great Lake, 'This boy who is singing them maybe knows the words but he does not know what it really means. I do not always know, I have to ask Red Star. See if you can understand this one:

> *Tuh ploh wah, pwa nar ta loh,*
> *thee ler lee kee bay er gho.*
> Golden Bud, he just wouldn't listen.
> Two cunts have killed him!'

'That must be about the dangers of adultery', I offered.
'No, no! It means, if Karen go to another country and love another culture, they will suffer. You cannot be loyal to both. It is poetic.'
I asked, 'How, or when, do you use the Jew's harp?'
'It is for making love', said Great Lake.

'Who can use it, anybody?'

'Anybody can play it, but this instrument is a woman. Red Star is going to make you a horn, which is a man.'

'Tell him the story', said Red Star, who was too shy to say much.

'Right, I shall tell you about the horn and the harp. A young man falls in love with a girl who lives alone with her father because her mother has died. He plays his Jew's harp to her, they are betrothed and everyone is very happy, but the young man then has to go off on a hunting trip. He says to her that he will be back in seven months. No problem, but he gives her the Jew's harp and tells her to play it if she is ever in trouble. Off he goes.

'Then her father marries again, and his new wife hates her step-daughter. She bullies her husband until she can get him to do anything she wants, and finally she insists that the daughter must be killed. Well, the father hasn't the heart to do it, but he doesn't dare to disobey. So he takes his daughter out into the forest and up to a cave on a high mountain, leaving her with seven months supply of food.

'But her fiancé is late back. Seven months and seven weeks later he returns – and she's almost dead of starvation. The father and stepmother have moved away. There's no one to be seen. He tries blowing on his trumpet and he hears the sound of a Jew's harp replying. He traces the sound and starts climbing the mountains. Each day he blows on his horn, each day the Jew's harp replies but the sound is getting fainter and weaker. At the end of seven days' climbing he finds her – just in time to save both her life and that of a new baby.'

Two weeks later, I found Red Star at Great Lake's house finishing the horn he'd made me. He'd promised to make it from a cow or buffalo horn, but what he gave me was much rarer. It was the beak of a hornbill, eight inches long with a glowing orange-red tip, light and translucent and in section shaped like an heraldic shield. Red Star had cut a small hole in it and was moulding a mouthpiece from beeswax into which he fitted a metal reed that he'd made from a brass bullet-case.

'There', said Great Lake, 'now you can go safely anywhere in the forest. If the Burmese hear this they will cry that the Karen are attacking and they will run away!'

Great Lake took my safety and my education seriously, and I became more and more reliant on his expertise – not to mention his humorous companionship. He could not only negotiate any rapids on the river; it was he who could strip the motor down in the middle of nowhere and make emergency spares from a bent nail and a piece cut from a tin can. He would instruct me in repairs to my own boat, and he fixed the leaks in my house roof. He would interpret for me if we met Pwo Karen, whose language he had picked up at GHQ. He fed me exotic foods and obtained samples of Karen weaving for me. He even helped knit a torch-cosy for me. Every well-dressed Karen man carries his flashlight in a knitted sheath. Gratitude did most of the work on mine, which is in red wool with green, pink and white zigzag patterning, a lens cover, two pompoms and two tassels, and the words 'Peace and Love' in the design. Great Lake plaited the long red and green shoulder string for it.

He helped me do a population survey of a village. The evening before, we divided the village between us. I explained how I wanted the questions and answers recorded, which he grasped immediately. In the morning, when I set off with the headman to guide me, Great Lake was lounging peacefully on the verandah sucking a cigar.

'What are you waiting for?' I called.
'I'm waiting until you are out of sight. Then I'm going to make up all the answers right here. I am so lazy, bloody fool *pwaken-yaw*!'

For all I know he may have done just that.

He could not prevent uncertainty and sadness surfacing through his gaiety. He would come to my house in the evening to listen to the BBC Burmese Service, sitting on my verandah in the dark, and it always made him restless.

'I cannot stand this, I wish to go back to my own place. My father is all alone now, I want to plant a farm and help him.'
'But you always say that you hate farming.'
'I will employ Burmese to do it for me. In one year from now I will go alone, I will make it ready and then I will call my family to join me.'

I wondered, but couldn't ask, whether they would want to. But there was another possibility which Lili might agree to. There was her sister who lived in Thailand just over the border from us. It was sometimes through her that Great Lake traded his more valuable finds from the forest. He asked me, just before I was about to leave for Bangkok in August, if I would buy him a comprehensive

Thai language course. For someone who usually spoke only of his forthcoming return to Burma, he seemed to be learning Thai rather seriously.

> 'Of course, I speak a little Thai already. I learned when I lived there.'
> 'I never knew you'd lived there. When was that?'
> 'I stayed with Lili's sister and family for one year and worked their farm for them. Then Lili and Bartholomew called me back here.'

He fiddled with the little black radio, running through the short-wave bands and pausing for a few seconds at a time on *Voice of America*, or *Radio Veritas* from the Philippines; jangle from a world that he'd surely loathe.

> 'Why did you stay in Thailand without your family?'
> 'To get identification papers. Now I have Thai papers for my whole family and it only cost me B.150 instead of B.2,000 or B.3,000 that many Karen pay in bribes, because I did it the slow and proper way. One day, maybe soon, I think we may need them.'

I thought of him, finally denatured, fading into Thailand. As the song says: two cunts will kill you.

They decided to build a new guesthouse for foreigners, and I moved into it from Bartholomew's for two months, leaving Millionaires Row behind.

The chosen site was on Health Department land at the far end of the village. As a teenager, I'd always wanted to be an architect, and I now thought that my chance had come. But True Love sketched the first design in five minutes, and then the Colonel's son-in-law, who had brought a diploma in engineering from Rangoon to the Revolution, made working drawings of a sort that few Karen houses can ever have had before. The Colonel himself arrived and considered the matter of orientation, urging that the verandah face east while pointing north himself. A carpenter had been called from Barterville, and a boy of fourteen with a Kalashnikov brought a workforce of prisoners – not PoWs, but thieves and adulterers. They spent three days bringing rafts of pale yellow-green bamboo down from the best groves, which some then split and flattened into wall panels while others put up a timber frame topped with corrugated tin. Another heap of bamboos were split to make the floor. It was assembled with kilos of nails, and all done in a few days.

Before any of this could be embarked on, however, the land had to be cleared. It was scrubby and tangled, having been an unkempt banana grove before. It needed long *parangs* and hard labour; there were tree stumps, tough grasses and snagged vines. All this was cut away by the schoolgirls from *Boarders*.

There's nothing like education for dividing, provoking and inciting. The Burmese always found the acquisition of learning by the Karen to be threatening. From the moment the American Baptists formalised their script for Sgaw Karen in the 1830s (see chapter twelve), village schools began to multiply in a remarkable fashion. W. S. Morrison, surveying Henzada District for the *Burma Gazetteer* in 1915, wrote that, 'Practically every Christian village possesses a good school building, and a paid teacher is usually kept.' The same is true in Kawthoolei today.

The Karen saw that, as with mission Christianity itself, the 'Silver Book' of Education was a potent means of strengthening their position *vis-à-vis* the dominant Burmans. The missionaries no doubt tended to exaggerate the extent of the uptake, but in 1887 Smeaton (p. 48) noted a new tension in Delta life: 'A Burman is wise in his generation. He never dreams of worrying an educated Karen, for he knows that he would catch a Tartar if he did.'

In 1851 the Burmese viceroy in Rangoon roundly declared to an American missionary that he would shoot any literate Karen that he met. The Karen sensibly did not flaunt their learning. Beyond village school level, the behaviour of Karen schoolchildren often puzzled early writers who described them as dull, slow students, concerned mainly to stay out of trouble by not speaking, but who would then surprise their teachers with their success rate. The main Christian seminary in Rangoon, Judson College, became in effect a Karen university, regarded by the Burmese government as a hotbed of sedition. Karen began to qualify in the professions; the Burmese response was to end all Karen language education after independence. The Karen reply to that was to make education a cornerstone of their revolution. Kawthoolei now claims to have more than 500 primary, fifteen secondary and six senior schools.

Christianity still dominates this system; the pupils pray and sing hymns and thank the Lord for Kawthoolei. But animist and Buddhist children attend also. Three forms of redemption go hand in hand: Christian faith, national liberation, and the salvation through knowledge of the 'bloody fool *pwakenyaw*' who'd tried to boil snail shells soft.

These were the forces that had created *Boarders*, some of whose occupants were now to be my trainee village paramedics.

> 'Who are they?' I asked, when I first saw my neighbours, two dozen teenage girls and two infants living in a large, gaunt shed near the river.
> 'They are orphans, they are in Bartholomew's care.'

The first story that I learnt was Waterlily's. The day she decided to tell me, she was visibly pining for her home village on the coast near Mergui. She was no orphan when she came to Kawthoolei, but a self-possessed thirteen-year-old.

'Some people came to our village, which is almost all Karen.

They had come to talk about Kawthoolei and to encourage young people to go. They had to be careful, because there were Burmese there who might have gone to the police. But these visitors came to my father's house one evening and talked with our family. My father is a respectable man; he has a job with the local administration, he wasn't going to abandon his position. But they said, even if parents couldn't go to Kawthoolei, they could send their children. My father felt that he had to agree to something, so he called us together and asked us what we thought. I was the only one who liked the idea – it wasn't the first time people had come asking us to join. I said that I wanted to go.'

Very good, but who would house and support the young girl in Kawthoolei? Who would feed her? Her father had not the capital to pay all the costs in advance, and once she was up in the hills the chances of getting a cash allowance to her with any regularity were remote. The Karen National Union could not afford to supply rice for every child who wanted a Karen education, however much they might like to. That alone would cost perhaps B.2,000 a year. But a deal might be done that would make it worth the KNU's investment; Waterlily could be supported through her schooling by a government department. When she matriculated, she would repay this with seven years of service to the Revolution. Thus would Kawthoolei build up its strength of skilled and educated Karen.

And on those terms she came, by boat and on foot through the forest:

'When I first arrived we were all at Barterville together. They'd hardly started this village then, it was just forest by the river. We were brought here and divided into work parties; I was with the Health Department. While the teachers were building the school, we started on the hospital. I did the floor, with Bartholomew showing me how. Then we slept in the hospital while we built *Boarders* for our home. And then we had to build air-raid shelters, and the kitchens and all these other buildings. Then at last we could go to school'.

Boarders was no palace; it was an L-shaped barracks. One wing was simply an ample thatched roof over a dirt floor where tools, spare roofing tin and the chest of rice were kept. The other half, where they slept, was a hall raised eight feet above the ground on twelve posts. It was windowless, but the walls were made of a single layer of split bamboo panels; they could see out easily, and light, wind and rain streamed in. There were no internal partitions. Each girl staked a claim to a patch of floor at the side, marked by the plastic sleeping mat which during the day would be rolled back, a thin blanket folded on top. Each girl had her tin trunk and a cardboard box for her possessions. There were two mosquito nets, but only for the babies; sleeping there was one of the few perks of being the children's nurse. From the horizontal lath halfway up the wall hung cords supporting shirts on hangers, spare sarongs, small mirrors and shoulder bags. Hang things in the wrong place and a rain squall would saturate the lot. It was a bleak and unlovely building.

By night, though, *Boarders* was transformed. Sometimes I would stand in the dark nearby and look at it for minutes on end. The light inside, provided by a single fluorescent strip run from the hospital generator (if there was diesel), would be replaced after eight o'clock by the softer glow of a dozen small oil lamps made from old milk tins, and this light would pour in stripes out through the walls, mixed with noise – the rhythmic droning of schoolgirls conning their lessons, or of gossip and laughter. Sometimes there was a borrowed radio to play, or rough cassettes of love songs by the stars of Karen pop. Sometimes there was a guitar and they'd sing together: gospel songs or battle songs of the Revolution, or the handful of older tunes that they knew and had perhaps been asked to perform at a function or wedding. Occasionally I would go up and listen, and eat with them the evening's rice cake or fritters. If they'd got the lighting right it could look homely – though there were usually one or two girls wretched under blankets, shivering with malaria.

Then lights out, and mostly they quietened down, though the babies might scream and there'd be nowhere for the girls to put their ears except under the thin blankets, and they'd be slow and ill-humoured in the morning.

Sam, as Bartholomew's son and deputy, kept order in *Boarders*. He knew where each of them had come from. Not all had crossed the Front Line for their education; some had come from villages way up or downriver where the little school with its single teacher could only take them to third or fourth grade. Their parents, anxious that they should learn but unable to afford the rice, sent them to Riverside under Health and Welfare Department auspices.

These voluntary exiles from home could be considered 'orphans'. Just one or two of them, such as Sam's girlfriend Lina, came near to what I understand by the word:

'Lina comes from a small village right down the other side of New Fields, two days away. Six years ago the Burmese raided the village. They were after her father; he'd been helping the KNLA with food. When the soldiers came, Lina's father escaped into the forest but they caught her older brother and shot him. Then they chased after the girls. Lina was only small, but they wounded her in the leg. Her sister was older. They were both captured; I think you understand what it was like for them. The Burmese retreated to their camp, taking the girls with them, and they held them for two weeks until some of the villagers came to the camp and pleaded for their release. The Burmese were bored with them and let them go. Lina came here to have her leg fixed and she's been here ever since. She's going to be a nurse.'

In theory they would all become nurses. But what if, after five years of schooling in Riverside, Waterlily or Charlie or Golden Bud hadn't wanted to be a nurse?

'They could work for any other government department', said Sam, 'but most of them really do want to be nurses. It's better than being a teacher, after all. Teachers are stuck in one village. Nurses get to travel.'
'What if they want to get married?'
'They must wait for seven years.'
'But what keeps them working?'
He grinned at me, not sure if he wanted to embark on a discussion of commitment to the Revolution. Then he said,
'We can stop their rice ration.'
'What about boys? Do any of them train as nurses?'
'Several have – me, for instance. But most boys want a uniform, so they go into the Army Medical Corps.'
'Who are the boys, where do they come from?'
'They are orphans too. You know the barracks up at Head-quarters? There are sixty of them there. They were separated from their families when their parents were forced to carry rice and ammunition for the Burmese.'

Ruth the Headmistress claimed that, of the 300 plus pupils at Riverside school, more than 100 were 'orphans'. I found this difficult to understand, in this low-key war; when I asked about, there were plenty who had family somewhere. I might have dismissed the term as a mistranslation, of 'homeless' perhaps. But others also used the word 'orphan' and insisted that it was correct.

It is a concept that the Karen apply to their people as a whole.

They were orphaned from the start, when they were separated from Toh Meh Pah in the forest on the journey from the River of Flowing Sand. Their plight has pervaded their history. They placed themselves, as 'orphans in the forest', under the wing of one colonial protector after another, whether it be the British colonial power, the missions, or the monarchs of Siam. But often the protector failed them – as in 1942 – and, deprived of patronage (that is, of a father's protection), they were orphaned once more.[1]

To be an orphan is for a Karen both a terrible and an admirable condition. Harry Marshall wrote in 1922 (pp. 133–4) of three classes of people who were condemned to live outside the village: widows, cohabiting but unmarried couples, and orphans. These were all considered to have offended their personal spirits and were thus contagious with ill-fortune. The Karen didn't want to risk orphans marrying back into the community, so they had to be kept away from nubile adolescents:

Left to range through the jungle, such orphans, if they survived, generally developed a daring and resourcefulness that inspired the ordinary folk of the village with wonder. Their deeds came to be thought of as due to a supernatural power. In short, they were believed to be magicians.

In many societies worldwide, diviners and healers have been recruited from just such marginal groups, who might be considered to be nearer to the spirits than usual. And here were the girls of *Boarders* being trained as nurses.

There are two terms for orphan in Sgaw Karen: *ser ghweh* means that the rest of your family are all dead, while *po ghweh* means that your parents are dead but you have other family still alive, and thus may be still counted as part of normal village structure: not threatening, in other words. The heroes of fantastic tales of cunning and heroism tend to be *po ghweh* (see page 66 for example) and are not complete outcasts.

What did it mean to have come from Rangoon to Kawthoolei and be thus irrevocably separated from your family, like True Love or many other friends? True Love had been warned that he would be arrested if he ever went home; he could well be considered to be an orphan. Even more so these girls, now under the patronage of the Revolution. They were *po ghweh*, part of the Family; they had been entrusted to Kawthoolei and Kawthoolei was on its mettle as the guardian of this trust – and, like a godparent, of the morals of its wards.

Discipline came first. As Manager, Sam attempted to impose a regime, and had posted a timetable on the wall upstairs, along with the cooking and cleaning rosters:

a.m.
5.00 – wake up
5.00–5.30 – washing
5.30–7.00 – work
7–8.00 – eat
(after which, off to school)

p.m.
1–3.00 – afternoon work
3–4.00 – play
4–4.30 – wash
4.30–5.30 – dinner
5.30–6.00 – rest
6–6.20 – pray
6.20–9.00 – read
9–5.00 – sleep

'Work' meant anything necessary for the survival of their community. Across the track was a plot of land belonging to the Health Department. The girls of *Boarders* cut and cleared the bush, dragged it into heaps, burnt it, painstakingly grubbed out the charred roots with *parangs*, seeded and weeded it, then built not very pig-proof fences all round it. Their own building needed almost constant maintenance. One week Bartholomew had them all splitting bamboos and replacing their own floor, wearing plastic bathcaps to keep their hair clean of shavings. The next week the Colonel declared that the roof needed replacing and that he was donating a stack of second-hand leaf-thatch shingles. They were full of scorpions. It took the girls two days to tie them in place, sitting in rows up in the rafters, an array of young heads appearing through the thatch. Then there were cushions to be sewn, pigs to be tended, children to be cared for, a new latrine to be dug at Bartholomew's house. They were recruited by Two Shoes to carry bamboos to his abortive basket-weaving operation – or rather, they were 'volunteered' by Morning Star who, as Bartholomew's second-in-command, thought it would be good for them. They were paid B.25 (60p) per hundred bamboos moved up from the river – and these were big bamboos, twenty foot or more. They would have preferred an afternoon off to play volleyball. When the school term ended, they might have hoped for a holiday – but the next day saw them trailing off through the village for a spot of road-mending. They were also one of four teams around the village who laundered the soft-furnishings of Bethany Church, and the washing lines would suddenly fill with blue cushion covers and altar cloths. They also dug air-raid shelters, and graves for the hospital.

Bartholomew personally took them through their tasks, or delegated Sam to oversee them. While Sam was brisk and efficient, convinced that he could do most jobs faster if left to himself, Bartholomew was an avuncular, comical tyrant, his sarcastic buffoonery at once frightening the girls and delighting them. He would not ask them to do anything that he shirked himself, and one might see the sixty-year-old head of the Health and Welfare Department stripped to his shorts thatching, hammering, digging with his students. He even cooked for them. They had a separate kitchen block, a shed with open fires and a single long table with pigs snuffling about beneath it and a baby urinating on top, and here he would sometimes announce that he was treating them, and would spend the morning making sweet parathas or coconut drinks for us all.

He had other responsibilities towards them. One morning they were presented with new pairs of flipflops, skirting material, shirts and a roll of green plastic sheeting embossed with patterns of roses, which he cut into lengths to make rain capes – their six-monthly issue. More solemnly, he would come to *Boarders* of an evening 'to give them a lecture', which meant a talk of an uplifting nature; duty, religion or revolution were the usual themes. Some said that Bartholomew had no control over his *Boarders* – but there were periods when he spent more time with them than with his own family.

The girls, meanwhile, were *in loco parentis* themselves. There were two orphan babies in their charge, Timmy and Lala. They were *po ghweh*, they had family still. They were the children of the wretched soldier at Headquarters whose gun had gone off, fatally wounding his wife in the stomach. He himself was said to be too shocked to care for them, but there were other relatives. Downriver with Bartholomew, we stopped for a few minutes at Black Turtle where he announced that he had to deliver a letter. On our return journey a few days later we stopped again and he collected money. It was from Timmy and Lala's grandparents, a contribution towards their keep at *Boarders*. There was, apparently, no question that they might simply go and live with their grandparents. Perhaps their ill-fortune was too contagious.

No, the orphans stayed with the orphans, under the Health and Welfare aegis. They were a sweet but somewhat sickly pair, very prone to malaria and colds. The girl who'd been given full charge of them was one of Bartholomew's handful of trained nurses, who had been called back from another village and who now lived with them in *Boarders*. What she thought of being presented with this role (for how long? years, perhaps) she never said, but she took every opportunity to farm them out. Their life and hers revolved around the shaded underside of *Boarders*, the siesta hammocks, the clutter of farm implements, a box and a bamboo or two, and the corrugated iron rainwater trap.

On his Health and Welfare Department land, Bartholomew gathered all the waifs and strays for whom he was responsible: the orphans, myself, one or two more than usually destitute Karen families (usually women with children whose husbands had 'run away' to Thailand) and my other neighbour, the *Pu Payor*.

The *Pu Payor* was not a Karen but an elderly Burmese miner (*Pu Payor* – Burmese Grandpa). He was tiny, wiry, with false teeth and a disgusting pipe. He'd come because he had no family, was destitute and knew and trusted Bartholomew. Given a patch of earth and dining rights at *Boarders*, he'd built himself a scrapwood and bamboo hut next to mine. It was a labour of love, for all its shanty appearance. He spent most of his day fixing things, borrowing (and snapping) my hand-drills as he made shelves, lamps, new water systems, doors and porches. A Buddhist, he felt the lack of a shrine. When one of the Thai sawmills ceased operation he purloined its spirit-house and brought it home, cutting a gap in his wall so that he could gaze into it from his bed.

Bartholomew gave the *Pu Payor* certain duties. When Vermilion brought half a dozen goats back from one of her trading trips down-river, the *Pu Payor* was made Master of the Goats. He knew nothing about goats and it was a while before he got to grips with either their voracity or their lechery. In the meantime they demolished vegetable gardens, and reduced the single, miserable nanny to a pale shadow of a goat. She was saved at last, and spent her nights by the fire at the *Pu Payor's* hut, enormously pregnant.

He was also the Head Gardener, and built stout fences around the lime and jackfruit trees, wheezing thin oaths at *Boarders* if the girls presumed to pick anything without his permission. He liked to keep the white man well stocked with bananas and limes, and jackfruit seeds boiled in red-black water in a greasy black tin over the goat's fire. Sometimes of an evening I visited him with a return offering of sweet coffee and a tin of pilchards. I speak not a word of Burmese and he not a word of Karen, but we did fine, pointing at the goat, the stars, his flowers or his shrine and grunting at each other in peaceable satisfaction.

To protect the Department's banana groves he built a barricade across the path so that the Army radio operators could no longer ride their motorbikes with quite such élan past *Boarders*. As they tried to manoeuvre round the fence they generally stalled and swore, and more than once the roadblock was mysteriously down in the morning.

With the *Boarders* the old man had an amicable relationship. Twice a day, grinning gummily, he'd stride across to their kitchen and collect his rice. In return he tended the fruit trees, and worked for them at Bartholomew's side on the patching and rebuilding tasks of the day. He drove away the cows that threatened to eat the flowers planted by the girls, and he beautified his own house and garden assiduously. He was a dead shot with a catapult; if he came out in the boat with us he had to be restrained from bringing down every fish-eagle on the river. He pottered, he tinkered – a new latch or ladder, an improved dog dish. I would ask (through the girls) what he was doing, and he would merely deliver cryptic grunts and more boiled jackfruit seeds in return. Great Lake, who thought him a silly old man and wouldn't have him in the house, referred to his patch as 'Little Burma'.

Inevitably, the girls teased him mercilessly. One morning there came howls of tragic rage from his hut, followed by the *Pu Payor* striding to the kitchen crying for justice. The children had wrapped a rotten banana trunk in his bedroll. He met with very little sympathy and much mirth. His attempts to terrify the girls into not picking jackfruit before he deemed them fully ripened earned him derision more often than respect. But it was certain that they were fond of him.

With others among our neighbours, the girls' relations were not always so happy. Behind the *Pu Payor*'s hut lived a sad family of abandoned women and children; their man had 'run away'. A particularly piercing whinge came from the four-year-old daughter if her mother went out of sight to the river. Their little boy was a shameless, compulsive thief. They too took rice from the *Boarders* kitchen, but they did nothing to help. They were resented for this. Worse, perhaps, was the helpless female destitution they stood for. The *Pu Payor* was, at least, the deserving poor in retirement. These people were an unhappy picture of Karen womanhood when its normal roles and support systems failed, reduced to dependency on the new-fangled state. Which was something the girls did not care to contemplate too often.

More difficult still were their relations with the military nurses who had taken over the hospital. It was painfully clear how much higher was the status of the military who now put on airs of professional disdain. This was quite understandable; women in a quasi-profession with few real skills to offer, with no economic or political prospects and no other way of impressing the society around them – how else should they behave? In Britain there is no group more obsessed with status and hierarchy than the nurses. Pecking orders were only to be expected in Riverside. But my orphan neighbours were truly second class. They were now excluded from working in the hospital that they themselves had built, but were expected to dig graves for the military's clientele. The civilian girls had no uniforms and virtually no equipment. In fact the Health and Welfare Department had no budget, while the Army was absorbing 60 per cent of Kawthoolei's revenues. Not very surprisingly, the *Boarders* regarded their own future with some scepticism.

Another of their duties reinforced their subservient position. Through a system known as 'family life', Army staff and civil servants could call on Bartholomew to provide live-in help at times of need, such as at childbirth. In practice, because he had no one else, this meant one of his nurses. What was, at first sight, not such a bad idea was really no more than a revolutionary perk, a way of letting friends, family and neighbours off the hook – quite apart from being an absurd waste of the precious few nurses. Girls sent to do 'family life' were in reality no better than skivvies. No one would admit to approving of this system. 'It is an abuse of the Health Department!' said the surgeon-director, visiting from GHQ. But it continued, and Bartholomew did not have the power to refuse the requests.

Among the distinguishing attributes of the early Hindu societies of S.E. Asia that (northern, male) historians like to list, there was,

says Georges Coedès (1962, p. 26), 'on the ideological plane, cosmo-
logical dualism and institutions based on the importance of women
and even matriarchal principles'. In the revolutionary State, the
benefits of womanhood seemed more negative. I was never close
enough to any Karen woman to know how she felt. This was a
symptom of my foreignness as well as my sex; female visitors
reported the same thing. It was only the *Boarders* that I could
approach easily. Otherwise, I could just observe and make mental
lists of the pros and cons of the situation. All I can say is that
it did not seem to be a very terrible thing, to be a revolutionary
Karen woman. There was drudgery, certainly. Arriving in a new
village with Timothy we saw, beneath a house, a teenage girl polishing rice in a tall wooden mill, the top half fitted with handles which
the girl turned backwards and forwards to bring the rice out at
the central seam. She rocked and twisted from side to side, rising
on her toes as she turned the heavy wood, sweating and tired.
Timothy grinned and said, 'Oh, one-lady-power disco dance!' But
the women in Riverside were not very hard-pressed, not physically.
They did not – as they would in much of Africa – have to walk
five miles for water twice a day; the river was only yards from
most houses, and men and children shared the chore. They did
not have to be up before dawn to grind flour for *tortillas* while
their husbands snored, as can happen in Latin America. Nor was
there a very firm division of labour. Women did most of the cooking at home, but True Love and Bartholomew could both produce a good meal, and would do so. In farming villages the hard
work on the steep hillsides was shared; the women got bad backs
from bending to weed the ground, while the men got hernias from
humping the heavy rice sacks. Rape was unheard of, and the in-
famous violence of Thai men to their women has no place with
the Karen.

There was certain work that one might expect to be naturally
done by women but with the Karen is not. Most of the village
midwives are men. They are spiritual supervisors as much as anything. They are not greatly interested in the physical state of the
mother or child before or after birth. They are there to see the
infant pushed smartly out into the world – often literally pushed;
two strong arms applied to the womb – with certain ritual observances properly made. It was no good asking them how they dealt
with problems, or if there were many vaginal tears or dangerous
bleeds. They denied that these ever occurred. I might as well have

asked a cardinal if the communion wafer transubstantiated success-
fully every time.

Frequently the women did without this help. Their resilience
was unfussed. Walking around Black Turtle I stopped at a large
but bleak and almost empty house seemingly inhabited by just
one woman. I wanted to know whether she'd called upon the local
midwife's assistance with her recent baby. No. *Why not?* I didn't
need any help. *You had no one else to help you?* No. *There was no one
here at all?* No, no one in the house. *What about your neighbours?* They
were at home. *Did you call for them?* No, I wasn't worried. *Weren't
you afraid at all?* No.

At GHQ they were now recruiting and training women to serve
in Front Line units. There were those who opposed this, but the
concerns voiced were less to do with physical or psychological
resilience, more that the women might undermine the morals of
the men in the trenches. We had none of that sort of thing at Riverside – only military nurses, wireless operators and official caterers
for the visiting bigwigs from Headquarters, or the foreigners who
came to preach and snoop.

In the modernist atmosphere of Riverside, few families would
insist on their daughters being (as Great Lake would wish) 'very
afraid' of me, and staying in the kitchen. Still, there were reserves.
If I ate with True Love, Silver would not usually eat at the same
table, but would serve and withdraw. I could not readily have had
a heart-to-heart with a family woman; a respectful distance was
maintained. In one village the schoolmistress washed and dried
my hands for me after dinner, on her knees. She acted with better
grace in giving than I managed in receiving her help.

I tried a more formal approach, and went about the villages
to meet the local representatives of the KNU Women's Organisation. This was established some years ago with President Bo Mya's
wife as the figurehead. She had fronted a tour of the Districts. They
went by boat *en grande dame*, big and blousy, amply padded, pro-
visioned and escorted and, like the rest of us, had from time to
time to get out in midstream and heave themselves and the boat
around the rocks – hardly Madame Mya's style.

They left a chain of representatives in each village. Notions of
what these should be achieving varied. In one village there seemed
to be little in it other than the occasional fund-raising stall by the
football field selling rice-flour cakes and pink drinks – a 'funfair',
this was called. Elsewhere the *Women* claimed greater clout:

'What powers do you have?'

'We have a health and hygiene officer who can go to houses and look at the kitchen, especially if there is a baby coming. Sometimes things are very dirty and we make suggestions.'

And not just any old dirt either. The Pastor (a woman) said,

'The women are responsible for the morals in the village. Karen mothers must be aware of their responsibilities for their children's thinking.'

What the hill-and-forest people considered right behaviour might not be what Delta urbanites were used to. Here at least, power was not in the hands of the newcomers. It was the women of the river villages who gave practical force to the view that the Revolution must live up to high and traditional Karen standards. True Love had nearly fallen foul of them: 'I was staying at Black Turtle with a friend and we went bathing, and I was wearing these very little pants to bathe and my friend walked back through the village still dressed in his trunks with his towel over his shoulder. Well, the women weren't having that. They gave me a warning and they fined him B.50!'

What other powers? I was told that if someone wished to sell medicines from their shop, they had to apply to the *Women's Organisation* for a permit. I think this ruling was taken about as seriously as the British take dog licences.

Over the mountains in the Western Valley, in the village of Gold Rock I was taken by the headman to see the local *Women's* representative at her house. It was before I'd learnt to speak much Karen, so the conversation was conducted through True Love. It was a four-cornered, but three-sided discussion. Faced with a bearded Englishman, an articulate Army officer and her village headman, the young woman clammed up. I posed a question, in English, looking at her. True Love repeated it in Karen, also looking at her. She said nothing, but looked timidly at the headman. He answered all the questions. I had been placed on the slightly raised inner floor, sitting in shadow. The woman knelt on the lower floor, fifteen feet in front of me. I thought our chances of communication could be improved, and I moved forward into the light and onto the same level as her. She moved back into the shadow, and we continued as before.

They weren't all so cowed. Elsewhere in the Valley, we stopped at a dark timber house that was home to a deaf and forceful grandmother called Sal. Mats were spread, she called for coffee and cakes from her family and decided that she was going to give me a

T-shirt from her shop. On the front of this it said: THE BOL-
LOCKS. The Animal Song.

In presenting me with this she had possibly blown the week's
profit. Her family, which included other KNU representatives,
listened impassively as Sal took the floor. She had, I was told,
pioneered the improvement in the position of women in Kawthoolei
in the 1960s.

> 'What has changed?' I bellowed. She roared back,
> 'Before, the men did not listen to us and were sometimes very
>   rude. They are not rude now!'
> No one was rude to Sal. In fact no one got a word in edgeways.

But of real power, to affect the course of the Revolution? No,
just a consultative role. Observers of Karen society describe a subtle
influence; women are there, in the shadows at the back. Their voices
are heard. The irony is that the establishment of formal structures
of village representation is exactly that which now prevents those
voices from being heard in higher echelons. Few women are elected
to Township Committees. The voices have been left behind in the
shadows.

There is one field in which the influence of women in Kawthoolei
(as opposed to traditional Karen society) is crucial, and that is
education. Perhaps they have simply inherited the British attitude,
that teaching and nursing are the professions suitable for girls. As
the pressures of the war increase, with boys frequently going straight
from school into the KNLA, the higher classes in the schools have
a steadily greater proportion of girls, and it is the senior girls who
are recycled as teachers of the junior classes. In Kawthoolei there
are, increasingly, two sorts of teacher: young men from the Delta,
possibly with some higher education, and young women produced
within Kawthoolei. In the Education Department itself, power was
fairly evenly divided. Edward was the administrative head, but
his wife Ruth was the Headmistress of the school, while the two
senior teachers were William and Dierdre.

In this situation, and given the chronic shortage of skilled labour,
it was of course the Education Department that challenged Bartholomew's hold over his *Boarders*.

The immediate issue was Bartholomew's right to take six of the
girls out of school early, before they'd reached the top grade, in

order to train them as nurses. Edward was furious. Bartholomew, he considered, had exceeded his prerogative. He had denied the girls the opportunity to finish their education, and what Kawthoolei needed was properly educated Karen. What Bartholomew believed Kawthoolei needed was more nurses as fast as possible. The matter came to a head at one of the Monday evening 'Free Discussions' at Headquarters.

Strain was telling on Bartholomew. His Department was under severe pressure. Burmese attacks had laid waste his plans; funds were sorely lacking. I met him, before the meeting, in the Colonel's house where, together with Arthur the Agricultural Officer, we were having lunch. I asked Bartholomew what he was going to say at the meeting. What would he do, I wondered, if the far more articulate Edward forced him to abandon his training plans? But Bartholomew was not feeling talkative; he sighed and gazed out of the window at the rain falling on the pigs and the forest behind the Colonel's house. Arthur sympathetically read his thoughts:

'You know, *Thera* Bartholomew has for years struggled to build up his Department and to provide a service for the people here, for the ordinary Karen people. And all the time these other departments are calling him to do things that he cannot do, and he has to give all his thought to the refugees and send his nurses with the Information Department tour, and they get married and so on, and however much he tries, now his Department gets smaller and weaker after all his efforts.'

I looked at Bartholomew again. For a moment I thought that he was crying; it may just have been rain.

Monday Free Discussions took place at 8 p.m. in a hall nearby. This was lit by fluorescent tubes powered by the main generator, which stood close outside. The result of this arrangement was that the room rapidly filled with termites, and that it was difficult to hear much of what was said. Anyone could attend, and some forty people did so, mostly senior administrators. This particular evening opened with a debate on Kawthoolei's relations with the Burma Communist Party, during which Edward remained uncharacteristically silent. He was saving himself for an onslaught, and Bartholomew shrank into his bench in anticipation. When his moment came, Edward fired a stream of accusing questions. The Health Department, he said, was threatening to undermine the whole policy of the Education Department. Why had the senior teachers not been consulted? How could a girl become a nurse if she was only half-educated? If they weren't prepared to stay the school-course through, what made anyone think they'd stick it out as nurses? Bartholomew, the simple man, could not cope with the tirade, and said hardly a word. Except that, he insisted, the girls had agreed that it was what they wanted to do. Which actually more or less settled the matter. The Colonel announced that permission would have to be sought from GHQ, which it was; it was granted, and Bartholomew was free to go ahead.

But what *did* the girls think? Did they really want to stay on in school? It was not as though they could win qualifications of any value in the outside world, and what I'd seen of classes was not vastly stimulating. But who was I to judge? I tried asking them, but they would only say yes, what Bartholomew said was the best for them and for Kawthoolei was of course their only desire. True Love, torn between his loyalty to Edward and his admiration for Bartholomew, was troubled. Some of the girls, he reported, resented being taken out of school; they had only come to Riverside for the education, after all. Perhaps Edward was only doing his duty – as one of their guardians.

As Bartholomew's course began, the chosen girls from *Boarders* seemed keen to do their duty, displaying uncommon enthusiasm and high spirits. Perhaps it was the novelty, or relief that a practical activity had taken over from the arguments at last. For Waterlily and her companions it was the next stage in a process that had begun years before; perhaps she was only grateful that its conclusion was now a year or two nearer. Perhaps, after all, she wanted to be a nurse.

Their desires were impossible to gauge, but they could be seen to dream. Of the outside world, for instance. I'd find Waterlily on my verandah, engrossed in tourist maps of Kuala Lumpur that I'd casually picked up in Malaysia. As we all bathed off the side of the boat one afternoon with the river in spate, Golden Bud asked if we had big rivers and floods in England, and how long did those jets we were forever seeing, coming out of Bangkok, take to get there? Well aware of a life beyond, but quite without expectation of ever seeing it, they would stare at magazine photographs like jailbirds re-reading old newspapers.

They were, in Karen terms, like women denatured – no swidden hill to work, no paddy to be husked under the house in the morning,

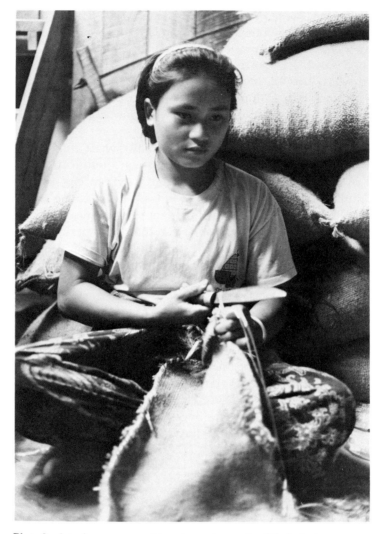

Plate 9. A trainee nurse making rice ration sacks. 'Their desires were impossible to gauge, but they could be seen to dream.'

no family to tend other than each other and me. No one to be 'afraid' of, and no privacy to withdraw into anyway. Even bathing in the river, there was a reserve about the proceedings; a dozen of them standing in the stream, delicately tipping small bowls of water down into the front of their sarongs over their breasts, coy even with each other. Sometimes they would borrow my boat to cross the river to the vegetable gardens, or to go fishing with rod and line (at which they were very proficient), and then, at least, they might relax, calmly poling their way upstream in late afternoon light, sleek and elegant and competent.

Most often I saw them sitting half-idle in the shade under *Boarders*, embroidering or mending, snoozing in a hammock or playing with the children. There was Mani, the senior nurse, cool and lofty in her manner, nominally in charge of these 'maidens' but often away on tour, leaving the others to tend her pigs for her. There was Waterlily, dark and plump, who took charge of my house and diet and rearranged both frequently. Charlie, maturely beautiful at eighteen, with a languid intelligence, prone to migraines and musically gifted – she composed as well as sang. Lotus, the refugee from the coast, badly schooled at some stage and 'behind', but quick-witted and self-confident, fond of punching me and laughing about it but with a smile that lit up dark Karen rooms. Lina, the fugitive who'd seen her brother shot. Golden Bud, Cool Shoot, Come Quick and Julia who, it was said, had eaten some leaves that she shouldn't have done while pregnant, so that now neither she nor her little boy were quite all there. Bathing, gardening, building or lazing beneath their sleeping hall, they preserved a measure of independence together with a refined sense of the demure and retiring. They could be hilarious and high-spirited in my house at times, and yet melt away into shadows when other visitors came. On the volleyball court between our buildings they were hopeless with laughter, but if the Colonel came they'd fall silent, and absent themselves fast.

They cared and cooked for me, and I bought them new volleyballs from Thailand. They would use my verandah as a cool and quiet place to read and sleep when the chatter and children back at *Boarders* got on top of them. We spent hours talking together. Once, after a long morning teaching, I went to Great Lake's house, tired and headachy from the linguistic strain, and calling for hot milk tea. He admonished me:

> 'It comes of sitting too long among maidens. Maidens smell very strong, and each one has her own smell. You have spent three hours sitting among the various smells of eight different maidens, and now you wonder why your head is spinning!'

A family man, he lit a cigar to provide a protective scent screen.

> 'We have a saying in Karen', he continued; 'Just when the baby deer is born, that's when the tiger eats it.'

'What does that mean?'

'Look at Bartholomew's department,' he said, without explaining.

But it was obvious enough. It wasn't just war and inter-departmental attrition that was wearing the Health and Welfare Department down; it was the way people have of asserting their independence by one means or another, even while seeming to be ensnared. By the end of the training course, just three months later, two of the putative nurses were already pregnant, and *hors de combat*.

We acquire moral and spiritual values by studying nature in rural areas.
Saw Moo Troo, (1981, p. 6)

OCTOBER 1986

The Karen month, *Si sah* – 'little starlight'[1]

The rains have begun to ease after (they tell me) two months of deluge. The roads have been destroyed. Given one or two dry days, someone was sure to try and drive between the border and Riverside, stirring the mud to the colour and consistency of toffee mousse. The mornings are cold. Colonel Marvel is sick and has taken to his bed, miserable and unspeaking under the blankets. The mist mills about in the forest until near eight o'clock, huge water particles like distracted rain that has forgotten where to fall. Drying clothes is a trial. If I do get a shirt dry, it goes straight into a sealed plastic bag.

I go to the river, to bathe in the rain. The surface of the water takes off around me, billions of big splash droplets rising three inches, a new top surface over the river. It is mostly gentle – although a sudden cataract has swamped a boat by the hospital.

The forest is close and claustrophobic; it has been growing hard since May, and every building is obscured and overhung – bad news if there are snakes in the trees. The rice fields are dense-packed but not yet ripe. Rats and wild pigs are the problem now. Boys with catapults sit in bamboo watch-towers overlooking the crop.

Everyone is waiting. When the rain stops, the harvest and the fighting will commence together.

NOVEMBER

La Naw – 'oilseed'

The rain slows. The level of the river falls, the water clears, and at night I shiver even with a blanket. The days are still very humid.

Plate 10. 'Everyone is waiting. When the rain stops, the harvest and the fighting will commence together.'

A flurry of building has begun, to be completed if possible in one or two weeks before the harvest starts. This is prime construction time; the bamboo is now well developed but still growing, and is thus green and supple. Karen are building huts out in the fields ready to stay with the harvest.

A green and black-checked tree snake in the rafters of my house this morning – pretty and peaceable, but not really to be encouraged. The overhanging mango branches will have to go.

In the compound, toads haul themselves from three-inch holes in the bare earth. Every form of wasp, every possible metallic sheen of beetle and bug makes its way through the house, some crawling slowly across the floor with long pauses, like connoisseurs in a gallery running their feelers over the walls, others going past my ears with as much noise and as little courtesy as the RAF in the Grampians. On a white starburst of flowers below the verandah, cobalt and magenta butterflies take lunch, the tails of their long wings trailing.

This house has too many scorpions. Timothy put his jacket on, and a scorpion in the sleeve stung him four times down the length of his arm. Last night there was a centipede the size of a small snake in the latrine, scuffling along the wall looking for an exit. They have crimson jaws and a bite the Karen fear more than scorpions. It is said that they climb into forest houses and lie alongside small children for warmth – until the child turns . . .

The campaign season is poised to go. There is rain still, and the roads are very difficult. But with elephants for food and munitions, the tracks are passable to the Karen. The village has suddenly filled with soldiers. The Gossips speculate that they will try and dislodge the Burmese from the top bend in the river, and so regain water access to the western valley. But the Burmese are reported to be moving, pushing downstream towards us. Fields above White Ponds have been abandoned – just before harvest – and in the south the season's refugees have begun to arrive.

This morning a company of soldiers, heavily armed, walked past the kitchen door. They made for the sawmill landing stage, and we heard the boats start off upriver.

DECEMBER

La Plu – 'eclipses'

The air is saturated, fat drops falling from the high trees onto my tin roof in the cold early mornings. But the rain has stopped. River travel is delightful, fast and easy, the water clear. There are big prawns to be had, and the small boys grope for them under stones. One or two of the boys have goggles, and pursue the prawns across the riverbed. The prawns make succulent, savoury eating.

The rice harvest is now in full swing, and the people I want to talk to are difficult to find. They don't return home in the evenings but stay out in field huts, and the villages are half empty. Children stay with their parents at the fields for weeks on end, and some of the schools have given up and closed.

There are other harvests. Older villages like Lama have areca groves, and at Bombshell and Black Turtle the sesame crop is in, innumerable minute black and blond seeds placed in basket-presses built into the sides of the houses, crushed with levers. The compressed pulp goes to the pigs, the oil to Thailand; there are Thai traders on the river now. At Riverside school they are clearing the compound of rogue vegetation and refencing it; scores of children mill about after lunch trimming bamboos and grubbing up weeds.

Walking through the forest and over the hills to the western valley, the track is still wet and the leeches bad. Wearing flipflops, you can at least see the leeches as soon as they latch on to your feet, and can flick them off before they do much damage. Fragrance tells me that she has never seen a leech – which shows how much walking in the forest she does. The slippery mud slows hill climbing. True Love has taught me a Burmese tongue-twister about sleek-coated squirrels skipping across mud:

> *Shoon baw, shint pye,*
> *shint mwe, shoon malu.*
> Over mud, squirrel run,
> squirrel fur, mud none.

Thick rain clouds like iron pyrites hang over Betelwood, low and lumpish. White Rock says, 'We believe that clouds like this mean there is heavy fighting somewhere'.

JANUARY 1987

Tha lay – 'Searching'

The harvest drags, the Karen are getting tired and bored. The men suffer hernias from lifting heavy rice sacks, and the women fret at the rats threatening the granaries.

We have brilliant sun by day, and the nights are warming up. Water still condenses on the tin roof before dawn, falling from the corrugated edge and drilling a neat row of small holes in the dirt below, as though the house were standing on a rectangle of perforated paper, like a postage stamp.

The level of the river is falling fast, and rocks are now a problem. But, with the road dry and open, we can buy in forty-four-gallon drums of petrol from Thailand.

Only the tin miners don't appreciate the weather. In the high river valleys behind Barterville, the streams no longer have sufficient water in them to wash out the ore. The seasonal mine labourers are redundant.

January 8: It is winter; it grows dark at 5.30 p.m. Everything is rapidly drying out. Bartholomew's compound is swept and shovelled clean of dust and leaves by the children each morning before breakfast. They burn small fires, before drifts of rubbish form. As leaves fall, as banana plants dry and shred, vines and creepers shrivel and subside, the village becomes more visible. How close the neighbours have been all this time!

Building of the new official guesthouse will begin shortly, as soon as the prisoners are free for the labour. They must get on with it. The building season does not last much longer because the bamboo is desiccating. It becomes hard and brittle, difficult to work; the chopper blade skids and bounces on the surface instead of slicing in.

I spent an hour towards evening sitting on the beach at Bombshell with True Love, listening to a curious musketry in the forest.

> 'It's the bamboo', he said. 'Now it is dead and dry, and as the air inside expands, it splits and cracks open. We're hot out here in the sun, but it will be very cold tonight. You see those?'
>
> He pointed to high-altitude ice clouds.
>
> 'We call those fish-scale clouds. The fish will be spawning in the river tonight.'

The massed bamboos, once bursting sprays of green rockets, are a sad sight now, an untidy jumble of dead pic-a-stics tumbling over each other onto the shingle beaches. The forest is collapsing, the great ferns yellow and sag in the sun, dragged down by a weight of stiff creepers. Sitting on the beach we can hear the small deer barking. In the high trees there are pendulous bees' nests; the swarms cross the river in clouds with a deep electrical hum. Honey collecting begins now, the young men climbing above one hundred feet up the exposed and featureless trunks on absurd scaffolds of single bamboos pinned to the tree with short wooden pegs. Not for anything would I do that – the scaffolds sometimes fail – but the honey is excellent, with a citron scent, and sells for anything up to B.40 for a litre bottle.

The *beho* (wild kapok) trees are fruiting, the pods swelling rapidly and darkening. There are Karen songs in which the *beho* tree figures as an image of the hard working life of the Karen, for its curiously sparse foliage that gives little shelter.

January 18: On the road to Thailand that leads up behind Barterville, vast expanses of black netting have been slung between tall trees, placed there by Thais to trap songbirds – there being not many left in the Thai forests. Thai traders come down this road in old Dodge (pron. *dodgy*) trucks, supplying the Barterville retailers and buying up all the sesame, honey and live monitor lizards the Karen can offer, while the season lasts.

I can distinguish a few varieties of drongo, dark and glossy birds, some with long pendant tail feathers hanging behind, two bare wires with feather buttons at the ends. There are supposedly six or seven 'common resident' species here. They are, says the book, 'Noisy; loud discordant chattering varied with melodious and harsh songs.'[2] True Love elaborates:

> 'The drongo once had proper tail feathers, you know. But it is a bird which likes very much the sound of its own voice; it can never stop talking. One day two drongos with fine long tails full of feathers, one male and one female, landed on the ground together and they began to show off to each other by chattering and singing, talking so much that neither noticed the white ants eating away their tail feathers, all except that little button at the end. The children of these two birds and all the drongos ever since have had those stupid tails.'

January 22: With the harvest ended, trade now peaks. Large herds of cattle are being driven out through the forest to Thailand. More refugees are being forced the same way: the Burmese Army is reported to have begun burning villages in the south – easier now that the thatch has dried out, presumably. My long-planned boat trip far downriver has had to be scrubbed; the Colonel says he can no longer guarantee my safety, the Burmese being within striking distance. Upstream, the KNLA assault on Burmese positions seems never to have happened. Are they going to spend the whole campaigning season on the defensive?

FEBRUARY

Tay Ku – 'Cutting'

River travel never ceases entirely but, as the water level falls off, so does boat traffic. You cannot go far without grounding on gravel or scraping over rocks. Experienced boatmen know the channels through the rapids, but no one can remember every rock. Between February and April wise Karen walk. From Bartholomew's house it is now possible to wade right across the river.

The heat is intense and unpleasantly dry. The roads are stirred up by cattle, flocks of schoolchildren and pickup trucks, and the fine dust irritates my nose until it pours mucus which the heat promptly dries and cakes; very uncomfortable.

The *beho* (kapok) trees, although quite bare of leaves, are now heavily laden with fruit, hundreds of heavy brown drops about to fall from the branches, expanding in the heat.

February 3: Scrub fires have started near Headquarters. Karen talk of hunters being careless with matches, but fires start on the remotest hills; many of these must be spontaneous and I find them described as such in the old books. Mostly it is just leaf debris that burns, the curling lines of small flame inching quietly through the forest which before them is fawn and ochre, behind them grey-black ash. Stout trees are singed but unharmed; even saplings survive. At the end of this month larger, controlled fires will begin, as the Karen start to burn off fields for next season. It is a matter of delicate timing; they must leave the forest that they've cut long enough for it to be tinder dry, but they cannot risk saturation by the first of the monsoon rainstorms. February seems very early to begin, but the onset of rain can, they tell me, go a full month either way.

Meanwhile, our chickens are being decimated. A wild cat has been carrying them off from houses near the hospital and, at the other end of the village, fowl pest is rampant. William is resigned to losing all his birds: 'It happens every year. Mine run around with their heads at a funny angle, or just fall asleep and don't wake up. We eat them if we can kill them before they die.'

MARCH

Thwee Kaw – 'Burning'

I asked William for a story about forest fires:

FIRE AND DISOBEDIENCE

A wealthy Karen once had a disobedient son. The man wanted the best for his boy and found him a pretty girl to marry who also happened to be rich. They prepared for the wedding but, at the last moment, the son refused to go through with it. He set off travelling instead. Coming to a poor village, he met and fell in love with a young girl. He brought her home. His father was horrified: 'She's poor, she's thick, she's lazy! Don't do this!' he cried, but his son insisted that he was going to marry the girl.

'She'll be the ruin of you', said his father sadly, but he paid for the wedding. They built a bamboo house in the forest for the young couple, and the father presented them with a large sum of money.

But the girl was indeed lazy. She never swept the compound or under the house, and dead leaves built up in heaps. Eventually there was the inevitable fire and the house was destroyed. The son applied to his father for more money, and they built a finer, stronger, hardwood house.

Life was fine during the rains. In the summer the forest dried out and fires began on the hills. The young man saw these and thought he'd take precautions. He went into town and bought several large clay water jars; he was going to place them round the house, full, in readiness. But when he reached home and took them off the elephant, he found that they were all broken. He could see the fires on the hillside getting closer, so he went back to market and bought tin buckets – but when he rushed home with these he found that they were rusty and full of holes. Now the fires were closing in, but he was exhausted.

'I can't do any more until I've eaten', he said to his wife; but she had done nothing about preparing food, and by the time he got his dinner it was too late. The fire caught their house and burned it down again.

The son and his wife moved to town. Once more his father provided money, and the next house was built of brick. With the remainder of his money the son bought two trading ships, employed the girl's father as his agent and sent them off to trade. But one ship was lost in a tempest, and the body of his wife's father was washed up on shore. The expedition made a loss. As a last, desperate throw, the son loaded the ship again and, taking his wife with him, set sail – but the ship was wrecked. Husband and wife were found clinging to a spar, drowned. The boy's mother died of a broken heart and his old father went mad with grief.

William and I agree that the morality of this tale is difficult. The boy was disobedient, but he married for love, not money.

The heat still grows, but the sky is overcast. The river is now so low that each night in my hammock I listen to it scuffling over the rocky gravel of the shallows by the school. The water is full of fish. In the absence of fresh vegetables (until the rains come), Karen energies go into fishing. I am sick of grilled perch.

There is still a thin strip of greenery at the river's edge, but the hillsides have turned to pinks and powder-grey. The trees are now full of hornbills – or perhaps they were previously just screened by leaves. Throughout the hills, swidden fires have been getting out of control. The Karen have a reputation for taking care, for cutting wide firebreaks so as to prevent wasteful destruction of the forest, but they're not doing too well here. Untidy stacks of smoke rise from the valleys on the Burmese side.

March 19: The first fire on this bank, on a hillside to the south of the village. By day it is merely a thin grey plume but at night the line of flame can be seen clearly as it moves across, stretching unbroken from top to bottom. Fragrance sits by me in the evening on Bartholomew's verandah, staring broodily at the fire.

Two days later, hills and flat-lands alike are burning. I cannot see what is to stop the fire entering the village but no one seems concerned. William says, 'We cut a break sometimes', without much interest.

Last night they hacked down all the vegetation between the hospital and the river, and then fired it. They nearly destroyed the kitchens and the drug store, and in the shop nearby the family were stuffing valuables into tin boxes ready to carry off to safety – but the fire abated as quickly as it caught.

March 14: Today was more spectacular still. They burnt off ten acres of flat-land between the prison and the church. I thought it was gunfire: a tremendous barrage of cracks and reports, an explosion of flame from the heaped debris lying in the sun. A bole of black smoke shot up over the village, intense fire sucking for air below. Squirrels careered about the fields, dazed and distressed as their homes were carbonised. Gangs of opportunist birds circled the smoke stack snatching insects – what a death! Woken, toasted, tossed into the air and swallowed by a drongo at 500 feet.[3]

I took photographs of men walking through the smouldering fields, in heat so intense that I could barely approach the margins.

By night the fires are beautiful. From Bartholomew's verandah, Fragrance and I watch a burning tree near the football pitch. The tree is dead and hollow, and the fire has caught inside the decapitated trunk. A fierce draft rushes up through it, a jet of sparks gushing from the top as though from an enormous Roman candle.

There are a dozen fires on the east ridge, vertical lines of flame in a slow march past the village in the dark. The lads sit out in the open, smoking cigars, strumming guitars and watching. Great Lake says that when the fire has passed, you can find roasted monkeys on the ground in the ash; they are paralysed by fear, shit themselves and fall out of the trees into the flames.

March 18: The Karen are preparing vegetable gardens, ready for the first rains: cleaning the soil, building pig fences, planting. A delicate point of judgement affects the siting. There is good ground on the riverbank – convenient if the rains prove as erratic as usual. But if too low, the plot will be washed out by the first flash flood.

Great Lake and I are building a store hut for the new house in which we'll be able to keep the Rotax and my two petrol drums. I wonder about tin-roofed petrol-stores and sun. The *beho* trees, on which the pods are opening with the first white fluff falling – they give no shade at all.

But the heat makes work difficult. The water is hot in the pottery storage jars (bought in from Thailand, decorated with dragons) and the inside of my black boat scalds bare feet. Almost any drink is refreshing. Village shops will send a boy up a coconut tree, cut you a fresh fruit and charge for sparing you the effort. As end of term exams approach, the *Boarders* can be found revising anywhere that's cool – lying on the cement floor of the hospital, or sitting in the river with their books.

March 24: Great Lake and I worked on the petrol store all morning. It is nearly finished, but the drums were still in the laboratory in the shade. At noon the heat was intolerable and we stopped. I sat reading on the verandah. At about 2.30 p.m. a fire started – someone burning off swidden to our south. The girls watched it nervously. When the flames broke through into a neighbouring field, they ran into *Boarders* to carry out their tin trunks. Sam and Great Lake paced about, watching the fire; it was out of control, the wind driving it straight at us. My roof is tin; one half of *Boarders* and most of the neighbours' are thatched. People climbed up, ready for sparks.

The fire moved rapidly across the field towards us. The only gap was the narrow road to the sawmill. The moment the fire jumped that, there was pandemonium. Sam grabbed my *parang* and began frantically hacking at dry vegetation. Some girls cut themselves fire-beaters of small banana trunks with the end frayed out, while others rushed to the river with buckets. The neighbours were in most danger, the flames surrounding their highly flammable home. Beating frantically, filling our mouths with water and blowing it onto the flames, we saved that house but by then the flames were approaching from two more sides, jumping from clump to clump of dry banana leaves, rushing through desiccated vine entanglements, crawling steadily across the ground towards not only my house and *Boarders* but also the laboratory and 400 litres of petrol.

We fought it for an hour. We seemed to have won, and relaxed – and then at once the fire burst out almost alongside the laboratory and the desperate beating and spraying recommenced, while Great Lake and I rolled the petrol drums away towards the riverbank.

It took all afternoon for the fire to die down. By 9 p.m. it was subdued, but small pockets glowed and sometimes tried to break out. We watched from our various verandahs, sending out control parties at signs of unrest. The petrol stays under Great Lake's house for now; the flames came within twenty feet of the new store. In the morning we cleared all remaining rubbish into neat and isolated heaps, burnt it off and felt thankful.

A sharp storm put out the hill fires, and has turned the river opaque brown, with a grubby scum of leafmould and ash. My boat was near-filled; the Rotax petrol tank has rain in it. I was sitting in Moscs' house and we were caught unawares when the rain began. It came in horizontally on a high wind, against which a Karen house, with half its sides open, is quite defenceless. Within seconds there was a chaos of wet papers blown into every corner. Outside, the deep, powdery dust drank up the water and turned to instant mud. A pickup which at one end of the football pitch was driving on a dry road, skidded, tried to manoeuvre and spun down to its axles before it reached the opposite goalposts. The leaves of the banana trees shredded, snapping and fluttering ferociously like the war banners of *samurai* cavalry. In True Love's house, with its inadequate single-layer walls, everything was soaked – cigars on the shelf, calendars on the wall, blankets in the bedroom. The water overwhelmed the ditches round this house; we now have a lake beneath us in which the ducks delight, and in the evening an astonishing roar of small frogs began, which thrilled them to their souls. All the air-raid shelters have filled with pale slime.

I have an umbrella, but Great Lake wages a campaign against it. It has alternate green and black panels and he calls it a woman's, even a *maiden's* umbrella. He says he won't be seen piloting any boat in which there is a white man under a maiden's umbrella – besides which he says umbrellas obscure his view of the rocks and also catch the wind, making the boat unmanageable.

With the storm, the river rose a foot overnight, then subsided as fast. The rapids are still impossibly difficult and many boatmen refuse to travel, unwilling to wreck their boats. But there is wind and thunder each afternoon; the river will soon be filling again. People talk of the mosquitoes breeding in the rainwater that will shortly be collecting everywhere, of the increase in malaria that will certainly follow. They are looking out their ragged mosquito nets. Yesterday evening the earth in Bartholomew's compound split open and for ten minutes a dense column of termites twizzled into the air on outsize wings, hatched by the rain.

The rain brings out less welcome livestock – the centipedes. Eight or nine inches long with legs like brackets, they squirm poisonously through the mud. A second storm caught me out visiting towards dusk, and trapped me at True Love's with flipflops and a torch whose batteries failed as I began to slide homewards – but not before I'd seen half a dozen centipedes. The sensation of that warm mud, so loathsomely populated, brought me to a near-tearful standstill. I took off my flipflops and ran – and I've not been bitten yet.

Also unwelcome, a plague of small black caterpillars has moved into *Boys Boarders*, obliging the inmates to shift into hammocks in the kindergarten.

Lastly, the Burmese – they have attacked and sacked Wali, a KNLA base and Township Headquarters in the north, destroying a new hospital in the process. This campaign season is going badly.

APRIL

La Kli – 'Yams'

April, they tell me, is the 'Karen month' – too hot to do anything but eat and sleep. Not at *Boarders*, though. Every day the girls go to their vegetable field again, digging out roots and rubbish and burning small fires.

Through the heavy matt ash that covers all the fields, vegetation is resurfacing. The little *Shy Princess* sensitive plants have sprouted, tiny seedlings in a green haze an inch above the black. On the paths down to the river, overhanging branches dangle new shoots in the bather's face. Burnt banana clumps sprout again from the base, and the village is full of splendid lilies, rich creamy orange, red and purples. The Karen love to have flower gardens around their houses, with wild and cultivated roses, the latter brought in from Thailand and sometimes grown over trellises as though in a Penang suburb.

The *beho* seeds are falling at last. Hanging high up in the sun the big pods, six or eight inches long, dry out and begin to split, then drop. When they hit the ground they break open and the kapok is released. Packed tight in woollen curls inside, it springs out as a ball of ethereal fluff like a dandelion clock. With a single black seed at its centre it bowls along the ground in the breeze. Less perfect specimens scud about in white fluffy lumps. It looks as though, somewhere in the forest, someone has put too much detergent in a washing machine.

Village women have been stitching pillowcases in readiness. At *Boarders* part of every afternoon is spent reclining in KNLA hammocks, embroidering. Waterlilly has completed one with a yellow rose at its centre and 'Home Sweet Home' in red. Charlie, nursing her migraines out of the sun, has beneath *Boarders* an old half petrol drum full of kapok which she fluffs out using a long cane with a bamboo propeller at the end, spinning it into the white fleece. The other girls take handfuls and stuff them into pillows.

Every group of houses has *beho* trees nearby, and there is kapok everywhere. Thai lorries come and buy it in the pod for a pittance – B.1 per kilo. People knock the lower pods down with broom handles and long bamboos, while Vermilion persuaded two boys to risk their necks climbing to the higher branches. Hard pods rained and rattled on the tin roof. She rewarded them with rice cakes, a pink drink and a cigar each.

When the *beho* trees have been stripped, they are pollarded, to make for vigorous and accessible growth next year. Sound branches are posted in the ground in rows. Six weeks later you have a new tree.

There are many other seeds that I don't begin to recognise. One, dropping from a tall gaunt tree, is a most elaborate structure, a green bell from which hang three pods that split and curl open like desiccated orchids, jettisoning little helicopter seeds. Another, which also grows and dries high up, is a firm brown case that falls hard, breaking and scattering black seeds. The case is covered in fine fur; if you pick it up, clusters penetrate and irritate the palm of your hand, like glass fibre. Then there are tree beans, tamarinds, jackfruits and faecal-scented durian. All of them are ripe and ready to germinate in the rains.

The whole forest is pullulating, rushing into leaf. The village, having been visible for the last two months, will disappear into the greenery and become close and claustrophobic again. But there is attrition too. The winds that blow most afternoons bring down the large trees; they have shallow, inadequate root systems and topple easily. One came down by the middle school, its top branches smashing part of the roof.

'I knew it would come down!' said Ruth, furious. 'I've been telling them for weeks, and now we have to repair our school!' But half the village is in the same danger.

Bartholomew delights in the new growth, and shows me medicinal plants each day; each one he calls '*pwakenyaw* vitamin', good for this, good for that. One fruit cures cancer. A tree bark is excellent for malaria. A certain 'red grass' is taken for strength. Dry it, grind it with chilli, mix with honey and take one teaspoonful three times daily. It protects against diabetes also.

The rice is shooting, and Bartholomew's family have left it very late to plant their maize. 'Should have done it a month ago', he said, 'but I haven't had one free day.' So we did it together, five children, Vermilion and myself, weeding, drilling and sowing. The older children went ahead spacing out holes with a *parang*, while Bi, Pu and Monkey followed dropping three seeds into each one. We knew that we were late and hurrying and not doing a neat job. It was a hot and somewhat bad-tempered afternoon.

Perhaps it's the weather. Now the atmosphere is damp and electrical, and the sky heavy. There is a short hard storm each afternoon. The days are much longer, light at five and dark at seven. In the early morning, condensation forms on the underside of Bartholomew's tin roof and drips into my face and hammock. This would not matter were it not that, after years of wood fires in the kitchen, the roof is coated with a thick layer of resinous soot; what drips onto me is a viscous brown liquid that stains my blanket. Embarrassed, Fragrance whisks it down to the river.

April 18: What I need is a charcoal evaporating refrigerator, for cold drinking water and film storage. Everything is here – timber, charcoal, chicken-wire easily available just over the border. I explained the principle to True Love and Bartholomew, Great Lake and Sam; a tray of water on top feeds into the charcoal-filled wire walls by means of cotton rag wicks. The charcoal drinks up water, and evaporation rapidly cools the interior. Neither Bartholomew nor Sam believe a word of it. Great Lake is cautiously interested; if it works, he says, he'll make one too and sell cold drinks. True Love the scientist is ecstatic at the idea and wants one now. Bartholomew muttered, 'Does he want me to make this nonsense for him?' No, I shall make it myself and amaze them.

MAY

De Nya – 'Lilies'

For the Thai traders the season is ending, as the roads will deteriorate rapidly from now on. Thais more or less resident in Kawthoolei in the dry months are abandoning their bamboo shops to be rotted and reclaimed by the forest, and are taking their valuables and families out to Thailand while pickups can still move. Several of the Barterville stores have closed. Great Lake and Lili are trying to put together enough capital to buy a full car load of stock, to last their shop until ... when, October? No one is ever quite sure how long the rains will last.

And no one is sure how the river will rise or fall. The rain may be here, or twenty miles upstream. The water can rise thirty feet in as many hours. Great Lake watches it carefully, sometimes having to retie the black boat two or three times a day, higher or lower.

May 9: The forest has come to life, a fresh green salad with a glass snake sliding through it. In the midst of the new growth, dramatic trees stand apparently quite dead, all grey, leafless, as though they alone find regeneration impossible. The sap has only risen half-way up their 150-foot trunks.

Cattle everywhere now; something to do with the new grazing, perhaps. They can't be left to themselves in the forest, but they are not always welcome in the villages; they wreck the gardens and foul the paths. At Bombshell a sign on the green in front of the church informs herdsmen that 'cattle may be grazed here free for one day, but will be subject to a poll tax of one *baht* per day thereafter'.

At Black Turtle, Great Lake and I came upon a pathetic sight – a cow, obviously dying, lying on its side in the scrub at the edge of the village. No one knew what had happened to it. 'Perhaps a snake bite', they suggested. The cow did not move, nor did it complain; it just lay dying. In the morning, when they butchered it, they found that it had killed itself by eating someone's jeans.

A traditional Karen cow, not recognising denim for the hazard that it is.

Another new-fangled peril – the headman of Black Turtle is going to spray his fields with a sack of 2,4-D – a defoliant that made its name in Vietnam. I begged him at least to put the sack, and his tank of paraquat, on a shelf out of reach of his babies.

May 14: In the old seasonal cycle, the onset of May rains brought hectic activity to the logging camps as the 'teak wallahs' and their Karen elephant crews struggled to have the logs in position in tributary streams, ready for flash floods to lift them into the main rivers and on, down to the plains. It was a task that went ill with mosquitoes and malaria. Now that the timber extractors work more with bulldozers and trucks than with elephants, by road more than by river, they can operate to political, not climatic seasons. They are here now, with caterpillars and chainsaws. We can hear them a long way off. The network of roads is extended week by week. By each new track, felled logs are stacked, numbers and letters painted onto their sawn ends. On the riverbank at Moha, Thai foresters camp under red-and-yellow plastic sheeting, trapping birds in their spare time and attended by a detachment of KNDO militia.

With both Thais and Burmese on their territory, the Karen are extremely nervous. To complicate matters, we hear that a battalion of the Singaporean Army is training on the Thai side of the border. Having no forest of their own, they rent a patch of Thailand to rehearse the invasion of Malaysia.

The Burmese are now not many miles from us upstream. As the roads collapse and the tributaries flood, making movement along the riverbanks treacherous, we hope that campaigning will pause until the monsoon passes. So, in past years, it would have. The recent difference is that the Burmese have not pulled back with the rains but have dug themselves into position, allowing the Karen very little breathing space at all.

However, I have finished the refrigerator. A solid structure of red hardwood, with double mesh walls packed with charcoal, the door similar, and a galvanised water tray on top with cotton wicks tucked into the charcoal. Today it has been thoroughly soaked, and my first two trial bottles of drinking water placed inside. Soldiers, nurses, children, KNLA wireless operators, village women and Departmental dignitaries inspect it and ask me, 'What does it do?' I explain as simply as I can. They nod, and walk round the house. They pretend to be looking at my lilies but actually they are saying to each other, 'Yes, but what does it *do*?'

I long for cool water. The clammy heat sends me to the river twice a day. On river journeys we regard all rapids as an excuse for a swim. Before getting into the boat I place my sunhat, full of water, upon my head. Great Lake declined a similar offer.

May 20: Marauding squalls, compact lumps of black cloud on a blue sky, raiding selected houses. You can walk round the cloudbursts. The hot ground steams when the rain passes. I am permanently damp; my sandals have rotted away, my camera is rusting and my shirts are growing black spots of mould. Sitting in a bamboo house in a hot and humid storm, it is easy to believe that you hear it decay about you. When the wasps are at work on the bamboo, you can.

Riverside is beautiful just now. The new vegetation doesn't yet obscure the views or block the paths. There are favourite evening walks, for which they have a phrase, *leh halokweh* – 'play-walk'. One good route takes you through fields towards the ridge, past flower gardens, fruit groves and fishponds. At the pond there is a curious sight; from bamboo fishnet posts standing in the water, rows of leathery bags hang. They look like slightly deflated morris-men's bladders, and appear to be glued to the posts. They are packed with frogs' eggs.

My own walk takes me downstream, behind the women's jail and through the scraggy backyards of middle-ranking militia families, with steep little ravines and the sinking wrecks of last year's houses, already half-submerged in flowering vines, many of the ruins now being used as frames for growing pumpkins. Bartholomew's own garden is well stocked with new vegetables, vicious little chillis, fresh bananas and fast-swelling papaya. Our pigs and ducks fatten happily.

May 26: Bartholomew is hardly ever home at present; he struggles both to maintain the flow of supplies and assistance to the southern refugees, and to hold together his fragile little organisation here. Sustaining the refugees keeps him up at Headquarters half the week. His future staff, at *Boarders*, require almost as much effort. He sleeps there or in the laboratory several nights a week, and by day supervises re-thatching, re-walling, gardening, training, even the absurd cycle of air-raid shelter digging. He is sixty years-old and he is nearing exhaustion.

He rarely sees his own family, who are often sick. We have disturbed nights; one or other child has a fever, is moaning and crying for more blankets. Vermilion is away trading, so the household falls on Fragrance's shoulders. She teaches all day, runs the home in the evening. Her small siblings could not be sweeter or more cooperative, but she too looks very weary after a night of comforting a malarial little sister.

At night the scrub is brilliant with lime-bright, green-white fireflies – one of the few silent insects in Burma.

JUNE

La Nwee – 'Seventh month'

I cannot get the refrigerator to work properly. The charcoal won't soak up the water from the wicks. A few drops trickle over the surface of the coals but mostly they are bone dry. Hence there is no evaporation and no cooling. Great Lake inspects it daily, doing nothing to keep the amused scepticism off his face. Passing soldiers ask him, 'What does it do?' and he tells them, quite accurately, relishing their incredulity. I shall try increasing the number of wicks and breaking the charcoal into smaller pieces.

Heavy rain. The river rises steadily, with no falling back between-times. The riverside gardens have vanished, as have most of the bathing beaches. We are forced to swim from halfway up the banks, off soft brown soil or low branches unpleasantly populated by ants. Better to use somebody's boat as a diving platform – and the *Boarders* use mine. Great Lake objects, 'I tell them I don't like it, but still they wash their clothes on our boat and you know what happens? If they use bleach it weakens the wood, and then we will hit a rock and break apart!'

But you cannot wash clothes on a mudbank. Or anywhere else, really, with the water in its present state, thick with silt and topped with debris on which ants stand marooned until the girls flick them off, to see how far they can run on water before a fish gets them. I rinse myself and my clothes in rain from the large jars by the petrol store. The front room is strung with yellow nylon cords hung with damp shirts.

Now the rapids are dangerous again; the mass of water hurtling over them gathers into waves that swamp and overturn boats. Coming upstream is slow, hard work. You creep by the banks but side-currents and whirlpools tug at the prow threatening to send you sideways into the flood stream. Journey time down to Barterville is halved, the return trip doubled. It was in water like this that Bartholomew's first wife and her children drowned; there are victims every year. Having risen far above its normal banks the water invades the forest; the margin of beaches, gravel and rock has vanished and the milk-tea river and the dense greens are entangled. We go boating through the tree tops.

June 5: Those tall grey trees, seemingly dead among the re-growth, are just coming into leaf weeks after everything else. On the ground there's another form of new life; it is baby snake season. Only inches long, they squiggle on the tracks. Some put on a show of ferocity. I have been confronted by a micro-viper, snapping dramatically at me with a strike range of perhaps four inches. At the roadside, hanging in shrubs, was the most beautiful snake I've yet seen, a metre or more in length but whip-thin and a pale olive green in colour, with a bulbous head like a spring onion, translucently delicate with a long thin snout.

Silver's baby is almost due. Alarmed that the road might be impassable at the crucial moment, True Love took her to the border early. Two days later I walked up also, in heavy rain. Out on the mud there were land-crabs of soft greys and magenta. Then I saw what at first I took to be a forest-lobster crossing my path, eight inches long and jet black – the most revolting, monstrous scorpion I ever wish to meet. There were more further on. As usual, I was wearing flipflops – which, indeed, I was about to take off because of the mud. My prize possession at Riverside is a pair of wellington boots.

This refrigerator simply doesn't work. The hardwood charcoal absorbs nothing, and the walls remain dry as dust. The only soul to appreciate my construction is Great Lake's dog, who likes to sit inside it. Otherwise it is useless.

I tried swaddling the entire thing in an old blanket in the hope that it might be more absorbent. That didn't work either. Charlie, coming back from the *Boarders* gardens, leaned on her hoe and watched me lashing the blanket down over the box. She asked courteously, as they all do, '*Thera* Jo, what does it do?' I felt ashamed and foolish and could only shrug in reply.

JULY

La Ho – 'Eighth month'

Walking with Bartholomew to a mining village up in the hills; the air is a sweet mix of cloud and woodsmoke in the high leaf-canopy. The forest is full of sound – water dripping from leaf to leaf, and the chugging of diesel pumps at the few mines now working; the streams are full and the mines working flat out.

It has actually rained very little recently. At Riverside the girls are kept busy bringing tins of water for their more delicate vegetables. Great Lake says he is glad he didn't bother planting this year. There is no possibility of carrying water a mile through the forest to water Vermilion's maize field.

July 7: Two Shoes and Janice gave me a lift back from Thailand. They are no longer working in Kawthoolei itself, but just on the border. We stopped off to inspect.

They are still interested in bamboo, but not for basket-weaving. They are taking whole bamboos to supply to builders in Thailand for use as scaffolding. The economics are tight. They hire ten-wheel trucks, and that costs B.3,000 a time. They have to pay the Thai Army B.500 on every load, 'and all the way to Ratburi we are paying the police B.20 here, B.30 there. We make perhaps B.1,500 on each trip and try for three trips a week. We think we've just fixed another deal to make toothpicks and chopsticks for Taiwan.'

At the bamboo-cutter's camp the men sleep on small bamboo platforms under plastic sheeting, like the loggers by the river. Janice delivered fresh vegetables and *Fansidar*, an anti-malarial, all wage-deductible. Although we were only a mile from the border, none of the workforce were Karen.

'These are all very poor men', said Two Shoes. 'I recruited them in north-east Thailand. They are very pleased to have this work. I gave up trying to get Karen. I don't know what it is with those people – too proud, maybe.'

There's no room for Karen workers now. There are two other cutting parties in the area, and not enough bamboo. 'There have been arguments', says Janice.

July 13: The floods have passed, the river maintains a steady high. The forest margins are tidier, the old bamboo gone, pushed over by new growth and grabbed by the water. A muddy smudge in the trees marks the high water line, as does a quantity of flotsam and jetsam in the upper branches, including one or two boats. Mary Kingsley remarked the propensity of West African boats for climbing trees; they do it here too.

The omnipresent mud reduces walking pace by half as we pick our route and try not to lose our flipflops. Now that heavy rain has been replaced by drizzle, we have a new obsession: the efficiency of each household's water-collecting system of bamboo guttering and pipes. People weigh the state of the sky against the levels in their jars and shift tubes quickly so as to catch everything – or be forced to use the brown river. Everyone knows that mosquitoes breed in the jars. Just one or two smarter families have tied netting over the necks.

In Thailand they are worried; it hasn't rained enough to flood the rice fields properly. Here the skies are heavy with unrealised deluge, brilliantly lit at sunset, beautifully turbulent. At night I sit on the verandah listening to *Parsifal* through headphones and watching the banana leaves waving, broad surfaces of hard black.

The cold and damp are returning. Karen with cattle build shelters and light fires for them to stand by; there are three or four on the riverside track, like Christmas cribs.

AUGUST

La Klu – 'Shut in' by the rains

Sick of my own company, I'm moving back to Bartholomew's house. They say there is still no rain in Thailand. In some northern regions they speak of drought. At Riverside it was torrential for two days; being full moon, everyone said it would rain all month. But it hasn't happened. What if the Thai harvest fails and rice prices go up dramatically? Kawthoolei has to buy.

Large numbers of monitor lizards have appeared; both they and their eggs make good eating except when cooked by Thais. Great Lake and I delivered Vermilion to Durianville for a week of trading. There were three Thais there, who had been searching unsuccessfully for aromatic eaglewood. They cooked us all a lizard curry, lit with chillis in the Thai manner. The Karen couldn't swallow it.

August 15: The Burmese, having held their positions in the forest when the rains started, are again harassing villagers. Bartholomew received a report this morning, detailing continued 'low intensity' pressure: 'At the village of K, the Burmese burnt the houses of the following families: (*six names*). One man, Saw Tha Nyah Eh, was shot dead. All livestock driven off . . .'

August 22: In such a humid atmosphere, the water would never have evaporated off the charcoal anyway. The refrigerator was misconceived from the start.

SEPTEMBER

Si Muh – 'Little sun'

Monday evening. Bartholomew is away somewhere, sticking fingers into dykes. Vermilion is away somewhere else, trading. So Fragrance is looking after everyone again. After school she cooks, irons clothes, attends to the pigs, ducks and water containers, gets her siblings to bed and moves amongst them with a lamp, tucking the blankets snugly. After which she attempts to sit with me at the verandah table and prepare lessons. She usually falls asleep. I wake her and push her off to bed. Full moon again, and drumming at Lama.

I'm tired of all this now, tired of the rain and the strains that I cannot properly share with them. I'm leaving, to spend a month looking for Karen in Thailand, where there is now an official drought and a state of emergency.

Interlude: from the Kok river

I went to North Thailand for a few weeks of walking in the hills, looking for Karen. There are tens of thousands of them along the border with Burma, but I decided to go elsewhere, to find communities well away from the war. I thought it might look different from afar.

The Kok river runs from west to east across the extreme north of Thailand, neatly snipping off the Thai sector of the Golden Triangle, heart of the world's heroin trade. This was beautiful but wild country not so long ago. Carl Bock travelled here in 1881:

The River Mekok itself is little more than a mountain-stream, filled with huge stones, between which the water eddies with a gurgling sound, making the navigation difficult for the shallow canoes. The scenery along the banks is very beautiful, hills of 400 to 500 feet rising abruptly from the water, thickly clad with trees and other vegetation. During the day I saw more wild animal-life than I had hitherto seen in any consecutive twenty-four hours.[1]

Now, from a village near the town of Fang, powerboats packed with tourists skid down to Chiang Rai in three hours, past settlements where, if only they could find a way of getting the boats to stop, they would love to sell you a Coke. I decided to take the regular water-bus, get out half-way and start walking south into the hills. A German woman in the boat thought the idea superbly courageous: 'But don't you worry! You just tell yourself that you can do it, and I'm sure you can!'

I disembarked at a small trading and police-post. Akha women, dressed in black and silver, came forward to sell bead-work. Another boat swerved in to the landing stage behind us and disgorged sweaty Italian men with paunches covered in cameras but no shirts, which is illegal in Thailand. Besieged by the little Akha women, they whooped and shouted with laughter, then clamoured for Cola at the shop. After the boats had gone it was very peaceful. A young policeman found me a room to stay in while bewailing floods that had spoiled his flowerbeds. Extraordinary homemade vehicles came through, engines mounted on bedsteads, laden with fermented tea – one of the cash crops of the hills. I began to walk in the cool, early next morning.

I had with me two maps. One, a sort of Thai Ordnance Survey, showed the way south to be along a small track over forbidding terrain, with hills up to 5,000 feet. The other, a chart of suggested walking routes, gave village and river names but little else. Neither prepared me for the reality of these hills, which is that they are desperately overcrowded.

Five hours of slog in drizzle up a steep muddy track, up to cloud level through blue-grey forest brought me to a place called Wawi. On the 'Ordnance Survey' map of 1973, Wawi does not exist; only a few nameless hamlets. Now there is a town. It has temples and tea factories, a large covered market and public washing tanks, shops and schools and a police presence and, at a guess, 3 or 4,000 inhabitants, mostly Yunnan Chinese (or, as the Thais call them, 'Galloping Haw'). Wawi has a cut-throat, frontier energy – the mud and unpainted clapboard buildings improved by the first gardens, the first traces of prettification.

I slept in a lean-to behind another shop. It was owned by a Yunnanese woman with a hard business eye, who sat in front of her store stitching new shoes. Hilltribe girls – Lahu, Karen and Lua – came to her with bags of maize which she measured out into a wooden bucket; then she dropped a few coins into the girls' hands. It was so few coins that the girls stood staring at them in speechless astonishment for a moment before drifting helplessly away.

The next day I crossed over to the Mae Suai river system, walking in bare feet – the mud being of a warm, sticky variety. The road rises and falls, through hills that until perhaps only thirty years ago were largely covered in virgin forest. Now there is hardly an unused slope. You can chart the progress of the swidden farmers year by year around the hills – this year's field rich with maturing rice, last year's under grass and thick camphor scrub, each previous year a little darker and denser.

I came to a Karen village. On the 1973 map it is simply marked *Ban Yang* – that is, 'Karen village'. I asked for the headman and ended up staying with the Catholic priest next door to a hostel for 'reclaimed animists'. He was called Bright Star, and to my delight he understood my southern Karen.

'My father came from Burma and we lived near Mae Sariang, not far from the border. But the land was getting crowded even then. We moved here ... when? It must be twenty-five years ago, to make new fields. Oh yes, I think about Kawthoolei. I have relatives there still. Maybe you know my cousin, *Thera* David at GHQ?'

No, but I'd certainly heard of him; he wrote much of the English language *KNU Bulletin*.

'I think sadly about my people in Burma, but I can't take my family back to a war. We are part of Thailand, my children were born here and have Thai papers. The problem is that there is so little land left here now that I wonder where we are going to make our fields next year. There are still people coming, Akha and Shan and more Karen, and where do they all think they're going to grow their rice? Maybe we'll end up going back to Burma just for the land.'

In the early evening, a stream of women came through the village, Akha and Karen. They were returning from a long, hot day of weeding the steep rice fields. Bright Star's wife came with them, exhausted, with hardly the energy to go and bathe. She lay down for half an hour while he cooked a pumpkin curry; then she sorted out lengths of fine Karen cloth that she'd woven herself, for me to use as blankets. I pottered about the village trying to work out where the Karen actually lived – a clump of thatched houses in a fenced enclave off the road. This 'Karen village' was dominated by anyone but Karen. Shan ran the two shops. There was also a smart new clinic, part of a 'hilltribe development project', funded by Germans, staffed by Thais.

I walked on, making detours to Akha and Lahu villages on the valley slopes. The next Karen community that I found was mostly animist, and I stayed overnight with the spirit priest and his wife. They ran a small shop and were not only tolerated by the official structure of Thailand; they were part of it. The shop was an official malaria information and mosquito control post.

Had escape from isolationist Burma broadened their world view? The priest was fascinated by my maps, never having looked at one closely before. He held it upside down to peer at it. His ignorance of the outside world was almost total; Russia and the USA blurred in his mind into 'the big country that is not China'. But he, too, kept in touch with Kawthoolei. He asked:

'Do you know *Thera* David at Headquarters?'

I obviously ought to. The priest had an up-to-date KNU calendar on his wall – but as he could read neither English nor Karen script, he could make little of it, pointing at the sentence KAREN NATIONAL DAY captioning a photograph and asking, 'Is that President Bo Mya's name?'

> 'Where did you get the calendar?'
> 'Oh, people pass through. Sometimes we can't understand the Karen they speak. Yours is simple.'
> 'Have you ever been to Kawthoolei?'
> 'No, never, but we hear all the news. We know what's going on.'
> 'Who do you get the news from?'
> 'The Thai Army.'

As usual, they fed me and found me blankets. The husband flatly insisted that I had the use of the official mosquito net. Karen hospitality never failed.

I walked on south down the Mae Suai river, through Arcadian valleys of broad rice and maize fields, fruit groves, thatched villages where Karen girls wore their traditional maidens' shifts over Thai jeans, by gentle hills and the remnants of forest, and the good works of the Thai–German Hilltribe Development Project.

Other Karen that I met that month knew Kawthoolei at first hand. There were ample reasons to go and visit. A young man at a guesthouse in Mae Hong Son told me about his family links:

> 'My father works the black market smuggling into Burma, and I sometimes help him. We take radios and food; that's what they want most. We meet all sorts of people going in and out. Lots of foreigners. I met a French doctor and a nurse going into Karenni two months ago. But mostly now it's Karen coming out. My country does what it can for them, gives them shelter, lets them build a village – but what else can we do?'
> 'Which do you call "my country"?'
> 'Thailand.'
> 'And you're Karen?'
> 'My mother is Karen from the border hills. My father is Burmese.'
> 'So what are you?'
> 'I am now Shan, because all the people here are Shan. Also I can speak Thai, because this is my country. My father sent me to school in Chiang Mai, and now I work for a logging company in an office in Chiang Mai. I wanted to be a doctor but I get drunk too easily. What I really wish to do is to go back to the forest and to live there like a Karen. You know, I have a little plot of land in town now – I'm going to build a jungle house on it!'

Another evening I found myself on the roof of a minibus with two young Karen. We were climbing high into dryer, starker hills near Mae Sariang, not far from the border. It was a dreadful road, cut by deep erosion gullies. But the sun was cool and soft, and we were riding over the top of the world.

One of the young men had a KNLA insignia tattooed onto his forearm. I touched it and said that I knew what it was.

> 'Oh yes', he grinned, 'I was in the KNLA for two years; my
> brother is still fighting – but the rest of my family is all out
> now.'
> 'Did you see much action?'
> 'Oh, lots of fighting! We could easily beat the Burmese but some-
> times they came round behind. I ... I got tired. I didn't want
> to be killed, so I came out. That is what usually happens. People
> come from the towns in Burma, they fight for a little while.
> Then they come out.'

No one really knows whether the Karen reached Thailand from Burma, or Burma from Thailand, or appeared independently in both, or indeed whether they 'came from' anywhere. What no one disputes is the direction in which they've gone ever since. Few Thai Karen enter Burma to stay; plenty of Burma Karen have fled to Thailand. The modern exodus began with the seventy years of wars across the mountains that started in 1752 – and it continues today.

They were generally well received, Thailand being, in the past, thinly populated. The Thais respected Karen forest skills, and found them to be invaluable border scouts. Although not given full citizenship until they came under the patronage of the reforming King Chulalongkorn in the late nineteenth century, they were not persecuted. Princes of northern Thailand took Karen as minor wives; other Karen made it into the lower ranks of the Siamese Civil Service.

In 1904, Lunet de Lajonquière described their position:

As regards those populations that are dependent on the Kingdom of Siam, there is a hierarchy with the Siamese at the top of the social ladder and the Kariengs at the bottom. They all live quite content with their lot, moving in their proper spheres with some degree of independence.[2]

They had many useful qualities. Thais didn't enjoy the work of tin mining – it offended the soil deities – but Karen would do it. Before Western medicine came to Thailand, Karen-prepared cures based on forest products were sought after even by those potion-connoisseurs, the Thai Chinese. Karen cloth was appreciated (partly because of the inordinate time it took to make). Above all, the Karen supplied most of the forest exotics that Siam both desired and exported.

Everything changed with the Bowring Treaty of 1855 and the opening of the Suez canal in 1869, which together turned Siamese trade towards Europe with a new emphasis on bulk commodities and manufactures – rice and teak exported, textiles and industrial hardware bought in. From that time, the Karen went into decline.[3]

The ruler of Siam included among his many titles that of 'King of the Karen'. Certain nineteenth-century Siamese monarchs took an active interest, especially Chulalongkorn, who liked to watch their bamboo-dances. It was Chulalongkorn who wrote the poems quoted in chapter three, describing Karen girls as pretty but smelly. He also admired their reclusive lifestyle:

> So tranquilly they plant their rice,
> birds in paradise, the dense woods.
> Glad bodies entice; minds at ease,
> they scorn worldly progress.[4]

But of Karen in the wild, the Thais knew very little. When the learned Siam Society was established at the turn of the century, one of its objects was to dispel myth and prejudice about the peoples of the hills by obtaining and publishing the facts. To this end they sent a questionnaire to a reputed *savant* in the north, Nai Chandr Gandasena, asking for details about Karen life. Here is some of Gandasena's reply:

They are not a quick-witted people . . . They have no games and no writing. Their tales all deal with love affairs . . . they have no drugs or science of medicine, but when ill they merely kill a fowl as a propitiatory offering to the spirits. They have no religious rites or forms of worship of any kind. They pay no respect to any gods and say that they know nothing of the relationship between gods and men . . . neither are there any priests . . . no particular rites, no prayers, no cults . . . they salute neither trees, rivers, streams . . .

Their belief in spirits is derived from old days but they have no written body of belief to refer to; they just believe what their fathers and mothers believed. They have no ideas as to how the world was made, who made it, or how the race of men arose . . . they have no fables or legends.[5]

Apart from the fact that the account distorts almost every aspect, it was hardly a description to inspire interest.

Neither the curiosity of the Siam Society, nor Chulalongkorn's kindly regard did the Karen much good. They entered into a long period of benign neglect that continued until the 1960s when wars in Vietnam, Laos and Cambodia, and the communist insurgency within its own frontiers, made Thailand acutely aware of the remoteness and vulnerability of its border forests, and the uncertain loyalties of the foresters. Official Thai patronage of the Karen, Akha, Lua, Hmong and other hilltribes became a blend of genuine concern with more urgent thoughts of Maoist insurgency and of opium.

Closely related to these worries, there are now acute problems of land use. All the hilltribes practise swidden agriculture. From the time of the colonial powers' first arrival until very recently, swidden farming was regarded as iniquitous, primitive and destructive; the farmers appeared to wreck the forest wilfully, grab one harvest and then move on.

The experts have in the last two decades realised that they were wrong. Swidden relies on a long cycle of fallow regeneration. You burn off and cultivate the field, harvest your rice, then leave well alone for anything up to ten or twelve years, moving on round to other hillsides. At first only weeds and grasses will grow but year by year other species, including trees, re-establish themselves and, at the end of the cycle, the soil is recovered and the plot ready for cultivation once more. So far from laying the land waste, there are hill tracts that have been farmed in this way for at least a hundred years, with no obvious detrimental effects.[6]

It dawned on the agriculturalists that these primitive hill farmers knew very well what they were about. The Lua people especially take great care of the land, constructing firebreaks and anti-erosion bunding, and ensuring that enough live trees are left to promote re-seeding. The Karen are good swiddeners, if not quite as fastidious. Karen arriving from Burma have also been rather predatory. For generations they've moved in on other people's land, at first asking permission to settle in the same area, then steadily overwhelming the earlier settlers by sheer weight of numbers.

The key to all this is population; as long as the level remains below the land's carrying capacity, there is no problem. But, if there is not enough land, farmers are forced to return to the same field after only eight, or seven or six years. There is leaching and erosion of the soil; the fertility falls. Crops decline and human malnutrition follows. Eventually the soil is ruined; only useless *Imperata* grass thrives. Hence much of the tension and anxiety that is now evident in rural Thailand.

From a guesthouse in Chiang Mai, two young Karen men ran 'hill-tribe treks' for energetic backpackers. They'd both taken Thai names – Tem and Sophon.

Tem had been in the KNLA.

> 'I was educated in Rangoon. My parents sent me to school there, though they were already in Kawthoolei. Then, when I was seventeen, they called myself and my brother to join them and told us that we should be soldiers. My brother joined up but I wasn't too happy about that so I became an army nurse; the doctors at GHQ trained me. I did that for four years, but I never went to the Front Line where my brother was fighting. He got scared, he thought he was going to get shot, and he came here to Chiang Mai. Our father didn't say anything and after a while ... well, I came out too. People do that. They pass through. I guess they get depressed.'
>
> 'Do you ever think of going back?'
>
> 'No. I could, you know. The Burmese never knew about me; I could go back to Rangoon quite safely. But no. I have a Thai girlfriend.'
>
> 'Not a Karen?'
>
> 'I wouldn't want the constraints of a Karen girl now. It's a serious business loving a Karen. But, you know, if I ever have children, even with a Thai woman, I'll make sure they learn Karen.'

Sophon's background was different, but the product was much the same. Born in Thailand, in a village in the hills, he'd been sent at the age of ten to a monastery in Chiang Mai to become a novice – and he'd never lived in the village again.

> 'I've been to Kawthoolei, though; I took a party of German visitors there once. But I'd not be happy about going again. I'm afraid they might ask me to stay.'
>
> 'Would that be so bad?'
>
> 'What would be the point? I can't see any end to the fighting. If the Burmese attack, the Karen just take everything of value into Thailand and wait until the Burmese run out of food and go away. How can either side win? The Karen leaders know it, and they're all bringing money out to Thailand. After a while the young soldiers find out and that's why they get depressed. We don't talk much about Kawthoolei now. When people come from there they don't want to talk either, they just want to be accepted by the Thais, so they keep quiet.'
>
> 'Have you got Thai citizenship?'
>
> 'No. It's very expensive.'

I went on one of their treks, to Karen, Lahu and Shan villages. There were seven of us, English and French tourists. Hilltribe treks out of Chiang Mai have been a growth industry of the last fifteen years or so. Every hotel in Chiang Mai offers them, and other people too. You walk through the hills for four or five hours each day, sleeping at tribal villages, sometimes with extras like elephant rides or rafting. My elephant *mahout*, another Karen, talked about com-parative love in Thailand and Kawthoolei in exactly the same terms as Tem – that loving a Thai girl was easier – and also about visiting Kawthoolei: 'I went once, but not again. They might keep me there!'

Treks are now much criticised.[7] The villages can become human zoos where the norms of tribal hospitality are thrown into confusion by influxes of gawping backpackers, pushing cameras at women in quaint and curious rainbowed homespuns. It's not only degrad-ing; it doesn't even make the villagers much of an income – no more than the lions get paid to live in a safari park. But, as the population in the hills increases and the land available to support them doesn't, people look anxiously for any source of cash. Just a little money finds its way from the trekkers to the tribes, via the families who hire out the elephants, for instance, or the men who build the bamboo rafts.

My companions, straight off planes from Europe, were polite and interested and did their best not to cause any offence. The English got grubbier by the minute, while the French had a clean change of clothes for each day of the walk and discarded the lot when we returned to Chiang Mai. We were scorched by the sun as we picked our way across irrigated rice fields, and were then saturated by stupendous rainstorms. Considering the mud, the jungle, the unaccustomed food, the humidity as we flogged up forested hills by day and the cold as we curled up on hard floors at night, they coped very well. Only the leeches upset them. They had insisted on wearing expensive walking boots (instead of some-thing sensible like flipflops), so they couldn't spot the leeches feeding between their toes, and squealed when they came to take off their socks in the evening and saw the consequences. The Karen helpfully suggested a preventative measure; the socks were placed in a bucket to marinade in a mash of tobacco in water. It didn't stop the leeches.

One thing the group were quite determined on; they were going to sample opium. At Sophon's own village, in his father's house, the opium lamps were lit and the pipes brought out, and some of the party tried unsuccessfully to get smashed by dint of spending a lot of money, lying in awkward positions and sucking at bubbly brown gunk through a tube. Three dozen children watched the attempt. The bars of the human zoo had become ambivalent.

'We had an English girl here last year', said Sophon, 'who smoked twenty pipes of opium. The next day we had to carry her on a stretcher to the bus.'

No one in my group repeated that feat. But in every village that we visited, Karen or otherwise, there was opium for the asking.

Back in Chiang Mai, I returned to the guest house to pick up my rucksack and to rest for an hour before catching the overnight train to Bangkok. I sat in the tree-shaded courtyard reading and drinking a pot of tea. There was an American man studying the *Bangkok Post*, and Tem was talking to the two Thai women at work behind the bamboo screen of the kitchen. A quiet but steady mutter of conversation persisted. I was engrossed in Tolstoy's account of the Battle of Borodino in *War and Peace*, and so I did not at first register the change in the sounds around me. Soon, however, it was inescapable.

The conversation in the kitchen had stopped – Tem and the women were watching something else, which I could hear but not see. Coming from behind the thick stand of banana trees in the centre of the yard was a man's voice. He was speaking Thai so I didn't understand a word, but he was evidently very angry. It was not shouts of rage that I heard but a cold, hard, vicious anger. There was another sound, which I realised was a hand slapping a face. Somebody was moaning.

The American was taking (or pretending to take) no notice whatever; Tem and the Thai women were watching but staying well behind the bamboo screen and were not going to interfere. Then there was a harder slap and out from behind the banana trees came a woman, sprawling across the gravel.

At this point another young Karen entered the courtyard; he helped out with the treks. He stepped neatly round the prostrate woman without looking at her, and went behind the bamboo screen muttering something. Then the Thai man appeared. He grabbed a handful of the woman's hair, pulled her up to sit and began methodically slapping her face, talking to her in a low voice. Her mouth and nose were bleeding and she looked dazed. She moaned again. I said to the American,

'Are we going to let this go on?'
He said, without looking up,
'Thais are famously rough on their wives.'
The assault continued. I went to Tem:
'We have to stop this.'
'No, it is not our business.'
'He's hurting her badly.'
'You must not do anything! It is his wife and she is drunk and
    it is very dangerous to interfere. Please sit down, John.'

He was angry – not with either the Thai or his wife, but with
me. But it was too late. The Thai punched his wife in the mouth:
she fell back hard against some concrete paving, her head smacking
onto it, her face covered in blood. I couldn't bear it, and shouted,

'That's enough!'
He looked up at me, showing no surprise at all.
'I don't care what this is about, but you'll stop that now.'

It was not the Thai husband who came towards me, but Tem
and the other Karen. They simply stood between me and the Thais,
pushed me trembling back to a chair and forced me to sit. The
husband walked to the gate, waved to a motor-rickshaw, bundled
his insensible wife into it and vanished.

'You should not have done that, John. If there had been a fight
    the police would have come.'
'Good.'
'Not good at all, not for this woman, not for you and certainly
    not for us!'
'Why not?'
'They would have asked for our papers. We do not have papers,
    John. You going to get us thrown into Burma for this woman?'

In the kitchen they went back to peeling potatoes for the tourists'
chips. The American went back to his room. Tem walked in a
circle round the yard, then suddenly sat down in front of me and
thrust out his right hand. It was bruised, cut and swollen.

'You see that? I was in a fight with some Thai boys last night:
    four Thai, two Karen, but they were very drunk so it was OK
    for us. One of these men is now in hospital. But it will happen
    again, you see? Too many people, too little money, no job.
    These people stop Karen getting a job now, they don't want
    us so much now!'

In August 1986, just before I first came to Kawthoolei, Roger P.
Winter, Director of the United States Committee for Refugees,

visited Thailand to look at the situation of the Karen in the camps along the Burma border, where some 18,000 people have taken refuge from the fighting. Afterwards, Winter wrote a concise but perceptive report:

Karen refugees have been received rather well in Thailand, in part because there is a substantial ethnic Karen population of Thai nationality there. However, the Royal Thai Government does not formally recognise the Karens from Burma as refugees ... Nothing of a developmental nature that might encourage the refugees to stay in Thailand or draw others, or that would antagonise the authorities in Rangoon is permitted.[8]

As the military situation worsens, there will be more and more Karen crossing into Thailand. Some will go to the camps, determined to return to Burma soon. Many will decide that there is no possibility of a return, that their future is in Thailand. There they hope that if they keep their heads down, behave themselves and work hard, they will be accepted as they always were before.

But the Thais are beset by such problems on all sides. The one country in the region never to have received the benefits of a colonial administration, Thailand is now seen by many as a haven of wealth, stability and security. From Burma, Laos, Kampuchea, the exiles creep quietly across to safety. But the pressures within Thailand are growing too – for land, for work, or for a piece of the action in the opium-substitution programmes anxiously funded by international development agencies. Many Thais have had enough of being everyone's bolt hole and, in October 1987, while I was walking the crowded hills, local Thai militia were taking matters into their own hands. They had moved into hilltribe villages and were burning crops and houses to drive the settlers back over the borders.

Some of the Karen would go back if they could, though most Karen in Thailand now regard it as their home. But in the refugee camps, Roger Winter found that Thailand plays little part in their lives: 'The preoccupation of most Karen refugees is not with their own circumstances, but rather with events on the other side of the border.' They live, he writes, in almost complete isolation:

The Karens manage their own assistance affairs as much as possible, and rely on private voluntary agencies to meet many of their assistance and medical needs ... Food supplies are tight ... Donated supplies are stretched by the use of leaves, fruits and vegetables gathered from the forest. The refugees are not allowed to garden and have no access to land for that purpose. Educational programs conducted by Karen teachers for refugee children at Wan Kha were observed to be disciplined, animated and operating at a high academic level, in English, Karen and Burmese.

The spirit in the camps is a strange mixture of hopefulness with vibrations of a fading dream.[9]

11 Last of the longhouses

My brothers and sisters, if you build a strong house together,
then, when the sky falls, you can push it back!
Build your house in the sky if you will. If it totters,
I'll help you support it.
If you have brotherhood amongst you, then when you
loose your bow, you'll shoot down something delectable.
So, have unity; build as the ancestors did.

Song recorded for me by Ku Wah and True Love

Where Thailand is at its narrowest, pinched by Burma to a few miles' width just above the Isthmus of Kra, half a day's drive south of Bangkok, there is a pass through the hills with a remarkable history. Easy routes across the 'dorsal spine' dividing Thailand and Burma are few. Those further north (Three Pagodas Pass most famously) have for centuries seen armies invading Burma from Siam or vice versa, intent on sacking capitals and rocking dynasties but not greatly interested in the hill peoples in between except as guides, porters and spies. But the southern pass of Maw Daung has more usually been a trade route – and a way of escape.

From the train, the Bangkok–Butterworth 'International Express' which is itself a favourite vehicle of young escapers, smugglers and myself, the landscape looks innocuous, even rather dull – low hills tufted with light scrub and half-hearted secondary forest. Stumpy, rotten-tooth rock formations add a little variety but, as the train runs south, even these peter out and it is difficult to imagine the low ridges of the hinterland as being an obstacle to anything very much. But they are. On the Burmese side the forest becomes rapidly inhospitable, the water scant, human habitation very thin indeed. It is known as the Land of Three Hundred Peaks, the *Samroiyot*.

For generations of traders, a rapid passage through this terrain from the Bay of Bengal to the Gulf of Siam was a short cut to profit.[1] Without it, merchantmen would have to sail down the length of the Straits of Malacca, rounding what is now Singapore and back up the eastern side of the peninsula to the Gulf – a voyage of the best part of 2,000 miles. The winds were unreliable, the waters full of shoals and alive with sharks. At Malacca and, later, at Singapore there were fees and taxes of every description. Worse still, the scores of islands scattered the length of the Straits sheltered innumerable pirates, amongst them the Selung, sometimes called 'Sea Karen'. The journey to Siam, if you ever got that far, would cost you a small fortune. Thus, the small Burmese port of Mergui and the relatively simple trail east from there across to Parachuap Khiri Khan on the Siamese side became an important stage on a commercial route that linked not simply Burma (or Pagan or Ava, according to century) to Siam, but also Madras to the Far East. One might even say it linked Europe to Japan. For centuries, cargoes arrived at Mergui, went on upriver to the town of Tenasserim and were there transhipped to smaller boats to be rowed on up the Little Tenasserim River until they could go no further. After which porters would carry both merchandise and merchants uphill through the forest for a few days more until, once across the Maw Daung Pass, they came to the eastern seaboard of the Isthmus and could take ship again up to Bangkok and Ayutthia. This was how fine artefacts from India reached the Siamese court, together with English woollens. On the return journey porcelain, dyes, incense and spices, silks and other exotics made up the freight.

Imperial Roman 'envoys' (probably Syrian traders) passed this way as early as AD 166.[2] A fifteenth-century Venetian, Nicolo di Conti, was the first European to describe a visit to Mergui and Tenasserim. Then, in 1511 a Portuguese ambassador of the Duke of Albuquerque made the crossing of the Isthmus and thereafter, along with the traders came a steady flow of Siamese civil servants (Siam ruled much of Lower Burma for long periods from the thirteenth century onwards), of English merchant adventurers and Portuguese and French Catholic missionaries, one of whom, the Bishop of Beryte, was in 1622 shipwrecked on the Little Tenasserim and found himself perched in a tree over the torrent.

The route was never easy. In his account of the exploits of Europeans here in the seventeenth century, Maurice Collis (1936, pp. 42–5), described the difficulties:

From Mergui to Tenasserim the journey was agreeable, for the scenery was good, the large boats tolerably comfortable and rowing with the tide, the rate of progress was reasonable. But eastwards from that city a dangerous section began ... I recommend it to any man who would like the sensation of traversing one of the last unexplored regions in Asia. No one knows what may be in the jungles extending for hundreds of miles north and south of the track. Besides wild animals and leeches, they reek of malaria. If you lose your way and escape the tigers, the ants will pick your bones.

I have on my wall a copy of the map produced by French *savants* who made the trip in the 1680s. If they had been relying on it, they would never have seen Paris again. Fortunately the route was well known to professional guides – many of them certainly Karen; these would also have guided the belligerent Burmese King Alaung-paya, who in 1760 led an army across Maw Daung that took the Siamese completely by surprise.

Steamships put an end to Maw Daung Pass as a continental link (although there persist today schemes to cut the Isthmus with a canal – schemes which the anxious Singaporeans as persistently subvert by one means or another). Traffic over the pass all but dried up. By the late nineteenth century the harbour of Mergui, once one of the most important in the Bay of Bengal, was visited by little other than the British administration's weekly mailboat. Tenasserim, formerly a cosmopolitan city with (as a cousin of Magellan wrote), 'its colony of Moors and Gentiles, its trade with Malacca and Bengal',[3] was by the turn of the century almost a ghost town. It was described by G. P. Andrews in 1912:

For several hundred years Tenasserim was the principal port of Siam . . . the overland route cannot now be traced . . . The village now contains a hundred houses. Opposite the landing stage the remains of the ancient shipyard are clearly visible.[4]

Inland, the staging posts that had provided shelter and refreshment had vanished.

For Kawthoolei the significance of the Maw Daung Pass dates from the early 1970s. The disgruntled ex-Prime Minister of Burma, U Nu, tried to lead a rebellion against Ne Win from (among other places) the vicinity of Three Pagodas and Maw Daung.[5] The KNLA had some not very serious involvement with the attempt, which faded quickly. Maw Daung was also favoured by the Communist Party of Thailand; they could easily retreat into the low hills without much risk of attack from either Thai or Burmese military. It became a 'sensitive area'.

But, during the Second World War, the Japanese had rebuilt or recut sections of the road into Burma, and illicit traffic had recommenced. Today there are two sorts of travellers: cattle smugglers, and Karen refugees. It was the refugees that I dealt with. This was the way Judith and Bismarck gained safety out of reach of Rangoon.

Bismarck was convalescing in the guesthouse up at Headquarters when I arrived; his wife Judith was the housekeeper. This was October 1986; my first evening in revolutionary Kawthoolei I was too tired to register much other than the ants that invaded my mosquito net at 3 a.m. The rain crashed through the forest to roar upon the tin roof of the guesthouse – a dark, dusty hardwood build-ing with a cold but prettily fretworked verandah where I had slung my net. In the morning I understood that I was sharing with a family of five refugees. They were not Karen but Burmese, of a sort. I had no choice but to wait there. I wanted transport down the hill to the river but the rain had overwhelmed the unkempt dirt road. When Bismarck started talking at 6.30 on Sunday morn-ing, I was glad of the conversation – even if it did concern torture.

The family were referred to by the Karen as 'Anglo-Burmese', with little reason. Judith was half-Karen, half-French. Bismarck was one quarter Burman, another quarter-Mon and the rest German from his father who had come to Rangoon after the Second World War and set himself up as a movie moghul. He'd bought a cinema ('now nationalised') and made his own Burmese films, love stories mostly. Then, with a lorry fitted out as a mobile cinema, he'd gone about the villages of the Delta projecting his fantasies.

Judith's father was a French businessman who, in scenes worthy of one of the German's films, had fallen in love with a Karen girl, married her and then killed himself with drink and tobacco. He had spoken excellent Burmese and had always used it at home with his family – with the result that Judith, sheltering now with the Karen, spoke hardly a word of the vernacular of these, her own people.

Judith was a young teacher when she met and married Bismarck, a student of Education at Rangoon University. He was a political activist, and by the time their first daughter was born he was already under police surveillance.

He was to be arrested three times. The first of these was on the occasion of U Thant's funeral. The celebrated Burmese Secre-tary-General of the United Nations died in 1974 – a spark that fired riots and shootings in Rangoon:

> 'U Thant was a great man, the first Burmese to be a great figure
> in the world. We were very proud of him, but Ne Win was
> jealous, knowing that he was not loved in that way. They tried
> to bury U Thant in a small place with no respect but we cap-
> tured the coffin and carried it in triumph to the University,
> calling for a state funeral. The troopers even fired at the coffin,
> there were even bullet holes in the United Nations flag!'

A number of students were seized, including Bismarck's:

> 'They gave me one helluva beating and torture! They sat me
> on a block of ice and gave me electrical shocks. They dripped
> water on my head, drip drip drip. It's quite nice at first but
> after one and a half hours the sound is like little hammers break-
> ing open the skull and I was ready to scream.'

By the time he'd been arrested and tortured a second and a
third time, his health was broken and Judith was badly frightened.
They now had three more children, and she was unable to work
to support them all. She told Bismarck that they had no choice
but to leave Burma. That is not easily done. If your request for
a passport is granted, you have to surrender all your property and
repay the cost of your education. But for dubious characters such
as Bismarck it was out of the question even to make the request.
They would have to escape across the border, and that meant passing through rebel territory, putting themselves in the hands of the
Karen. Judith went to her Karen relations and was introduced
to representatives of the KNU in Rangoon who said that they'd
be most welcome in Kawthoolei. It was agreed that they should
leave as soon as possible.

The eldest daughter, now of school age, could stay in Burma
with her grandmother, but the three little children would have to
make the journey with their parents – out along that same route
which in 1662 had nearly killed the French bishop.

Judith's memories of the journey were clearer than Bismarck:

> 'We travelled down the coast by bus, then upriver to a small
> village in the hills. Then we began to walk. We were escorted
> by KNLA soldiers and there were other Karen with us, going
> to Kawthoolei. Bismarck was really sick now; at times his
> malaria was so bad that he was unconscious and the Karen
> had to carry him. We had our three babies with us too! I carried
> the little one, the other two walked the whole way, they did
> not complain. When Bismarck was able to walk he carried our
> one small bag. It was a real adventure. We had to walk through

thick, thick forest for three days and I was very scared – there were snakes and so many monkeys!'

I said that I thought the Karen generally more of a threat to the monkeys than vice versa, but Judith wasn't having it:

'How could we know? We are from Rangoon, we'd never done anything like this before. I thought the monkeys would come and steal my baby. Bismarck was worse, he was really very funny; if he saw a wild buffalo he'd run and hide. We had no guns, nothing at all. But these Karen looked after us.'

They reached Maw Daung in June and were at once taken north to Headquarters. The theory was that Bismarck would teach in a new middle-school there but, almost as soon as they arrived, his health gave way altogether and they found themselves in the guesthouse with Judith nursing him. Within moments of meeting Bismarck you could see that the story was true. Nervous, excitable, physically enfeebled (and now with a new kidney complaint) but talking his precise English in rapid, staccato periods, he was in effect just another child for Judith to care for. He was unable to sit still, but could do nothing of much use. Indeed, his arm was scalded from an ill-judged attempt to intervene in the kitchen.

Moreover, in the malarial damp of the forest at Headquarters, the health and morale of the children was deteriorating. I asked Bismarck:

'What will you do?'
'When I am quite recovered I will teach here. I must repay these people somehow. When the babies are bigger, Judith will teach also. But she has a sister in the United States. If that woman will send us some money, a lot of money, we can buy Thai passports and go to the United States. That is the only thing for us now.'
'What does Judith's sister do there?'
'I think she is a waitress.'

I went down to the river next morning, and it was four months before I saw them again.

Colonel Marvel announced, at one hour's notice, that we were leaving for a week with the refugees at Maw Daung. It was now February and, after the post-monsoon chill at Christmas, the air was parched again. Burmese dry season campaigns had burned more villages and pushed new groups of refugees east, up into Karen territory.

People at Maw Daung were falling sick, there were difficulties with the water supply. Also, security was lax, the Army needed a shake-up and the school an inspection. Rice reserves were low and the administrators didn't seem fully to understand their duties. There were delicate legal matters to be gone into. Lastly, the Colonel thought that the refugees weren't pulling their weight; he'd hoped for more commercial enterprise. He thought he could sort it all out in five days, and said to me, 'I want you to see the conditions that they are in. I want you to understand what we are doing for all the Karen people. Bartholomew will come also.'

Within Kawthoolei the Colonel would always drive himself – nobody else drove with sufficient élan for his liking, and he enjoyed nothing more than to materialise out of the forest in his new blue pickup (with *Colonel Marvel* in silvered plastic letters stuck on the dashboard) with the driver sitting redundant by his side and a clutch of bodyguards up on the back. But, when we crossed the border in the morning – because to reach the southernmost Township of Kawthoolei required a full day's journey through Thailand – it was with a Thai driving; the Colonel didn't have a licence.

The Thais, knowing that they cannot stop the Karen crossing in and out of Burma at will, attempt at least to keep some check on their movements, and so a special vehicle had been authorised. Beside the Thai driver sat a Buddhist monk who was also vice-chairman of the Kawthoolei Refugee Committee – it had once been the Karen Christian Relief Committee, but they were becoming more sensitive to charges of bias. On the back of the truck huddled Bartholomew, two nurses and myself, with the Colonel squatting amongst the luggage trying his best to look like any Thai peasant going shopping in town. The Highway Police took one glance and were thoroughly suspicious. Our papers, of course, were not in order, and we spent part of the morning at the police station.

Many hours of driving later, stopping for lunch and to buy water-melons for the Township Committee, we neared Maw Daung. Again, the Thai soldiers on the border decided to be meticulous and searched every bag. The Colonel declared that it was a reflection of our importance.

'They know who we are, and they are showing us that they too know their duty.'
(Or, perhaps, that we were subject to them.)
'So what are they looking for?'

'They will say that they are looking for drugs, but they know that we Karen do not carry drugs.'

One of the Thai soldiers found something that interested him more than drugs. It was the rockclimbing karabiner that I use as a keyring. It has *Stubai 2000 Austria* stamped on the side. He held it up excitedly.

'Oh, snaplink! Snaplink, yes?' I nodded. He showed the whole squad.

'Snaplink! OK, snaplink!'

With that, we were in. Morse radio messages were sent to report the safe arrival of Colonel Marvel. Such are the lines of communication between the Colonel's Headquarters and the outposts of his authority.

The camp – with the caution, born of experience, of most Karen bases – is only just inside Burma. There is a Township office building, staff hostels, rice stores, all of roughsawn hardwood. We settled ourselves in the office, a thatched and cramped room with an open-sided meeting hall in front. The Colonel took one of the two wooden beds, Bartholomew the other, and I slung my hammock between two posts in the hall. Immediately, the Colonel called a meeting of all local officials. Never mind that we'd been driving all day; one cup of tea thickened with condensed milk and he was ready to give them a lecture.

'On the governmental structure of Kawthoolei. They don't know how it works yet.'

And for the rest of the evening he drew charts of the power structure on the blackboard. After which they all sang in honour of Ba U Gyi and we went to bed.

The Colonel began his working day at 5 a.m., at which time a small parade of overawed Township officials came to the office and presented their reports and such documentation as he had required, held out to him in the manner of an offering – presented in the right hand, the left hand supporting the right forearm. The Colonel's response was curt but highly effective; a stream of peremptory instructions sent the officials about their business as though they had only been awaiting this release for their energies.

'They do not think much for themselves, but then I expect a lot of these people. They are just villagers. They have lost everything; they must build for themselves now. I cannot do everything for them.'

One man, the Secretary, seemed to be doing rather more than his share of the rebuilding; a quiet and gentle person, he ran most things from forestry to food issue. Moving with slow purposefulness about the dark office from the typing desk to the silkscreen duplicator between stacks of curling files, boxes of *Satellite* soap for the refugees and used stencils blotched with vermilion correcting fluid, he was shy in front of me but deeply respectful of Bartholomew as he brought him up to date – here, as almost anywhere, refugees come under the aegis of the local health officer and were thus Bartholomew's responsibility. He spent an anxious half-hour with a calculator, then announced that the refugees were costing his Department 22,000 baht (*c.* £550) a month in rice, salt and medicines and where was that going to come from? He looked across at the Colonel, but the latter had developed a new technique for not hearing; he'd borrowed my Walkman, clapped the headphones on his ears and, playing or not, hardly took them off in all the five days that we were there. Bartholomew saw no relief from that quarter, and closed his files. He then decided that we'd go on a tour of inspection of the sawmill.

We walked for a change. Here too there had been brush fires, the singed bamboos – their sections striped and exaggerated by charring of the rough flesh at each node – stood in fields of black ash. People had been careless with matches, said Bartholomew; the soil was lousy anyway – just look how stunted the surviving banana palms were.

Not many years ago there was nothing at Maw Daung except marijuana fields, cultivated (the Colonel had insisted) by Thais who crossed the border looking for free land away from the gaze of their own police. There had been few residents. The water in the vicinity being poor, the nearest Karen villages were two days off, down near the Tenasserim River. Only the cattle smugglers and lumbermen had passed this way. At that time the whole district was even more a backwater of the war, the fighting patchy and small-scale. But, as the conflict in the north had intensified and gone against the Karen, the Government of Kawthoolei had decided that a more regular presence was required – to watch the back door, as it were. A KNLA base was established in the forest, and the militia burnt the marijuana.

Then, in 1979, the Burmese extended their *Four Cuts* campaign against the Karen in the south. Soon, new groups of refugees from the forward areas began to arrive. They required support and administration. Township Headquarters were built, many of the Thais left and the new Karen arrivals moved into the ready-made beginnings of small villages. In 1984 the numbers coming up through the forest swelled again. There was no more accommodation for them so they took over the sawmill and turned it into a longhouse.

There was a time when many hill Karen lived in longhouses. A few dim memories of these persist; only in the accounts of the early ethnographers do we find them described.[6] The last report of a longhouse in what is now north Thailand dates from *c*. 1920,[7] though that may simply mean that none of the 'teak wallahs' or Thais working in those parts later on were interested enough to write about them. In Burma too they survived into the twentieth century. Smeaton, in 1887 (p. 157), described enormous structures:

The village is, so to speak, the federate unit. Among many of the clans it is simply a big barrack, containing eighty to one hundred families. The roof is nearly flat, shielded from the rain by split bamboos cut in lengths and laid like tiles. A long hall runs through the entire building, and the separate suites of rooms occupied by the different families open into this hall. Each family has two rooms and an open verandah for drying and cleaning paddy.

To the officers of Indian Civil Service Settlement Party No. 5, preparing the *Gazetteer* of Tharawaddy District in 1920, a longhouse was already an anachronism:

In the hills the primitive Karen customs still exist almost untouched by the outside world. There are a number of one-structure villages where the whole village is a single long bamboo structure without a board or a nail in it ... The whole is raised above the ground and enclosed in a stockade to afford protection from wild animals and dacoits.[8]

In 1922 the American missionary Marshall described a Karen longhouse as simply 'a bamboo apartment house on stilts'.[9]

The design and construction of longhouses in different parts of the world can have widely differing significance. Certain Amazonian types, for instance, embody an entire cosmology. But they may have an urgent practical purpose also. A longhouse, by its very existence, implies a state of simultaneous threat and security. It is a response to outside menace, a gathering-in for mutual protection under one roof, while at the same time it suggests that the danger is not sufficiently overwhelming to warrant more than simple measures. Faced with a devastating invasion by superior forces – a professional army, for instance – a longhouse becomes a liability, trapping its inhabitants and their vulnerable goods and food stores in a high-profile target. Marshall records a Karen war song describing a raid:

> I go with a host of men.
> We will reach the steps of the house
> and fire muskets and shout aloud.
> The men will come with wives and children.
> Raise the spear and draw the sword.
> Smite the neck and pierce the side.
> The blood is gushing purple.[10]

If this sort of thing goes on, the villagers will take the opposite solution and disperse; it's better to spread as thinly as possible the risk of your whole clan being massacred.

Why the longhouses of Burma died out I don't know; they can, after all, still be found in forests as far apart as Borneo and Brazil – but the hill Karen accommodated themselves in many ways to the lowland cultures around them. From the point of view of the authorities, a longhouse may be threatening by its very essence – as Indonesia's treatment of the Dyaks has demonstrated. Karen have long felt an affinity to the indigenous peoples of Borneo whom they see as sharing important elements of their culture and who must, therefore, be distant cousins of some sort.[11] The Dyak tribes include Borneo's longhouse dwellers *par excellence* but to their Indonesian rulers, quintessentially Muslim Javanese and obsessionally anti-communist, the longhouses imply a dangerously collective frame of mind – and almost certainly lax morals as well – and so, from Kalimantan (Indonesian Borneo), there have been stories of local police shooting into and setting torch to the Dyak buildings, forcing the people into villages of neat single dwellings in the Javanese manner. There was always in my mind a strong suspicion that the Javanese were simply jealous – either of what they secretly imagined to be a diurnal round of orgy, or more simply of the affectionate internal tolerance of the tribe (dangerous, easy to convert to exclusive solidarity) which made life at such close quarters possible at all. The 1920 ICS surveyors noted of Karen longhouse living that, 'they show clearly their peaceable character in doing this without continual quarrelling'.

The surrounding stockades and internal design of a Karen longhouse, with its rigidly separate family units, suggest that on this practical level at least, the structure's purpose was protective, and that it was the physical expression of a mutual support system between the families – by no means the same thing as communal living, or communism.[12]

But policemen, Baptist missions, public health officials, twentieth-century 'progressives', pan-Karenists (for whom the tight cohesion of such a small unit was inimical to broader nationalism) and of course anti-communists – all these had their reasons for mistrusting longhouses.

To Colonel Marvel, the sawmill at Maw Daung represented a variety of problems. He saw it as a focus of disease, a symbol of the flight of Thai economic investment from Kawthoolei, and as a distressing state of suspended normality for his people, in which they neither lived like decent modern Karen nor organised the building of a proper village. But for all that, it was the timber and steel embodiment of shelter, the umbrella of refuge that Kawthoolei offered to dispossessed Karen, under which it gathered them all in.

It's much like any other Thai sawmill in Kawthoolei; like most of them it's idle, as squabbles between Thai entrepreneurs and those military politicians who in one sense or another control the border, shut down the lucrative hardwood trade that was stripping Kawthoolei's forests. There is a huge expanse of tin roof on wooden joists, crudely built and sagging like a broken-backed turtle in a sea of scrub grass and wild camphor plants growing on the site of old fields. Inside, all the machinery is still there – unguarded circular saws fed by trolleys on rails, tall band saws mounted over concrete pits, capable of reducing a centenarian hardwood to little more than chopsticks. Overhead, pulleys roll along massive I-beams; whole trees are swung into the path of saws this way. Underfoot, the floor is padded with accumulated wood dust stirred into the dirt. The power-plant is there, a ton of Broomwade diesel. In spite of all this redundant tackle, the place is now a Karen longhouse – possibly the only one anywhere.

There were some two dozen families there when I came. Each one had built its own living quarters inside, under the wide tin roof. The 'separate suites' are all bamboo, raised on stilts like the

'apartment block' that Marshall described. Each consists of one
or two rooms of a few square metres, with woven bamboo or thatch-
panel walls rising three or four feet above the raised floor, enough
to give privacy, to contain babies, to exclude draught and dogs
and to hang a few bags and clothes from. These dwellings are all
around the sides of the sawmill, forming outer walls. In the centre,
stacks of rice in jute bags can be watched over by the whole community. Here in the shade there's space for work and for children
playing in amongst the pits and saws – which no one seems to
touch at all. Some corners of the community dwelling are shambolic,
cluttered and ill-used. Others are neat and orderly. It is simply
a revised version of village life.

In many other settlements of refugees – the camps of Salvadoreans
in Honduras, for example – the population may be almost entirely
made up of women and children, as the men have either been killed,
or have escorted their families to safety and then returned to the
fight. Not so at Maw Daung. Kawthoolei's 'People's War' is not
of that sort. At the sawmill the men were in under the KNU umbrella
with their families.

But, as far as much of the rest of the world is concerned, there
is no such thing as a Karen refugee.[13] Those who flee the Front
Line but remain in Kawthoolei are regarded by the UN High Commission for Refugees as 'displaced persons' within their own
country: Burma. Those who cross into Thailand become illegal
immigrants. Nowhere do they qualify for official refugee status,
and consequently they get little official assistance. What help they
do receive all comes from private charity – although, such is the
current sensitivity to the very word 'refugee' in Thailand, surrounded as it is by actual or potential conflicts on every frontier,
that even the private charities insist on referring to the lesser breed,
'displaced persons'. The charity is not negligible; to the north,
Karen camps in Thailand receive large shipments of rice.

Here, in a far corner of the sawmill was a room with a padlocked
door: a clothes store. A Thai church organisation had presented
a heap of secondhand garments for villagers arriving with nothing.
A man with a key approached, and a queue formed. A few minutes
later there were men and women in outsize business suits moving
amongst the bamboo platforms in the mill.

Bartholomew counted the neat stack of rice bags hard up against
the powerplant, running his hand over the coarse jute as he regarded
his stock and his clientele. 'We shall have to feed them for the

remainder of this year, until next harvest. I think perhaps we can. It depends how many more come.'

Then the Colonel arrived, banging the smart blue-grey pickup from ridge to pothole, grateful for a break in his interminable meetings and anxious to be in on any action. Three young men with M16s clambered out of the back of the pickup. The Colonel removed my Walkman headphones for a minute, tucked his shirt and shoulder holster more comfortably and began to pace about like a man who, if he could only see the problem, would charge it and knock it down. The refugees watched him, perhaps wondering which part of their lives might be stood on its head today. The bodyguards watched him with a certain admiration – and an alert apprehension that they might find themselves doing goodness knows what in half a minute's time. The Colonel took the towel from his neck and wiped his face thoroughly.

> 'And so, Mr. Jo, what can you do for us here? You see how many
> people we have to care for? Kawthoolei must protect anyone
> who comes to us, Karen or anybody. We have Burmese houses,
> we have Bengalis, we have Mon. We have said, we will feed
> and protect you. In Burma, we call our people, they know there
> is Kawthoolei for them to go to. So now I am asking you,
> what can you do to help us? What do you think? Shall we
> write a letter to Mrs Thatcher? Will she receive my letter? I
> do not know your procedure.'

He looked over to Bartholomew who was rummaging in the refugees' cooking pots. 'Why don't you have a clinic now?' Bartholomew jerked his head at one of his nurses who produced the stethoscope and a plastic box of medicines. Bartholomew placed an empty sack on the dirt floor, with a block of wood as a pillow, and an old woman scampered forward, lay down and said she had 'wind'.

The Colonel went back towards his car, saying again, 'We have promised these people our help'. His guards backed out of the way, one of them prematurely climbing back into the pickup for departure. But the Colonel only wanted to raise the tone of the clinic. He propped the driver's door wide open and put on a tape of Jim Reeves, very loud: 'It is no mystery what God can do'.

While Bartholomew de-wormed the refugees, the Colonel examined the community's manufacturing industry. He was unimpressed:

> 'They cannot support themselves on bits of grass . . .'

But they were trying. The women were making thatch-panels of grass and palm leaves which could be sold for a few baht to visiting Thai traders. There were castor oil nuts to be shelled, chillis to be dried. In the morning, the men went out to the new fields – but there too the Colonel was dissatisfied:

'They just do not see that times have changed, that they are no longer growing rice for their families alone, but for all the other refugees who are coming, for Kawthoolei. We *must* go into wet rice now; but what do we leaders know about wet rice? We are soldiers! We have to study and then we can make them do it. Send me an agriculturalist from England, Jo, one who can teach us this.'

The trouble, he announced, was that, 'We Karen are too individualistic', with no idea of working together:

'Look at how much rice we give them! The first year they were here they had to work together in a hurry to make new fields, and they got a fine harvest, they got nearly 1,000 baskets. This last season they have all worked as separate families again and what happens? 300 baskets. They blame the weather.'

The Colonel checked this near-communist talk, and drove us back to the office for a cup of Ovaltine. And there were Janice and Two Shoes.

The Colonel had called them to Maw Daung to see what they could do to stimulate the local economy. They'd come by motorbike, were dirty and tired. Janice – whose Sgaw name is 'Flower of the People' but who is about as far from 'traditional' Karen as a woman can get – pulled cigarettes from the pocket of her catsuit, smeared one with a few drops of menthol, then stretched her stiff muscles, extending one limb at a time. Janice could make urban sophistication for the Karen seem an attractive idea; I found them a charming pair. But the Colonel's operation of Maw Daung as a Priority Development Area left them bemused. He began without ceremony:

'So, what can you do for us here?'
'Well, what is your policy?'
'What policy?'
'Do you want us to work here or at Headquarters? And what sort of things ...'
'There are 200 refugees here, What shall they do?'
'So, we must discuss ...'
'But I have another meeting now.'

The Colonel stumped outside to issue some orders. Janice sighed.

> 'We must come here, we must come there.'
> But Two Shoes was losing patience.
> 'So before, he tells me to start something at Headquarters. He
> tells his Secretary to help me, but what do they want to do,
> these people? Eat rice, eat fish paste! These people really are
> ... (he searched for his word) ... inert.'

Not so the Colonel, who came bustling back. It was lunchtime,
and he announced that we would eat Indian; we went to the local
takeaway. On the Japanese forest highway to Burma stood an
Indian store. A scruffy-white-haired Bengali with a sweet smile
made us all some more Ovaltine to sip while he fried up two dozen
parathas which we then took over the road. A Karen mechanic
lived there, from up north. His Burmese wife had prepared us a
venison curry. The Colonel, a former mechanic and *soi-disant* gour-
met chef himself, was back with things that he appreciated, and
announced that today was Karen National Union Day.

> 'So we are having this special lunch. You see how I respect these
> people. They, too, have come to us for protection.'

Everybody, it seemed, needed protecting from something. The
Bengali shopkeeper was a double refugee. He was a Muslim, and
things had become so rough for Muslims in Burma that he and
his wife had finally fled through Kawthoolei to northern Thailand.
But there, in a small town near Chiang Mai, their house had been
attacked by thieves and his wife murdered. He married again,
another Bengali woman, and they returned to the only place in
which they felt safe, which was Kawthoolei. And now they'd set
up to corner the market in hot parathas for cattle smugglers, working
their shop together in a calm and competent silence.

The Colonel was on the verge of resenting them, muttering again,
'Where is such initiative in *my* people?' But he had a weakness
for hot parathas, and besides, he needed the shop for interrogations.

For the Colonel himself was vulnerable. He had throw-away lines
about the 'unnecessary' bodyguard that had been foisted on him
and his pickup, but there were, it seemed, real dangers. The militia
had a man in the lockup. He was held there on suspicion, and
this afternoon the Colonel was to be an examining magistrate. He
established himself at the largest table in the paratha shop. 'That
man was going to murder the Township Chairman for money; that
is what they think. There is a price on my head too, from the Bur-

mese government. Ne Win has offered cash for the head of a Central Committee member like myself: K.100,000 (£2,000) for the man who guns me down. Do you know there is a price list for murdering Karen?'

The price dropped steeply below District level: the Township Chairman was worth a mere K.10,000. Very little for a murder, really, considering the scarcity value of skilled administrators in Kawthoolei.

The accused was a broker in the cross-border cattle trade. If found guilty he'd be shot. But the Colonel only had sixteen days – that was the maximum that the man could be held without charges before release on bail: 'We have Rule of Law, you see?' That afternoon it was the suspect's wife that he wanted to question. She came with an armful of accounts in exercise books; a lot of money had been found in the house and she was anxiously trying to prove that it was legitimate profits on cattle, not an advance on the assassination. Her story was jumbled, her performance poor. But the Colonel showed himself to be a humane interrogator.

> 'She is scared and not thinking clearly, but that does not make her husband guilty. I am not a trained detective. It is very hard to prove an intention, but these are the dangers of refugees. We have said that anyone may come here – but who can tell what criminals and spies may come too?'

Later that afternoon, exploring the KNDO militia compound with Come Quick, following the eighteen-inch-deep slit trench around the perimeter of the parade ground, I came to the prison. It was small and wooden, and the one inmate lay face to the back wall upon some blankets. In the guardhut nearby was his warder, curled up on a high bunk with what – given Karen scruples about these things – I took to be his wife.

But the Colonel wasn't letting me out of his sight for long. There came a reedy blast of a battle horn, and the militiamen came running from huts and kitchens around the compound. The Colonel had brought his camera.

He formed them up in front of the command post – two dozen of them, armed with an assortment of M16s and AK47s, a grenade launcher and a number of carbines. Some of the militiamen were so young and so small that even the diminutive carbines looked like howitzers in their hands. The Colonel fussed about amongst them, and I took most of the photographs for him as they posed

Plate 11. Militia at Maw Daung. 'I thought they looked a sad and feeble bunch. They proved me wrong later.'

together like a football team with its coach. He had them retie their sarongs and straighten the occasional red neckerchief over their battledress. He took the youngest aside, placed his own beret on the boy's head and showed him how to look his sternest with a rifle. Frankly, at the time, I thought they looked a sad and feeble bunch. They proved me wrong later.

An Army car came for us at midday on Saturday. The KNLA camp was eight kilometres further into Burma, after which the old Japanese road gave out again. The track was wretched; stumps and roots tried hard to smash the pickup's suspension. But the camp itself was large and well-ordered. A high wooden archway bore the Company insignia. Timber houses and offices, with split bamboo walls and tin roofs, lined up neatly across the wide compound, surrounded by a slit-trench – a rather more serious one than that encompassing the militia camp. There were machine-gun nests, a church, a small hospital.

All around the camp were swidden fields worked by the service families, watched over by a string of observation posts, each with an old motorcar hub or similar resonant scrap as an alarm clanger. The Army was nicely settled.

Beyond a small stream full of children and buffaloes, the Second-in-Command lived up on a hillside. Climbing the hill I passed a hut with the chalked slogan, 'KNU loves KNLA'. The 2IC's house was enormous, hardwood and lofty on its stilts, extending back and back towards the forest edge, full of rooms and family. Brothers and sisters and spouses throughout, children underfoot, over whom the young 2IC presided with a cheerful lack of apparent authority. He was said to be a stern but caring commander; here he was a genial paterfamilias. His brother, the Lieutenant, told silly jokes all afternoon.

Bartholomew declared another clinic, upstaging the military nurses in the camp hospital below. Plastic matting for the examinations was laid at one side of the verandah. By mid-afternoon the sick had filled the other side, waiting and watching; the 2IC sat amongst the crowd gossiping amicably. There were casualties: a boy of nineteen with persistently infected sores on a leg badly hurt by a landmine two years before; another man with a wooden leg which was hurting the stump – same cause; another man blinded – same cause. Always mines: always legs and faces.

It took too long to see them all; we'd have to stay the night, but had brought nothing with us. While half a dozen women killed chickens and stirred fish curries at the rear, the 2IC brought out a new sarong and a heavy army jacket for me to sleep in.

At Mergui, at the far end of that near-vanished trail, the Burmese army was rumoured to be impressing Karen villagers as porters – which was usually a sign that something was going to happen. But, with the rich hospitality and a most substantial-looking camp below, from which, later, came the sound of hymns, I was feeling smug.

Sunday morning church parade – Bartholomew did not attend. We sat about on the verandah at a loose end, only joining the Company for tea after the service – brewed and served from an enormous wok out in the open. I decided that I would start the journey back through the forest by myself, on foot, leaving the others to follow as they pleased. Bartholomew remained at the 2IC's house, irritably turning through back numbers of the KNU *Bulletin* while waiting for the vehicle. I didn't get far. There came an emergency summons; the Colonel was obliged to leave for GHQ in a hurry, and wanted me to go with him, but I'd had enough of his scuttering about. Anyway, at the Township office I'd met Bismarck again:

> 'Yes, we are back here now. Our babies were getting sick all the time at Headquarters and so we returned. It is quite dry here; perhaps my health will improve also.'

He asked me to bring aspirin; the youngest child had a fever and Judith was suffering migraines. It was difficult to feel much optimism for them. They'd been given a cramped and squalid hut – just a sheltered dirt floor with a small sleeping platform at the rear. The children, meek and sweet, were being as little trouble as they could but the youngest was flushed and unhappy. Judith, between giving her drinks and wrapping her tighter in blankets, sat on the ground in the open shelling castor oil nuts. I gave her my supply of aspirins. Bismarck, as nervous and twitchy as ever, hung about chattering.

> 'There are many cobras in the long grass here. Also there are wild cats which are taking my chickens. Also we are sent here to work, you see, they have a school here now and they need me. I am almost well although I am hellish tired sometimes. Judith is almost well . . .'

We didn't dwell on it, but talked of America instead. Then Bismarck took me to see a family who'd built themselves a larger house along the same ridge: more refugees. The old father, a watery-eyed sexagenarian soldier, had been on the border customs post for the last two years, dunning the cattle-traders. Also in residence was a fat-faced young pastor from Headquarters.

> 'There is no pastor here for the refugees. I am to inspect them; I think I will be sent to work here.'
> A sigh of very weary anticipation. Then he brightened up.
> 'I do not think that this will be a permanent place. We all hope to return to our homeland.'
> 'Isn't Kawthoolei your home now?'
> 'My goodness, I am from Burma! This Kawthoolei is an illegal, temporary place. When our fight is over we shall go to our own land. How can I be at home here? I am of the Delta, I don't like these mountains. I want wide fields! Do you know

the history of Israel? Israel was in Egypt forty years before they won back their homeland in Palestine. Toh Meh Pah will lead us home: that is what we believe.'

I wondered if that was how he would teach the second coming in the refugees' Sunday School.

That evening, in an attempt to make it seem a little more like home, the Township resorted to a familiar tactic: a video in the schoolroom. It was a three-hour Indian version of *Aladdin*, in song. Janice and Two Shoes made their excuses and left. I lay awake in my hammock most of the night, listening to the heavy lorries rolling south to Malaysia down the tight strip of Thailand a mile or two to my east, passing Kawthoolei by.

There are records of Karen fleeing Burma for Siam as early as the eighteenth century; flight is part of the culture now, like being an orphan.[14] In the weeks following our return from Maw Daung, I spent more time with True Love, Great Lake and Bartholomew out on the water, and I began to see how deeply the whole District was permeated with the idea. One Township headquarters, a village that had been there since well before the Second World War, had replaced its population with refugees; most of the present inhabitants had fled from a town upstream which had been captured by the Burmese a few years back. That was where True Love's wife Silver had come from. Downriver, a Buddhist village had come *en bloc* from the Front Line after the Burmese army had repeatedly forced them to carry rice and ammunition through the forest, and here a monastery and two schools had been built, as well as experimental wet rice fields – failed, but nonetheless tried. They had built up reserve rice stocks against the arrival of more families. No patient inertia here; they showed every sign of flourishing, with a determined reconstructive energy.

A third village had moved back from the Front Line five years before. Here was an atmosphere of struggle, of such cashless helplessness that there wasn't even a small shop to sell torch batteries and tins of pilchards. 'We are refugees, we have no money at all!' they would tell me, although I noticed that the shop a little way downstream seemed to be thriving on somebody's custom. It was a cynical observation, because there were sickness and shabby clothes in most houses, lacklustre children, a mother attempting to keep on working in the fields even as fulminating sores on her legs burst open and spilt pus down her thigh. But their hospitality never failed. The Sunday morning that I was there, the deacon gave thanks in the Baptist church that God had seen fit to send an Englishman amongst them once more; such a pity that the visitor had not seen fit to come and join them in worship.

There were Burmese refugees too; a colony appeared on the river-bank in June, running not from warfare but from economic disaster in Ne Win's Burma. They camped among dense trees near Barter-ville, their pots of lukewarm rice lopsided on the sand, their children squealing in the water. They were cheerful enough, they were wait-ing for a lorry to come and take them off to seasonal wage-labour in Thailand. Bartholomew almost smirked, telling me that, siege notwithstanding, rice was now seven or eight times as expensive in Burma as it was in Kawthoolei. The Burmese refugees were welcomed. Their sick sheltered in the little hospital and received treatment from the midwife. And their truck did come.

Kawthoolei holds out its emaciated arms in welcome; individuals, families and whole communities respond. Some arrive with cattle, cash and heirlooms; others come destitute. We met a woman of sixty-plus who had carried a sewing machine for four days through the forest, her equally venerable husband carrying the iron under-frame.

But, on all sides, the strain showed. It was not only the physical and financial burden; the fabric of Karen social morality was, some felt, threatened by the influx. Saw Moo Troo (p. 5) wrote:

Honesty is decreasing markedly among our people. Beehives marked are no more respected. Fish pools reserved by private persons are no more treated as private. Properties hidden in jungle store-rooms are ransacked and stolen. Vegetables and fruits in gardens and paddy fields are regarded as common property. This moral decay is due to the increase in numbers of refugees and armbearers from remote areas.

In Bartholomew's house there was an evening ritual. Squatting on the bamboo floor with his children, his glued-together specs, his abacus and his lists and charts, he totted up the refugees as they came, all neatly categorised by sex, age-group and place of origin, then pushed the papers at me, stabbing at a figure with a pencil. 'Two hundred and thirty-seven!' he'd exclaim fiercely, as though it was something inexplicably overlooked by the rest of us. And afterwards, the endless tense meetings up at Head-quarters and the allocation of an ever-higher proportion of ever-scarcer resources, time and manpower to the clinics and the sawmill.

> 'Why send all that to Maw Daung', I asked, 'when you've got whole villages upriver with nothing at all? People are just as sick up here ...'

As I began to appreciate Kawthoolei's role as a refuge, Bartholomew betrayed exasperation, pointing at packs of mongrels, saying, 'Those are refugee dogs! Go on, photograph them, bring them aid, why don't you?'

He himself had no choice. Politically, symbolically, emotionally, the promise of shelter had to be made good. The umbrella, however, had begun to rip in the storm. Two weeks after my return from Maw Daung, True Love said:

> 'You remember the 2IC you stayed with at Maw Daung camp? You remember his brother, the Lieutenant? A friend of mine, one of our best fighters. He has been killed. He took his section to a village they thought was safe. He left his men in the forest and went into the village alone to check – but the Burmese were there. He tried to escape but he was recaptured, and then they cut off his head.'

At Maw Daung, tension increased as new reports came from Mergui of Burmese preparations for an offensive. At the Township, three Burmese were arrested as spies. They'd been visiting before, carrying Buddhist bronzes for sale. This time, when all three came together and seemed far less interested in hawking images than in asking questions, they were seized by the militia and Harvest Moon the Justice set off south to deliver judgement on them. The putative assassin of the Township Chairman was smarter. He persuaded his amorous guard to let him out for a shit and, while the latter's attention was, as usual, taken up with his woman, the prisoner vanished into the forest.

Meanwhile, three Thai farmers had also been arrested. They'd been caught with marijuana growing in the middle of their fields. But the local Thai border commander had presented the Karen with irrefutable evidence of the dope-gardeners' good character and, in the circumstances, they had no choice but to let the men go. It was not the moment to be prejudicing the open border.

The attack came in March. Villagers who had been forced into porterage for the Burmese troops sent warnings up ahead to Maw Daung. The non-combatant population left, crossing into Thailand; I heard that they were camping under plastic near Parachuap Khiri

Khan, and catching cold in the rain, and that the Thai authorities were not allowing foreigners to visit.

At Maw Daung there was a vicious battle. The KNLA estimated that 1,300 Burmese soldiers had come towards them through the forest; several hundred then made a frontal assault on the pass. From the Burmese point of view it was a shambles. When they reached the Township they found themselves with the Karen militia (that sad football team, as I'd thought) on one side of them, and the KNLA on the other. Maybe as many as forty or fifty Burmese were killed, including four officers: 'They were looking at a map – one mortar shell!' crowed True Love. Retreating hurriedly, the Burmese disappeared into the forest and for a while we thought they were cut off, trapped in unfamiliar terrain without food or water. But there was no further engagement, and some days later villagers reported the hurried withdrawal of a large force carrying many wounded.

There was, said True Love, another explanation: 'If the Burmese soldiers are given orders for a two-week operation, that means exactly fourteen days, and they know they will be punished if they return early. So they hide in the forest until it's time to go home.'

There had been just one casualty on the Karen side. As the KNLA retook the Township, a Burmese mortar lobbed a bomb at them. It landed near an officer and buried shrapnel in his back. They tried to get him out to hospital at Parachuap, but the spinal cord was cut and he never made it over the border. He was the best officer they had in the District, said True Love; it was the 2IC, whose brother had been killed ten days before.

A week later, with the Burmese gone, the refugees were back in the sawmill. At about this time I learned that there is no single, simple way to express the idea 'safe' in the Karen language, without suggesting what it is that you are safe *from*. The general concept of 'safety' does not interest them.

12   A delicate bamboo tongue

Costard: O, they have lived long on the almsbasket of words!

Love's Labour's Lost

I made my first attempts to learn Sgaw Karen at my mother's house in Oxfordshire. I had two books,[1] the *Introduction to the Study of Sgaw Karen* by Saya Kan Gyi (Rangoon, American Baptist Mission Press, 1915), and a *Grammar of the Sgaw Karen* by D. C. Gilmore (Rangoon, 1898). Both these began by requiring me to study a new script, similar but not identical to Burmese. Because of its predominantly rounded forms, this is sometimes called 'apple script'. To me it looked like an optician's fantasy of spectacles, monocles and long-handled lorgnettes. The grammar asked me to convert these little curls into meaningful noise, assuring me that, 'If the learner will remember to breathe hard in pronouncing the aspirates သ , and ဟ , he can hardly fail in getting the correct sound.' The *Introduction* cheered me up by asking me to translate grubby phrases – 'Who soils my book?' and 'I drop the ink on the organ' – as light relief from more serious matters: 'The light is in me but darkness is in you.' The history of Karen literacy is imbued with a high moral tone throughout.

Some Karen believe that they once had a script and a written literature of their own, but that they lost it. Lt Col MacMahon (1876, p. 188), quotes traditions that speak of an old 'palm leaf book that is written in circles' but there is no sign of it now. An inscribed metal plate found among the Bwe Karen is said to be a specimen of the old script and the KNU *Bulletin* reproduced it in 1986. The clusters of straight lines on the plate, resembling twigs and claws, tell us nothing; the only progress towards deciphering it has been to suggest that certain small asterisks mark the periods. Its provenance is equally mysterious; it was supposedly one of seven, made out of a bucket and given to seven brothers.[2]

'Lost writing' myths are common world wide. The Karen version is perfectly in character; the loss was, they say, entirely due to their own laziness and stupidity. In the simplest version, someone gave 'the Book' to a dog to carry, and the dog dropped it while crossing a river. In more developed versions, God bestows gifts upon each of three brothers – a Karen, a Burmese, and the 'white younger brother'. The others take good care of their books, but the Karen places his on a tree stump while he gets on with the rice planting, and the 'white younger brother' removes it overseas. The Karen are thus obliged to wait for the white brother to return, bringing them both the Golden Book (which the Baptists equate with the Bible), and the Silver Book, which is often taken to be Education. There are many variants on this theme but the conclusion is always the same: bloody fool *pwakenyaw*.

They do seem to have missed an early opportunity to gain, or regain, literacy. The various historical scripts to be found in Burma derive from Sanskritic models. By the eighth century AD, both the Mon (who controlled Lower Burma) and the Pyu (dominant in Upper Burma) had adapted a script from Madras known as Pallava. But in *c*. AD 718 the 'Cakraw' – very possibly Sgaw Karen took part in the sack of the Pyu capital. The Pyu were dispersed and soon faded from history. The Cakraw learnt little from their triumph, and certainly not the Pallava script. When, however, the Burmans seized the Mon capital of Thaton in 1057, they were smarter. They took the most learned Mon monks and scribes back to their capital at Pagan and set them to adapt the Pallava script to the Burmese language. Apart from rounding out the square Pallava forms into the characteristic Burmese apples and lorgnettes, the system needed little alteration. The first inscriptions in Burmese date from the following year. Having missed their chance, the Karen had to wait a full millennium before at last getting their script – derived from those same Burmese apples and lorgnettes for them by a quite new race of priests, from America.[3]

For the Karen, the nineteenth century was the Baptist century. The story of the Karen conversions, once a Sunday school favourite, is little heard now. Even to a sceptic, however, it is a remarkable tale and bears another brief retelling.

The first American Baptist missionary, 'the great' Adonirum Judson, arrived with his wife in Burma in 1813, and for many years struggled for converts in a hostile atmosphere. The Judsons came close to being executed by the Burmese during the First Burma War of 1824/5. After the war they were allowed to move to British (Lower) Burma, and were joined by another couple, the Boardmans.

A new base was established further south, at Tavoy, where they recruited a Karen house-servant called Ko Thah Byu. The Boardmans had no more success among Burmese Buddhists than had the Judsons, who had managed one convert in seven years. They had, however, begun translating the Bible into Burmese. The servant, Ko Thah Byu, showed great interest in the book that the missionaries were making – rather surprisingly, since he was a self-confessed bandit and multiple homicide. He started to ask questions, and with a sudden access of enthusiasm declared that this was the Lost Book of the Karen which their songs promised would be brought back to them by the white brother, the book which they had been so disappointed to find that Captain Michael Symes' embassy had not been carrying in 1795 (see chapter two). When the Boardmans opened a school for illiterates, Ko Thah Byu studied to become a gospel preacher in his own right. From then on, the Baptists never looked back. With Ko Thah Byu as their advance guard, heralding the return of the Book in the villages, the Americans converted and baptised entire communities. They then sent Karen preachers to work on the Kachin, Lahu and other tribes who had similar prophecies. Conversions ran in the thousands, peaking with the 4,419 Lahu baptised in a single year (1905/6) by William Marcus Young, a feat which even the Baptist authorities found suspicious.[4] In the meantime, perhaps one quarter of the Karen were converted and became, if today's Karen Baptists are any measure, very devout Christians.

In this spectacular success story, the written word was paramount. The Bible in Karen – the tangible Book – and a network of Christian-run village schools were the backbone of the endeavour. Without an actual volume in the pastor's hand, the Karen would have taken no notice. In 1828 George Boardman was taken to a village where twelve years previously a passing Muslim had given the people a book which they had been worshipping ever since:

With a long train of followers, the chief appeared, bringing with him the sacred relic. The basket was opened, the muslin unrolled, and taking from its folds an old, tattered, worn-out volume, he reverently presented it to Mr Boardman.

It proved to be the Book of Common Prayer and Psalms, of an edition printed in Oxford.[5]

At Tavoy the Boardmans now had another colleague, the English-born Jonathan Wade who had joined the American Baptist Mission.

Wade began the translation of the Bible into Karen and compiled the bulk of the *Anglo-Karen Dictionary* that is still used today. Wade began work on a script: '... before I could speak a sentence in Karen ... I adopted the Burman alphabet ... for the simple reason that we had Burman type and no other in the printing office at the time'.[6]

Fortunately for Wade, Sgaw Karen is related to Burmese.[7] They are both monosyllabic, and also tonal; in Sgaw Karen a word may be said in one of six rising or falling tones, radically altering its meaning. Burmese 'apple script' provides a system of marks for these tones. While the sounds used in Sgaw are not all the same as in Burmese, there were enough symbols left over to cover the Karen anomalies. The only other change that Wade needed to make was to introduce a little punctuation in deference to the verse structure of the Scriptures. The script as finalised by Wade was logical, consistent and thoroughly practical. The production of printed books could begin as soon as the translations were ready, and school teaching could follow close behind since some Karen could already read Burmese. Thus, almost overnight, Sgaw Karen became a literary language. Wade's associate Francis Mason adjusted the script for Pwo Karen a few years later, and in 1843 they launched a Sgaw newspaper, *Sah Muh Taw* (*The Morning Star*), which Mason claimed was 'the first native newspaper ever published east of the Ganges'. The *Morning Star* thus preceded the Burmese *Sun* (*Thooryah*) by sixty-eight years.

MacMahon (1876, p. 74), wrote:

The effect on them was electrical. Tottering old men and aged matrons, as well as youths and maidens whose pleasures were hitherto aimless and profitless, if not absolutely vicious, vied with each other in endeavouring to acquire even a smattering of learning.

The fruits of this work may be seen everywhere in Kawthoolei. Among Baptist Karen, literacy is the norm. Among the Buddhists and animists it is not, and that alone accounts for much of the power of the revolutionary Christians, who have access to government communications (they have even fitted Karen into Morse code), and to letters and news bulletins. In Riverside virtually every house possesses – and uses – at least a New Testament in Sgaw Karen, and one or more Karen hymn books as well. In Bartholomew's house there were several of each, his own Bible being wrapped in camouflage-mottle plastic.

In a bamboo shack at Barterville I bought myself a copy of Jonathan Wade's *Anglo-Karen Dictionary*. I found it on a shelf heaped with new Bibles and hymn books, and gospel stories illustrated with nineteenth-century engravings. The hymn book is smart and practical, in a plastic cover closed with a zip, to be carried through the monsoon rains to church. It is printed by Christian Communications of Hong Kong and, with a wary eye on the Burmese ban on imports of non-Buddhist religious literature, is inscribed, 'For the use of Karens in Thailand'.

Such delicate considerations didn't trouble Wade and Mason. Liberal British civil servants wanted government officers to learn the languages of the tribes they were dealing with: 'Let the Karen language be officially recognised as the vehicle of communication between the officers of Government and the people', demanded Smeaton in 1887 (p. 220). But it never happened, and for all their 'advocacy' of the Karen, the missions were not much concerned that it should. Their sole concern was the Gospel. To my knowledge the only available primer in Sgaw Karen is the Baptist *Introduction* of 1915. Though the Karen had supposedly made great advances in the public service by then, little in Saya Kan Gyi's lessons has any bearing on administrative life. As public functionaries, Karen worked in Burmese and English. The only reason a white man might have for learning Karen was for propagating the Word – and that always closely related activity, healing the sick.

I took the *Introduction* to Kawthoolei with me. Edward at once asked me to obtain a photocopy for Education Department use. Bartholomew turned the pages and read out the specimen sentences quietly. Nothing much had changed, he said. Thus encouraged, I tried to reconcile Saya Kan Gyi to the Revolution.

The primer includes a vocabulary of priority words: vinegar, violate, violence, virgin, virtue, vision, visit. Sentence construction begins with fundamentals, that is sleep, food and guns. The specimens give pause for thought about Karen life at the turn of the century: *I eat rice in the cup* (lesson 3), *My flower is on my head* (lesson 5) and *I shoot the gun in my house* (lesson 8). Thereafter, the focus shifts: *I shall read the Bible. I read six chapters. How many verses do you read?* We learn to distinguish between *John told us that he was not the Christ*, and *John talked with my father yesterday*, although only as regards syntax. These are interspersed with further fundamentals: *Today it rained very heavily. We got much rainwater*, together with exhortations: *I shall conquer if I try.* The last few lessons are mere lists of families of vocabulary, of fruits, of animals and of diseases

Plate 12. Pastor Moses reading from the Sgaw Karen New Testament at an
evening prayer meeting.

– Arcady preserved by the healing touch of the American Baptist
Mission.

This view of Karen life excludes not only any suggestion that
Karen might be dealing in their own language with persons in
authority, but also any thought that Karen might visit the towns,
let alone live in them. The Mission had a firmly rural view of the
Karen, to which they added their own form of social organisation.

Placing heavy emphasis on literacy, they spread their remarkable network of village schools throughout Karen territory. In doing so, the Baptists introduced a new concept into that loosely allied society of intermarrying villages – the idea of pan-Karen organisation. At the same time, in order to make the most of the prophetic traditions, the Mission annexed the oral literature.

I have no way of knowing what the full range of that literature might once have been. The Baptists held a monopoly on the collection and publication of verses; everything that has come down to us bolsters the idea of a flame of proto-Christianity burning in expectant village hearts, nourished by the certainty of white saviours. The vast majority of the recorded verses can be found in a handful of books by Francis Mason, Alonzo Bunker and their immediate colleagues. Even a Karen writer like Saw Moo Troo quotes the American Baptist renderings of his people's poetry. Most of the verses refer to God as *Y'wa*. However firmly historians discount ancient Karen links with the Nestorians and the 'Lost Tribes of Israel', Baptists have never ceased hinting that *Y'wa* is simply a mispronunciation or echo of *Yaweh* or *Jehovah*.

There are hymns of praise:

> Y'wa is eternal, his life is long.
> One aeon – he dies not. Two aeons – he dies not!
> He is perfect in meritorious attributes.
> Aeons follow aeons – he dies not!
>> (Quoted by Mason)

There is an 'Old Testament':

> Y'wa formed the World originally. He appointed food and drink.
> He appointed the 'fruit of trial'. He gave detailed orders.
> Nu Kaw Lee deceived two persons.
> He caused them to eat of the 'tree of trial'.
> They obeyed not; they believed not Y'wa.
> When they ate the 'fruit of trial',
> they became subject to sickness, ageing and death.
>> (Wylie)

Other verses admonish:

> O children and grandchildren! If we repent of our sins,
> and cease to do evil – restraining our passions
> And pray to Y'wa, he will have mercy upon us again.
> If Y'wa does not have mercy on us, there is no one who can.
>> (Mason)

Of the original Karen we have no trace, only these Psalmic translations. Of a rather different significance was this:

> The sons of Y'wa, the white foreigners,
> Obtained the words of Y'wa.
> The white foreigners, the children of Y'wa,
> Obtained the words of Y'wa anciently.
>
> (Mason)

Not everyone was so readily convinced. J. G. Scott, in his 1900 *Gazetteer of Upper Burma* (p. 524), remarked churlishly, '... it can hardly be amiss to point out that savage fancy in many places recalls Biblical statements,' (or, indeed, vice versa). Others asked why, if this really was a long-lost Christianity, Nestorian or otherwise, was there nothing resembling a Christ figure? Even the Baptist authorities had their moments of doubt. Faced with William Young and his Karen colleagues' astonishing conversion rate among the Lahu in 1905, the Mission sent investigators.[8] Their conclusion was that Young was pandering to pagan myths. But as that could be said of the entire Burma enterprise, and as the congregations in the United States were so enthusiastically contributing large sums to continue the work, nothing was done to hinder it. Burma was the first overseas project of the American Baptist Mission; their excitement was understandable.

Since then, attitudes have changed a little. The verse examples above I have quoted indirectly, from the modern American Evangelist Don Richardson's book *Eternity In Their Hearts* (1984, chapter four). Richardson regards the verses as divinely inspired prophecy, and discounts the various 'Lost tribe' and 'Nestorian' theories. I read Richardson's book on the verandah of Ruth and Edward's house in Riverside, where it had been deposited by a visiting Californian.

I never met a Karen, in Riverside or anywhere else, who could actually recite 'the old poems'. They know them now in printed form. The one aspect that has been perpetuated orally is the goodness of the 'white younger brother' – rather oddly, I felt, as this brother had actually purloined the Book in the first place. True Love and I went to visit Silver's grandmother with a tape-recorder, and she sang a little rhyme which updated the tradition further:

> Look out to sea! The English are coming
> in planes and ships.
> You'll see them coming with golden ships,
> bringing the Golden Book, the Silver Book
> and the Laws.
> These are our lost books.

> 'Have you ever seen the *Golden Book*, Jo?' asked Bastion.
> 'You mean the Bible?'
> 'The Bible, yes, but also we have this other *Golden Book*.'

He went into the bedroom of his small house and could be heard rummaging. Rose, his wife, sat making clothes on a Jones treadle sewing machine. Their son had the baby suspended in a sling from the ceiling and was pushing it to and fro. A senior school student who lived in Bastion's house sat in the corner fiddling with a radio searching for Burmese news. Bastion re-emerged with a small green paperback.

> 'This is the *Golden Book*', he said, 'which a Karen man has collected. This has all the prophecies in it, and all about our Karen poetry. I really want you to know and understand our Karen poetry.'

He turned through the first pages of dense 'apple' type. The book was dated 1955.

> 'Who wrote it?'
>
> 'A famous Baptist teacher called Thera Htoo Hla E, who has gone to all the villages and written down all the old poems that people can tell him. Here, this is the introduction which I shall read to you. He says: "We must teach the young about the poems because they are the gift of our ancestors, their promises and their warnings. The young must not forget their ancestors. Their poems are precious, the greatest achievement of the Karen people. The ancestors loved poetry and communicated in poetry because it is profound. It is said that they sometimes made poems together for seven days without rest." Now you see, Jo, here are all the chapters ...'
>
> He read me the list of contents: 'The history of our ancestors, their true and fulfilled prophecies. God creates Adam and Eve. Sickness and death. The Flood. Satan. Our ancestors' warnings. Karens' expectation that Literature will come to them. Our ancestors' exhortation to their children. The Bible reflected in the poems ...'
>
> 'Can you help me work through it?' I asked.
>
> 'We shall read it all.'

We began with the verse forms. There are two basic Karen verses: *Ta law pwee* are quatrains with lines of seven syllables. *Ta daw yuh* are longer.

'You see', said Bastion, 'he explains every one. This is a little one':

> *Hsaw mi O, O ler pwa puh.*
> *Y'wa hay kay ner ta nar huh.*
> *Hsaw mi O, O ler pwa kla.*
> *Y'wa hay kay ner ta thay nya.*

When there are wild chickens in the forest,
You don't hear Y'wa coming.
When there are wild chickens in the jungle,
You don't know of Y'wa's coming.[9]

'It is a poem about God, you see, Jo? Thera Htoo Hla E says that the wild chickens are Satan, who prevents us from hearing the word of God.'

Bastion began a longer example that spoke of the noble and beautiful mountains surrounding us, the myriad trees to be found there, and how Y'wa loved to walk there and farm this beautiful land. But again, the wild chickens came to scratch up his good work. And again the editor paraphrased; Satan has undone all the good work wrought by God among the ancestors. Biblical references are given for comparison, to Isaiah (6:9–10) and to John (12:37) – 'But though he had done so many miracles before them, yet they believed not on him.'

Other verses do not always mention Y'wa directly. The imagery is charming, and Bastion grew excited:

> 'In this poem, Jo, it says that you cannot follow the flight of flies through the forest because they are too fast, and you cannot follow a wild goat because it is too quick. Not even with a dog will you be able to keep up with it. But the goat will leave a trace that you can follow with your dog. And now, the Editor explains this, Jo; he says that the mystery of God is unfathomable but still our ancestors felt its presence, although they did not yet know that the Gospel was coming to them.'

Another chapter deals specifically with Toh Meh Pah. After re-telling his story, verse prophecies alluding to Toh Meh Pah's return are explained. Bastion read them out:

> 'Before Toh Meh Pah returns, three things must come to pass. The first is that the Karen lands must be joined to other lands by great highways. And you see, Jo, this is true and it has already happened, for now we have the Burma–China High-way, and there was the railway to Thailand also. Then there is the prophecy that a great bird-shaped rock shall sing. I don't know about that.'
> 'What's the third one?'
> 'I am not so sure; this is very difficult old Karen language. Now look, here are the ancestors' prophecies about the English':

Lee tuh lee say, lee pa Y'wa,
Lee law mah plah ler kola.
Lee pa Y'wa, lee tuh lee say,
lee law mah plah ler puh deh.

Gold Book, Silver Book, book from Y'wa,
The lost book found by the English.
Book from Y'wa, Gold Book, Silver Book,
The lost book found by the younger brother.

Another verse identifies the enemy: 'Before the white brother brought the Golden Book, in the time of the Burmese Kings we were taught by Burmese Buddhist monks. Beware! This is not true Karen literature.' On occasion the Karen are themselves equated with the Satanic chickens. 'Because we have lost our literature, we're like wild chickens wandering in the wilderness. When the white younger brother brings the Golden Book, there will be peace among the Karen, see Psalm 126 verse 1: "I will lift up mine eyes unto the hills, from whence cometh my help."'

If the parallels were sometimes a little free, it was not for want of trying. Later chapters set them out in detail, and Bastion read them to me by the light of my failing torch, stumbling and hesitating often and stopping to ask his wife Rose and the schoolboy in the corner what the 'poetic old words' meant.

Twelve parallels are drawn between the Karen and the Israelites:

1 Just as the Israelites trace their descent from Adam and Eve, so the Karen have two original forebears, Saw Ther Ner and Naw Ee U.
2 Both the Israelites and the Karen are clearly elect and beloved of God.
3 Prior to their decline into animism, the Karen worshipped one all-powerful God, like the Israelites.
4 Both made sacrifices to that God.
5 The Karen prophetic poems are equivalent to the Psalms.
6 The old Karen also had communion with God.
7 Both peoples acknowledge his sovereignty.
8 Both tribes had prophets. The most famous Karen prophet was Wee Maw Leh (early nineteenth century) who, a few years before his death, foretold the coming of the missionaries.
9 The trials of the Karen, their poverty and their oppression, are the result of disobeying God – as with the Israelites.
10 Israel in Egypt, the Karen in Burma: similar servitude.
11 Both nations have been promised a land of their own.

12 As Israel awaits a Messiah to bring them to the Kingdom, so
the Karen await the coming of Toh Meh Pah. He is a parallel
to Christ, and is eternal.

The presiding spirits of the *Golden Book* are, however, not Toh
Meh Pah but Adonirum Judson, George Boardman and their colleagues, whose careers are recounted and whose portraits are reproduced in the little volume.

What, I wondered, did the Buddhists and animists think of this
wholesale requisition of the traditions? Perhaps by now they have
been persuaded that the prophecies are the property of the Christians only. Within a few years of Wade's script for Sgaw Karen,
and Mason's for Pwo, two other Pwo Karen scripts came into existence. Neither of them were Christian work, and neither was used
for the old poems, which only appeared in 'Mission' script and
thus became part of the Christian domain. Of the two other scripts,
one is said to be the work of Pu Ta Maik, reputedly the first Karen
to be given Royal permission to enter the Buddhist monkhood in
Burma. The other belongs to the *Leke* sect, a quasi-Buddhist group
who combine distinctly Karen elements with millenarian expectations of the coming of Ariya, the future Buddha. Their sacred
text, which is now preserved only in a copy in a school exercise
book, is written in a script known as 'chicken scratch', because
that is what it looks like. But, while thus establishing some measure
of literacy for their adherents, neither the monks nor the Leke
teachers shared the Baptist realisation that writing meant power.
The Baptist script is simple, easily taught in schools and easily
put to widely different uses. The Buddhist monastic script is (says
the scholar Theodore Stern (1968b), who compared the three), idiosyncratic and 'less explicit', while the *Leke* version is 'lavish', difficult
and exclusive; few can read it. The Buddhist script is taught almost
exclusively to Buddhist novices, *i.e.* males. 'Its main uses', writes
Stern, 'serve personal ends, in writing letters, in jotting down the
words of songs, and in recording chronicles. As such it enhances
the style of life and invests the Karen with the dignity of a writing
system of his own.'

But the limitations are obvious. For example, the monastic script
was no good for writing heterosexual love letters if the girl concerned
couldn't read it. The Christian girl could read hers. Broadbased
education gave the Baptist script unmatched authority, and gave
the Karen a unity beyond traditional norms. As the majority of

those who became Christian were Sgaw Karen, so it was Sgaw that became the dominant language of Christianity, of the schools – and, now, of the Revolution.

Ein Volk. Ein Reich. Eine Sprache. In 1887 Donald Smeaton (p. 221), wrote, 'No people can long survive the extinction of their own language . . . If the [Karen] language is perpetuated, the national customs will probably take care of themselves.' Smeaton never specified *which* Karen language. 'The Italian of the Orient', Harry Marshall called Karen, partly for its beauty but also for its more than twenty distinct variants. Sgaw, Bwe, Pwo and the others are mutually incomprehensible and when I found myself with True Love in Pwo villages, he looked most uncomfortable at the chatter going on around us.

'I haven't a clue what they are saying', he confessed. 'I am not sure how we will get on here.'

Saw Moo Troo lists eight attributes of the true Karen, including language – but he doesn't specify which language either; in fact he avoids discussing it at all.[10] The French scholar Georges Coedès (1966, p. 10), calls language, 'the only criterion for distinguishing the various ethnic groups that share the soil of the peninsula'. But on those grounds, Kawthoolei's claim to represent a common Karen cause looks rather thin. In many units of the KNLA – in which many of the senior officers are Delta Sgaw but a high percentage of the rank and file are Pwo – the language of communication has to be the only one they share: Burmese. This use by allies of the language of their enemy is not new in Burma. When the Japanese invaded the country and made common cause with Burmese nationalists, they often had to communicate in English.

Sgaw Karen, the language of the Christian leadership, is the 'front' language of the Revolution, of all formal documents and proceedings. It is the language of the education system, and thus presumably a unifying force. Even within Sgaw, however, there are variations. It is very typical of emergent states that priority is given to establishing a national language. In many post-colonial countries, National Academies have been set up to standardise and dignify the chosen language (often selected on very delicate political grounds, from many contenders.) In standardising the language, some model of the 'best usage' is identified. But they do not necessarily choose the language of the metropolitan power centre. Often some other cultural focus – Florence, for example – is seen as having more linguistic authority.

'So where do they speak the best Karen?' I asked True Love, wondering if he would propose Papun or Pa-an, traditional 'capitals' of the Karen.

'Tavoy', he said, firmly. The little port of Tavoy, in Lower Burma, has never been a predominantly Karen town.

'Why so?'

'Because that is where the missionaries first worked. They made their studies of Karen at Tavoy and wrote their grammars there, their dictionaries and their translations of the Bible – it's all in Tavoy Karen.'

'You're not from Tavoy,' I said.

'No, I'm from near Rangoon, and I do not speak very good Karen.'

'But that goes for most of the teachers here.'

'That's right, we're from Upper Burma. We have different pro-nunciation, and we don't understand many of the old words. Only people from Tavoy know them.'

Which explained why Bastion had been having trouble with the *Golden Book*. Neither he nor Rose knew the vocabulary.

'Perhaps we could ask Pipi Dierdre?' I suggested. Pipi was univer-sally respected as the most senior and cultivated person in Riverside.

'No good', said Bastion, 'She's from Rangoon.'

Only the schoolboy in the corner, a local lad, knew the answers.

Bastion had actually refused to teach Karen in the school, on the grounds that he didn't speak it well enough. He wasn't the only one who felt uncomfortable. One of my tasks was to prepare a short course of simple language lessons for future health teams from Britain. I was making tape recordings of specimen passages in Sgaw, one of which Ruth, the school headmistress, had written for me. But when I took out my cassette machine and microphone, she protested; she couldn't do it, she said. Her Karen pronunciation was terrible. I must get one of the students to record it.

The very last sentence given for translation by Saya Kan Gyi's *Introduction* is this: 'Enemies do not sit side by side. They always sit one in front of the other.' In 1954 Edmund Leach (pp. 11 and 17) suggested that many aspects of a culture may be 'unintelligible' except through reference to another culture. He wrote, 'The main-tenance and insistence upon cultural difference can itself become a ritual action expressive of social relations.'

Leach was writing particularly of the confrontation between sub-groups of the Karen's northern neighbours, the Kachin, and between the highland swiddeners and the lowland wet-rice farmers. For Kawthoolei, of course, the confrontation now is military. Sgaw

Karen has been the official language of that confrontation ever since the foundation of the Karen National Association in 1881. But even after a century of nationalism, even within Kawthoolei many of the revolutionaries freely speak Burmese. This is not wholly surprising; before they left the towns of the Delta to come here, for many of the Karen the language of daily life was Burmese. Karen nationalism has never outlawed Burmese. Edward and Ruth spoke Burmese to each other at home. Pastor Moses remarked that he liked talking with True Love because he spoke such good Burmese. For the young élite from Rangoon, Burmese was the modern prestige language they liked to speak among themselves.

Burmese is taught in Kawthoolei's schools, and True Love was happy to teach it. 'There are so many things we cannot say in Karen', said Great Lake, 'so many words we need to take from Burmese.' He and True Love liked to point out that Karen was often very close to Burmese, but not too close. William gave an example:

> 'We Rangoon people have a Karen language that is also Burmese. For example, our word for coconut:
>
> > Burmese *on"thi* (*thi"* – fruit)
> > Rangoon Karen *U thi" tha*
> > Sgaw Karen *ghwaw tha*. (*tha* – fruit)'
>
> Thus the Rangoon Karen is a tautology, doubling the general 'fruit' but leaving out the specific 'coco' part. I asked True Love why he thought this happened:
> 'It is because our mouths cannot make proper Burmese sounds.'
> 'But True Love, everyone says that you speak excellent Burmese.' (Laughter.) 'Perhaps you don't want to get it quite right?' (Further laughter.)

You find it repeatedly in Kawthoolei: the desire to return, to be part of Burma, and the little markers of distinction and opposition. Hugh Tinker, a British historian who has little time for the Karen, wrote in his *Union of Burma* (1957, p. 179), that the Burmese policy of excluding 'lesser languages' such as Karen and Kachin from schools and public life 'is certainly the right policy for the long haul. There is no place for parochialism and clannishness in Burma today, and nothing will create a true sense of solidarity so surely as the acceptance of a common language.'

Since Tinker wrote, Burmese policy has been a little more subtle. In 1964 an Academy for the Development of National Groups was created. General Ne Win declared that, although the state had responsibility for matters such as economics and defence, the various ethnic groups would now be responsible for all matters relating to culture, language, literature, religion and the like. In July 1987 I listened to a conversation between a Canadian lawyer and two representatives of Kawthoolei's Foreign Office. The lawyer asked:

'Have the Burmese offered any cultural concessions? I mean, it's very common, it's a way governments try to defuse separatist issues, by seeming generous in cultural matters. Have they ever offered anything like that?'

'No', said the Karen, 'nothing at all.'

A cursory glance at a history book would have told the lawyer otherwise, but the Karen were in a dilemma; how can you define yourself by opposition if the enemy tells you to do as you like?

It was quite different with the Thai language. Karen have been in Thailand for centuries but, in his *Introduction*, Saya Kan Gyi lists the Karen for Englishman, Burmese, Indian, Chinese and Jew but not Thai. Something in Karen–Thai relations made it unnecessary. The main difference in the situation of the Karen in Thailand is that they have not usually been in a state of violent confrontation with their hosts. Of course Siam/Thailand was no paradise, and had its own racial tensions. But the Karen did not, at least when Saya Kan Gyi was writing in 1915, feel any need to counter-distinguish themselves from the Thais.

They learned to speak Burmese, but they did not learn Thai. In 1904 Lunet de Lajonquière noted that '*mes bons Kariengs*' did not speak Thai at all, even though they were working for Thais. The pattern is less firm today, but still holds. A modern Thai ethnographer, Preecha Chaturabhand (1987, p. 195), writes of Karen in northern Thailand: 'The primary mark of identity for Karen seems to be language, and they frequently comment that they do not like to speak Northern Thai even though they know some of it.'

In our District, hard up against the border over which traders, refugees and others went to and fro, hardly anyone spoke Thai, nor could they read the quite different script. It often made for problems with, for instance, medicine labelling. Edward spoke very little, though he of all people knew how important it was coming to be. Neither the Colonel nor most of his Headquarters staff knew Thai, though delicate negotiations with Thai border officials became more critical by the day. Thai is certainly not taught in Kawthoolei's schools, although its importance for business now, and mere survival in the future could not be more obvious. But they don't want to admit that. As with exiles anywhere, to learn the language of the country of exile is an admission that you are going to stay there, that you are not going home, that you have lost whatever war it was.

> 'Why don't you teach Thai in the school?' I asked William.
> 'It is not Central Education Committee policy. If we decided to do that, it would have to be out of hours, in the evening.'
> 'It would be difficult', said others. 'We would have to have native Thai teachers.'

This was not a consideration that had stopped them putting enormous energy into teaching English. Besides, there was hardly a shortage of readily available Thais. But the authorities wouldn't hear of it.

On the quiet, though, several of my friends were learning Thai. The Colonel had bought himself some tapes. True Love had a Thai grammar, and studied it in the evenings just as he did English. Whenever his brother-in-law, a soldier in the Thai army, came to visit, True Love would use him to try out his pronunciation. Karen has less in common with Thai than with Burmese, and in Thailand someone who muffs their tones and drops final consonants is said to 'speak like a Karen'. True Love was not very good as yet, but he was sticking to the task. Great Lake asked me to buy him a very solid Thai grammar in Bangkok. He used to have a big Thai dictionary once, he said, but he'd hidden it somewhere in the forest and had been unable to find it again. In the meantime he made do with my Thai phrasebook for tourists, which told him how to order wine, dry cleaning and prostitutes in Bangkok hotels, and how to say to your girl-friend, 'I name you Queen of the Southern Seas'. Just as the Thais are now, at last, becoming alarmed by the numbers of Karen entering their country, just as tension and xenophobia are increasing, the Karen are beginning to learn the language.

As their situation in Burma worsens, the assertion of the Karen language as the essence of national identity has relaxed. Kawthoolei needs all the friends it can get, and cannot afford to be too fussy about their conversation. Full Moon, the senior school student who told me that his ambition on leaving school was to kill his enemies, was also a decent singer and guitarist. He recorded a song for me, in Burmese:

The mountain's beauty, the waterfalls,
the song of the birds – that's our people's home.
Frank and honest they are, so
even if you don't speak Karen, come to us!

Please believe it, here we're all equals.
We'll welcome you with smiles.
O, my far away friends, come to us!

'It's a nice song', said True Love, who translated the Burmese for me, 'but he's got a lousy accent.'

The more I was told of Karen and Burmese chauvinism, the more I saw the linguistic boundaries crossed. At every crossing, the Karen indulge in a blend of pride and mocking self-deprecation.

Great Lake was one of my more meticulous Sgaw language tutors. I had a lengthy set of model English sentences for translation, designed to elicit certain characteristics in a second language, and Great Lake did most of these for me. The work ran over several days, not least because he was so concerned to give me the exact, the very best Karen equivalents. Often he would go into his house and consult with his family. At times he was humiliated by the realisation that there were things that Karen could not neatly express which, to be idiomatic, would have to go into Burmese. At the same time, it was Great Lake who was fondest of bilingual jokes and the macaronic mock pidgin that he and I developed together. 'Bloody fool *pwakenyaw*' was one of his, as was 'another *ke daw ter blaw*' ('try just once more'). He would ask me to pronounce the names of fruits, howl with derision at my bungling of the tones, and thereafter we would know that fruit by the literal English re-translation of what I had said:

Mango *ta kaw tha* 'foot fruit'
Papaya *mah tha* 'son-in-law fruit'
Chilli *mo hay tha* 'mother come fruit'

Our conversations were a bilingual babble. James Matisoff (1969), found that bilingual misunderstanding is the basis of a whole class of jokes among the hill tribes in the region. Many of his examples are close to jokes that Great Lake told me, and usually the essence is self-mockery. A wife asks her husband to buy her a cake in town, and his inadequate Burmese leads to her eating a cake of soap. A favourite story, which Bartholomew acted out with all his finest buffoonery, concerned a British Army officer employing Karen workmen to construct the telegraph wire from our river valley out to Thailand. A party of Karen are attacked by a rogue elephant who demolishes their work and the thickets nearby. A terrified Karen runs to the base to find the officer but can only splutter out, 'Elephan bamboo *taw* bong bong!' (*taw* – tear up). The Englishman, well used to the Karen, knows just what he means. Just occasionally the jokes were more apparent to me than to them – such as when one of Bartholomew's nursing students, in a test question on skin diseases, managed by a slight mistake with the Sgaw tone marks to change 'boil' into 'saw'.

The normally well-disposed Lt Col MacMahon (1876, p. 51), described the Karen as 'so utterly devoid of humour as to be unable to appreciate a joke of any kind'. But the Karen have kinds of wit that MacMahon failed to recognise. The language is rich in playful counterpoints and subtle imagery. Learning it was a delight. For example, a monosyllabic language has only a limited number of basic morphemes to carry contrasts of meaning, even when the possibilities are multiplied by the tone system. Sgaw Karen, therefore, have to construct new words by elaborate combining and recombining of the limited set of units of possible form and meaning, the monosyllabic morphemes – as though the language were a verbal bamboo, extremely simple in its basics but capable of endless flexibility in new uses. One only had to learn the most effective patterns of combination.

Some of these patterns allow for the creation both of new phrases and also of delightful perceptual concepts. They can be found in a number of related S.E. Asian languages. In one, a four-unit structure is built around a simple anchor word. In Karen, a common anchor word is *po* – 'person' or 'child'. Some examples:

> *hee-po-haw-po* 'house child ladder child' that is, family, household.
>
> *sah-po-kaw-po* 'star child land child' large animals, such as cattle. Other examples created new categories:
>
> *twee-po-toh-po* 'dog child pig child' that is, the sorts of animals that live under Karen houses.
>
> *to-po-li-po* 'bird child squirrel child' that is, the sorts of creatures that frisk around in trees.

'You cannot split the phrases up!' protested True Love, when I asked him to confirm my understanding of *sah-po-kaw-po*. 'This is poetic, the small words have no meaning on their own.' But in examples such as 'dog child pig child' or 'water child land child' (citizen), the words obviously do have a literal meaning that is perfectly consistent with the whole phrase. True Love meant what he said, though. In combination, they have an elusive, extended nuance. In another pattern of combined words, there is a 'balanced pair':

Ke re koh, ke re nar the village elders.

The phrase is made up of *ke re*, a gathering or community, *koh* (head) and *nar* (ear). Thus it means 'the village head, the village ears'. Plain *ke re koh*, 'the group head', is just the village headman. The addition of *nar*, 'ear', is firstly a joke at the expense of the language itself, guying the metaphor of 'head on a body' as applied to officials. At the same time, the 'ears' obviously have a very good meaning in their own right, since the elders are both the talking shop of village politics and, supposedly, those who listen to and are sensitive to village opinion, and those who hear and pass down instructions from government. The subtlety of mind involved is only apparent when the phrase is spoken as a whole and is, as True Love said, 'just beautiful'. The monosyllabic language uses these elaborate expressions (says Matisoff: 1986, p. 76), for two reasons: they give 'phonological bulk', and have 'elegant stylistic value'. True Love convinced me that they were poetry.

The Karen, says Saw Moo Troo (1981, p. 11), are not a people 'clever in twisting words'. But such a language, of double shadows and bilingual laughter, is not one that need be called 'lesser', or that need be nervous of its future. Indeed, for decades the Karen have been consciously equipping it to meet new demands. At breakfast, I asked Moses:

> 'If you don't have a word that you need in Karen would you just take it from Burmese or would you ever look at other languages, or what would you do?'
>
> 'We have a committee! To make new words in Karen. It is old now, the origins go all the way back to the Karen National Association before World War One. And then, after that war, there were Karen scholars who had been trained by the Baptists. Have you heard of Thera Than Byah? He wrote a book called *The Karens and Their Progress* in 1913. These people were very concerned about our language. Saya Kan Gyi, who wrote those lessons that you study, he was another. Our National Association had meetings until the Second World War and then, when our national feeling was very strong in 1947, we formed a Karen Cultural Committee to make the language strong too. We still have this, it is called the *Pwakenyaw ta ketoh athaw ke re*, the "Karen New Words Committee". The Baptist missions gave

them advice and they made lists of new words they said we
should use instead of Burmese words which were common in
Karen.'

'Where did they get the new words?'

'Some were quite new, which they made up. Others were very
old words which they brought back, perhaps with a new meaning. The man who wrote the *Golden Book*, Thera Htoo Hla E,
he collected many old words as he went around the villages
collecting our traditions.

'I will give you an example. Now we have a revolution, and we
wish to tell our people that they have a duty to fight for their
freedom. But there was no word in Karen for "duty". When
I was a seminarist just after the Japanese had gone, we used
the English word with some Karen explanation; we had to say
dutee ta mah ler er law bah ('duty the work that must be done').
Now, that was too much to say, not a good slogan. So we found
an old word, *mudah*, and this was reintroduced about 1951.
This is the word we now use.'

'True Love wrote a song', I said, 'called *Ta eh daw ta mudah* (Love
and Duty).'

'Well, he could not write a very good song called *Ta eh daw dutee
ta mah ler er law bah.*'

'How does the committee tell the people about the new words?'

'There is a paper published by the Baptist Convention, called
Leh Suh Nya (Go Forward!). They used to put an extra piece
of paper inside that, with the new words. It is still published,
but not so many words now.'

For a few minutes we ate in silence. Then Moses said,

'You are humming again.'

'I'm what?'

'When you eat you make a little humming noise.'

'I'm sorry, I'll try and be quiet.'

'It is all right, but you will marry an old woman.'

'Thank you so much.'

'Yes, this is what our proverbs say about a man who sings when
he eats. Not an old spinster, I mean, but a woman who has
been married before.'

The Karen New Words Committee has not yet had the nerve to
issue in Burma coinages that would be useful in a revolutionary
state. Such new terms are required, however, and Highlander told
me several of them. The names of official Departments, for example.
Some are simple and straightforward: *suh klay / mah ser / we klo*
– the Health/Assistance/Department. Others are more luxuriant,
for example that of the Transport Department. There is no single

word for 'transport' in Sgaw Karen, so they put all the different words for 'carry' together: *wee soh daw sher we klo* means 'back-carry hand-carry head-carry and dispatch department'.

Highlander's own office, which I call the Information Department, is more properly the 'Organisation Department'. They are responsible (amongst other things) for publishing news and propaganda both within Kawthoolei and to the outside world. New coinages were the least of their problems.

> 'Where do you get things printed?'
>
> 'Oh dear, such trouble! We bought a press, you see, and that was fine but then with the new Burmese attacks we decided that it was in danger and we should move it out to Thailand. We did a deal with a Thai company. We gave them the press on condition that they would do all our printing for us at cost price. But now they are saying that the prices of paper and ink are going up so much, and that they have to charge us more than we can afford. At the moment we get our printing done in Chiang Mai where it is cheaper – cheaper than our own press!'
>
> 'That's not the only problem', said Edward. 'We would like to bring our press back, but we don't have anyone who really knows how to use it properly, or at least to fix it when it goes wrong.'

He wanted me to recruit a printing instructor from England for the KNU.

> 'This is a big problem for us', said Highlander. 'We had to close down our radio station at the same time because of danger from the Burmese. So now our people can only listen to news from the BBC Burma Service or from Rangoon or the Catholic radio in the Philippines. We need our own.'
>
> 'But you do still publish?'
>
> 'As much as we can. We publish a news sheet called *Ta Nuh Tuh* (*The Golden Horn*), 3,000 copies each month, and the *KNU Bulletin* in English, 1,000 copies each quarter, if we can. Sometimes we can do a magazine for the Women's Organisation, or the National Democratic Front. It always depends on money.'

Highlander and Edward, Arthur the Agriculturalist and the Colonel himself all shared a dream: to see their schoolbooks and technical manuals printed in Sgaw Karen. Until that happened, they felt, neither their people nor their language could develop. Bartholomew, for instance, was far more fluent in both reading and writing

Burmese than he was in Sgaw. This was not because he preferred Burmese; it was simply that everything that he was interested in was published in Burmese.[11]

If better translations could be done, and if the money could be found for printing, the KNU would still face a difficulty that was bequeathed to them by Jonathan Wade and the first Baptist linguists. It is the problem of typeface. For obvious reasons, very few Thai printers possess a fount of Karen type. Those that have one can dictate their terms to the KNU.

Even as the early Baptist missions worked on their script, their dictionaries and Gospel translations in Tavoy, others involved with the Karen began experiments with a Roman script. They never made much ground in Burma but in Thailand, visiting Karen communities north of Chiang Mai, I found Romanised Karen in use. For the tone marks, it simply employs those letters of the alphabet, such as z, of which Sgaw has no other need. I don't know if, in point of detail, the Roman script permits as accurate a rendition of Karen sound as Jonathan Wade's converted Burmese – but it works.

Wade, Mason and their colleagues were fine scholars and linguists; they were also passionately pro-Karen. Had they been active a century later, and seen the worldwide predominance of the English language and Roman script that was undreamt of in 1830, it is unlikely that they would have chosen to adapt Burmese. As it was, the foreigners who did most to stimulate the Karen national identity also isolated revolutionary Kawthoolei, by means of a typeface.

True Love in love 13

Saw Ter Kwa (O my beloved),
Listen to what I tell you.
Remember how, in the old stories,
Toh Ki Baw and Naw Tho Mu
Loved each other faithfully;
How Ku Naw Lay tried to save
Naw Muh Eh from the serpent's jaws.
My love will be as strong as theirs.

Song recorded for me by Ku Wah and True Love

I went on tour with Come Quick and True Love. Come Quick could not sing this particular song. She was a nurse from Bartholomew's Department who had got her name by virtue of an easy birth. In sterner quarters she was regarded as a shameless hussy; I thought her delightful. She was attractive too, in a tomboyish way. But she had a gap in her front teeth, and this was the reason that she couldn't sing *Saw Ter Kwa* – it always came out as *Thaw Ter Kwa*, or so said True Love who (if he could stop laughing for long enough) would imitate Come Quick singing and reduce her to foot-stamping rage. She was very easily teased.

But Come Quick did nothing to dispel her own reputation. Indeed, she was a prize flirt, and was teased for that too. This particular tour took us walking up a side stream to a village where there was a young teacher called Milly. True Love declared that I was in love with Milly and that Come Quick was crazy with jealousy. I grinned at the latter, hissing softly through my front teeth – and she came after me with a *parang*, chasing me round the compound and succeeding in cutting my finger, after which she went off penitently to gather certain salving leaves, rubbed them to a pulp with her spittle, and dressed the wound.

She had other endearing games. I had at this time some nasty sores on my right ankle, the result of infected leech bites, and Come Quick's favourite joke was to kick or hit these wounds with a stick when I was halfway up a house ladder. She offered me a bargain one evening in Black Turtle; I could pull the scab off her knee

243

if she could squeeze the pus out of my ankle. In spite of this she was, I thought, rather a good nurse.

When Colonel Marvel took myself and Bartholomew to visit the refugees at Maw Daung, the latter brought Come Quick and her friend Rosepetal to help him with clinics. On our return, we left them there for a tour of duty that might last anything up to two years. But a week later Come Quick reappeared in Riverside. She was pregnant. She had made a full confession to Bartholomew and he had ordered her back in a hurry. The village lads were merciless and racked the information from her. Young John the Justice's son came to report, announcing that he knew all the facts, 'We insisted: Where? How many times? We got it out of her. Six times, out in the forest. She told them at *Boarders* that she was going to gather vegetables!'

Before I had a chance to see her, or to hear who the father was, Come Quick disappeared from view once more. She had been sent to jail for three months for pre-marital fornication. Her lover was a soldier who was dispatched in disgrace back to the Front. There were four women in the jail at the time, all for sexual offences, and True Love said that they could sing, or thing, *Thaw Ter Kwa* together.

Karen folktales are frequently tragic, and the two stories referred to in *Saw Ter Kwa* are no exception, though it goes to a gentle, pretty little tune. Toh Ki Baw (Yellow Parrot) is the typical Karen hero, a poor orphan boy who falls in love with a rich girl, Naw Tho Mu – but her father kills him, and she throws herself on his funeral pyre in despair. In the other story, Naw Muh Eh is seized by a giant python; the snake will only release her if it can drink Ku Naw Lay's blood instead. So Ku Naw Lay cuts his own throat to save his wife, who dies of grief anyway.

These grisly tales have other common features, one of which is that the proper setting for romantic love is the solitude of the forest. One hero finds the woman of his dreams, a demi-goddess, bathing naked in a forest pool. In a motif familiar to folklorists, he traps her on Earth by stealing her clothes. In another tale, a young man caring for his aged mother in a remote forest clearing goes to look for food and finds hen eggs. Nearby he discovers the camp of a princess who, oppressed by court sycophancy, has retreated there. They become lovers.

The anthropologist Theodore Stern (1971), collected Karen harp songs in an area of Thailand not far from Riverside during the 1960s. One of the purposes of the songs, he decided, was to express in melody and metaphor your feelings towards someone in your audience, when such feelings could not with propriety be said direct. He quotes an example of a love song in which the secluded forest pool is now an image of love itself, cool and refreshing, shaded from the prying eyes of the sun and the public.

'This tribe is strictly moral', asserted a recent book on Thailand,[1] echoing a long tradition of similar judgements by missionaries, civil servants and the Karen themselves. Gaining a reputation for morality depends, of course, on whether your morals happen to coincide with those of the observer. The Karen and the Baptist missions suited each other well. The Baptists must have been delighted to see the close rein on which romantic passion was apparently held. They may not have realised what went on by forest pools, and public courting was restricted to a very few settings. At funerals, however, propriety could wear thin:

these are regular homeric orgies. Both sexes are seasoned, since they begin drinking strong drink before they are weaned, and staid married people shake their heads at the amount of flirtation that goes on between the unencumbered at these festivals.   J. G. Scott (1916, p. 35)

The Karen writer Saw Moo Troo (1981, p. 3), says that, among the Karen, 'There is no such thing as spooning or dating. They have no idea what dating is except through imagination.' Come Quick's imaginings seemed fairly concrete. Traditional courtship steered a fine line between asking parental permission and presenting them with a *fait accompli*. Marshall (1922, p. 176), says that marriages used to be arranged between young children but that even when he wrote, in 1922, it was a thing of the past. Romantic negotiations could begin very early, the engagement could be very long. Gandasena (1925, p. 77), claimed that, among the Red Karen, it was common for a boy of eleven or twelve to pick out his girl, win her consent, inform her parents and then wait until they were both twenty or twenty-one before marrying. Gandasena's information is most unreliable (see p. 188); nonetheless, a protracted courtship is still common.

For long-distance courtships, intermediaries used to be employed and romantic songs composed. These could be highly elliptical. As well as the imagery of forest pools, a favourite means of declaring one's love was to write a sort of Karen *Song of Songs* and call it an exercise in Buddhist devotion. Love messages could be sent between villages. Before the advent of literacy, these consisted of small paper packages containing locks of hair, seeds and other symbols that referred to traditional adages, and which had to be decoded by village elders for the recipient. With literacy, the proverbs could be spelt out. This did not make for any greater privacy, however, as the sayings were often so obscure that they had to be read out in public and debated.

In a traditional village today objections to a courtship normally only arise when someone (not necessarily a relative) thinks that there is a risk of offending the spirits, perhaps because the couple are already kin in some restricted way, such as first cousins. Such an offence endangers the village as a whole. Almost any taboo, custom or prohibition in Karen life may be explained as placating the spirits. Offend them, and the crops will fail, the pigs and buffaloes will die and the people sicken. The word is *chai* – broken taboo, leading to ill-fortune. It falls to the village elders to keep a close watch for anything that might incur the spirits' displeasure – the wrong members of a family living in the same house, or inadequate observances made to the rice goddess before harvesting, or sexual misdemeanour. If the elders fail in this duty, ruin will swiftly follow. What the missions have called 'morality' could equally well be described as fire-watching.

For the revolutionaries, the details of courtship and marriage have changed considerably, but beneath the surface familiar patterns may be glimpsed. The guardians of public morals have simply put on camouflage uniform; their probity is as pragmatic as ever.

A wedding tomorrow in Millionaires Row; glamorous and extravagant it will be. A man from the Mines Administration at Headquarters is marrying a very beautiful young woman from White Ponds, near the enemy. He is in his thirties, she is still a teenager; that is not so unusual. The Mines Director has his family home down here in Riverside, so that's where they'll marry from. Throughout today there have been people arriving, friends and relatives from Headquarters, half the Mines Department, all of them looking for a verandah with space to sleep on, while most of her friends from White Ponds have moved into the hospital and are camping there. Bartholomew's house gets its share; the conversation hasn't been so varied and splendid for weeks, all fuelled by betel.

Naw Bi, Monkey and Pu are in clover, staring at strangers and getting under everyone's feet, while the older girls grow short-tempered as they desperately try and keep pace with their mother's directions to produce cup after cup of sweet tea, or to go to the shop for cakes, while at the same time cooking the afternoon meal. Vermilion, born gossip and socialiser, lies on the bamboo floor smoking a Burmese cheroot and looking charmingly languid, gazing contentedly at each arrival.

They're cooking for 200 at the wedding. Behind the Mines Director's house, down the path leading to the river, fireplaces have been cut into the earth. In the morning, the animals are slaughtered. A pig is quickly dealt with but this is a truly lavish wedding and we're to have beef also – a rarity. The cow has no suspicions before it is suddenly hit very hard on the forehead with the back of an axe, falls, its throat slit promptly.

> 'Who's in charge of the cooking?' I asked Moses, noticing that
> a number of soldiers seemed to be involved.
> 'The KNDO militia, It's part of their training.'

In front of the house a booth or arbour is being built of flower-decked bamboo, big enough to seat the immediate wedding party. The families and principal guests will eat in the house. Down in the shade of the trees at the back, the soldiers are building two long tables of bamboo with fixed benches, to seat another hundred at least.

The large kitchen of the house is stacked with every aluminium pot they've been able to lay hands on, with heaps of broad new banana leaves as platters for the chefs. In one corner there is a pungent stack of meat, already moving with flies. In another, a heap of yams. Everything is to be scrubbed and chopped by this evening. The bride's father and her brother are steadily working through the meat, cutting it up small. Nearby a woman sits and chops the yams. Everyone uses *parangs* with eighteen-inch blades.

There is more activity beneath the house, between the mats and hammocks, farm tools, baskets and motor parts. The bride's mother and the Mines wives make cane and cardboard baskets for the ceremony, covering and trimming them with white crêpe while children cut out little white flowers for the women to sew in place. A white heart cushion has been made too, embroidered with the names of the couple, and is now being finished off with lace.

At the kindergarten the decorations are being installed. A rich blue banner hangs the length of the back wall, criss-crossed with crêpe streamers and tinsel. At the centre, there is another heart with the names of the bride and groom in gold paper. Chairs for the bride and her maid, the groom, the best man and the page have all been covered in white cloth embroidered with orange flowers, while the table for the register has a new cloth also and three sets of plastic flowers in wooden holders. Outside, streamers and bougainvillaea, purple and creamy orange, are being tacked and taped to the doorway.

In the late afternoon the soldiers light the cooking fires. They have cut four fire-trenches and on each there is now a wide steel wok into which the pork and beef are placed. An hour later, everything is managed by one man stirring each wok with a wooden oar. There's not much for the others to do now. They sling their hammocks between the trees and laze, nursing radios. But, as the evening draws in, people begin to converge in front of the senior school where, on the usual tiny television screen linked to the generator by an unwise arrangement of flex, there's to be a programme of Thai martial arts movies provided by the Mines Department.

Pre-dawn activity in Bartholomew's house. A row of sleeping guests fills the verandah, shapeless under cotton blankets. Fragrance is making bright yellow sticky rice with coconut as a first breakfast. The wedding is billed for nine o'clock; at the kindergarten there is a slow accretion of spectators. True Love is there in clean military uniform; Bartholomew is there in full Karen dress. There are a number of smart gentlemen in crisp tropical suits: the Mines Directorate. Several have cameras. A group of young schoolgirls in blue skirts and white blouses are hovering near the doorway, each carrying a pair of wands tied with ribbons of pink and red, orange, yellow and blue. The half-hour gone, voices are asking if the bride has changed her mind. Then the first procession appears.

The groom and his best man come from the Mines house. They come with a small choir behind them, blowing along with cheerful hymns accompanied by a guitar. The groom and the best man are identically dressed, with bright red Karen tunics over long-sleeved white shirts, white trousers and white shoes too. On their striped tunics each wears a pink rose grown here in the village, with a spray of ferns cut in the forest. They walk quickly over the 200 yards to the hall, and take their seats.

Two minutes later the bride's party comes from a neighbour's house – another musical band, but with more attendants. Her parents are with her, her father has an enormous yellow kipper tie hanging down the front of his Karen tunic. His wife has on a deep blue lace blouse over a long, flower-patterned sarong. In front of the bride walk the two little maids, one carrying a basket of flowers, one the heart-shaped cushion trimmed with long bows. They are very young; they must be shepherded and encouraged by their aunt.

The bride and her first maid are both in the long white dresses of a Karen girl, with three delicate stripes of green, orange and red at the throat, bordering the small V-neck and then falling straight to the bottom hem, interrupted only by a band of colour forming the high waist and bust. They wear white socks and plastic sandals. Both girls carry large bouquets of pink and white roses. The only difference between them is that, whereas the maid's hair is kept in place with a simple white satin bow, the bride is wearing a long nylon veil that reaches the back of her knees and is trimmed with sweet-scented white *mali* flowers. Her face, lightly powdered, is pale and silken.

Again, there is no solemnity in the procession. The accompanying songs and hymns are quick and joyful, and the party moves rapidly across the main village road and up the dusty path to the kindergarten. As they came into the compound, the six schoolgirls with coloured wands are waiting, forming arches for them to pass under – then scampering in front again to form the arches three or four times.

Inside the crowded hall, the guests are standing. As the bridal group enters, a very old man playing a very old fiddle performs 'Here Comes the Bride' uncertainly, accompanied by Julian on electric guitar. The bride, her maid and the two little girls with the flower basket and heart cushion take their seats, and the service begins.

There are prayers, there are hymns from Riverside School choir, a choir from White Ponds, the bride's village and another from the Mines Department. They simply stand up in their groups among the benches and sing. And then Harvest Moon the Justice, his fine belly swelling out under the stripes of his tunic, begins an address. He refers to a folk song in which the Karen people are exhorted to follow the example of the black and white cranes, which do not mix and keep strictly to their own sort; thus, says Harvest Moon, a man and women become one at marriage and should remain that way. And if the wife sees some crows flying overhead and says that they are cranes, her husband should agree with her that they are of course cranes. That is the way to harmony.

Then Moses performs the ceremony proper, just as at any Baptist wedding anywhere in the world: rings and blessings and vows and, at last, the signing of the Register.

Then, straight back to the Mines house for the wedding breakfast. Now the procession is followed by a crowd that scuffs up a thick cloud of dust as they go. As the new couple approach the house, there is an obstruction. Friends of the groom have erected a low fence across the path and they will not let the couple cross until the bride has allowed herself to be kissed. They hold up a large mirror so that she can see herself assaulted. She is intensely embarrassed. It is the first time in her life that she has been kissed in public and it will certainly be the last; it is something that Karen simply don't do, and of all the imported details of the wedding, this to me jars most crudely, is vulgarly out of place. But the groom's friends are adamant; she gets no breakfast until she submits, and the crowd are shrieking at her to comply. At last there is a roar of applause; she has allowed a tiny, rapid peck – he snatches it and recoils like a chicken taking grain. The barrier is removed and they pass through, and the family party are seated in the little flower-hung arbour where they are served with green and pink soft drinks chilled by a twenty-kilo block of Thai ice, together with small, brightly coloured cakes and cream buns. The bride and groom feed each other cake, the groom gets cream on his tunic. They are, at last, relaxed and grinning broadly.

Just outside the arbour is a small table on which a few wrapped presents and some banknotes have been placed. The bride's mother goes to count the money. And then, with no warning, the groom stands and leaves the arbour. He's had enough of ceremony, he wants a real breakfast and goes into the house to find one. The guests follow, and they sit down to beef stew and fat pork, plantain curry and pints of pink sugary fluid. Outside at the long tables, scores of friends, soldiers and freeloading village children do likewise. An hour later there are second and third shifts at the long tables, while up in the house latecomers are still eating and the betel and cigars are circulating. But the groom has disappeared. It's over, as far as he is concerned. The bride wanders around outside, still in her long traditional maiden's dress, surveying the debris of her wedding.

Plate 13. 'Moses performs the ceremony . . . just as at any Baptist wedding anywhere in the world.'

'Was your wedding like that?' I asked True Love.
'Nothing so grand. That sort of wedding costs a lot of money; I have no money and nor do Silver's family. Nothing about our marriage was very grand.'

We were travelling downriver. As usual, the counterfeit-Rotax motor had packed up and, as Great Lake took it to pieces once again, we sat on the beach staring at the water. The occasional small fish got up on its tail, ran across the surface for a yard or two and then dropped back in, True Love described a revolutionary courtship:

'If you wish to get married, first of all you must get to know the person very well. Then you must inform the head of your Department, so I told Edward as I was a teacher then. If you are both in government departments then at least one of you must have worked for seven years before you marry. In fact I had only worked for six years and Silver for less but we were given special permission because I was getting old and because we were both going to continue working afterwards. So, you must find the person that you love, and then you propose. I was very nervous, and Silver refused me the first time; she wasn't sure. Later we made a trip on the river together and stopped in many romantic places and she said yes. So we went to see her parents. You don't ask their permission, you just inform them. We wanted to be married very soon, but some people wait a long time, maybe three years, to be sure that they really like this person; we cannot usually get a divorce if we have made a mistake.

'We don't get married in church here, not even the Christians. We use a hall or somewhere like that. Because Silver and I are both teachers, we were married in the school. For us a wedding is really a civil ceremony. Any senior official can per- form it − a head of Department, for instance, or the Justice. Of course, I am also a soldier, so I asked the Lieutenant-Colonel to marry us. Silver's parents were there but mine are in Burma so they could not come. Edward stood in for my father. So all our employers were there as our sponsors. Good tactics!'

'What did you wear? Karen dress? Or a grey suit like Sasi?'

'Oh no, we could not afford anything special. We wore Karen dress − and I did *not* have a shirt on under my tunic; I think that is ridiculous. Silver looked very beautiful in her white Karen dress.'

'She does anyway.'

'Oh yes. And we had the school choir, and some little cakes and drinks. It was very simple. And the next day we went back to work. I was living in the *Boys Boarders* at the time. We moved in with a teacher friend until I could get my house built. I have some photos of the wedding. Can you get me copies made in Thailand? And I'd like one of me in uniform with Silver in Karen dress, because she looks so lovely.'

When a shooting-star passes overhead, the Karen say that a boy in the heavens is going to visit his lover. On Earth, 'getting to know the person very well' involves strictly decorous visits and restrictive public protocol, and love letters. These at least are now reasonably private – although in Bartholomew's house anything addressed to Fragrance would be seized upon by her mother and siblings and read aloud while she hid in the bedroom, stamped her foot and moaned with chagrin. True Love and Silver had also exchanged letters, but a great deal more discreetly.

The next stage, asking the permission of your department head, is no mere formality; a commitment to the Revolution is not that easy. A month or so later, Rosepetal caused considerable embarrassment.

Rosepetal was a nurse in Bartholomew's Health and Welfare Department. It was she who had accompanied us, together with Come Quick, to Maw Daung and the refugees. Come Quick had returned, pregnant, almost at once. Within a month, Rosepetal was back too.

> 'But I thought she was going to be staying with the refugees two
>   years', I said to Bartholomew. He gave me a black look:
> 'I take you south with two nurses and look what happens.'
> 'What has happened?'
> 'She wants to get married.'

He went off muttering to himself, and the Gossips had some suggestions as to why. Rosepetal's lover was a young man at Headquarters called David, who manned the border customs post. As such, he reported to Edward in the latter's capacity as General Finance Officer. David had asked Edward to go on his behalf to Bartholomew, to ask his permission to marry nurse Rosepetal. But Bartholomew had refused. His Health Department, which was desperately short-staffed, had supported Rosepetal throughout her schooling, and she had served only four of her obligatory seven years in return.

That was two months ago. But now, here she was back from Maw Daung and about to get married. 'She has to get married', said True Love, 'for the same reason that Come Quick had to go to prison.' Hence Bartholomew's fury. But this time there was no incarceration.

Rosepetal's wedding was a joyless affair. They were supposed to be entertaining all the village to a pig-feast breakfast, but the soldier ordered to execute the pig wasn't equal to the task. He missed the animal's heart; it escaped and ran off into the forest.

'Terrible waste of B.600', said True Love, 'they should have let me do it.' The wounded pig was found later and dispatched, and we all got a bit.

The wedding was held in the senior school, by virtue of Edward's Education authority. They were both in full traditional dress. Rosepetal processed from the women teachers' hostel, David from his sponsor Edward's house. The choir of girls from *Boarders* was under-rehearsed and sang badly. At Edward's request, I took a lot of photographs. He at least was determined to see the thing done properly. Pastor Moses officiated.

'Well, at least the Church has forgiven them', I said to my neighbour, who replied, 'He doesn't know.'

After the service they sat down to a rather hurried tea in the junior school but Harvest Moon wouldn't touch it, saying that he only ate real Karen food, not those prissy little Thai cakes. David and Rosepetal left as soon as they decently could.

But Bartholomew's heart had softened and his anger with Rosepetal faded. She had promised to continue working for the Department. That evening, Bartholomew held a prayer meeting for them in his house. It was a sober but not unpleasant occasion. Moses spoke of the marriage at Cana; we drank sweet tea. I took a photograph of Bartholomew listening impassively to the homily. In the lamplight it required a four-second exposure, but he didn't move a muscle.

I was discussing weddings with Great Lake when a pattern occurred to me. Weddings that were in the least suspect took place not in the church hall but in any other public building. It was understandable that, in unions where the girl was already pregnant, the Church might feel it wrong for the ceremony to be held in even a marginally sacred place. But there were other differences. The most 'modern' weddings, those in which the couple wore grey suits and full bridal dress with all the panoply of a Saturday morning in Sheffield or Rouen, were always held in the church hall. The more 'traditional' the ceremony, in costume at least, the more likely it was to be held both under a cloud and in the school. We ran a swift check of a dozen recent marriages and the pattern seemed to hold. It was as though these eager Delta revolutionaries, for whom the establishment of a traditional Karen identity for Kawthoolei was such a priority, felt that they must atone for their offences against inherited sexual mores by looking as traditional as possible.

Great Lake was unimpressed by this theory. He wanted to point out something more fundamental:

> 'Why are all these girls pregnant in the first place? I tell you, all they know how to make in this place is babies. Is that what Karen maidens should be thinking of? In my village, if a father catches his daughter talking to a strange man he is very angry with her and sends her back to the kitchen at once. It is this village, it is a wicked place. They are not so free at GHQ. There they have soldiers who patrol at nightfall, and if young girls are found out with young men they are reported and there is big trouble. Here they can get away with anything.'
>
> 'What do you want, more soldiers?'
>
> 'More soldiers, and less grass and bananas.'
>
> 'What?'
>
> 'There are too many places to hide here. They like to go out and ... well, get married among the bananas.'

For once, Great Lake was running contrary to tradition – or at least, to traditional reality, if not the ideal. Everyone who has investigated marriage customs among the Karen reports the same thing: that 15–20 per cent of couples pay a small fine at their wedding, the penalty for premarital sex. Non-Christians may be required to sacrifice a chicken. Again, the great danger is that the spirits might be offended and the crops fail.

When Come Quick went to jail I asked Highlander of the Information Department, who had sent her there? He said:

> 'This is a special law made by our President, General Bo Mya. He is, you know, a Seventh Day Adventist, and a very strict man. He believes that our Revolution will not prosper if we behave improperly. The penalty is from one to three months in jail. Anyone can complain against a couple like this, but usually it is a senior official. Perhaps Bartholomew himself reported her, I don't know. He may have felt obliged to; he is responsible for those girls.'
>
> 'Isn't the man sent to jail also?'
>
> 'Oh yes, sometimes, but not if he is a Front Line soldier. We need him too badly.'

I asked True Love, 'Is there any homosexuality among the Karen?'

> 'I don't think so. I have never heard of such a thing among our men, although there was a case a few years back at Barterville. A woman there ... she did something, I don't know what. But

the *Women's Organisation* wrote to the Colonel to complain about her. We have a word for it in Karen, *ta eh puh ker*. It's not a real Karen word; it was invented by the missionaries.'

Down in the Cities of the Plain, Marshall wrote of Karen transvestites living in the Delta, some of them in steady cohabitation. True Love said,

'Of course, they do many things in Burma. I was at a boarding school where the boys all walked around naked, and a friend of mine who was a medical student in Rangoon says that the girls do the same in their hostel. He used to creep across to see what he could see.'

They wouldn't stand for that on this river – not even walking through the village in your swimwear. Captain Low (1839 p. 229), reported that Karen women 'adhered to their own fashions in dress, alleging that the lower garments of the Burman and Peguan fair are not only unbecoming, but indecorous. These assertions are, unluckily, too true.'

It is easy to understand the Karen feeling that their hills are surrounded by festering stews of lowland vice. I bought myself a Thai phrasebook which, in the shabby way of the Thai tourist industry and its clientele, told me how to instruct the hotel porter to bring prostitutes to my room. Great Lake was intrigued by it. It seemed to him that, if it was printed in a book, prostitution must be Thai government policy.

'Many foreigners are doing this in Bangkok.'
'What about Karen?'
'Some, maybe, when they go to Thailand.' He named one or two people that we both knew, one of whom ran a girlfriend in a Bangkok nightclub though devoted to wife and family in Kawthoolei. 'And there are some young Karen women who live in Thailand who are taken as young girls to do this; they become just like Thais. Burmese do, of course, and some Karen women in Burma. Not in the Karen towns like Papun. In those places a Karen girl will never speak to a foreigner, she will go to the back of the house. In the Burmese towns, though, I do not like what Karen girls do.'

A 1952 Burmese government report claimed that 25 per cent of the adult population of the cities of the Delta carried a venereal disease.[2] In Bangkok, just four hours by road, AIDS is pullulating – but Bartholomew said that he had never yet had to deal with a single case of VD in Kawthoolei.

One morning in May an old man with a creased face, grey hair and a mouthful of betel could be seen walking about the village together with a young woman in jeans. That in itself was enough to make people stare. Apart from the occasional military nurse, the only other Karen woman who ever appeared in trousers was Janice, on business visits with Two Shoes her 'husband' – and everyone knew that Janice was a loose woman living in sin.

But this was the old man's wife, and not his only wife either. In fact, he was reported to have ten. He was a Karen *doctor yangu*, a healer and potion-peddler, who lived just over the border in Thailand. I asked Great Lake, why should ten Karen girls want to marry this man?

> 'He is very powerful, he has many sorts of magic. These women are not forced to marry him; they want to be near him to absorb his power. The more wives he has, the more his reputation grows, and the more wives want to come to him.'
> 'Have you ever seen such a thing elsewhere?'
> 'Oh yes. I had an uncle who got married, and after his wedding discovered that his new father-in-law had gathered many wives like this – and was about to get another when my uncle decided that he had enough wives now, and killed him. Then the soldiers killed my uncle.'

Polygamy is not something that the state condones. Another *doctor yangu* who arrived at Barterville met and married a Karen woman there. But it was then reported that he already had a wife in Moulmein whom he had abandoned. He claimed that he was divorced, but the KNU demanded a B.15,000 surety from him against documentary evidence of the divorce. It was all very well harbouring Burma's refugees, but they weren't going to be a dump for Burma's loose morals and broken marriages as well. The man set off on the uncomfortable and dangerous return journey to Moulmein; whether he hoped to find the validating certificate, or was simply cutting his losses, I never heard.

Here is one of the stories referred to in the song *Saw Ter Kwa:*

THE ART OF ADULTERY

Ku Naw Lay was a famous Karen craftsman and sculptor. One morning he took his gun and went out hunting in the forest, but he lost his way. After hours of walking, he at last lay down under a tree and went to sleep. In the morning he was woken by the crowing of a cockerel; he looked up and saw a rooster, perched in the branches above him. It flew off, and Ku Naw Lay followed it. The rooster led him to a hill on which stood two houses. Ku Naw Lay approached and called out. He was answered by a woman's voice. Ku Naw Lay asked her for shelter and food. The woman replied, 'My husband, Say Blu, is out in the fields but let me give you a meal anyway. My name is Naw Muh Eh.' And that evening, when Say Blu returned, he of course welcomed the visitor and told him to sleep in the empty building next door, which Ku Naw Lay did.

In the morning, Say Blu went off to the fields again. Naw Muh Eh prepared food for Ku Naw Lay again, who asked if he could stay there a day or two and rest. He realised that he found her very attractive, so much so that, after a day of talking with her, he said, 'Why do you live in this lonely and dismal little house? If you would come away with me I would build you the finest home that a Karen woman ever saw.'

Naw Muh Eh was unmoved. In the evening Say Blu returned and they ate together. The next day, when Say Blu left for work, Ku Naw Lay continued his approaches to Naw Muh Eh. Again, she rebuffed him, but she did not tell him to leave.

After three days, Naw Muh Eh began to show signs of giving in. That night, Ku Naw Lay made a fine wood and clay statue of her, lifesize. The next day, when Say Blu left, he began his seduction again. Naw Muh Eh resisted at first but late in the afternoon she gave in and agreed to go away with him. They decided to flee together at once. Before they left, Ku Naw Lay placed the statue of her in the house by the fire, looking as though she was cooking. They left together. When Say Blu returned he saw his wife cooking by the fire and for some hours left her alone. Only when it grew dark did he speak to her and, when she made no reply, went over to touch her. By then, the fugitives were well away.

Say Blu set off in pursuit. In the course of his journey he met with many adventures, one of which resulted in him being turned into a giant python. In this form he made a long and difficult crossing of the mountains. There he came upon a beautiful house. It was so fine that he realised only Ku Naw Lay could have built it. Say Blu the python went into a deep cave nearby.

That night, Ku Naw Lay suffered terrible nightmares of disaster and ruin. He instructed Naw Muh Eh not to leave the house while he was out hunting. But, when he had gone, the python attacked a pig under the house. Hearing the noise, Naw Muh Eh descended the steps of the house – and the python grabbed her, pulling her into the cave.

In the struggle, a silver chain fell from Naw Muh Eh's neck. Her tame dove saw this, picked it up and flew after Ku Naw Lay. When he saw the chain, Ku Naw Lay ran back to his house, and heard his wife's gasping cries coming from the cave. When he saw her plight he pleaded with the python to release her, but the python said, 'I will let her go on just one condition – I must drink your blood.'

Ku Naw Lay hesitated only a moment; then he cut the palm of his hand and dripped blood down the hole to the python's mouth. But the snake demanded more and more, squeezing the woman harder until she was nearly dead. At last, in despair, Ku Naw Lay cut his own throat and fell dying at the entrance to the cave. The snake drank up the blood and now, his revenge complete, released his own former wife and crept away into the forest.

But Naw Muh Eh was not to be consoled. The villagers came and helped her carry her lover home, then built him a funeral pyre – onto which she threw herself to die beside him.

Many of the stories told me by William concerned adultery, and the guilty parties always die. It didn't seem to me that Ku Naw Lay was made out to be an especially wicked man, although a wife-stealer. Indeed, the song presents him as a model of self-sacrificing devotion. But in other tales, adulterers are executed by the king to the applause of the populace. They are never forgiven. I asked William:

> 'Why do you think Karen are so strict about adultery?'
> 'Maybe it comes from living in longhouses, as we used to. If you
>   lived that close to each other, you had to be very moral, to
>   keep the peace.'

Nothing brings out their wrath so quickly. From the first western contacts, writers have remarked the severity of the punishments handed down by the village elders. As described by Saw Moo Troo (1981, p. 3), the penalty is humiliation. A meeting is called:

Everyone, young and old, has to attend this meeting. Here pungent and vehement oration is delivered by the spiritual leader of the village directed primarily to the offenders and generally to the congregation. It is a stern rebuke addressed in this wise: 'We are assembled now to do a thing which we hate to do, to punish the wrong doers. They have committed immoral acts which are most shameful, loathsome and repugnant to our folks. We are cautioned by our ancestors and elders constantly to avoid sin, and indecent acts considered as moral and spiritual degeneration ... The present visitation of evil and misfortune is a curse which befalls the entire community. A severe punishment is called for. Now, strip. (The culprits have to undress.) You the mischief makers have to measure the walls of the hall with the length of your arms before the audience naked ... This is a warning to you all ...'

After this the couple are allowed to put on their clothes, and are expelled from the village for at least a year. They have also to supply one full grown buffalo for sacrificial offering for the atonement of their sin ... This operation is meant to purify the village to appease the evil spirit, and to cool and cleanse the land.

Other writers have recorded far more drastic procedures. Major J. P. Anderson reported on the Karen to the Siam Society in 1923. The punishment for 'illegitimate love affairs', he wrote, began with the guilty pair being brought before the village headman. On a table were placed three identical pills. One of these was harmless, the others contained a deadly poison. The man and woman were required to select one each and to eat it. They then walked out into the forest together. After an hour the elders of the village followed, to find either two corpses or a corpse and a survivor. In the latter case, that person was allowed back into the village to lead a normal life. The last known case, says Major Anderson, (1923, p. 56), was in 1912, near Chiang Mai.

British colonial moral norms were inadequate by Karen standards. Lt Col MacMahon wrote in 1876 (p. 335), that 'Bwe Karen ... who have come under British rule declare that profligacy has increased among them owing to the British law viewing breaches of chastity more leniently than their own law did'. The KNU have remedied this. Of the work party of prisoners that built my new house, three were adulterers. At the time I arrived in Riverside there were twenty men in the jail. Three were murderers. The other seventeen were all guilty of illicit love.

'They're not just adulterers either', said Great Lake. 'Three of them are Baptist pastors!'

Over the road in the little women's jail there were four convicts. Apart from Come Quick, they were all there for adultery, and their sentences ranged from ten to fifteen years.

> 'The problem with punishing adultery in that way', I suggested to Highlander, 'is that you make the situation worse. You remove any chance of reconciliation or a return to family life, and you often hurt the innocent as much as the guilty. Look at White Rock. He still loves his wife, but she's in jail for ten years. He'd take her back if he could.'
> 'There can be special dispensation, you know. But also he can now obtain a divorce. White Rock is a free man.'

In the old days, if not poisoned, adulterers were expelled from the village to avoid giving offence to the spirits. Now they are swept away into jail. 'Our President believes that our Revolution will not succeed if we are immoral', Highlander had said, 'He is a Seventh Day Adventist.' I wonder what the spirits would have thought of a story that Great Lake told me, and which several others corroborated. A woman at GHQ abandoned her husband

and took not one but two new men. The President, Bo Mya, got to hear of it. He had all three lovers shot.

Bartholomew set off for the jail one Sunday morning and returned twenty minutes later with Come Quick. All was forgiven amidst welcoming laughter. The child, a daughter, was born in the hospital and Come Quick was thrilled, walking round the village showing her to everyone, enormously pleased. At the time of her release Bartholomew grinned at me and said, 'Who shall we send you to Maw Daung with next?'

But it was not something for me to trifle with; Karen take marriage seriously. They are, the anthropologists say, protective of the reproductive capacity of their women. J. G. Scott (1916, p. 35), found that the Red Karen could be as fierce in this matter as in adultery. They used to have, he wrote:

very strict rules of endogamy, and the penalties used to be very severe. A large hole was dug in the ground; across this a log was placed, to which two ropes were fastened. The ends of these were noosed around the necks of the man and woman, and they were made to jump into the pit, and so hanged themselves. Now the custom is to excommunicate the woman, and both are forbidden ever to enter the village again. There are said to be two villages in the hills entirely inhabited by eloping couples.

The Burmese government is well aware of the value that the Karen place on racial cohesion, and would be only too happy if more Karen, Burmans and others would intermarry. Bastion, the teacher, had once worked for Kawthoolei's radio station, before Burmese attacks had threatened the transmitter and forced them to dismantle it. He played me a tape of ferociously energetic propaganda songs, accompanied by a clamour of shawms, drums and cymbals that he had recorded for the radio at Wan Kha Karen refugee camp in Thailand. One song shrilled, 'The Burmese chauvinists are trying to sexually obliterate the Karen by marrying our women!'

> 'It's rather odd music', I said. 'I've not heard anything like that here.'
> 'No, no', said Bastion, 'That's a Burmese style they're playing in.'

Like any other notion of racial purity, the pure Karen is a myth. Captain Low in 1839 (and others since) described villages of Mon husbands with Karen wives.[3] There's no reason to suppose things have changed. But the notion of purity comes and goes, focussed more or less sharply as circumstance and politics demand.

> 'Find Nelli a nice white man, Jo!' said Ruth the Headmistress.
> 'She has heard that babies of mixed race are very beautiful
> and intelligent. She is so beautiful herself: can't you introduce
> her to someone? She wants to ... how do you say? Broaden
> her horizons. It is very difficult for these girls to have broad
> horizons.'
> 'You want to marry a Karen girl?' asked True Love.
> 'He wants to marry that girl Milly', said Great Lake.

The two of them teased me all evening to the point where I
had to put my head under the blanket and declare myself asleep.
The idea of a Karen wife – so tempting, so easy, and yet what
would I be doing: either condemning myself to live in a non-state
fighting an unwinnable war, or condemning her to pushing trolleys
around Aberdeen supermarkets. I put the thought well out of mind
until one day I saw a wedding photograph pinned to a wall. The
bride was in Karen dress, as were all her family. The groom was
a tall white man. I asked True Love who this model of selfless
commitment could be.

> 'His name's Marcel. He's a French mercenary.'
> 'Let me sing you something', said Great Lake. 'We have a song
> about people like you. It is a warning to our Karen girls:

> Little girl, your mother tells you,
> Never love a white-skinned man.
> If you do, he's sure to leave you,
> and go back to his wife at home.'[4]

> 'If I was Milly's father', he continued, 'next time you came to
> the village I would tell her to go to the kitchen.'
> 'Did we meet Milly's father?' I asked. 'I don't remember him.'
> 'He wasn't there', said True Love. 'He's one of the pastors now
> in jail for adultery.'

Fermented monkey faeces 14

'To the Buddhist Bishop of Toungoo we are indebted for a suggestion that "Karen" is derived from a Pali word meaning "dirty eaters".'
Lt Col MacMahon (1876, p. 45).

But the Bishop was surely wrong. However once well deserved the Karen reputation for filth, in one tiny respect they have always been fastidious – as Capitaine Lunet de Lajonquière discovered in 1904:

Personally I never saw them wash anything other than the very tips of the fingers of the right hand, with which they took the sticky rice from the communal pot to knead it into balls – though this hygiene was never extended to include the whole hand.[1]

There is no doubt about their enthusiasm for rice. Sam, Bartholomew's son, would pack the soft white mass into his mouth with a frenzy that even the girls of *Boarders* found repulsive; they wouldn't sit next to him at meals. Sam could perhaps plead *force majeure*; even before the outbreak of war, the Karen would say to their children, 'Eat fast, the Burmese are coming!' Medical Officer Timothy had a capacity for rice that I hope never to see equalled. On our tours together he would sit himself down to supper in someone's thatched kitchen and devour five large platefuls in the time that I took over one and a half. Afterwards he would rise from the meats with a beatific smile – and then suddenly clutch his belly and start groaning, after which he'd have to lie down in pain for an hour. He claimed to have a hernia, and one could see why. Many Karen suffer agonies of indigestion; 'wind pain', True Love called it, swearing that it sometimes rendered them unconscious.

In view of their rice consumption, this was quite credible. A number of researchers have attempted to gauge Karen daily intake of rice and, while the estimates vary considerably, some say that an adult male Karen requires, each day, two-thirds of a kilo of uncooked white rice.[2] Think of that cooked – overcooked, to British taste – imagine the sheer bulk involved, and you have some idea of why they treat rice with such respect.

The urge for rice comes over Karen at any hour of the day or night. In the houses there is almost always a battered aluminium pot of it, hot or cold, sitting in the kitchen in case of need. On the road, the call must be answered in other ways. Lunet de Lajonquière's Karen *mahouts* spoilt his sleep:

> Towards one in the morning our Kariengs, hungry again, got up, lit a fire of twigs and set about cooking rice ... Woken by the noise, I rose, thinking that we must be about to set off – but I found that my good Kariengs, having swallowed their rice, were sleeping peacefully once more, curled up in their blankets.[3]

On our forest tours, if we didn't finish all the rice at one sitting, the lads would stuff it into plastic bags and carry it along for little wayside snacks.

Rice is the very core of Karen culture. That crowd of stars we call the Milky Way, is to them the Rice Bin. Where, on meeting an acquaintance, we might enquire after their health, Karen ask 'Have you finished your rice?'[4] Lt Col MacMahon reported that they knew forty different varieties of rice by name. In a people much given to storytelling, the 'story about storytelling' concerns rice. After I'd been importuning him for more stories William told it to me one evening. His wife cooked us a large plate of rice-flour banana fritters as he talked.

The story relates how a king who had a passion for stories issued a challenge. He would give up his kingdom, and present his daughter in marriage, to anyone who could tell a never-ending story. Failure was punishable by death, so no one would take him up until one day a poor Karen came forward and offered such a tale, on one condition:

> 'You must hear the story out for as long as I can keep going.'
> 'Agreed', said the king.
> 'Very well. Once upon a time there was a great emperor who was very greedy. Everything that he saw, he wanted, and anything that he demanded, he got. One year he collected so much rice that he ordered the building of a vast new barn, into which the rice was poured, filling it to the roof. That year there was a terrible plague of weevils in the land. They besieged the barn, because they could smell the rice but couldn't find a way in. At last one bug found a hole big enough for a single weevil to pass through carrying a single grain of rice. A first bug went

in, took a grain of rice and brought it out. Then a second bug
went in . . .

'One year later, the Karen was still there, carefully describing
the movement of weevils in and out of the barn. At last the
King could bear it no longer. "Enough! I'll be dead before
this is over. You can have my kingdom, you can have my
daughter – but promise me you'll never tell that story again!"'

'What is that about', I asked, 'if not an unending capacity for
nonsense?'

'It is about appropriate punishment', said William. 'Greed for
rice and greed for stories, both punished in fitting ways.'

And of course, it is also about rice and power politics. Rice is
at the heart of the Karen Revolution.

In *Karens and Communism*, Saw Moo Troo cites a proverb: 'The
rice we get with the sweat of our own brow tastes delicious.' He
intends it as an illustration of the improbability of the Karen accept-
ing a system of common ownership. Equally, the point is one of
dependence and self-determination. The problem for Kawthoolei
is that the hill Karen do not normally produce enough rice to feed
themselves. Every investigation has shown that farmers of the low-
lands produce a surplus of rice but those of the hills a deficit which
they have to make up with cash purchases. The hills and the plains
thus live in symbiosis, which is fine until war separates them. Having
declared that war, the KNU are responsible for the consequences.
The problem is not serious as long as the Thai border stays open,
allowing access to the markets there. If the border closes, they're
in trouble.

But it's more complicated still. Who is going to feed the Army?
The farmers, generally speaking, *could* produce more rice, but do
they want to? Theirs has been called an 'economy of sufficiency':
farm for what you need, not for profit.[5] They have little interest
in growing more than enough. Producing a surplus takes time and
effort that they regard as better spent elsewhere. Feeding the Army
thus requires a shift in attitude. And that, in turn, requires political
persuasion.

For the villagers it is also dangerous. The Burmese Army knows
very well that the KNLA is fed by the villagers, and therefore when
the Burmese seize a village, they confiscate all the rice. Hiding
it puts the villagers at risk of being caught and punished. Surrender-
ing it condemns both the KNLA and themselves to hunger.

There are limits, of course, to what Kawthoolei's government can expect of its farmers. There are points of pride, propaganda and history involved. The British, particularly in the 1860s and 1870s, made Burma 'the granary of Asia', to satisfy demand for rice in Europe and India. To do that they encouraged rice production by allowing Indian moneylenders to move in, providing capital for the drainage and cultivation of new land. The consequences were profound. Traditional social ties and structures broke down and many farmers found themselves with debts they couldn't meet – all because the British wanted more rice. The Saya San rebellion of 1930/1 was a revolt of Burmese who had lost their lands in this way, and the fact that the British employed their old friends the Karen to suppress the rising was ironic, since in many areas it was actually Karen who'd suffered most from British-induced money-lending.

Thus, even before the Second World War, only at its peril did government put pressure on rice farmers to grow more. Since Burmese independence, rice production has fallen catastrophically. Worse still, said Pastor Moses, the Burmese government takes rice from the villagers to export, to earn foreign exchange. Discussing the matter, usually after a good dinner and now seated around the table on Bartholomew's verandah, smashing up the areca nuts with shears and chewing hard as they spoke, Moses, Bartholomew and True Love would grow angry at the thought of Burmese government impositions on the poor, Burman and Karen alike: 'Do you know how they do it, Jo? They give you an allowance from your own rice and if you grow more they just take it. And do you know how much they allow you? Fifteen tins per head per year! That's unhusked rice. Is that enough for a Karen? Are they trying to starve everyone to death?!'

From what I'd seen of Karen intake, it sounded enough for a week. Kawthoolei has to tread with care.

Other pressures are felt already. The military situation being what it is, cash is increasingly hard to come by, and villagers have been forced to make up their own rice shortfalls by growing more. Families calculating their needs for the coming year allow a certain percentage for visitors. In one or two energetic villages they have managed to accumulate a small reserve to assist a new sort of guest: Karen refugees, fleeing the war zones. Elsewhere, feeding the refugees is another burden for the government.

Then, of course, there are all the civil servants, the forestry officers, the nurses, the Department secretaries, the teachers ... the KNU has to feed them all. To do that it has to use its own tiny reserves of foreign exchange, from the tollgates and from the sale of timber, to buy rice in Thailand.

For most Karen revolutionaries, a rice and salt ration is all the pay they can expect. Predictably, the ration is known by a British Army term, *Scale*. Any 'member of the Revolution' is entitled to it, drawing from a central store once a month. Each is allowed half a basket a month per head of immediate family living with them. 'Silver and I could claim twice', said True Love, 'hers from the Education Department as a teacher, mine from the Army. But of course we don't do that.'

Some did, perhaps, on the quiet. I embarked on a series of village demographic surveys, with True Love and Great Lake as intermediaries. After one or two of these, True Love began to look unhappy and finally told me that there might be trouble:

> 'Some people think that you might be a Burmese spy.'
> 'Oh, come off it, we're only asking how many children they've got. Anyway, what do you tell them?'
> 'I tell them that the Colonel has approved this survey. But still, they are not happy.'
> 'What are they really worried about?'
> 'They think you're going to reduce their *Scale*.'

Great Lake wouldn't accept a *Scale* ration at all, although as Health Department boatman he could take one. To his mind, the whole thing stank. 'I don't like it. All these people who give nothing to the Revolution but take food from it. That is not loyal, that is quite wrong. I will do what I can to make money; I will grow as much rice as I can, the rest I will buy. Anyway, if I don't take their food, I'm a free man.'

Just bringing the rice to Riverside could be a problem. The village granaries were not large and needed regular replenishing. But during the rains, when the 15 km road turned into a mud-wallow at the top end and a series of tricky crossings of the swollen stream at the bottom, there was no possibility of the Colonel's pickup truck carrying sufficient rice down from the border. Elephants could bring some, but an elephant's carrying capacity is quite small.

At the end of October I saw one of the solutions. There was a great racket in the early morning. The girls of *Boarders* were up, eating and laughing, before dawn. The school closed for the day and everyone walked off up the hill. Late in the afternoon we saw them returning, a steady stream of adults and exhausted children who'd gone three and a half hours up in the morning, and back down in the afternoon heat, each carrying a bag or pillow-case full of dry rice on their head. Some were very young and very tired indeed. It was food for two weeks only.

The Army had its own stores, but all civilians drew their *Scale* from a wooden shed on the far side of the football field. Another solution to the transport problem was to stock everyone up as much as possible before the rains started. At the end of each month we would collect our rations for the next, but at the end of June (when I was living in the new guesthouse next to *Boarders*) it was decided to move three months' supply in one go. Rats were attacking the main store; it needed emptying, repairing and refilling while weather permitted. For the *Boarders*, that involved shifting a full ton of rice, which would mean the twenty girls trailing down a mile of hot track with heavy bags, back and forth all day. I suggested to Sam that we could borrow one of the Thai logging lorries from the sawmill to shift the whole lot. He liked the idea, but said it wasn't possible.

> 'I can't ask them.'
> 'Why not?'
> 'I don't speak Thai.'
> 'But anyway, won't the rats get it here too?'
> 'We've got cats.'

(Well, I had the cat, in fact, a formidable ratter. It liked to bring its victims into the house at two in the morning and eat them directly under my hammock, waking me with the sound of the crushing of rodent skulls, and a peculiar acrid smell. In the morning there would be a tail on the mat just where I put my feet.)

In the event, the District Car was persuaded to take some of the *Boarders* issue of twenty sacks. The rest we carried ourselves – although some of those dependent on rice from *Boarders*, the families of waifs and strays, did not take part. Everyone was there. Bartholomew's children scuttling to his house and back with pillow-cases, teachers and pastors and public servants of every sort with their households, all milling about the door of the shed for their share. Tiny women staggered off with huge sacks on their heads, visibly compressed by the weight. I did it with a rucksack – a relatively easy way to carry 70 lb of grain. Once we'd got it back to *Boarders*, most went into a big wooden chest. The waifs and strays came across and helped themselves, but not without remarking on the poor quality of rice that had been delivered. It's true; the

Revolution cannot afford to buy good rice, and instead buys cheap, cracked grain. Those who can, grow their own for special occasions, and at Christmas in Bartholomew's we had good rice. On the first of January we went back onto the ration; dreadful pap it made. 'Do you know what they do with this stuff in Thailand, Jo? Feed it to the pigs.'

Arthur the Agricultural Officer had the unenviable task of trying to increase local rice production – though it was he who had defended the schoolchildren against the charge that they should be doing farm labour, with the words, 'That is not what childhood is for.' He was in his thirties, and a son-in-law of the Colonel. One of his projects was an attempt to introduce irrigated rice terraces to the swidden farmers of the hills. It's not as though Karen don't know about irrigated rice. On the contrary, it is thought that when the Burmans first came to the Irrawaddy Delta, they took over irrigation systems that had been built by Sgaw Karen. But in spite of the arrival of steady numbers of Delta Karen in our hill district, no one knew how to do it – which is an indication of who was arriving: not farmers, at any rate.

Arthur had a junior diploma in engineering. He had tried one irrigation system already, the season before I had come. It hadn't worked:

> 'We decided to try near Durianville, because on the other side of the river there's a settlement of Buddhist refugees who are energetic and usually make a go of things. It wasn't a big scheme, just a dam on a small stream and a few acres of fields. Manpower is always a problem here. We calculated that we needed forty people to take part, who would then get all the rice. I thought it would be easy enough at Durianville but, when I tried, I could get only eight or ten people interested. So the dam wasn't big enough or strong enough, and when heavy rains came it was destroyed.'
>
> 'But you are trying again?'
>
> 'Certainly. We have found a solution to the labour difficulty, I think. There are many Karen who are being ... what can we say? They are not refugees exactly, they are being resettled in safer areas. I think we can use them. We have also found some new land and a stream, and we have started work. It's difficult. None of us actually knows how to do it, and I am studying books as we go along. But there are many more people now, and who knows how many more may come as refugees. We have to do this to survive.'

A story about food. I heard it, as usual, sitting on William's high verandah overlooking the school compound. His small children crawled about between us threatening at any moment to drop off the edge into the black night.

FLESH AND FAMINE

There was once a poor village family with two children, a daughter and a baby boy. The daughter was called Naw Ler Ker.

The rice crops had failed and there was famine in the area. Each day the parents went out to look for food – berries, wild vegetables, anything. One morning they set off together, but they hadn't gone far when they remembered that they'd not told their daughter to feed the baby boy. They turned back. When they thought they were near enough for her to hear, they shouted that she should cook the baby some yams. But they were further from the house than they thought. Between them and their daughter, a witch heard their call and thought of some instant mischief. She came near the house and, imitating the parents, called to Naw Ler Ker and told her to cook the baby.

Naw Ler Ker could hardly believe it. She hesitated a long time, but then thought, 'I must obey my parents'. So she killed her little brother and curried him. Still, she felt there was something wrong, and she was afraid. When her parents came home in the evening she didn't know what to say. They asked, 'Where's your brother?' and she replied that he had gone to play at his grandmother's house. The father called to the boy but there was no answer. 'Oh well', he said, 'I'll go and get him later. Is there any food?'

Naw Ler Ker set the table and her parents sat down. Seeing the curry, they wondered, where did she get the meat? But they said nothing until mother found a little foot in her dish, and then found a little hand. When Naw Ler Ker claimed that they had told her to cook her brother, her father was furious. He fetched a long stick covered with big, sharp thorns and beat Naw Ler Ker until she was bleeding, full of thorns and near insensible. Then he kicked her out of the house.

Sadly, the little girl crept off into the forest and wondered what to do. She built herself a small shelter because, she realised, in this famine no household would want an extra mouth to feed. But how to eat? She went to some relations and begged the loan of an old fishnet. Deep in the forest she found secret pools and there she fished. When she had plenty of fish she went back to the village and paid people to pull the giant thorns out of her back – one thorn, one fish.

But one especially big fish and one beautiful prawn she kept in her pool. She fed them on ants each day and, to call them, she recited a little poem.

After a while her parents, regretting the loss of both children, came looking for their daughter. As they approached the water they heard her recite her poem and saw the fish come. Naw Ler Ker moved away and her parents stopped by the pool. They were still very hungry and the fish was, by now, very big. The father picked up a spear and recited the poem, killed the fish and pulled it out. The prawn escaped, diving to the bottom.

The father and mother sliced up, fried and ate the fish – all except the oil sac which they tucked back up in the bamboo roof. Then they left, feeling guilty. When Naw Ler Ker came home she called the fish but it didn't come. When she saw the prawn skulking at the bottom of the pool, she knew that something was wrong. There was a crow circling over her house, trying to get at something in the roof. She went to see, and found the oil sac. She was very upset. 'Everything on this earth is against me!' she cried, 'so I'll go to heaven instead!'

She searched the forest until she found a very rare bamboo. She tucked the fish's oil sac inside it. Then she struck the bamboo hard on the ground, and it began to grow. Each time she struck it, it grew taller. She planted it and watched. The bamboo grew up towards heaven.

Naw Ler Ker climbed up the bamboo and said to the Thunder, 'Will you marry me?' The Thunder replied, 'No, you'd be frightened'. 'Test me!' demanded the girl, placing chicken shit in her ears so that she'd not hear the noise. The Thunder raged at her, but she didn't flinch. Most impressed, Thunder agreed to marry her.

After a while, she asked Thunder if they might visit her parents, and perhaps help them. Down the bamboo they both came and found her parents, who were delighted to see her and welcomed her husband. But they wanted their daughter back to look after them. Looking at Thunder, her father thought, 'I know how to scare off these celestials: dog's head soup!' He killed and cooked a dog and served it for dinner. Sure enough, when Thunder tasted the dog, he leapt back up to heaven in a fury. But, to the old people's dismay, Naw Ler Ker felt the call of love to be stronger than filial duty. She followed her husband, and never returned to Earth again.

They eat twice daily in Bartholomew's house, crouched on the floor round a low circular table. Each person has an enamel plate heaped with rice, with spares nearby. Further plates and bowls cover the centre of the table.

As the family sits, each person touches the rice in front of them, breaking up the clods. Physical contact with the food is established by this light fingering, but nothing is eaten yet. Bartholomew says grace, calling our attention with a soft *kay* . . . He mutters the prayer quickly, the family chorus *Amen* and we begin. In polite society, the first move is to eat a little rice with fishpaste, which registers appreciation of the staff of life. The next stage is to drink soup, of which there are two communal bowls with just one large common spoon in each; we all slobber a mouthful or two. Then, the process of packing in rice together with whatever garnish is there, as fast as possible. To be courteous you delve in the curry for a succulent morsel of chicken or pork and place it upon your neighbour's plate. Bartholomew does this for his children, quietly insisting that they eat some protein.

Often the meal is taken in shifts, with Fragrance (or whoever has cooked) sitting to one side to keep the family supplied with rice and curry. She eats afterwards, far more casually, sometimes just squatting by the back steps. On tour, four or five of us might arrive together at anyone's house asking for shelter and a meal; the family would hang back, serving us but rarely eating with us, deferentially waiting until we'd had our fill and had subsided on the verandah with the betel tray, then moving in to make the most of what had, at least, been a good excuse to kill a chicken. There are strict rules of hospitality. The traveller is entitled to unlimited food and shelter, and I never saw it skimped.

In the revolutionary state, these things are partially formalised. Government officers will go to the headman or the pastor's house, and sleep and eat there for as long as their duties keep them in the village. At the headquarters of any Township, the government office doubles as a guesthouse for visitors, and the KNU *Women's Organisation* will cook for them. There are no charges, and apparently no time limit to the official hospitality available. Some effort might be made to reduce the imposition; we could bring or buy meat, or supply coffee and tinned milk and biscuits for everyone's breakfast. On our first tour, True Love and White Rock announced that we were taking with us a girl called Roly, a trained laboratory assistant. 'What's Roly going to do?' I asked. 'The cooking.'

Often, if our circus was large, or if there was only an old man or woman in the house, we'd take over. Most Karen men can cook, and don't hesitate to move into someone else's kitchen and start doing so. The unwritten law is clear: no one begrudges food contributions to the State. Timothy would point at pumpkins, tamarinds or limes and say, 'Can I take some of those for the hospital?' and the householder would simply nod, 'Of course.'

I worried about my impositions and consulted True Love and Edward; if I was going to be visiting villages regularly, shouldn't I carry my own food? Rice, at least? Or should I pay? Edward said; 'The first time you come, they will give you a feast. The second time they'll kill a chicken. The third time you'll probably just get rice and fish paste and they'll hardly notice that you're there. Don't worry; as long as we have rice we'll feed you.'

We never reached that final stage, and I was still feasting a year later. Merited or not, this was very reassuring. Disgrace as well as approbation can be expressed through food:

One of their curious customs which appears to be dying out, is their procedure in a case in which a man betrays a maid and she is found with child. If the betrayer will not or cannot marry the girl, he is obliged to give her a buffalo in compensation. But the curious part is that the girl in no way benefits by the gift, as the animal is immediately slaughtered and the meat divided among the whole village.[6]

They may then eat it together. The pork feast is an essential component of religious life, held to mark the rites of passage or to atone for some spiritual offence that has brought disease or poor crops to a village. The harm is 'eaten away' by the people together. And weddings, as almost anywhere, are celebrated by village feasting, and are given communal witness and approval. Today, the need for positive solidarity being greater than ever, pork feasts are central to any National Day. Colonels and Departmental Heads make sure that they are seen eating with the people. Even small villages build bamboo tables in order to eat together at Karen New Year. They can't afford to do it too often, and the State doesn't insist. Animism has lost adherents partly because the provision of ritual food is so expensive, and there is, in 'national' feasting, a fine line between the successful expression of popular cohesion, and a resented imposition. But as the song (quoted in chapter eleven) says: if you build together in a fraternal spirit, something delicious will come your way.

'But what', my correspondents at home asked, 'do you actually eat?'

I began to keep a culinary diary of Bartholomew and Vermilion's table, of which the following is one week. These dishes accompany the staple of rice and fish paste:

MONDAY

Breakfast   Green beans with duck egg yolks, vermicelli and cabbage soup with the egg whites. Small fried fish. Green papaya cooked with turmeric.

Dinner   Fried fish, onion and papaya soup, sautéed banana flowers.

TUESDAY

Breakfast   Fish steaks. Fried noodles and fried green beans. Clear soup. Dried shredded venison.

Plate 14. 'The need for positive solidarity being greater than ever, pork feasts are central to any National Day.'

Dinner   Fish curry. Chopped long beans with duck eggs.

WEDNESDAY

Breakfast (with Moses)   Fish, grilled and curried. Fried eggs with groundnuts. Wild cat curry. Braised fat pork. Stir-fried cauliflower and pork. Spring onion soup. Raw onion and cucumber. Good quality rice.

Dinner   Grilled and curried fish. Papaya sauerkraut. Lemongrass soup.

THURSDAY

Breakfast   Fried rice with baby mangoes and chilli pickle.

Dinner   Grilled fish, papaya sauerkraut, fried noodles and vermicelli soup.

FRIDAY

Breakfast   Fried rice and a riceflour blancmange sweetmeat.

Dinner   Fried fish. Various greens, boiled and raw. Sautéed cauliflower with pork. Lemongrass and fish soup.

SATURDAY

Fried rice early, then a village breakfast in honour of military service induction (pork).

Dinner   Cauliflower and pork, fried green beans and boiled tree beans.

A noticeable absence from this particular week is another Karen staple, the tinned pilchard. This is not, I think, a new taste. B. W. Swithinbank, in the *Burma Gazetteer* for Toungoo District (1913 p. 24), reported that, 'they also indulge largely in imported provisions, biscuits, sardines and fruit'.

I described the cuisine to an English friend who had also visited the area. She said, 'It certainly wasn't like that when I was there. All we ever got was rice and fish paste. Mind you, I was travelling with the Army.'

Quality and variety did not necessarily reflect wealth, since most of the real delicacies came from the forest, available to anyone who had the time and skill to find them. The locals were never at a loss for an exotic titbit but the Delta newcomers were often in the position of Toh Meh Pah's brother, trying to boil snails.

As hunters, they were enthusiastic amateurs rather than professionals. No one made a living out of hunting, but everyone liked to enrich their tables with forest treats. For the Delta sophisticates it was a matter of morale, a way of asserting their ability to survive in the jungle. In May we travelled downriver with Harvest Moon's son John as *klee koh*. A lad of around twenty, he'd spent far more time in Thailand, even Bangkok, than most people at Riverside and there were now plans to send him to school in Chiang Mai. He knew that we thought him a nice but ineffectual urbanite. Half-way to Barterville he managed to shoot a large monitor lizard. He exulted, 'You thought I couldn't do anything, didn't you?'

They were watching for food at all times. We ate venison, we ate black mountain bear. We ate green pigeons curried and wild goat, wind dried. An Army radio operator cooked me an otter – tasty, but extremely tough chewing. Succulent fungi, and fermented tea pounded with garlic and peanuts, eagle, anteater, snails, squirrel and turtle were all available. Lt Col MacMahon reported that old men liked to carry edible snakes in their shoulder bags as a convenient snack. Lizard eggs were good, like a large roast chestnut. I only wished that I had seen them hunting tortoises with trained dogs, as Captain Low described in 1837.

Monkey meat is a favourite; they like to keep it a day or two in the tropical warmth until it is very high. In the past they dispensed with even that minimal preparation. A nineteenth-century British Army officer on tour through the forest wrote of being sickened, 'by seeing the Karen devour the raw and bloody entrails of a monkey I had shot. They swallowed the intestines *au naturel*, like macaroni.'[7] By the time I arrived, intestines were being prepared with more art. Monkeys are predominantly herbivorous; their guts contain a fragrant mash of greenery and gastric juices. This the Karen squeeze out and pack into bamboo tubes, allowing it to ferment. The product, a grey-green paste with an acrid, faecal savour, can then be diluted and taken as soup, or blended with rotten fish as a condiment. Either way, it is near the margins of what I consider edible. As were the large, fat yellow grubs I saw being dug out of a tree stump one morning, which were served up later. In themselves they might have been passable; it was eating them with glutinous rice and warm, liquid lard that I couldn't face.

'Almost omnivorous', Smeaton (1887, p. 77), called them: 'Every animal from a rat to an elephant, every reptile from a sand-lizard to a serpent, ants, grubs, every bird, every fish and the whole vegetable kingdom adorn their tables.' In one of their commandments, the ancestors are recorded as saying, 'O children and grandchildren! we may eat anything without sin, for God created them all for us.'

But they are not so undiscriminating as this suggests. Goat meat, by and large, they don't like. Beef they cannot afford – they keep the animals for export, not home use. Their palate is sweet but not too sweet; they contrast themselves to the 'Mandalay Shan' for whom nothing is sweet enough. And there are taboos, to which pregnant women especially are subject. They may not eat the flesh of certain monkeys, nor the pods of a vegetable called 'alligator's tongues'. Great Lake claimed that, in their ritual foods, Karen were quite modest:

> 'It's only the animists who eat really peculiar things. When they get married they each eat a baby chick without any dressing at all, just held over the fire.'

He grimaced: *roasting* meat? No, he never did that.

I asked True Love what he would, and would not eat:

> 'Well, not dog – though the Chin and other tribes eat dog which they feed up on sticky rice, and I have eaten dog in Burma, with plenty of beer. Dog meat smells strong, so you have to spice it heavily, so then it makes you sweat. There's a sort of dog with yellow spots over its eyes which we call the four-eyed dog – if you boil the meat and drink the juice it's good for malaria. We eat wild cat, but not domestic – too soft and sweet. We eat snakes, certainly. Some Karen will only eat poisonous snakes, others only non-poisonous snakes; I don't know why. Python is good, like chicken. There's also a long thin brown snake which is good. What else – baby bees! Oily and sweet – make you sick if you eat too many. We eat grasshoppers, but other insects only as medicine. We'll eat any bird except vultures; they're too ugly. And personally I cannot eat turtle. I'm allergic to it.'

On two occasions the KNU has attempted to influence the people's diet. Monitor lizards are an increasingly endangered species worldwide and the KNU, anxious to uphold the image of responsible government, once tried to ban the hunting of them. People took little notice, the ban was dropped, and I saw Karen shooting, trapping, even running lizards down in pickup trucks. At Barterville I found a heap of them ready for export to Thailand. They were alive. To disable a lizard you take its tail round to its front legs – under one leg, over its back, round the other leg and back again. The lizard is completely immobilised by this. They were being weighed, for sale by the kilo, and a dozen or more of them were piled on top of the shop scales, tied up in their own tails and blinking sadly, like some victimised creature in *Alice in Wonderland*.

There was also – after the international spate of controversial reports that it was dangerous – an attempt to ban monosodium glutamate food seasoning from Kawthoolei's shops. That didn't work either, and MSG continued to be imported from Thailand, sold in remotest villages and used everywhere, by government families also. It's not that anyone was flouting, denying or defying authority in this; it simply hadn't occurred to them that government might tell you what not to eat.

But one ban *was* enforced, after a fashion. True Love's friend Dan also assured me that no one in Riverside ate cat – but he gave a different reason. Dan said, 'Cat is only delicious if you eat it with alcohol, but we cannot do that here because we're not allowed to drink alcohol.'

Rarely was there such a notorious race of drunkards. Major Snodgrass (1827, p. 148) wrote that 'Carians are remarkably fond of ardent spirits and, generally speaking, will do more for a glass of brandy than for a sum of money'.

J. G. Scott (1916, p. 31) noted this trait when he described the Red Karen to the Central Asian Society in London in 1916: 'In the old days ... a Red Karen never went out of doors without a bamboo of liquor slung over his back. From this a tube led to his mouth and he was able to go about his ordinary avocations without wasting any time.'

The American missionaries took the matter seriously, although Mrs Judson found cause to be indulgent: 'Though greatly addicted to drunkenness, extremely filthy and indolent in their habits, their morals are in other respects superior to many more civilised races.'[8]

Other colonial writers were rather pleased at the effect that alcohol had on the Karen. W. S. Morrison (1915) wrote of the Karen male: 'He has none of the vivacity and lightheartedness of the Burman, but is sombre, slow of speech and much inclined to be sulky ... He is much inclined to liquor, and in liquor finds that lightness of heart that is naturally so foreign to him.'[9]

Alcohol had its serious uses. For non-Christians it had – and still has – an important religious role, as an offering to the spirits, or in oath-taking, in which metal scrapings from spears and firearms would be dropped into a bowl of alcohol and drunk by all parties to the contract. But the new religion changed everything. Had it been Catholics who had the success in converting the Karen, things might have been different, but the nineteenth-century Baptists (and twentieth-century Seventh Day Adventists) found Karen drunkenness intolerable and set about redeeming them.

But, once again, remember that the Christians are only one

quarter or less of the Karen population. This makes the ban on alcohol in Kawthoolei much more remarkable. I assumed at first that the ban must be the work of the Baptist and Adventist KNU leaders; just as illicit love jeopardises divine sanction for the cause, so drunkenness perhaps besmirches the purity of the Revolution. But what an extraordinary political risk to take, the possible alienation of three-quarters of your people!

It is, however, a gambit and a fanaticism familiar in regimes with their backs to the wall – a call for sacrifice coupled with a plea for purity. Nor is it the first time it has been seen in Burma. King Bodawpaya, Burmese King of Ava from 1782–1826, over-reached himself in attacking Siam and taking on the British and the Mon and the Arakanese, all at the same time. The strain on his kingdom and his mind turned him into a religious bigot who decreed the death penalty for smoking opium and drinking alcohol. Now it is the Burman's old adversaries who uphold the bans in Kawthoolei; even if the penalties for consumers are not so harsh, trading in opium is a capital offence in the rebel state.

I never saw anyone in Kawthoolei take opium (though plenty of Karen in Thailand do: see p. 191). Alcohol, however, is consumed on the quiet. The authorities cannot forbid the religious use of spirits, but try and license it while allowing small quantities of whisky to be imported for medicinal purposes. It was hardly surprising to find young soldiers drinking, or to meet Karen in Thailand calling for iced *Mekhong* whisky with their lunch before coming back across the border into Kawthoolei. It was more surprising to be offered alcohol in the house of a senior Riverside teacher who was also a leading church member, or to be told how the Revolution and Christ had saved a certain government official from serious health problems, only to watch him later cracking a bottle with the border guards. And all of these Baptists. I asked True Love who it was that insisted on the ban. The Church? 'No, I think it was originally the Army. It's because, in the early days of the Revolution, we lost some battles because our soldiers were drunk. Some of our best commanders were killed like that.'

I asked another soldier who had been drinking if he was scared of being caught. 'Certainly not', he said, 'They'd only put me in jail for a couple of weeks. They'd not dare to do more than that, because most of the officers drink too.'

People *were* punished. One of my journeys with True Love had to be abandoned because a colleague in his already overworked office had got drunk one evening, started shouting and fighting and ended up with a dishonourable discharge from the Army. I heard of other soldiers, officers included, being disciplined with a week in jail.

In the old days, Karen warriors arming for a raid would prepare themselves with liberal quantities of spirits, and would then rush the enemy with unstoppable impetus. 'Our battles was all won on beer', said Stanley Holloway's Private Samuel Small. Even British Army manuals approved it:

Alcohol is quite unnecessary for the youthful, but probably is beneficial in the tropics to those over thirty since it affords psychological relief from unpleasant surroundings, but it should be taken well diluted, in strict moderation and only after a day's work has been completed. *Field Service Hygiene Notes*, India 1945.[10]

The KNLA leadership do not lightly go against the written recommendation of the army that trained them.

Fermented monkey faeces, fermented rice, fermented fish; I have never eaten so much fish. A meal could well include small fried fish (eaten whole, like whitebait), fish curry, fish soup and a bowl of fermented fish condiment. It is quite nice fish. Everyone fishes. Small boys dive for big prawns under the rocks, the girls of *Boarders* drift downstream in my boat with rod and line, and Great Lake places long nets across the river to snare the bream and the passing boat propellers. Others go groping in the puddles and long grass after rain for frogs; wet slimy creatures are regarded as a class of food together – *dee o nya o*, or 'frog-and-fish'. The frogs have a miserable time; you see them in the kitchens, alive, with their legs broken or sewn together. They are dried and sold by the half dozen, held in a split bamboo.

Fish paste is the other half of the staple diet, and when the lid is put on the rice pan to keep the steam in, a ball of paste is pressed onto the top to warm through and release its well-rotted flavour. It accompanies every meal, and they import it from Thailand in plastic sacks. I once rode for four hours perched on a leaking, reeking heap of it, in the back of a pickup.

I asked True Love and Dan how it was made. They looked abashed:

'We don't know, we are ignorant town people and we cannot make it. None of us can. I was on the river recently and I

met some hunters who had caught a lot of fish and they offered
me some, saying that it was the best sort for paste, and I was
so ashamed because I didn't know what to do with it.'

At breakfast, Pastor Moses insisted that he and his wife made
their own:

'You catch lots of little fish and you dry them in the sun. Then
you pound them up with salt and pack them into bamboo tubes
and keep it. That's all.'

'So, did you make this fish paste that we're eating?'

'Well, no . . .'

Thomas, the Karen missionary from Thailand, didn't trouble to
hide his exasperation:

'I can't believe these Karen!' he said, 'They are short of rice,
they are short of bullets, they have a river swarming with fish
and yet they *buy* their fish paste! How can they expect to win
a war like that?'

'I will try to learn', said True Love. 'But you know, everything
changes with a war, nothing can be as it was. Great Lake wants
us to be old, traditional Karen and to eat traditional food. But
we have moved around and we have eaten so many things,
Burmese food and Thai food and western food. We cannot pretend that we have never tasted these.'

Great Lake accepted, at least, that war was disruptive of tradition,
and he taught me an old rhyme which expressed the most heartfelt
desires of his people:

Kola hay, payor thee,
pwakenyaw aw mee aw mee!

With the British returned and the Burmese dead,
The Karen will do nothing but eat, sleep, eat, sleep!

15   Perfect hosts

> For the Karens hospitality is not merely obligatory out of courtesy. It
> is the duty of the host to provide shelter, protection, facilities, comforts
> and privileges wherever practicable. The host has to help the guest by
> showing him the way to the next village, to provide a guide [and] to
> carry the bags of the guest if he is old and cannot carry his own bags.
> There is no charge for the discharge of these duties, no monetary remuner-
> ation whatsoever.   Saw Moo Troo (1981, p. 6)

'I'm Alice, this is Honour, and you'll be Jo, right?'

A fair and solid woman from Perth, Western Australia, standing
on the river bank trying for the first time in her life to bathe in
a muddy river without taking her clothes off – which, in black
polyester slacks, was proving difficult. In my absence downriver
with Great Lake, nine of them had come to Riverside, under the
baton of Greg. He was a real missionary, but his party were ordinary
churchgoers, mostly middle-aged farming men and women. They
were here for two weeks and they were eating the Karen into submission.

'These are just church people who have never been outside
Australia before', said Greg. 'They've come to experience faith in
another land.' As usual, it was Ruth and Edward's house that they
came to, and most of them slept in a row on mats on the verandah.
Two of the women went to Pipi's teachers' hostel, while one man
said firmly that he hadn't come all the way from Perth to sleep
in a row of fellow Australians, and took himself off to Bastion's
house. But it was Ruth's kitchen that fed them, three times a day.
Continual shifts of Karen girls worked without pause upon heaps
of vegetables and a score of chickens. To be fair, the Australians
had brought supplies of vegetables and coffee, and did pay for the
chickens.

In return for this hospitality, they taught geography. As none
of them knew anywhere else, it was Australian geography that they
taught. True Love interpreted for their classes. I said that I thought
there were subjects duller than Australian geography:

Plate 15. 'These are just church people who have never been outside Australia before.'

'Don't you find it interesting?'
'Not at all. We've had groups of Australians three years running now and they all talk about the same things. Bushfires, kanga-roos ...'

The Australians, however, were interested in everything that they saw. They had a video camera with them, and filmed the building of my new house day by day, with a running commentary. They came to a wedding and were ushered to the front seats, but they didn't have the nerve to shoot film there, so they got True Love to do it. Then they were sent upriver to White Elephant in four boats – half the village fleet.

'I hope they behave themselves at White Elephant', said True Love. 'They had an unfortunate experience of missionaries there once. The village has its name because there used to be a huge white rock in the river which looked like an elephant. White elephants are sacred to us and the village people thought that this rock was sacred too. Well, there were six or seven of these mission-aries, and they wanted to be photographed sitting all together on this rock. But some were women, and the villagers asked that if any of the women were menstruating, would they please not sit on this holy rock. No, no, said the women, no problem. So they all sat on the rock and had their photographs taken and the next morning the rock was found to have split in the night and collapsed into the river.'

The Australians returned from White Elephant without mishap. Really, they were as harmless as could be, apart from the disruption caused by their level of food consumption. The only person who thought them suspect was Pastor Moses. He, one evening, asked if I would buy or order some religious publications next time I was in Malaysia. I suggested that he ask the Australians, who would have access to better shops when they returned home, and might know something about the books. But no: 'I'd rather not', said Moses, 'They are Pentecostalists, and they get far too enthusiastic.'

A few days later their enthusiasm was put on display. A farewell concert was given for, and by, them. Senior school pupils danced the rice-planting dance, illuminated by the headlights of a pickup so that the Australians could shoot their video. Then the visitors began to sing. Tom, the younger man who had moved in on Bastion, performed 'Sound the Alarm in Zion', accompanying himself on an electric guitar. My last sight of them was in a clump about the microphone, blinking into the headlights and roaring, 'When the saints!' with dreadful intonation and fearsome passion.

In 1876, Lt Col MacMahon (p. 339), reported an unsettling trait in the Karen: uncontrollable mirth in the face of foreign visitors. Since then the joke appears to have worn off, and their habitual courteous reserve has been reasserted. In some areas, their traditions of unstinting hospitality have, in recent years, led to new problems. In the last two decades or so, 'hill-tribe trekking' has become a boom tourist industry in northern Thailand (see p. 191). Villagers who had moved to the cities now bring back a steady flow of young foreigners with rucksacks, to 'glimpse that most elusive of states – happiness', as Preecha Chaturabhand puts it.[1] Custom demands that visitors be housed and fed free of charge – but the customs of a recluse tribe were never meant to cope with a tourist industry. Equally puzzling is the fact that the white guests once wanted to convert them all to Christianity, but now seem to find them interesting only if they are *not* Christian.

The Karen are not entirely naive about foreigners, in spite of their reputation for timidity and seclusion. They saw at an early date that the missions offered them an alliance against the Buddhist Burmese, with economic, political and security advantages which they duly made the most of. By contrast, missionary work among the Thai Karen has never had much success. This is sometimes ascribed to mere bad tactics, a choice of white men 'ill-equipped in mind and character',[2] or the tactless assigning of Sgaw evangelists to work with Pwo Karen. A simpler explanation is that, in relatively hospitable Siam, the corporate strength offered by the Church wasn't needed.

In Burma, the Karen repaid the Baptists with a satisfying conversion rate, demographic leverage in Burmese politics and the thrill of having perhaps found a 'Lost Tribe of Israel' which they would now protect and nourish. This last was not, for the nineteenth century, the absurdity that it might now seem; the French were investigating the origins of certain Cambodian tribes in similar terms.[3]

The Karen, thought Smeaton, owed all they had to their missionaries under the protection afforded by British rule. The Karen are not ungrateful. They received schools, literacy and hospitals and a focus of political cohesion in a time of need – and, through Dr Vinton, the guns with which to assert it.

Were the missionaries, then, in any way responsible for the war? Some say yes:

the success of Christian missionaries among the Karen must be seen as one of the most significant causes for the emergence of the Karen rebellion.
Charles F. Keyes (1979, p. 20)

Others say no:

The American missionaries deprecated the wartime feud from which the rebellion developed, and were in no position in 1947–9 to tell the KNU leadership what they could or could not do.   J. Cady (1958, p. 596)

Remembering Dr Vinton's Gideonesque leadership of that 'plucky little nation' in 1886, it is difficult to excuse the missions entirely. Today it is not their power that is striking, but the very muted role that they play. Restricted in Burma, and thus no longer able to act as a focus there, the missionaries that reach Kawthoolei from Thailand now bring some material assistance with them, but are politically impotent.

In Riverside we met them week by week, the scouts of a would-be influence that did not dare throw itself wholeheartedly into the affair. I cannot imagine the evangelists of the nineteenth century being so timorous, however 'delicate' the official position in Thailand. A curious selection appeared. One morning a party of a dozen Japanese Baptists came to call. Another day I was introduced to Gary of *Word International* of Tulsa, Oklahoma: 'Basically we're involved in training National Christian Leaders. Our courses are customised to the circumstances.'

Gary wanted to extend *Word International*'s operations to Kawthoolei – but he never returned. A Malaysian lady faith-healer turned up, and reduced some of Pipi's hostel girls to hysterics. And there was Thomas, the Karen who now worked for the Assembly of God in Chiang Mai, Thailand, with his Australian wife. Thomas came regularly and organised many of the others.

Sometimes they brought gifts. Thomas gave True Love and Silver household and kitchen equipment. The Japanese gave Moses a large banknote. Thai Baptists gave Bartholomew clothes for the refugees, some of the less practical of which ended up on Monkey's back. In receiving such donations, the Karen often unwittingly gave offence, because they have very different ideas of gifts and their protocol. For Karen, gifts lack that specific, carefully targeted mystique with which we endow them. Once a gift leaves the giver, it can be used, abused or redirected with no reference to the donor. This is true at every level. When I gave Sam a shirt from Malaysia he promptly gave it to someone else. I took a portrait photograph of the Colonel and had it enlarged in Penang, entrusting it to True Love to pass on to him. It was intercepted by his family *en route* and the Colonel never saw it. When the Australians gave ducklings to the schoolchildren for the long-term improvement of their diet through stock-raising, the ducklings ended up under the houses of several teachers, and of Bartholomew. An Australian gift of pork to the school similarly went astray. A medical mission in Thailand donated two years' supply of anti-malarial drugs to the Education Department for the benefit of the children. Some of that went to village dignitaries, some of it to the Army. The Karen saw nothing wrong in this. If a gift was seriously intended to benefit the people, surely the people should direct it where it was most needed. The Army defended the school, after all.

But donors don't see it like that. Sally, a Californian mission teacher, brought a microscope and gave it to the civilian hospital. When, shortly afterwards, the Army took it for use down south, Sally was incensed and wanted it back. The Australian Pentecostalists, having promised to send an agriculturalist, gave a large rotivator instead, presenting it to the Education and Health Departments jointly. But when Colonel Marvel saw it sitting under *Boarders* he at once declared that he would be taking it down to Maw Daung, where the refugees had greater need. I said that I didn't think that would go down very well with the Australians, but he replied that it was no longer their business. The rotivator was saved for Riverside by two things. First, Thomas (who delivered it) forgot to bring a vital bolt. Secondly, it was so large and powerful that many of the little Karen were unable, or didn't dare, to handle it. The one time they started the motor, near *Boarders*, no one knew how to steer or stop it, and it ploughed relentlessly through the rose garden before True Love, trotting alongside and reading aloud from the book of instructions as he went, managed to grab the right lever.

These gifts were small beer compared to the continuous presence and enormous influence that the Missions used to have in Burma. The most useful form of support that they can offer Kawthoolei has changed also. The loyalty of the common soldiers, many of whom are Buddhist or animist, is based more on identification with General Bo Mya as a Karen hillsman than it is on religious sympathies. What the churches can provide now is a link with an international community, for which a permanent presence is not required.

There are plenty of other visitors. Some are no more nor less than tourists. That is nothing new. Many of the earliest European ethnographers were simply interested private enquirers. In 1904 Lunet de Lajonquière (p. 208), reported *deux globe-trotters belges* in the Karen hills. Today, excursions are organised for tourists from Thailand who pay heavily for a day trip to Kawthoolei GHQ. Others are taken for an expensive forest walk through what they are told is 'rebel territory' – in reality never leaving Thailand.

Other arrivals believe, with the missionaries, that they have something to offer the Karen. Some find their own way over the border, some are employed by the rebel state. A woman was brought to GHQ to teach English. After two years, they said, the children's English had not improved at all but the woman spoke excellent Karen. Everyone talked about agriculturalists, the Karen of hiring them, foreign agencies of recruiting them. It seemed rather unlikely to me that a white northern agriculturalist would have much to teach that a Thai wet rice farmer couldn't. But the Karen didn't want a Thai farmer; they wanted the support of an international community. Researchers into this and that, tin mining experts, pharmaceutical botanists, lawyers – all received a cordial welcome. Who knew that one of them might not produce a miracle to save Kawthoolei? Journalists and photojournalists, English, Dutch and German television crews and Filipino video makers all made their way across the border, unable to resist the showmanship of Colonel Marvel. When a South Korean airliner disappeared in the area, trailing clouds of correspondents, the Colonel was at his most imposing, showing them all the pistol he had taken from a former Burmese defence minister (see p. 308) and saying, 'We do not expect many survivors from the plane. Our soldiers have reported many tiger tracks.' I doubt that there's been a tiger there for decades – but never mind, it got into *The Observer*.[4] From time to time the Burmese protest to the Thais, who make a show of deporting a journalist or two. These usually return a week later.

Medical teams, French and English, set up laboratories, surgical hospitals and health care schemes. In this, however humanitarian the work, we are still outsiders organising another people. We place ourselves in direct line of descent from a host of improving colonial administrators, and of missionaries; in certain of the hilltribe languages (though not Karen) the word for 'missionary' and 'doctor' is the same, and in some areas, 'the first conversions of ... village people (and many of the subsequent ones) were of families needing medical attention'.[5] I am not a Christian, but I was there at the invitation of a political and military élite that is dominated by Christians and headed by a Seventh Day Adventist. My image was fixed before I and my KNU escort appeared in any village, and I need not have wondered why I never got close to the poorer, forest-dwelling animists who kept themselves to themselves and for whom this war and its pan-Karenist leadership have at best an uncertain appeal.

We did not have too many illusions about these matters when planning the project and looking for funds. There was little doubt about the need (I'm sure missionaries and mercenaries tell themselves the same thing) but we would never be able to reconcile the irreconcilable – our doubts about the viability and validity of the rebellion, the inescapable truth that even confining treatment to civilians still adds up to support for the war, as against the fact that people *are* sick, and do need help, and won't get it from the Burmese.[6]

This sort of ambivalence is something I've learnt to live with, as I once had to in educational publishing in Java (which I suspect benefited British publishers more than it did Malay students), and in food aid to East Africa (arguably an elaborate form of commodity dumping by rich governments). Whoever I hoped I was helping in the long run in Kawthoolei, there is no question who benefited first. The KNU were never far from any class or clinic. Every quinine tablet dispensed, every suture sewn under foreign supervision is an international vote of confidence in the KNU, that has sought out and brought in this aid for its people. 'We cannot train your army medics', I would say. 'Our mandate is strictly civilian; I'm here to work with the villagers.' At which the Karen smiled and replied that their nurses *are* villagers, that the soldier is a teacher, that the army boatman is a farmer, that the farmers feed the troops...

'Why do you try to divide our people from the Revolution, Jo? That is what the Burmese do, that is Ne Win's *Four Cuts* policy. Whose side are you on?'

Some visitors don't give a damn whose side they're on, as long as it's lucrative and exciting. These hills are a demi-paradise for 'soldiers of fortune'. There's something for everyone: war, women and wildlife, drugs and danger unlimited.

Burma, though, has never been a physically healthy place for foreign soldiers; the First Burma War of 1825 cost the British (Indian) Army 40,000 dead, mostly from disease. European professionals had found their way to this fertile battlefield three centuries before that. Forty years after Vasco da Gama rounded the Cape in 1498, Portuguese mercenaries were in Burma defending Pegu from its enemies – unsuccessfully, on that occasion. Across the mountains, Siam began in 1686 by inviting a French army to oppose the threat of the Dutch, and went on to employ Danish officers and artillerymen to fight the Chinese. The Karen themselves were recruited (when not conscripted) by Siam against Pagan, and *vice versa*, and are no strangers to the idea of mercenaries. Several of the 'ethnic' rebellions in Burma are more a matter of warlords hiring private armies to defend their opium trading interests.

But foreigners have been involved with the Karen struggle for more altruistic reasons also. In the war against the Japanese, British officers worked very closely with hilltribe counterparts, especially in Force 136, the group that parachuted agents and organisers back into the villages to sustain tribal resistance to the Japanese. At the end of the war, certain officers of Force 136 felt deeply ashamed and angry at what they and the Karen agreed was a betrayal by the British government. Retired officers attempted to assist the KNDO insurgents, notably Lt Col J. C. Tulloch (known as 'Pop'). True Love told me that when Ba U Gyi was killed in the forest in 1950, a British Major called Young was killed there also – but I've not discovered any more about him. The Karen believed that these individually loyal friends represented the spearhead of massive foreign support, but it never materialised.

There was a touch of the cargo cult about their hopes, and predators and opportunists closed in. At Durianville, walking with Bartholomew from the village towards some outlying houses, he paused and waved vaguely around the flat scrubland that we were crossing and said,

'I built an airfield here once.'

It was in 1953, he said. He'd been an energetic young KNDO cadre at the time. Two foreigners had come – he supposed they were British, though some said they were French; there was no shortage of French regular and highly irregular military in Indochina at the time. They promised the Karen guns and said that if the people built an airstrip a plane would come laden with arms. So Bartholomew was made responsible for organising the villagers and hacking down the forest. But the plane never came.[7]

'We get the lot', said Edward on my first day in Kawthoolei. 'We've had the CIA, the French DGSE, the British SAS, the Australians – they all appear from time to time.'

They didn't seem to do a great deal other than ask questions. But there had been exceptions. In October 1985, at a time of particularly intense fighting, there were reports of mercenaries fighting with the KNLA. One, a Frenchman called Jean-Phillippe Courrèges-Clerq, was killed in a Karen assault on a Burmese position. In retrospect, the Karen now say, it was his own fault. He'd encouraged the Karen to attack a well-defended hill top which their own commanders had doubts about, and the assault had been repulsed with heavy casualties. There was an Australian too, one Martin Donnelly who went under the alias Sonny Wingate (was he trying to suggest a relationship to the Chindit commander Orde Wingate?) who had been wounded in the head by shrapnel and woke up in a Thai hospital. When the Burmese demanded to know why the Thais were allowing such men to cross the border, the Thais replied that the mercenaries had claimed to be staff of the French charity *Médecins sans Frontières*.

The *Washington Post* of 22 October 1985 said:

According to Western diplomats and relief workers, as many as a dozen mercenaries have been reported ... The Karen deny that they are paying foreigners, some of whom are described as young idealists searching for a cause.

I met one such idealist in a guesthouse on the Thai side of the border. Andrew was English, and twenty-seven years old. His father was a nuclear physicist with the Central Electricity Generating Board, his brother a biochemist and he himself had read engineering at the City of London Polytechnic. He had then joined the Army and had served for two years, mending helicopters in Northern Ireland. But he had taken to heroin.

> 'I was always into drugs. I lived in a squat in King's Cross at the beginning of the punk era, about 1976, and there were several floors of punks and the like, an alright sort of place if you like lots of fighting and don't mind sleeping with an iron bar by your bed. Up top there was an amphetamine factory making speckly blues, the very best. Anyway, I got back onto the heroin in the Army. Then I had this accident, you see?'
> There was a long, contorted scar on his right leg, deep and muscle-deforming.
> 'I was completely doped up one night and fell asleep on top of an electric fire; ended up in Billericay burns unit. They offered me methadone to come off the heroin but I went cold turkey and I'm fine now. I'm really into fitness.'
> He was walking fifteen or twenty miles a day around northern Thailand.
> 'So anyway, I'm invalided out of the Army of course, but I'd some money saved so here I am. I'm sort of on the soldier circuit, pick up bits here and there, Afghanistan and so on. Moonies were paying me $300 a day there.'

What Andrew was most interested in was women – or at least, their bodies. He claimed that a village headman had given him the use of his daughter for a night, a snip at B.200 (£5). His long-term goal was uncomplicated:

> 'I'm screwing my way to Australia.'

Just now he was looking for a route into Kawthoolei.

I couldn't see Andrew risking his neck against the Burmese for no pay, but some did. There was an Australian who spent his leave from active service with the Australian Army to come and train the hilltribes, for fun. And what of the Frenchman who had taken a Karen bride and was settling down in Kawthoolei? Surely his relationship to the Revolution must now change: was it possible to be both a committed family man and a cynically aloof paid killer with the same people? If he really loved the Karen, he'd not drain their pitifully scant funds, would he?

Others had a clearly professional interest. Jimmy the Belgian, who had been at Riverside handing out *Soldier of Fortune* badges, was said to have recruited white mercenaries for the KNLA and to have received $3,000 per head, he himself paying them rather less. The main French contingent, a permanent feature at GHQ, gave True Love sleepless nights. There were persistent rumours that they would be sent down to our District to run training pro- grammes, for which he would have to be the interpreter. 'Not so good at the Front', he said, 'Things can get dangerously confused.'

The French had, at least since the Courrèges-Clerq débâcle, won a reputation for professional competence that not all the mercenaries shared. If Kawthoolei wasn't paying them, somebody surely was. Nobody was saying who.

In July 1987 an American arrived at our Headquarters. I met him in the Colonel's house, but he wasn't talkative. In fact he said not a word, and as a result rumour had a field day. Timothy said he was called Captain Jock. Someone else said that he came from the Delta Force, others that he was an ex-Vietnam Green Beret. He was here to train commandos who had already received some instruction from the French at GHQ. True Love had shown him around the camp at Headquarters.

> 'Come on, True Love, you're doing the Army accounts at the moment, you must know. Is the KNLA paying this man?'
> 'No need to pay!'
> 'So who is?'
> 'I don't know ...'

The Gossips were in no doubt; it was the CIA. But when Trevor the New Zealand photojournalist came to stay, he disagreed:

> 'It's nonsense, I know that guy, he's absolutely straight. He's just an ex-Vietnam GI who took his discharge money and now lives in Bangkok. He's got a Thai wife and children. Lots of GIs did the same. They've got enough money to live on but nothing to do, so they get back into the only thing they're any good at, which is jungle fighting. He sometimes just goes walk- about in the forest on his own for a laugh. He's only trying to make himself useful.'

The Gossips were not convinced. They didn't want to be convinced. They wanted to think that the CIA was backing the Revolution.

As a rule the mercenaries are there to train Karen troops, not to fight battles. It is a vexed issue. The most efficient use of such skills as they might have would be in upgrading Karen officers who would then be able to multiply the benefit. But that is not what usually happens. Instead, the KNLA want them to train Front Line soldiers, or 'commandos'. Mercenaries are rather like tattoos and elephants – a magical asset to make the boys unstoppable. The problem is shared by visiting teachers and health workers; the Karen are desperate to learn but appear to have no faith in their ability to teach each other. Aid workers the world over are familiar with 'dependency-syndrome'; in the case of the Karen, the inferiority complex of the insects of the hills has been developed to a high degree. Smeaton quoted Karen as saying that, 'we live between the legs of other men'.

The Karen are still prey to some illusions about foreigners, and con-men feed on those illusions. A few years ago the KNLA shot down a Burmese aircraft. An American appeared saying that he was an aircraft mechanic and could fix it for them – they could have their own air force! But of course, he would have to return to Bangkok to buy spare parts and for that he would need quite a lot of money. They gave him the money . . .

Then another American arrived. This man said that he was a lawyer and he claimed that, for a small fee, he could secure for them recognition and representation at the United Nations. His fee would be $6,000 dollars. They gave him the money . . .

Maybe these stories have been exaggerated in the telling and retelling, but plenty of Karen believe them. They believe themselves to be honest and gullible: just as at Insein in 1949, 'We were tricked, always we are tricked. Bloody fool *pwakenyaw!*'

These days they have their wits about them more. The most comical figure to appear was a British peer of the realm – so he said. He left us a fund of stories that lasted for weeks. The Gossips told me all they knew; he'd arrived at GHQ claiming to be the son of an English earl. He was Commander RN (or was it Royal Marines?) He'd been everywhere. There was talk of Eton and Oxford, Pall Mall clubs, Borneo, the Falklands, Ulster. And now here he was at GHQ, all military bearing and hauteur in smart new battle fatigues with a smart new survival knife at his hip and a smart and newly pregnant Thai wife in tow. He talked of beginning with fifty men: 'Then, when I have evidence that you people are the real thing I shall be reporting back to London where, I assure you, funds are available.'

But for once the Karen were suspicious, not least because the noble Lord got extremely drunk one night and insulted everyone in sight. He then departed, but reappeared shortly afterwards saying that General Bo Mya had called for him. When Bo Mya declined to see him, His Lordship was livid.

'He's got just the right manner to intimidate them', said Trevor, who had also met him. 'He goes stiff as a ramrod and barks, "This really isn't good enough, you know, I've got people in London waiting for replies". I think they told him to get stuffed.'

But they've got to talk to someone. Trapped in Burma,[8] unable to pass through Thailand to the outside world for lack of a passport, access to international opinion-makers is a major problem for the Karen. 'If only we had a port!' said Highlander. 'Then we could go wherever we liked. Would your country let us in? How else can we speak to the world?'

Sensitive to complaints from Burma, the Thais will grant the Karen residency papers but not passports. Only on very rare occasions would they give travel papers to a representative of Kawthoolei. One such toured Europe and the United States in 1987, and for the first time, an 'indigenous person representing the Karen National Union' spoke to the United Nations.[9] Such direct communication is rare. While there is much truth in Karen complaints that they have been forgotten by, for instance, Britain, they have themselves failed to present their case effectively to the world. Although the *KNU Bulletin* may be found in a few specialist libraries abroad, no press agency ever quotes from it. Only when journalists cross the frontier into Burma do accounts of Kawthoolei emerge. Thus the international image of the Karen is left in the hands of half a dozen sympathetic writers and lobbyists. Some are genuinely concerned. Others represent allies that the Karen should think carefully about – the World Anti-Communist League, for example.

The Thai ethnographer Preecha Chaturabhand (1987, p. 198) remarked a particular handicap:

The desire to have a spokesman in an unfamiliar situation is characteristic of Karen ... Anyone who is assumed to be more powerful – whatever his calling – will be pressed into service for this purpose and, without such an intermediary, hill people are very reluctant to seek services from lowland authorities.

Such spokesmen meet the outside world in Bangkok. In mid 1987 I sat in on a discussion with the Canadian lawyer specialising in indigenous rights. The spokesman was one of the two qualified Karen doctors from GHQ, accompanied by his brother. Both Karen speak excellent English and are quite at home in Bangkok and with foreigners. But neither said very much. Nor were they very anxious to take the lawyer into Kawthoolei. What was the need for such an awkward, uncomfortable journey? Why should first-hand impressions or contact make any difference? They would tell him the truth. They said, 'Please ask us all your questions', and waited quietly. The Canadian, a friendly and sympathetic man, felt that he was swimming in a void: 'Where does one start? If you ask at the UN about indigenous populations in Asia there is quite simply no one who knows. They refer you to the International Labour Organisation which claims to have the best social sciences library in the world. And they have *nothing*.'

Perhaps for all the welcome, Karen always knew that whites would have a deleterious effect in the long run. One of the first things anyone learning the Sgaw language is told is that the Karen for 'Englishmen' – *kola wah* – means 'white Indian'. Actually, it doesn't. *Kola* means 'caste person' – those who cross into Burma from India being marked by their stratified and hierarchical societies.[10] This was not something that the Karen shared – until their Baptist-educated and British Army-trained élite declared independence.

In general, writes Preecha Chaturabhand (1987, p. 198), 'Karen do not take an open attitude with respect to the outside world. They define their world as a Karen world in which the boundaries between ethnic groups are or should be closed.'

The Karen expressed something similar to D. M. Smeaton, in melancholy and xenophobic sayings: We are the leaf, other races are the thorn. If the leaf falls on the thorn, it is pierced. If the thorn falls on the leaf, the leaf is pierced all the same.

Might it not be better, even now, to withdraw to a secluded fortress and wait for Toh Meh Pah?

16 Old guard, young Turks

Edward was very slow to forgive. During the weeks after the acrimonious Monday Free Discussion at which the fate of the girls of *Boarders* had been debated, he and Ruth found many opportunities to make their feelings felt. Seeing me to be in Bartholomew's camp on the issue, Edward cut me and refused to answer any questions. On other occasions both he and Ruth quietly but firmly remarked that they thought the whole procedure, whereby the girls had been taken out of school without their permission, to have been thoroughly disrespectful. They felt hurt, and said so; not, it seemed to me, without some justice. But for Edward it was not merely the lack of consultation, the slight to his office. There were deeper issues for him. It had been a conflict between two Departmental patriarchs, and of their ideas of what mattered for the Revolution. It was a trial between two equally dedicated but quite different views of the Karen – the one looking for intimacy with village people and their local knowledge, the other concerned with the modern state and an outward looking future. And for Edward it was another round in his own battle for personal prestige and political survival.

Edward was the archetype of the Karen urban élite from the Delta, and in the terms of that élite he was much the best-equipped administrator in the District, a man familiar with modern accounting, office procedure, printing and audio-visuals and Thai bureaucracy, vehicles and firearms, the English language and international politics. All this competence he had brought with him to the Revolution.

As a student he had been a political activist and had got himself into trouble. He told me that he had spent three years in jail. When he met Ruth, he wanted to bring her straight away to the Karen Revolution. She was the daughter of a Baptist pastor, one of ten. Her parents objected to her going, alarmed by the impetuous and intense young man who proposed to seduce their daughter off to a war, to live among the primitives where, they warned her, life would not be easy, would bear little resemblance to a middle-class

Delta existence. But Ruth had accepted him and gone anyway, captivated by his convictions and energy. She had begun her forest education alongside Edward; on the way to GHQ they had toured on foot across a wide area of the Karen hills. Ruth had been nervous, she now admitted, and would send Edward into new villages ahead of her to ensure that they were friendly before she would enter. But they had, as a result, a more extensive knowledge of the situation and the lives of different groups of Karen than many of the Delta radicals who came to Kawthoolei.

Edward had been employed at GHQ where his organisational talents won him rapid promotion. To everything that he undertook he applied the same furious energy; no cause could have asked for a more industrious servant. But it was not simply zeal that drove him. Edward's father had been a Karen leader before him – but had been one of a faction called the Karen Revolutionary Council which had agreed peace terms with Ne Win's new military government in 1963, and as such his name was reviled by the present hierarchy. Edward had a mission: to restore the good name of his family as Karen revolutionary loyalists.

But this had proved to be an uphill struggle, and his own character was partly to blame. He was transparently ambitious; he was also supremely tactless. As do many S.E. Asian peoples, the Karen take the art of circumlocution to a fine pitch, and political negotiation is normally conducted in the most deferential, tangential manner. It appeared that Edward had never noticed this – or perhaps he disapproved of it, as incompatible with rapid progress. He liked to state his opinions forthrightly to anyone who cared to listen – and his opinions of the policies and performance of many of his colleagues were often far from complimentary. It was not long before he began to arouse jealousy, resentment and suspicion among both his contemporaries and the senior leadership.

'Did you know that Edward was once under sentence of death?' the Riverside Gossips said. 'He'd been shooting his mouth off as usual and it got too much for our leaders at GHQ.'

He was only saved, the story went, because his wife Ruth saw the sentence lying upon the President's desk awaiting signature and she had interceded, pleading for his life and winning for him a pardon and a chance to prove himself again. But from then on he had been marked and watched. His posting to our District was as a political exile; he had been placed where his efforts could bear fruit without his ambition constituting a danger.

He had found plenty of employment, as head of both the Finance Department and the Education Department. It was the latter job that fired his excitement. It suited him perfectly, because he believed passionately in education as the salvation of the Karen. It also fitted his perception that the Karen struggle must be internationalised to have any chance of succeeding. The Karen have been poor publicists of their cause, and their obscurity and isolation are to some extent their own fault. Edward saw this, and saw that it would take educated people with a command of modern English and some cosmopolitan nous to improve the situation. Education, the 'Silver Book', was a vital link with the outside world. In the name of education, links could be made with churches and charities abroad, in Asia, Europe and the United States, attracting supplies and money, interest and visitors.

But, ironically, it was precisely 'internationalism' that Karen education could never achieve, because no qualification or certificate granted by the Kawthoolei education authorities would ever mean anything in another country. No one spoke of this, but everyone knew it, and in the mining villages nearest the border the families sent their children walking across the frontier to schools set up by the Thai royal family especially for the benefit of the hill tribes. It wasn't just the free uniforms and twice-weekly curry lunch that drew them.

What is the object of education in Kawthoolei? The hill Karen hardly need telling how to grow rice and shoot monkeys, after all. Implicit in the schools is the aspiration to nationhood; or is it just a nexus of social control – education and the Revolution being synonymous? Is it a preparation against the return of Kawthoolei's Karens to some negotiated status within the Union of Burma? Or is it perhaps just a ploy to persuade young educated Delta Karen that Kawthoolei is a place and an idea worthy of serious consideration? Many of the young arrivals from the Delta go straight into teaching, if only for a year or two before being moved on to other departments. It is an immediate role for them and as such it has considerable importance, because it is these people that the Revolution needs most but finds hardest to keep.

As the war first of all stagnated, and has now run increasingly against the Karen, many of the young have grown impatient with the older leaders. Those veterans of the Burma Rifles who have been in charge since 1949 sometimes seem to the young to have no policy at all other than dogged resistance in the hills, waiting for a hitherto inexplicably silent world to take issue with Burma over their fate, or for the Rangoon dictators to drop dead. This, the young feel, can hardly be called dynamic strategy. The 1949 generation calls to younger educated Karen to join them, but few are recruited. They either see little future in the Revolution on its present course, and so ignore the call, or they come to Kawthoolei and find themselves unable to influence the old guard's planning, and in frustration pass on to Thailand. Hence the painfully obvious lack of middle generation leadership. Of the thirty-to-forty-year-olds, only those with strong personal reasons or axes to grind stay on, or those with a wildly optimistic view of their chances of influencing events. There are very few Edwards.

He was, I think, in his late thirties, a slim but muscular man whom I imagined to be capable of violence. He loved to wear military uniform and a gun, but was never in a position to use either. He had a weak face with a slightly silly smile. It was often very difficult to decide whether his expression was serious or joking – and there was a sly side to this; it allowed him outrageous calumnies and half-truths, falling back on laughter if challenged.

I could rarely persuade Edward to talk seriously; an entanglement of barbed facetiousness was his protection against saying too much. On a very few occasions he relaxed and spoke of his hopes. He saw clearly that the war was going nowhere but downhill. It could not be won. The only thing to do, in his view, was to exploit the enemy's weaknesses and these were not military but political. As Ne Win, 'Number One' of Burma, grew older and more eccentrically dictatorial, so the forces for change, Burmese and otherwise, manoeuvred for the succession. There lay the Karen's best hope, thought Edward: in underground propaganda, persuasion, alliance, bargains struck with the future. His arguments had considerable force because Edward acknowledged what most Karen know in their hearts: that Kawthoolei is not viable as a separate political or economic entity. The future of the Karen had to lie either within Burma or within Thailand, and the Karen would only survive if they were equipped by education. But even as Edward threw himself into the task, the senior leadership still spoke of 'winning', of independence, of a Burmese Yugoslavia, Monaco or Luxemburg. For a man as shrewd as Edward, there could only be frustration beneath such a regime of day-dreamers. He worked his heart out to secure some sort of a future – if not for himself, at least for the person he loved most, his small son.

Whatever doubts Edward may have felt himself or aroused in others, there was no question of his energy or effectiveness, nor of the imagination and skill that he brought to bear on the Education Department. It ran far more efficiently than any other. Edward moved fast, shuttling between offices on a bright yellow motorbike. In the morning he'd be at Riverside allocating his teaching staff for the new term; in the afternoon, up at Headquarters supervising the printing of a little geography booklet for the junior schools. The next morning he'd depart for Bangkok to negotiate with an international charity for rice and textbooks, and then back to Kawthoolei the following day with boxes of ballpoint pens. There were days when he travelled from Riverside to Headquarters and back three times, a forty-five minute motorcycle ride on a rough track each way. He might still be at it – shuttling, or working – in the early hours of the morning. Somewhere he also found time to write the Christmas pageant performed by the teachers and schoolchildren, to organise recordings of revolutionary songs, and to strip down and repair the motorcycle. On top of all this, he also ran the Finance Department, with considerable powers to promote or block other people's projects. Not surprisingly, he was often ill.

Such frantic industry is not common in Karen; they do not subscribe to a 'do it yesterday' work-ethos. Edward felt that most things would run more efficiently if he did them himself. This conviction, allied to a natural inclination to gather power to him, made for a highly centralised Department in which Edward, and Ruth as headmistress, took all major decisions. Little of importance was ever delegated, and a predictable inertia could be felt among the underlings. Edward was not only an empire-builder; he even called himself one. His house, close by the junior and senior schools, looked across the compound to the smaller houses of his teaching staff. From his verandah he could watch over all the comings and goings in his department, and he grinned at me and said, 'I like to watch over my empire'. On that verandah he held court, ostentatiously dispensing coffee and other costly imported luxuries, receiving visits, representations, reports and submissions from great and small, and issuing instructions. Or he would pace the compound in front of the junior school running a cordless electric razor over his chin – an extraordinary gesture in a beardless people.

With the concentration of power there went a familiar syndrome of patronage, privilege and favouritism. He had creatures and clients whose loyalty he rewarded with material assistance, job preference and 'insider' status. Of course, he had antagonists also, people who chafed under his rule and who attempted to evade his control. One teacher petitioned Colonel Marvel for a transfer to another department, any other department. He claimed in public that he was tired of teaching but in private he admitted that it was the regime that he could no longer tolerate. Other independent spirits were sent to far corners of the District, to Maw Daung or the Western Valley, often several days' travel from their families.

True Love and Silver were protégés of Edward and Ruth. In return they gave their loyalty, and there were times when it made me furious. Silver, seven months pregnant, was asked to assist in preparing food for the naming ceremony of Ruth's new baby. Silver's previous pregnancy had resulted in a very late, life-threatening miscarriage and she was now anaemic once again. The weather was at its hottest, and she should have been in a hammock in the cool beneath her house. Instead, she spent twelve hours in a hot kitchen. I told True Love what I thought. He replied: 'These women love each other. They have been through so much together, and Ruth too has lost a baby. When Silver was ill last time, Ruth sent people to help her, and now they are arranging for Silver to go and have this new baby of ours in Thailand. You must understand, we are very close to them.'

True Love, meanwhile, acted as Edward's factotum. Presentable, articulate, and with his own frustrations to spur him on in sympathy, he ensured the smooth running of not a few of Edward's projects.

I don't say that Edward abused his power and privilege; but he exercised it freely. Of all his favourites, his own family took clear precedence. He made no secret of his enjoyment of trips to Bangkok and the opportunities they presented for combining official duties with private advancement. The duties were more than adequately performed, so why not? He spent much time in cultivating business and political contacts in Thailand and abroad, but if these brought economic gain and international support for Kawthoolei, so much the better. No one that I heard objected to his Department staff being required to perform certain services for his family; it was commensurate with his position. The household did not require the 'family life' services of Bartholomew's nurses, for the simple reason that they had their own ready supply of help – the senior students and the junior women teachers under Ruth's authority, who could frequently be seen in her kitchen – 'receiving their training', as Ruth put it. No one complained, except Ruth herself when things were not running as smoothly as she wished. I met her one afternoon sitting on a bench in front of the school in a foul temper. What was wrong? 'Oh, the pump is broken, and so now these people have to carry water up from the river and I have to behave like a Burmese soldier' – that is, shouting orders at Karen girls, whom I now saw coming up from the river and hurrying to Ruth's kitchen and bathroom with old kerosene tins of water on their heads.

Edward was uncompromising and fervent on behalf of his people, but there was nothing egalitarian about him. While Bartholomew struggled against the odds to provide basic health services for the villages along the river, Edward thought nothing of sending his wife to Bangkok to have her baby, or returning her there at frequent intervals for check-ups and vaccinations that were certainly not available to the populace. They would have nothing to do with the normal health services of Kawthoolei, but independently obtained supplies of malaria prophylactics for the schoolchildren in their charge. And they set themselves apart in other ways. Ruth in particular was a devout Christian, involved in missionary activity among her own people and support programmes for Christians in Burma. But she kept aloof from the Baptist establishment in the village, not becoming involved in their conventions or the consecration of the new church, not even attending most of the imposing special services that marked national and revolutionary days.

Between husband and wife they spoke Burmese, not Karen, while Edward liked nothing more than to have his Thai business contacts come to his house in their white Landcruisers, to sit with him on his verandah and discuss cross-border deals in rare timber and aromatics. All of which negotiations were conducted in English since, to his enormous chagrin, he spoke very poor Thai.

It could be that such a display of confidence and capability was a source of strength and encouragement to other revolutionaries. It could also be that it left the underlings nervous as to what might happen if this patron and example should desert or fail them.

They worked for their position, Ruth and Edward. I had good reason to be grateful to them in my first few weeks. Edward himself met me at Bangkok airport and ensured my safe arrival in Kawthoolei. He also collected mail for me in Bangkok. Their house was never empty. Edward had made himself the unofficial foreign minister of the District; he was probably the only one who could do it. Apart from his fluent English, he had an international *savoir faire* that other Karen lacked. He knew what foreigners needed and what they wanted to know, and so it came to be accepted that it was with Edward that they dealt. Quite a few of these visitors were offering assistance, both to the Education Department and to Health and Welfare, or to the Army or the Church. Journalists and film-makers, teachers and missionaries all moved into that not very large house at one time or another, filling the verandah, waiting to be fed, needing information, interpreters, assistance, coffee, sleeping space, boats and boatmen. Everything was provided or arranged by Edward and Ruth, who had no privacy other than the cramped bedroom in which their suitcases full of coffee, cameras and cough mixtures for their little boy were stored. It was a room which, most unusually in a Karen house, was kept padlocked. It had a hardboard door which, even when open, was never agape, just a narrow chink through which they would slip to order their secrets. And when there were no foreign guests, anyone from soldiers and farmers to school-teachers and doctors might be found on the verandah, looking at the pictures in *National Geographic* (to which Edward subscribed), or talking politics, or fiddling with the radio, or watching Edward cleaning his pistol, or doing nothing at all, simply being there, paying court.

But for all Edward's apparent domination of village life, for all his dependants and his organisational energy, his true power was not unlimited. The old guard were less flamboyant, less fluent self-publicists and less conversant with the English language and the ways of the outside world generally, but within Kawthoolei they held sway and they were not people to let the likes of Edward usurp their positions. The higher Edward raised his public prestige, the more attention he attracted, the more the older generation quietly closed ranks against him. Colonel Marvel was merely the head of that archaic order but, given Edward's outspoken ambition and the Colonel's arbitrary and eccentric rule, it was inevitable that there should come a personal clash. They were, in many ways, direct rivals.

The generation gap in Kawthoolei public life may be explained by the frustrations and disappointment of the younger generation, but it would be wrong to blame the elders entirely. Many of them have ideals and a clear vision of how a good Karen society should be, based on traditional values, not on commercial internationalism. Many of them have spent much of their adult lives working, and fighting, towards that vision.

On Karen Revolution Day, the 31st of January 1987, Colonel Marvel came to Riverside to address a parade of the people. In his usual manner, which gave nothing away to Edward in terms of hard work, he began his day by driving down the hill at 4 a.m., arriving at Riverside three-quarters of an hour later and summoning Bartholomew and others to a quick meeting before the ceremonials began. At 7 a.m. we assembled in the mist on the parade ground. The villagers mostly stayed at home, but the attendance of the schoolchildren and their teachers was compulsory, and it was to them that the Colonel spoke from the little white podium, with True Love once again in charge of the public address system.

It was a simple speech, but in its way rather moving: 'On this day, thirty-nine years ago, when the Karen people took up arms for their freedom at Insein, I was there. We have been building Kawthoolei ever since. I was young and vigorous then; today I am a much older man. But my belief in our future has not dimmed one bit.'

I have a photograph of the Colonel taken that morning. He is in full dress uniform, crisply pressed, with three stars on his shoulders, the drum-and-horn badge of the KNLA on his peaked cap, his commemorative medal from the battle of Myawaddy and his long-service medal on his chest next to a ballpoint pen sticking from his breast pocket. Only his very battered black boots are less than smart. In another photograph taken at the same time, the Colonel stands with a group of his closest associates – Major Richard, Major Baldwin of the KNDO, 'Devourer of the Country' of the Information Department, the Quartermaster, the Transport Chief, the Secretary and others. They stand posed tightly together, staring appraisingly into the distance. There's no doubting the solidity of purpose in the faces. These are not men who are making small deals in exotic forest products with traders from Thailand. These are not men who really know much about Thailand, except as a source of vehicle spares, rice, uniforms and disadvantageous timber sales. Edward is not in the group; I photographed him separately, dressed in clean battledress with the sleeves neatly rolled and a woollen commando hat. He alone is carrying a gun. After the speeches there were prayers and then a public pig-feast. I was taken to the Justice's house to eat with the Colonel and his team, but Edward paced about among the schoolchildren and the teachers outside.

Colonel Marvel shared other traits with Edward, apart from sheer

Plate 16. Colonel Marvel instructs a young militiaman. 'I was young and vigorous then. Today I am a much older man. but my belief in our future has not dimmed one bit.'

energy. There was money behind both of them somewhere. The KNU does not pay allowances for coffee and biscuits, but they were both munificent providers. The Colonel, of course, took the lead in hospitality, and his house was even more open than Edward's. I stayed with the Colonel often. Here too there was coffee for the asking, with white Thai bread and pineapple jam in the cupboard and large jars of purified Thai drinking water which the Colonel took on medical advice. The dark, hardwood house was unlike any traditional Karen home in having an upper storey. Downstairs, the reception room was lined with hard wooden arm-chairs in a horseshoe facing the Colonel's grey steel office desk. The walls were covered with pictures of Ba U Gyi, Burmese calen-dars, photographs of the Colonel, his family and of fighter aircraft. One never knew who would be there, passing in or out of Head-quarters or of Kawthoolei, exchanging news or copies of the *Bangkok Post*. The Colonel, like Edward, was a relentless self-improver. Edward went about it with more system perhaps, but the Colonel filled his house with imposing technical volumes that he bought in job lots in Thailand. He was very keen on medicine, and had got hold of *The Radiology of the Paediatric Elbow*, *Emergency Care in the Streets* and *School Psychology*. He also had a fine library of the classic literature of Vietnam, and over the months I read most of it: *Despatches*, *365 Days*, *Friendly Fire*, *Nam*, *Sideshow*, *Decent Interval* and others. Given the considerable differences between that war and ours, I wondered what he had learnt from these. Also, the Colonel's English was not outstanding; what did he make of 'spooky', 'gooks' and 'Puff the magic dragon'?

Other volumes in his library were more surprising. He had a grandiose coffee table history of *The American Chair*: 'Oh, I thought that our people might make furniture from all the timber here in Kawthoolei. But I don't think these patterns are appropriate for us.' No, it was difficult to imagine them turning out reproduction Chippendale and Shaker rocking chairs. But he had given it some thought.

In spite of its facilities, his was not a comfortable house. It was full of scorpions, and it was lit by neon tubes without switches, so that one had no choice; they came on with the generator at 6 p.m., went off at nine and came on again at four-thirty in the morning. So, they imposed regular hours. The Colonel needed to be up and about. There were new schemes and projects to be managed, reports to be considered, junior officers to be bawled out and a war to be won. Relaxation was his least talent. He was only still if reading the *Bangkok Post* and chortling over the dicta of his much-admired Mrs Thatcher, or when lying prostrate having his calves massaged by the wife of the Forestry Officer. Otherwise, he slept as little as Mrs Thatcher. His day, like Edward's, was a cycle of vivid imagination, impetuous decision, inability to delegate, impatience, frustration and exhaustion, followed by a few hours' sleep. Like Edward, it was hardly surprising that he was often ill. Except that Colonel Marvel had been living like this for twice as long and was twice as damaged.

When I first arrived in Kawthoolei, with the October weather cold and damp, the Colonel was sick. He was diabetic and over-weight, his blood pressure was high and the cold made him so miserable that he had taken to his bed. This was the reputation that I had heard in Bangkok; that he was elderly and infirm and in no way equal to the tasks that he set himself. Perhaps the Bangkok Gossips had only met him on cold, wet mornings. On other days he left us breathless in pursuit. As with Edward, the hectic enthu-siasm of his presence tended to create inertia in his absence. If he was at Headquarters, bags would be minutely checked at the border. If he was away, they'd be ignored. Keenly practical, he said that he never travelled anywhere without a set of carpenter's tools in his car – but he was never still in any one place long enough to use them. He would arrive at any hour, send his bodyguards up a tree for coconuts and say:

'So, Mr John, shall we go?'
'Ah, right. Where are we going, Colonel?'
'Anywhere; where would you like to go?'
'Well, I have things to do here, actually . . .'
'Good, so tell me: what can I do to help you?'
'I'm not sure . . .'
'You ask my secretary for any help that you need. I have to go to GHQ tomorrow. Why don't you come with me?'

He would appear one day in green fatigues, the next in a silver-grey jump suit, or a new blue tropical outfit. He would have been Burma's best-dressed insurgent were it not for the blue towel that he carried round his neck to mop the sweat from his brow.

The Colonel told me something of his past as we drove through Thailand one day in February. In his late teens at the time of the Japanese invasion of British Burma, he had accepted a brief training in mechanical engineering from the Japanese army, only to enlist promptly with the British forces when they reinvaded. He had become an Armourer Third Grade and, along with many other Karen soldiers, had been drafted straight into the army of the Union of Burma at Independence. But he and his comrades deserted to join the new Karen National Defence Organisation for the fight at Insein. He rose through the ranks with a succession of military and political roles, assisted by his reasonable English: 'I was with the Kawthoolei Foreign Office in Bangkok for several years, and I didn't speak a word of Thai. I'm trying to learn now, from cassettes.'

And then, back to military commands at the Front where, he said, 'I took the very best care of my men. I had to be their doctor as well as their commander. I had no such training, so I learnt medicine as I went along. I had to do everything.'

As we drove south towards Maw Daung, he recalled different periods of Kawthoolei's history – and many of them aroused in him acid regret: 'It is a terrible thing to be disunited. We did well in the first years, but then in the late fifties we had all those factions and leaders who were like warlords, not true nationalists, and what happened? We lost all the territory that we had won. And then our leaders went so far to the left and it made things worse. We needed a strong political philosophy, of course, and Mao Zedong's was the best available. But when our leaders began insisting that our movement should be led by illiterate farmers, against the clever politicians of Burma – how could that work? And so the movement split again, and we had the Karen National Liberation Council and the KNU and all these new names and we have wasted so much time on these things.'

It was not only time that he felt had been wasted, however. The Colonel loved to wear a gun, a pistol in a shoulder holster, and he also liked to tell you where he had got it: 'I took this from a former Defence Minister of Burma, Let Ya. I am now looking for an opportunity to return it to his widow.'

Behind the rhetoric lay, for him, a sorrier story. In the 1970s the Burmese ex-Prime Minister U Nu and his confederates, the men who had been ousted by Ne Win's 1962 coup, were briefly allied with the Karen in confronting the Burmese government. Let Ya, U Nu's Defence Minister, was seen as a good and powerful friend of the Karen but he was caught in the crossfire when U Nu and the KNU finally fell out. Sent to disarm these Burmese allies, Colonel Marvel had ordered a few 'warning shots' to be fired into their camp – and Let Ya had been the casualty. He was the one person the Colonel should not have killed. The latter now lived with the suspicion that the incident had irredeemably spoilt his chances of political seniority in Kawthoolei. Thus, like Edward, he had something to live down.

Colonel Marvel had been sent to take charge of our District some five years before I arrived. Strictly speaking he was Chairman of the District KNU, but he was usually referred to as the Governor. The posting could be seen as a rest cure in what was then still a back-water. His kidneys were failing, he'd needed two operations, and he was relieved of his frontline command at GHQ for his own good. In the course of the year, I began to see other reasons that the GHQ leadership might have had for his transfer. Frantic activity, impetuous decisions and short-term expediency are understandable in men who see the enemy advancing towards them and their own memorials unfinished, but finally they are just as destructive as the opposition. The Colonel and Edward could see this in each other, but not in themselves. To post them together was rather unkind. Like the sinners in Sartre's *Huis Clos*, they'd been condemned to occupy the same space.

Edward's Education Department was the most extensive and the most consistent state presence in the villages of the District. In theory, every child had access to a village school and the reality almost matched that. Those not attending were poor forest animists who lived well away from the villages. Whether they would have wanted to attend, I cannot say.

Most villages could provide only primary education. For the secondary level, children had to move on to the main centres at Riverside or Betelwood in the Western Valley. At Riverside there was also a senior school with some thirty pupils; if there were enough teachers that year, they could go up to grade ten.

At every stage the children were drilled and tested. Those who failed their exams stayed down a year; some were in their early twenties and still trying. The children took the exams quite as seriously as the teachers. The only time I saw Bartholomew's granddaughter Bi crying was for an exam failure. She was five at the time. For days beforehand you could hear them revising, in *Boarders*, in the schoolrooms, in houses throughout the village, rote-chanting their lessons. Many of the key words, especially in the sciences, were of course in English. But one also heard names from European history and even the plays of Shakespeare in the hubbub: *na na na* nitrous oxide *na na* Goebbels *na na* Duke of Albany. The girls of *Boarders* got up well before dawn and sat in their kitchen, cramming. As the weather grew hotter and hotter towards the end of the school year, they lay full length on the concrete floor of the laboratory or the hospital, or took their books down to the river to sit in the water, muttering. As British children once used the dandelion clock, so Karen use the croak of the *tokay* lizard to predict a pass or fail: *to-kay!* I pass, *to-kay!* I fail, *to-kay!* I pass ... When term and exams were ended there were celebrations and picnic outings, volleyball tournaments and music.

For one star pupil a year from each District there was a special higher course at GHQ, lasting for ten months. It was still experimental, and the first grade ten girl was sent to take part in 1987. Fragrance, Bartholomew's daughter, was to go next. On their return, these graduates would be expected to teach and to take a lead in raising standards in the schools, perhaps to become full-time teacher-trainers.

But for now, the many village schools were staffed by people from almost as many backgrounds. The teacher might be the Pastor, or the Pastor's spouse. It could be the daughter of the headman, brought back from Riverside to work at her home. It might be an elderly retired civil servant from Burma. It might even be a Burmese-trained teacher. Young men from Burmese secondary schools or colleges, such as True Love, were concentrated at Riverside and Betelwood.

Nineteenth-century ethnographers noted that, within a few years of the arrival of the American Baptists among them, Karen villages were building schools and supporting schoolteachers from their own community with food and small funds. In Kawthoolei today that tradition continues and accounts for perhaps the majority of village primary school staff. But there are also the 'revolutionary teachers' like True Love and White Rock who, having been appointed by Edward, received only an official rice and salt ration to keep them going. Any other cash they might want for themselves or their families was left to themselves to find. So we met teachers on trading trips, passing through the forest with cattle, Burmese jewels or specimens of increasingly rare wildlife to sell to the Thais. Materials were scarce in the far-flung schools, so on their return journeys the teachers carried packs of books, inks, chalks. It was the only way the schools in the Western Valley could be supplied. The teachers carried twenty kilos each, slung from their foreheads, and it took three days of hard walking.

There were plenty of other problems. The war shut the school at the Front Line village of White Ponds; they were afraid to have all their children in one vulnerable clump together. And the harvest didn't help. From November to January many families moved away from home to live in huts near the far-flung fields. There were too few teachers, and in larger villages they had impossibly large numbers. Chanting and songs were often the easiest option, but they *did* learn in these schools; the literacy rate remains high – among Christian Karen at least.

To prevent total isolation, and the decay in standards that would inevitably follow on the teachers' loneliness in the outposts, Edward organised an annual upgrading course in Riverside. Everyone came; it was the high point of their year.

The course was held in May, but the start was delayed a week while essential materials were obtained and instructors from GHQ coped with the financial and practical hazards of travel through Thailand. In that week, Riverside filled with several dozen teachers. They all had to be lodged somewhere. Several moved into the already crowded *Boys Boarders*, others stayed with friends. At Bartholomew's house we received the eccentric old gentleman who taught at Durianville, and who now unrolled a mat next to my hammock. Tall, gaunt and fastidious, he spent half an hour brushing his hair each morning, and then packed it in under a green knitted hat. He talked to himself incessantly, and liked to have the family together for prayers under his direction each evening – something unheard of at Bartholomew's, and a little embarrassing because no one in the family knew any of the hymns he chose. He made up for this solemnity in the children's eyes by standing out in the back yard singing his head off in the moonlight, a wild medley of songs religious and less so, which the children accompanied with make-believe guitars and screams of laughter.

Other teachers contrived bedrooms in the school itself, suspending curtains from the ceiling. The delays dragged on and they hung around at a loose end, playing volleyball or singing together, or cooking meals in the school kitchens, or washing their clothes in the river.

At last the promised materials arrived, bundles of textbooks of a new English course for the entire District. There was an opening ceremony in the church hall, with patriotic hymns and saluting of the flag. And then, hectic activity for three weeks.

Their best efforts went into the new English course; it was the first that they'd ever seen of it, and they were now expected to take it to their villages and teach it. It was not quite the latest in language education, but for Kawthoolei – perhaps, too, for Burma – it involved a dramatic change of style and teaching technique, employing flash cards and other visual aids, games and songs. Many of the vocabulary cards were prepared by True Love who was able to start work on the illustrations only when the new books arrived, and was thus employed throughout the three weeks in sketching cats, mats and rats onto stencil sheets, a task that annoyed him intensely as he was proud of his ability to draw and now complained that he had no time to do a decent job. The teachers sat till late in the evening in the classrooms, colouring in the printed cards with crayons and copying vocabulary lists off the blackboard. Then they went to the Californian mission-teacher's 'phonics' classes which several Karen proudly disapproved of: 'We speak British English. Why are we being taught these noises?'

The Secretary of the National Education Committee came from GHQ to supervise the adoption of the new English course. I found him sitting on a bench in front of the school late at night; he'd been writing word lists on the blackboard for the teachers to copy, and was now resting his eyes in the darkness. I said that I was impressed by the activity, but hadn't it been very expensive to make the change?

> 'It's paid for by each District as they introduce the new book, not nationally. Yes, the printing is expensive, but that is not our biggest problem. We need teaching staff, and not just good teachers but staff who can train others. I have just finished training thirty new teachers at GHQ and, frankly, there are only six who could train other teachers and only two that I thought could be trusted to do it well. Another reason why we can't do anything too quickly.'

I mentioned the hard revision I had seen going on before exams, and my surprise at hearing the Duke of Albany in conjunction with nitrous oxide. He almost lost his temper.

> 'That's an even better example! The teachers have completely misunderstood the reason for those stories being in the course at all. They were meant to be simple stories as examples of the language, but half the pupils have been learning the stories by heart. It's because the teachers don't know what they're doing.'
>
> 'Where did the new course come from?'
>
> 'An Australian teacher prepared it for us, so you can see it is very Australian. (*Mr Kent, Mrs Kent, John and Susan, Tabby the cat and Kip the dog.*) This teacher had been to some of the refugee camps where people from Cambodia were having to learn English very quickly so that they could go to new countries, and this is their crash course which has been adapted for us.'

He stood and went back into the classroom to see how his staff were getting on with their cards. Once they had finished there would be entertainment – a video: *Streets of Fire*.

True Love and William sat down in the shadows with me, exhausted. I asked William if it was true about the Shakespeare stories being misused.

> 'Yes, I'm afraid so. But that is what happens when you just tell people what to do without explanation. Nobody told us what those stories were for.'
>
> 'Do you get any say in the school curriculum?'
>
> 'Not a lot. It's very centralised. But there are ways in which we can control things a little. If there's an instruction that the teachers don't like, they just avoid doing anything about it.'
>
> 'Many of the teachers prefer it this way', said True Love. 'It makes our work much easier. I have a long teaching day, six classes, but I know exactly what I will have to teach in each one, and so I have to do very little preparation the night before. At most I sometimes have to simplify the lessons a little bit.'
>
> 'Because the students can't keep up?'
>
> 'Or because I don't know what it is about.'

And he went off to find the leads to connect the video-machine to the generator. Children and teachers and soldiers had already packed the classroom in front of the television. The vocabulary cards lay unfinished in heaps on the desks next door.

There were other classes each day, apart from language, and some were aimed at the teachers themselves. Flow charts were drawn on the blackboard illustrating the relationship between the responsible teacher, the good pupil who grows into the good citizen, and the prosperous state. Meanwhile, all around them as they worked, the old hardboard walls of the junior school were being taken out and replaced with cement blocks. Edward and Ruth appeared not to sleep. If not arranging classes or giving instructions for the preparation of meals, they'd be issuing stationery to be taken back to the village schools, and soap.

'We all get an issue', said True Love, collecting his from the school office. 'One and a half bars per teacher per month. Very dirty, teachers. These are mine, those are Silver's.' He walked out with a stack of *Satellite Soap* jammed under his chin.

At the end of three weeks, the flashcards were done and the teachers weary. There was a closing ceremony. Once more they saluted the flag, prayed for Kawthoolei and sang the anthem. Edward, dressed in a snappy tropical suit, gave out prizes that

looked as though he'd had them gift-wrapped at the Central Department Store in Bangkok. Then there was a demonstration of the
new English teaching system with a 'class' of teachers being put
through the games and dialogues, with a song:

> One man and his dog,
> in a car together.
> One man, two men, three men and a dog,
> in a car together.

Outside the door, six young teachers gathered in white maiden's
dress, holding presents tied with bows. At the front of the hall,
a schoolmaster began to play 'What a Friend we have in Jesus'
on a home-made slide guitar, accompanied by True Love on bass.
Edward sat at the front waiting, smiling sweetly as the six girls
came into the hall and approached him. They placed a garland
of flowers about his neck and laid the presents on his lap, and
he rolled his eyes contentedly. Colonel Oliver, deputising for Colonel
Marvel, made a short speech.

As we rose to go for breakfast, a motorcycle drew up outside
the hall. The dispatch rider entered quickly and silently and, with
a slight bow, handed the Colonel a slip of paper. The Colonel read
it, folded it and the two of them left promptly on the motorcycle.
We went to eat fat pork in the school.

For Ruth and Edward the upgrading had been a triumph. Its
objectives had all been achieved, a vast amount of work had been
done, the new walls were very smart and the organisation had been
good. For three weeks the Education Department had taken over
the village completely, and the teachers' morale was high as they
prepared to set off for their homes.

But the fragility of their plans and achievements was thrust at
them at the very moment of their satisfaction. The dispatch rider
who had interrupted the closing ceremony had brought frightening
news. The Burmese Army had attacked and captured our District's
northernmost Township headquarters and had wrecked it completely. The KNLA had expected the attack for several days, and
had taken up positions in the forest to meet the enemy, leaving
just one section in the village. But they had been outmanoeuvred.
Moses told me what he had heard:

'We have a radio station there on top of the hill, right by the
border, so that we thought at least our communications were safe
enough. The people's houses are all around the base of the hill.

But it seems that the Burmese went through Thailand and were able to come behind our soldiers and take them by surprise. We think they must have had an arrangement with the Thais who we thought were our friends – it is the worst possible news. Apparently the section at the village put up a good fight but then the Thai soldiers intervened, saying that they wouldn't have fighting on their border, and they disarmed our men and handed them over to the Burmese. There was one Karen soldier who was over in Thailand when the attack came, and when he saw what had happened he got into a car and came here to tell us. Everything else is rumour.'

Which was plentiful. Sam told me the latest:

> 'We all have friends there and we don't know what has happened to them. Maybe ten Karen have been killed, and a hundred or more taken prisoner, pregnant women and small babies too. Everything has been wrecked, the radio station, all the buildings. My father's Department had four nurses there and we have no idea what has become of them. The Township Secretary has been captured and two of his officers are dead. There are many wounded at Sangklaburi hospital in Thailand . . .'

True Love was more cautious about rumour, but he too speculated miserably as to why the Thais had allowed the Burmese through.

> 'We have heard that the Burmese paid the Thai soldiers on the border – it is said they paid two *lakhs* of *baht*.' (That is, B.200,000, or £5,000.)
>
> 'But who were the Thais who disarmed the Karen? Army? Rangers?'
>
> 'We don't know exactly. But not all Thais support the Karen, you see. Thai businessmen don't want fighting on the border, they want it quiet and wide open so that they can take all the trees without trouble.'

As usually happened after a Burmese attack, everyone spent the next few days polishing up their guns. Edward stripped and re-blued his Luger. Shortly afterwards it was Edward that the Colonel sent north to investigate the situation. But, as that involved a journey through Thailand, he had to leave his gun at home.

Colonel Marvel could not dispense with Edward's talents, but nor could he stomach his success. The blow in the north merely underlined the weakness of the KNU claim to protective authority, even as Edward appeared to be achieving great things in education. At just this time, the Colonel began to move against him.

It began with a cruel cut. For several days Edward was in a particularly foul mood. Whereas this normally meant that he stone-walled my attempts at conversation, he was now so awash with indignation that he couldn't help but tell me why.

> 'I have been told that I am not to have anything more to do with foreigners coming to our District. Nothing at all. The District Secretaries will be dealing with all external affairs. If you wish for any information now you will please ask someone else. Also, I ask you to have your mail redirected. I am not a postman, and I do not want you to use my Bangkok contacts now.'

He was very bitter, both at the arbitrary manner in which the decision had been made, with no effort to consult him and no consideration of his years of hard work in establishing international contacts. In the next few days he became surly and rude. When I was at last able to sit and drink a cup of coffee with him, while he cleaned yet another pistol, he suddenly looked up and said:

> 'Do you know what they did with Mussolini, Jo? They hung him upside down!'

I reminded him that the German officers who had plotted against Hitler had also been hanged, with piano wire if I remember rightly. Though Edward did his best to be offensive, I couldn't help but sympathise with his position.

Others were worried. The Gossips reported that Edward and the Colonel went through a daily charade of mutual support and appreciation at the Headquarters offices, and maligned each other constantly once out of earshot. Their respective allies thought it both childish and serious.

'Edward's been in trouble before', they told me. 'Not just at GHQ. Our President, Bo Mya, came to visit us here last year and he was very angry with Edward about something. The Colonel supported Edward then, but God knows what would happen now.'

It was painful to watch. I saw the Colonel in a spectacular fury one afternoon when the assistance and the health services he'd arranged for the Maw Daung refugees appeared to be falling apart through departmental inertia. The Colonel let off some steam by washing his new car – which the Finance Department had not very privately called a gross waste of scarce public funds. The Colonel roared instructions and abuse at miserable youths who'd had the temerity to walk, not run, when he sent them for more water, or who had left smudges on the chrome – and Edward was there, fussing about at the Colonel's elbow, nodding energetically to everything the Colonel spat out about foreigners (me, principally), refugees, inadequate officers and all the incompetents by whom he was surrounded. And, behind Edward's sycophancy, I could see exasperation writ large. What did the Colonel expect, if he issued half a dozen contradictory orders and wanted each one executed immediately? The office staff all vanished. They knew about these tantrums and kept well out of sight until the Colonel calmed down.

In June I went briefly to Penang. On my return I expected that the new school term would have started and normality have been restored to village life. I was quite wrong. The day that I walked down from the border, a minor coup was in progress at Riverside. The Colonel had come and had called a grand meeting of the Education Department. It was not a discussion, just a series of announcements. Edward was to be relieved of all his education duties and was to concentrate solely on his work in the Finance Office. Ruth was to 'rest', William was to run the school, and the new head of District Education was to be none other than Colonel Marvel himself.

> The Gossips were not surprised: 'It's been coming for a long time. Our leaders have been watching Edward and they have been thinking that the more power he had, the more of a liability he became. The Colonel found out that Edward had gone to GHQ and denounced him to Bo Mya as a madman. What will happen now is more interesting. There is a rumour that the Colonel is to be recalled to GHQ and that a man called Bo Gyi will take over here. It was Bo Gyi who once sentenced Edward to death. We think that if Bo Gyi comes here, then Edward will run back to GHQ – and then Colonel Marvel will return here ...'

The affair grew more Byzantine hourly. After the short-lived high of the upgrading course, morale in the Department was sinking rapidly. 'We do not like the way this was done', they said, 'Edward didn't deserve that. Some teachers are now threatening to leave.'

> For True Love it was a matter of personal loyalty:
> 'I love Edward, we are very close. He has his faults but he is very talented, and he is prepared to face anybody and any situation. Why can't our leaders see the good in him and make an ally of him? I only came back into teaching because he personally asked me to.
> 'And anyway', he continued, 'who else can really do the job?

> The Colonel cannot – how does he imagine that he will have the time? William is a fine man, but he has no experience of Bangkok and foreign charities and these people whose support we need. Also there are some teachers who do not like to work with William either, because they are more senior . . .'

And so they bickered, while the Colonel, having taken this new role to himself, did nothing about it at all, being far too preoccupied with the refugees and other problems. I went for a protracted and delicious breakfast of wildcat curry with Moses, at which he said that he was praying that they would all come to their senses and remember the common cause that they were supposed to be fighting for.

> 'Of course, the ones who will lose most are those who were Edward's special favourites. They will no longer have protection and privileges. It is very dangerous to place too much reliance on a patron like that. They are out in the cold now, with everyone else.'

As we talked, Edward rode past on his bright yellow motorcycle, heading up the hill to Headquarters and the unrelenting labours of the Finance Department.

A few days later I found Edward sitting on his verandah once again, in a surprisingly cheerful and welcoming humour. He was civil to me for the first time in weeks, and made me coffee himself. He had a brighter picture to paint of the situation:

> 'Have you heard, and what do you think? The Colonel has assured me that none of my policies will be changed. Ruth will be going to Bangkok for her rest but she will still be the real head of the school. I have left everything in a good condition for William to take over. The school is on a sure footing, they have plenty of materials and the teachers' morale is high, the upgrading was a success. What do you think? What are people saying now?'

That was what he really wanted to know. He had suddenly had a perception of himself as a man without friends, only dependants whom he was no longer in a position to reward. He was not, however, going to let himself seem cowed:

> 'I have new projects. I shall build a house up at Headquarters, and live there with my work. I have something to show you.'

He went into the inner sanctuary and brought out a neat blue-grey plastic box which he gave me to examine. It was a file of microfiches on Appropriate Technology, loaned him by friends in the United States.

'I have this until October. I am going to read it through and arrange translations of everything that will be useful to us. And look, I have something else ...'.'

Back into the bedroom, and out with a grey camera case. Inside, a new Nikon.

'What do you think?' he asked again.

He returned to Headquarters, staying with the Forestry Officer while his new house there was built. Ruth, their little boy and their new baby went to Bangkok. True Love was left for weeks not knowing whether he was meant to be a teacher or a soldier in the coming year. And the house that was the heart of Edward's empire was taken over by senior school students, who cooked for themselves.

17   True Love and White Rock

> We are music lovers but our infatuation for music is only shallow. One British Major Nolan put it this way. The Karen have an aptitude for music. But they do not work hard enough or go deep enough to master the art and to attain international recognition. There are no artists among our people qualified to go to other countries for money making, fame and for display of propaganda stunts.   Saw Moo Troo (1981, p. 1)

In Communist-ruled Krakow, playing the lute was a subversive activity. To assert the existence of an historical Polish music culture was tantamount to separatist sedition. Music has been closely associated with many revolts, violent and peaceful, grandiose and plebeian. Verdi's opera *Nabucco* incited Italian patriots to noisy demonstrations against the Austrian army of occupation and his name was chanted as an acronym of 'Vittorio Emmanuele Re d'Italia.' A less exalted musical flowering, but still one of the most remarkable in the twentieth century, was that initially associated with Salvador Allende's government in Chile in the 1970s, and in other Latin American countries since: an upsurge of *nueva canción* expressing hopes for, and sometimes the triumphs of, social liberalisation and reform, and whose chief exponents are now to be found in Argentina (the glorious Mercedes Sosa) and in Nicaragua.

Saw Moo Troo speaks of propaganda abroad, but it is within the country of insurrection that music counts for most. 'Populist' uprisings make use of music to communicate with people who may have been downtrodden for years, even for generations, and who are often illiterate. Songs provide a ready means of spreading a message. Woody Guthrie said of his 'Ballad of Tom Joad' (a retelling of Steinbeck's *Grapes of Wrath*) that the poor people he wanted to speak to couldn't read the book and couldn't afford to see the film, but they might just hear and learn the song. The Indonesian singer Mogi Darusman, once a star of European Country and Western, went home to Java in 1978 to sing about issues otherwise banned from public debate by a heavily repressive government. In El Salvador, the mere fact of congregations of the poor coming together

in church to sing is an act of communal solidarity that can constitute
subversion in right-wing eyes. If such disaffection develops into
armed conflict, the role of the musician changes; in Nicaragua,
the Sandinistas used song to teach their illiterate soldiers how to
strip and clean machine guns, as well as to keep up morale. Although
the rhetoric and even the tunes may seem superficially repetitive
from Revolution to Revolution, with unsurprising lyrics about freedom or death, and emergence from the dark night of slavery, the
problems faced by composers, the tasks required of their songs and
the choices they have to make vary widely. Are the oppressors internal or external – if internal, how to distinguish your music from
theirs? Do the people (or disparate peoples) actually have a common
musical culture at all? Once the tyrant is removed, how long should
one persist with rousing battle cries before turning to more thoughtful, perhaps self-critical songs about the problems of new nation
building? Is there to be any place for sadness in the songs, or does
the need for morale-building preclude it? These may seem unmusi-
cal, manipulative considerations, but to composers serving groups
who need to muster every resource that they can if they are not
to be crushed altogether, they are important. Few societies can
go for long without some form of corporate spirit-lifting; the more
dire the circumstances, the greater the need.

And yet few would deny that they prefer to see local cultures
behave *as* local cultures, to make it new in their own language,
not in bland international clichés. There is a uniformity about parti-
san music that can be most depressing and, if you love the variety
of music that humanity has produced, it can be hard to like tub-
thumping battle hymns that sound remarkably similar whether sung
by goose-stepping fascists or the most spirited of popular liberators.

I didn't know what to expect of the Karen. I had been warned
that our area was denatured, but I had also seen illustrations of
a fine array of instruments, harps and Jew's harps, bronze drums
and flutes and bamboo mouth organs a metre long – things I love
to listen to and collect, and learn to play if possible. With forty
years of revolution now part of their culture, what might they have
done with their music?

Red Star the Elephant Man made me a harp and I brought it
back to Riverside, but no one there could play it. True Love, an
excellent guitarist, told me that the Karen name *ta nah kee klaw*
meant 'bent guitar', but he had no idea what to do with it, having

never seen one before. I had acquired a very similar instrument in Uganda in 1981, and was thus able to improvise a simple melody with three chords – which caused some astonishment in Bartholomew's house. Sam exclaimed, 'Only one in a thousand Karen could do that!' As no one there knew any of the harp songs either, my technique did not develop very fast.

In other districts of Kawthoolei, the old music survives. Animists and Buddhists in the north sing and play the old songs, and the frenzied tunes for mouth organ (*pi ba*, or Thai *faen*). In Riverside I asked after a mouth-organ player. I was told that the only one in the entire District was an elderly man in the Western Valley. On my tour there I went to find him, hoping to make a recording. But he was sick with malaria – and I was never able to go back.

Some slight traces of the old music persist. For national festivals there are performances of two or three traditional dances, accompanied by (they assured me) 'very old songs'. Even these seemed blurred and questionable. One of the most popular, *Do pu weh* (quoted in chapter eleven) has a tune that sounds suspiciously like an English or American children's game-song. Another, *Kwe Ke Baw* (see chapter four) has a more unusual melody which has been firmly disciplined by diatonic harmonisation. Perhaps both were once traditional melodies, but a century and a half of mission culture has jammed them into a different mould entirely. As for Karen children's song, such as the one recorded by Silver's grandmother describing pupils coming to school, there was no doubt at all. The rhythm is no longer dotted, but the tune is 'Here we go gathering nuts in May'.

What was it that destroyed traditional music among the southern Karen? Christianity, very largely – although music is the foremost tool of both the Baptist Church and the Christian-dominated school system, and although, from the very outset of their ministry, the missions cultivated Karen musicians. The Baptist ethnographer Harry Marshall (1922, p. 61), admitted in 1922:

It is to be regretted that, with the acceptance of Christianity, the Karen have almost entirely dropped their own music for that of the West...

Marshall is not telling the whole truth; non-Christians haven't dropped it, and the missions played a far more active role than he implies. But the Karen were not passive either – anything but:

they [Baptist and Catholic Karen] show towards one another all the zeal and intolerance of converts. They are very fond of music, and frequently have village brass bands; and it is on record that villages of rival faiths on opposite sides of a valley met on one occasion in the middle and broke one another's heads and the band instruments with fanatical enthusiasm.[1]

Of the tunes in the *Karen Hymn Book*, a handful are in fact Karen; for example, No. 536, 'Angel Voices – Karen air harmonised by Professor J. G. Hamilton', and No. 542, 'Benediction – Karen air'. That a thoroughly musical people with accessible, strophic, easily harmonised tunes should get to contribute at most 1 per cent of their own hymnbook is hardly an encouraging sign of cross-cultural sensitivity, but no doubt the Baptists would have argued that time was pressing, that they should make use of material ready to hand in the West. Whatever their thinking, they had the infrastructure, the mission presses and the harmoniums on their side. 'The girls all play the harmonium', wrote MacMahon in 1876.[2]

Just as Christian communities had been the rock on which nineteenth-century Karen nationalism was built, so Christian music provided the basis for a new Karen music. Christian music in its broadest sense, that is. The first wave of influence was from hymns, but secular Christian music became increasingly important. Layers of changing fashion in imported gospel song can now be heard there.

One evening in May 1987 I heard music coming from *Boys Boarders*. It was a close harmony quartet. I tried to creep up in the darkness to listen, but was spotted at once and told to come inside and sing. Four teachers from outlying villages, in Riverside for the annual Education Department upgrading course, were crouched around two candles and a battered volume of gospel songs: *Radio Favorites* by the Blackwood Brothers Quartet, a group that flourished in the United States in the 1940s. 'We are rehearsing, *Thera*', they said, 'Tonight Julius will be holding First Birthday prayers for his little boy, and we ask you to join us in singing for him.'

And so, later that evening, we crossed the way to Julius' dark house and sang 'The Royal Telephone':

> You can get your Father on the line,
> Connections through to Jesus are just fine . . .[3]

barber-shop harmonies drifting through the rainforest to charm True Love in his house fifty yards away, and to inspire Moses to ask me to seek out a copy of the songbook, next time I was in Penang.

Since the days of the Blackwood Brothers, the Karen have absorbed the piously soulful sentiments of Jim Reeves and Pat Boone wholesale, together with the slower-moving side of Elvis Presley. These are the tapes to be found in Colonel Marvel's car and in half the cassette players of Riverside, cherished by the older generation but enjoyed by the young as well. And then there are the moderns, Country and Western singers of the smooth school, John Denver and James Taylor, in which a strongly Christian element out of the southern United States is never far below the surface. True Love and White Rock between them could sing the works of John Denver, and a mass of similar songs. When we stayed together at White Rock's house over the hills in Betelwood, these two displaced 'orphan' rebels in the rainforest sat on the back porch, picked up guitars, put their feet up on the wooden rail, lit cheroots and crooned their way through 'Nobody's Child', 'Fire and Rain' and 'Country Roads, Take Me Home'.

These favourite songs are uniform in character – smoothly mellifluous, invariably major-key and unflinchingly sentimental. Even those that aim for pathos are upbeat in melody and rhythm.

Christian faith is never far away, consoling the wounded and oppressed Karen:

> Other peoples have sweet water,
> rich land because they bought it
> with their sweat.
> We'll put our faith in God
> who will heal our country, the Bible says.
> Listen to it!
>   Recorded for me by Ku Wah and True Love

But though the KNU élite is Christian, there are plenty of rebels who are not, to whom the hymn tradition will mean rather less. It is another aspect of the unanswerable question about the rebellion as a whole; was it really Christian in inspiration, or did the Baptists just provide a needed matrix for nationalist sentiment, for newly awakened political aspiration? Although the music sounds Christian, that does not mean that it was adopted just because it was Christian. Only a very foolhardy theorist would claim to explain precisely why a particular idiom should turn up as an influence in another culture – and yet who could deny the appropriateness of Country and Western for Kawthoolei? Implicitly racist, distinctly conservative and with its roots firmly in the Baptist Bible Belt,

Country and Western has never (*pace* Johnny Cash) been noted
for its opposition to war, and it answered a need in Burma. For
whom? The sophisticated hicks of Rangoon gone to fight in the
forest, the heirs of Toh Meh Pah. And what need? The need for
a musical idiom that was quite distinct from the Burmese and,
together with the hymns, well suited to carrying didactic messages.
Combine these with a stiffener of military music left over from the
British Army, and you get modern Karen song.

In the new Karen music, the influence of the church remains
strong. There are other, practical reasons for this. It is still the
Christian church that sponsors most literacy, that is almost entirely
responsible for music reading and keyboard playing, and fluency
in the sorts of melodies that make for easy pop. I bought a typical
example in Thailand, where by no means all Karen are Christian.
It is a commercial cassette recording called *Deh Deh* (Brother), and
is subtitled in English, 'The first perfect original hill-tribe modern
song of Karen'. Guitars and electric keyboards back a sweet-voiced
girl gliding through conventional 'western' songs, sung in Karen
but of cosmopolitan blandness and Christian-derived sentiment:
'Golden Ring', 'Momma', 'God's Command'.

It may have been 'the first' in Thailand, but in Burma this has
been the mode for years. We had a tape in Bartholomew's house
which I got to know very well over the months. It was by a Karen
singer called Lionel. He'd had (said White Rock) an interesting
career:

> 'Oh yes, I know him. He was a student, studying and singing
> around Rangoon at the same time as me. He came to Kawthoo-
> lei too, but then he had a misfortune. He was on a visit to
> Thailand and he killed a Thai policeman, so he fled back to
> Kawthoolei. But our leaders said that they could not protect
> him from Thai justice because we must be friends with Thai-
> land, and so Lionel left us and went back to Burma. Of course
> he was arrested for being a Karen revolutionary and he spent
> two years in jail. But he's out now and is a famous singer.'
> 'So who paid for this recording?'
> 'His family live in the ruby-mining region and they are quite
> rich, I think, especially his uncle and his two sisters, and they
> gave him some money to produce it. The other singers come
> from his local church choir.'
> 'But can he perform in public himself?'
> 'At the church fairs, yes. Every Karen church in Burma has a
> funfair in about November, and the bands can perform then.

Lionel writes songs which tell the Karen people to preserve
their culture and their dress. Everyone knows these songs.'

White Rock kept in touch with musical developments in Burma,
and he obtained for me half a dozen recordings by, for example,
the Choir of the Theology School (Insein) and a band called Julia
and the Creation. The songs include a translation of 'Silent Night',
a Karen version of the Christmas pop song 'Jingle Bell Rock', and
a good deal of 'Love Your Neighbour', 'Get Hope from God' and
so on.

He taught me a song which he regarded as one of the finest
modern Karen compositions. The composer was a friend of his
who has taken melodic elements from a number of sources including
the Lennon-McCartney song, 'Something', with lyrics that are
firmly in the Karen Christian tradition. The song is called (in
Karen) 'God Bless You':

> As you go through life, you'll encounter many things.
> Face them all with firm resolve in your heart.
> Because I pray for you every day,
> my love for you will never die.

It is a professionally calm composition. Like many of the modern
songs, it is designed to be played sitting among friends.

There is another side to Karen music: the brisk marching songs
of the Revolution such as 'Forward, Karen Soldiers'. The Karen
have inherited this music by a more direct line than some of the
world's rebels; it came to Kawthoolei with former soldiers of the
British and Burmese Armies. It is quite recognisable as such. The
Karen have their own version of 'Lili Marlene', with words remind-
ing the people of the atrocities committed against them in the past
by the Burmese, which must be avenged. The schoolboys doing
their military training recorded for me a stirring march on the subject of Kawthoolei's natural beauties, which musically could have
belonged to any army in the world. At Betelwood, where the last
of the mouth-organ players lay sick, I spent an evening with a
KNLA sergeant-major who had studied music with a military band
in Tavoy and could play the clarinet, saxaphone, cornet and sousa-
phone. As a child, I went to a primary school in London that was
next door to the Kneller Hall College of Military Music. Every
day we heard the bands practising – and the tunes bawled out
by the Riverside boys took me back to my own schooldays.

Good tunes may be taken from anywhere, as long as they are

upbeat and uplifting. The Beatles 'Oob la di, Oob la da' has been rewritten in Karen to rousing effect. Just the thing for a dank night in a rainforest camp.

True Love, White Rock and friends have synthesised their own idiom from these sources. Their tunes are often of easily recognisable parentage: True Love's 'Kawthoolei ler yer eh' ('Kawthoolei that I love') is a direct descendant of the Tom Jones song, 'The Last Waltz'. The texts are optimistic, the music major-key, with lightly syncopated rhythms and plenty of sevenths in the harmonisation. The tunes are reliable, never throwing you with dissonance, chromatics or unexpected modulations. They are excellent vehicles for clear, simple messages: love your people, your country and your flag. Go forward without fear. Trust in God. Trust in the KNU.

As pop took over from the old harp and mouth-organ tunes, so it had perforce to take on other social functions of music culture: for death and funerals, for instance. In traditional villages, when a person dies the family and friends gather at the house to make as much noisy music as they can, all night, to drive the newly liberated spirit off and ensure that it doesn't hover about the village, bringing ill luck. When an old gentleman died of a throat cancer in Riverside hospital, the military nurses sent for the KNLA radio operator. He brought a bulldozer battery, a cassette player and a crude old amplifier, pointed the loudspeaker at the corpse and played it Pat Boone until dawn.

Although the old mouth-organ player was too sick to record for me, he was prepared to talk a little. There were, he said, formerly three types of Karen song that he knew. There was music for funerals, love songs and a third group which True Love translated as 'political history' – that is, epic stories.

The first two of these, love and funerals, are closer to each other than one might expect, funerals being one of the few social occasions when the young courted openly. Music at funerals therefore contained romantic overtones, with teenagers holding flirtatious verse-capping contests to the accompaniment of harps.

The old musician said that, of the three styles, 'It's only the love songs that anyone is interested in now, and they only want to play guitars'. He was noting a change in ritual patterns as much as in musical taste. In our District, where Christianity is predominant, the grand old manner of animist and Buddhist funerals, with the slaughter of many animals and festivities for the whole village, has faded away, while the Christian majority are buried with a minimum of public fuss. Where and when, at what sort of occasion can romantic love now be expressed in song, without offending conventional decorum? Apart from weddings (the end product), the only large gatherings are the nationalist and Church events of the KNU calendar. Thus, on these public days, music's function is multi-layered: the overt (funerals having become national cere-monials, e.g. Martyrs' Day), the communal, and the romantically covert.

In the course of the year there were six or seven concerts. They were held to mark the consecration of the new Bethany Church, or KNU Women's Day, or the Karen New Year or the departure of the Australian missionaries – anything that called for community celebration.

The favourite venue was the bamboo stage behind the church, which had been built for the consecration but which lasted out the season until the rains came and drove us back into the old hall. The stage was large, raised four feet off the ground with an area of some twenty-five feet wide by twelve deep. It was lit by a neon strip and two brilliant footlights, and had drawing curtains of red cloth. I performed on it. Many people did, at one time or another.

True Love organised, taking charge of the amplifiers and guitars on stage while White Rock drew up lists of performers, and com-pèred. White Rock sang, but True Love never would. He preferred to play with the backing group, sitting discreetly at the side of the stage with an electric guitar. Dan played a second guitar, Robert the silver-haired KNU treasurer played the drums. A single micro-phone stand occupied the front of the stage.

The village schools sent choirs to the concerts at Riverside. Anyone who wanted could do a turn, from the smallest pupils to the KNDO Major. White Rock introduced them and True Love smiled admiringly at the children. One after another, singly or in small groups, they came to the microphone and sang. Mostly they were girls in school uniform; just a few older boys took turns. Songs of praise alternated with calls to youth to stand up for Kawthoolei. They had curious stage manners. No one was shy of the microphone, not even the six-year old girl who couldn't reach it. Few of them had learnt the words to their songs; they stood clutching lyrics pencilled onto scraps of paper torn from school exercise books. They all sang clearly and loudly but no one knew how to end their act

– they just reached the last chorus and sidled offstage. The band backed each song in the same manner, which was not difficult as they were all in duple time with uncomplicated tunes.

In front of the stage, children and elders sat staring at what was, after all, a rather remarkable scene in a rainforest. Stallholders sold their noodles, cigars and sweetmeats. A crowd drifted and chatted and, at the back, standing in the shadows for decency but with no concealment, young couples stood together as they never did elsewhere. They talked together, private in the throng. One or two even held hands. True Love pushed me onstage.

> 'True Love, what shall I sing?'
> 'Whatever you like.'
> 'All right, tell them that this is a love song.'

'Scarborough Fair' was a bad choice. For a start, it was in triple time and I forgot to tell Robert the drummer, who provided a relentless two beats to the bar throughout. The song confused everyone else by being in a minor key. They clapped politely. True Love said,

> 'Now sing a song about freedom.'
> 'I only know one. It's Irish.'
> 'Fine. I'll say that.' He turned to the microphone. ' *Thera* Jo will sing a song about the Irish people fighting for their freedom.'

The awkwardness of the situation grew on me half way through the first verse of 'The Bold Fenian Men'. Who were they fighting? The British. What happened to them? They all died:

> 'And wise men have told us their cause was a failure . . .'

I put my all into the chorus:

> 'Glory O, glory O to the bold Fenian Men.'

It went down a little better than the first, but I should have stuck to James Taylor.

The anthropologist Thomas Stern (1971) collecting traditional Karen song near Kanchanaburi in the 1960s, remarked that many of the songs disguised declarations of personal romantic love in a decorous Buddhist garb. In Kawthoolei, love songs serve the Revolution, and vice versa:

> A young man was going to the front,
> and he was singing a beautiful song:

> I must go to the battle, I must fight
> for my country and my people. When the war is over,
> I'll come back to you, and everyone
> will call you *Muh Bo Gedaw* (a commander's wife).

This is an early revolutionary song of the 1950s, recorded for me by Silver's grandmother. The sentiment is repeated in True Love's 'Ta Eh daw Ta Mudah' ('Love and Duty'):

> I hope to see you someday – life will be wonderful then.
> But now duty calls. Someday, sometime,
> when I come back from the Front,
> I hope to see your welcoming smile.

None of this is unique to Kawthoolei. Comparable lyrics can be found in Nicaraguan *nueva canción*: revolution and romantic love go hand in hand. The difference is that, in Nicaragua, the young girl is supposedly fighting at the front also.

It is easy enough to find sources for the romantic element in modern Karen song. There are traces here of the traditional culture. The old song 'Saw Ter Kwa' (see chapter thirteen) calls upon the beloved to remember Karen heroes. But, just as throughout the colonial period Karen society absorbed not only Baptist missionary but British secular influence as well, so they were exposed to popular as well as church culture, especially in the Delta. Karen went to the cinema, and they listened to the radio. Moses learned 'Paper Doll' from British soldiers and Silver's grandmother sang for me songs that she had learned as a young girl, songs of a Victorian flavour, even if sung in Karen:

> When the moon is shining in the evening,
> in my garden I think longingly of you.
> It shines through the flowers, soothing me.
> It reminds me of when we were here together,
> and you promised me to return quickly ...

By one means or another, the Karen have been exposed to most of the pop music fashions that have appeared in Britain and the United States, as well as a good number from other parts of Asia. In a house deep in the Western Valley I found a fat volume, printed in Thailand, containing the words to several hundred hit songs of the last twenty-five years, from Pete Seeger to Michael Jackson, the Beatles (all five of them, in the accompanying drawing) to Bob Dylan and Linda Ronstadt. Thai commercial stations pump it out, while the pirate cassette industry flourishes all around. Local variety might seem doomed under this onslaught, the planet apparently sinking into a syrup of banal international pop. But the availability of such a wide range of potential source material shows how exceedingly selective the Karen are in what they absorb. They want song, not dance; they have no interest in rock-and-roll. They listen admiringly to Elvis Presley singing devotional songs but never did like 'Jailhouse Rock'. The jollier Beatles tunes, like 'Oob la di, Oob la da', are popular; most of the rest – and the entire Rolling Stones canon – are rejected. Knowing him to be inquisitive, I played True Love a typically quirky recording by Talking Heads, wondering how he would react to its dissonance and drive. He turned it off. I played Fleetwood Mac to Bartholomew's family; they gave it two songs, then firmly removed it from the cassette player and put on their favourite Country and Western gospel singer, louder than usual.

This is not simply a rejection of the remote; I played them little that was altogether unfamiliar. They would, equally firmly, turn off the radio when certain Thai styles which they disliked were broadcast. Had they been less selective with regard to modern Thai music it might, paradoxically, have led to a revival of their own traditions – since a feature of contemporary Thai pop is the use of updated traditional forms and instruments.

Bartholomew couldn't stand the sort of music that True Love and the boys played. But this wasn't exactly a generation gap; there were complaints from some of the young too, that this electric pop was being foisted on them against their will when sometimes they wanted the old songs. The divide was more between the local villagers and the Delta newcomers. Bartholomew sided with the former, who included most of the girls of *Boarders*. Those who really pushed the new, electric music were usually men, and very often teachers.

The schools of Kawthoolei rely heavily on song. It is at school that the children learn how and what to sing, not at the family hearth. They learn to sing in groups under a teacher. Thomas Stern described the process by which the traditional Karen bands and dance troupes that he saw performing learnt their new material. Each group had two teachers – an elder guru, and a junior *répétiteur*. At Riverside, where so few people were familiar with the old forms, we did not have a guru but we did have Ku Wah. She was the teacher still in her early twenties, who recorded many songs for me, who was now regarded as the village authority on traditional dance, to be called on whenever public ceremony required a performance.

Edward considered that it was the responsibility of the teachers and the Education Department as a whole to keep interest in the old music and dance alive – a familiar official response in cultures under siege. Edward had encouraged Ku Wah to learn traditional dances (whenever someone came by who knew one) so that she could pass them on, and he had tried to revive other forms also. If Karen traditions were ever to be part of the future, he believed it could only happen through the schools:

> 'I tried to bring a flute teacher here. We have a traditional flute with six holes which we use in a small orchestra – four different sizes together with a drum.'
>
> 'What would you use it for?'
>
> 'I wanted it taught in the schools. I thought it would go very well with our new revolutionary songs. The flutes can use Western notation, so Ku Wah and the teachers could learn it without any trouble. They could use these flutes in class, in church, anywhere. All we have now are guitars, which are expensive and don't last long in this heat and damp.'
>
> 'So what happened?'
>
> 'I brought an old man from near Mandalay who could teach us, but he died on the way. I'd like to find another, but I don't have time to organise everything.'

In Karen tradition, playing musical instruments was predominantly (though not exclusively) a male occupation. The same tendency still applies. There's nothing to stop women playing guitars, and a few girls do. But whenever I recorded a group of teachers and pupils, the boys played and the girls sang. One consequence was that Ku Wah and her female colleagues had collected the words of the songs. Each woman teacher possessed an exercise book, in which she had carefully written down the lyrics of the few traditional songs remaining, together with more or less contemporary compositions, Christian and otherwise. Ku Wah's book contained several dozen songs.

I mentioned these books to the Colonel: 'Wouldn't it be a good idea to make a collection of these? You could make a little book, and distribute it all over Kawthoolei.'

'Please propose this to Edward!' said the Colonel enthusiastically, assuming that this too was work for the Education Department.

But there were all the usual problems: the organisation, the work, the printing, the money. It never happened.

Ku Wah and other school teachers invariably filled part of the classroom day with singing. Not only did they enjoy it; there was a practical point. It provided a change and a relief in classes with no other resources for practical work and no alternative to reading aloud and rote-learning. And it was the readiest means of inculcating national spirit, through songs to the glory of Kawthoolei, its natural beauty, its past heroes and its present patriotic youth. They sang every day, morning and afternoon. Arriving at one village school I found the entire establishment, all six classes, singing their heads off to different tunes; it was the end of term concert the next evening and they were rehearsing their turns. One small class of four boys stood in front of their teacher, a young man energetically strumming a very poor guitar. They sang in English:

> We are the people!
> We are the jungle people!
> Hey! Hey!
> We are the jungle people!

Only in imported songs is the rainforest ever referred to as 'jungle'.

Another teacher, an eccentric old man, was one of the keenest exponents of imported pop. He was headmaster of the school at a mining village, with no immediate family of his own but with a magnetic influence on the pupils in his charge. He had created a style and a discipline in his school that no other village could match. When I first came there, I walked up a short hill to the headman's house. As I passed by the building next door I was spotted by the headmaster and a dozen of his pupils. One by one they jumped off the verandah to stand in front of me, gave a crisp military salute and said in English, 'Good morning, Sir!', then extended a hand to shake.

I stayed with the old teacher that night, smothered by the attentions he pressed on me, making up a bed behind specially rigged curtains on his verandah, making me sweet Ovaltine with biscuits just as I was falling asleep, and playing me his collection of 'Paboo' (Pat Boone) and Cliff Richard tapes. This cost him considerable effort, since to extract the last quiver of power from his failing batteries he had to fit twelve of them in a row inside a split bamboo. I had been asleep for an hour or more after a hard day's walking when he finally fixed the circuitry and I was woken by Elvis Presley's 'Wooden Heart'.

On another visit there in True Love's company, I coincided with a Sunday evening village music-making at which everyone did their turn. The teacher, never one to miss an opportunity for technical research, tried out his home-made guitar pickup which he pressed to the body of the instrument as True Love played, producing a blizzard of distortion through an antique loudspeaker. Some months later he came to Riverside to the teachers' upgrading and there performed at the closing ceremony upon a Hawaiian slide guitar of his own devising. A short, stocky man, he walked about the village in an enormous bush hat and, each time we met, grabbed and pumped my hand energetically and started to sing.

The one thing he didn't do was compose. Of the modern songs actually produced within Kawthoolei, almost all are the work of schoolteachers. Several of the staff of Riverside school had written songs, and it was Edward and the Education Department who decided that they should make a recording. The songs that they were writing were propaganda, and propaganda has no value unless everyone gets to hear it. In a building that normally housed Silver's kindergarten but which was now renamed 'Thu Da Nu Studio' after a legendary Karen hero, the tape was made.

It is called 'Ta Kee suh Ta Ker Paw', or 'Darkness to Light'. I have, incidentally, a recording of educational songs from Sandinista Nicaragua called the same thing. The Karen performers include True Love, White Rock, Dan and Wilf – the group of friends that Edward had recruited together from GHQ – together with Robert the KNU treasurer and two young women teachers, Thoolei Paw and Caroline. The songs are by True Love, William, Robert and White Rock, and the titles include: 'Love and Duty', 'Darkness to Light', 'Our Blood Calls Us', 'The Time Is Nigh', 'Youth and Duty', 'Set an Example', and '12th August 1950', commemorating the death in an ambush of Ba U Gyi. The five-colour cover (predominantly pink) shows the drum and horn symbol of the KNU, and a military beret over crossed commando knives.

There had been considerable problems in producing 'Darkness to Light'. The cover had been printed with the help of a Thai business friend of Edward's, and a thousand copies had been delivered. But copying the tape itself was a different matter. They had wired three cassette decks together but it was a slow process; they could only make ten copies a day and, in all, only about one hundred

Plate 17. 'These were the most contented afternoons that we had together.'

had been finished. One of these days, they kept saying, we will do the rest, and sell them cheaply to our people.

White Rock in particular had a passion for cassettes. In Bangkok he bought all the hit tapes and, when he could, tracked down and met the singers. His favourite, a woman whom he regarded as the best singer in Thailand, ran a coffee shop also and he would go there to meet her and look for encouragement. Her name was Nan Ti Dah, and White Rock had all her recordings.

> 'She sings superbly, and the harmonisations are very original. They are all her own songs.'

To me they sounded not original but merely slick. To White Rock, however, the mere achievement of such polished recordings was as important as anything. Nan Ti Dah's latest cassette had been sponsored by a manufacturer of boiled sweets.

> 'I have to make another tape, professional this time, with proper equipment. The sound of 'Darkness to Light' is not so good.

I want to do it soon, me and True Love and Robert, and we'll
ask Nan Ti Dah to sing some of the Karen songs on it.'
'What would it cost to do?' I asked.
'Maybe B.30,000 (£750). And no, I don't have that, or not much
of it. So, I am looking for some opportunities in trade.'
'Does Nan Ti Dah know any Karen?'
'Actually, I think it would all have to be sung in Burmese. If
we are to sell this tape it must appeal to all the other people
fighting their Revolutions in Burma. We must sell it to the
Mon, the Kachin, the Wa, everybody. So it must be in Burmese,
in a style which they will like.'

As White Rock pursued musical novelty with laid-back persist-
ence, coming forward to sing the lead, compèring concerts and seek-
ing out recordings from Burma for me, he threw into contrast True
Love's diffidence. A fine musician and composer, and a better singer
than White Rock, True Love never performed his own songs in
public and, when he played to back other performers, he always
sat discreetly out of the light at one side of the stage. It was not
that he was stage-shy; at least, he could teach a large class in school
to sing, or face a public gathering, or lead the homage to the flag.
But in the activity at which he excelled, he was retiring. He had
not even sung his own songs on 'Darkness to Light', but had left
them to White Rock.

'Why don't you ever sing in public, True Love?'
'Oh, but I prefer to see the children sing. I love my students!'

Something in him would not come out in the open with his own
opinions – just as he would never go to speak his mind at the Monday
Free Discussions. The only times that I heard him sing were when
he recorded for me in private.

These were the most contented afternoons that we had together.
Ku Wah came to True Love's house, bringing her fat school exercise
book of songs. We borrowed a guitar from *Boys Boarders*, we drank
coffee and we smoked cigars, the baby crawled between us and
the pigs and chickens snuffled about below, the cicadas racketed
and we recorded songs, True Love singing his own and Ku Wah
everything else. Afterwards, Ku Wah would go to rehearse the
church choir and True Love would help me work out a translation
of the lyrics, sometimes referring for explanations of old terms or
references to Silver's grandmother, who sat chewing betel and nodding happily in the shade. There was only a handful of songs that
he would confess to having written himself.

'When did you last write a song?'
'It has been some time.'
'Are you going to write any more? They're good; you should do.'
'Why don't you write a song for us?'

Why not? The excuse that I couldn't write the verse in Karen did me little good since he could easily have translated it. But, if he was now ambivalent about these things, was it for a foreigner to do it for him? Besides which, I hesitated to concoct a dishonest message of unequivocal commitment. In the delicately melancholy atmosphere of Kawthoolei, with the possibility of defeat always there, the future at best uncertain, anything less than unambiguous encouragement would have been unfair and unwelcome.

'I'll teach you one', I said, and taught him 'Somewhere' from *West Side Story*, which seemed admirably suited. He rapidly practised it to perfection.

'I also want to learn that most beautiful Irish song', he said, meaning 'The Bold Fenian Men'.

Silver's grandmother listened, enjoying the tune, humming it. Finally, because the guitar-picking style was new to him and a little complicated, True Love asked me to record it and leave him the tape. We wrote down the words and taped the song. When we played back this proud Irish elegy for a lost cause, the background was filled with a blend of ducks and chickens and the voice of an old lady, repeating the refrain over and over:

'Glory O! Glory O! Glory O!'

18 Insurgents in a landscape

Kawthoolei, my beloved Karen land,
You are so rich in everything.
Such beautiful scenery everywhere,
streams and mountains to gladden my heart . . .
                                        Song by True Love

I walked to the Western Valley with True Love. I was informed
that an elephant would carry the baggage, but then there was no
elephant spare. I was assured that there would be porters instead,
but on the morning of departure they were all otherwise engaged.
So we just went anyway, with rucksacks and no problems – but
you never know until you do it.

'Everybody loves to camp!' said True Love, who walked in
camouflage fatigues and flipflops, carrying his M16. He became
a teenager again, laughing his way over the mountains. But in the
evenings – when I imagined that there might be some fireside con-
viviality – he retired early to his hammock and read his prayer
book. So, we were all exhausted.

The first afternoon we merely crossed the river and walked an
hour and a half on an old logging road to a camp at the foot of
the first mountain, so as to be ready for an early start on the slope.
The loggers had left a vast slab of sawn timber there, six metres
long, and on this the travellers assembled. There was Baldwin and
his daughter Eve, both of them teachers returning to Betelwood
with 20 kg packs of school supplies. There were traders and professional porters with even larger loads of shop stock, torch batteries
and pans, Thai sweets and nylon T-shirts, all to be retailed at
stiff mark-ups for the porterage (even stiffer during the rains). And
there were government officers on errands, soldiers coming or going
to their posts. In all, a dozen or more gathered in the bamboo
grove, ranging their packs on the slab, spreading plastic sheets to
sleep on by their goods, and cooking rice.

Some of us had Army hammocks, and by the one large tree on
the campsite, stout bamboo posts had been driven into the ground

338

in a row. One end of the hammock went to the tree, the other to a post. Conscious of the weight of my pack, I had brought no blanket, imagining that the nights would be mild and that I'd sleep fully clothed anyway. It was a stupid mistake; these were some of the coldest nights I've ever spent. I lay in my hammock staring upwards at Japanese decorations of bamboo leaves on a bright sky, the moonlight slowly giving way to mist. Soon after midnight, the shivering Karen cooked themselves more rice for comfort. We started climbing early, and walked for ten hours the second day.

Thera Baldwin and *Theramuh* Eve were carrying too much for the terrain. They could scarcely haul themselves up that stiff climb and within half an hour were sweating hard and staggering. The hill was greasy, but KNLA elephants had been over the mountain two days before, their huge deep prints in the mud turning the track into a three-hour flight of steps. Near the top there was a spring of fresh water, and the first leeches on the path.

The party spread out and we moved on in silence. The track was narrow, single file, rising or falling steeply so that one hauled oneself from tree root to tree root. Or it ran along ridges between a tedious series of peaks. It was claustrophobically enclosed, in spite of the altitude. Occasionally I glimpsed open air through the trees and realised that I was almost in the clouds, with deep valleys below me, mountain ranges stepping away into Burma on all sides. At such a height in Scotland I'd be able to see for forty miles. Here, visibility was twenty yards.

A perceptual dislocation sets in. You walk through a vast forest over a grand mountain sequence, and your own field of perception is more intimate than in a crowded town. The person walking ahead of you may be only thirty paces in front, or less, but is often invisible, hardly there at all.

Marshall (1922) says that in the forest the Karen measure distance by betel-chews. You rarely see the sun. I marked progress by my watch and by matching what I knew of the day's itinerary to the rise and fall of the path. I had kept my cotton sunhat on, to keep leaves and twigs, ticks and spiders out of my hair, and it acted as an acoustic reflector to my footfalls; each step sounded loudly, and I became mesmerised by the endless repetition, step by step, hours on end. The track is mostly free of obstructions, passing Karen having hacked away shoots and branches as they go. But they cannot chop off a sapling exactly at ground level, and there is always a two- or three-inch stump in the middle of the path to stub your toe on. You walk with your eyes glued to the ground six feet in front. Often the first indication of a change in the vegetation is a new quality in the light on the ground. High, thick-layered canopy mutes and dissipates the sun's fall. Groves of smaller trees give a sharper focus, scales of white slipping and flicking over one another. When the gloom of the ground suddenly brightens, you look up to see low but unpleasantly dense grass or shrub. And then you quickly pay attention to what is ahead, in case it is that most awkward of obstacles to a person carrying a rucksack – a dead and toppled bamboo grove that requires crawling under.

The walk was, to me, far more exhausting mentally than physically. Constant attention to where you're putting your feet is a strain in itself and precludes any other interest. Hour by hour, step by resonant step, thoughts become repetitive, tunes go round and round. I took to singing, to keep down recurring thoughts and phrases; one of these, which dominated my mind for half a day in the hills, was 'at the interface of incomprehending cultures, new forms of loneliness appear'. I struggled to shake this junk out of my head. Describing his wartime expeditions through Burmese jungle with the Chindits, Richard Rhodes James wrote that for the British soldiers one of the problems was the monotony of the march and the psychological strain it imposed. It was no trouble to the Gurkha troops, but the British just didn't know what to think. He says that, at each evening camp, many of them had recourse to reading the Bible, like True Love.

Other sounds moved with us. A rhythmic rushing in the air overhead, a glimpse of huge black and yellow wings – hornbills, tracking us for ten minutes as we crossed their hills, seeing us off. Choirs of monkeys, mynahs replying, and the aching rub and creak of crowded stands of bamboo – all these making for patterns of perception around me, but not for intelligent thought.

The walking fell into clear stages of two or three hours each – up the hill, up a river valley, down to a vale, up again. Each stage involved a different activity and different problems. The mountain streams were still full. Moving along a valley meant crossing the stream perhaps every fifty yards, on slimy rocks or deep drifts of sharp gravel. I had a strong walking stick and never fell, but there was always the risk of losing flipflops – which sent True Love running through the forest to try and intercept his as they floated round the next bend.

A one-hour stretch of track, ill-reputed, I named the Slough of Despond. It was in a high valley of dense forest in which a small and lethargic steam malingered, and it was alive with leeches, dark little groves of them upright in the path, waving, waiting for your feet to pass within reach. With no more than fifty paces from crossing to crossing, you could be sure that at each ford you'd find a leech swelling with blood between your toes, and another on the back of your calf. Thorns too. Everyone hated the Slough of Despond. The Karen ran through it where they could, but the stream had thick mudpacks at each bank which there was no avoiding. We moved faster and faster, skipping along the dank, shaded path – until we reached a patch where the water had settled on a soft, pale grey clay slime, and made it thigh deep. You took your shoes off and floundered, trying not to grab at the fat-spined tree trunks, trying not to worry about the neat round holes (snakes?) in the mud, just pushing forward, thinking about how nice it would have been to be riding an elephant at this point, if you could have avoided being swept off by the overhanging branches.

At the end of the Slough of Despond, a little rise, a small clearing and a fireplace. It was smouldering (from a previous group), and we used the embers to scorch off the last of the leeches.

> 'We have a medicine to make them fall off,' said True Love.
> 'So the entire population of Riverside took pleasure in telling me. Salt, tobacco and lime on a rag tied round the end of a stick. Every house has it, they all said, but somehow no one ever produced any. Does it work?'
> 'It works!'
> 'Why haven't you got any?'
> I forgave him more readily than I did Timothy, who had thought to cheer me up with an interesting item of natural history:
> 'You know, we have special leeches that like buffaloes, and when a buffalo comes they climb up its leg, go in its bottom and suck and suck until it dies.'

Two small hills; then another river section, crossing and re-crossing, making our way up the headwaters, the gorge narrowing until there was no room for a path at all and we could only wade upstream. Where the path took off again up the next mountainside, there at the foot was the evening's camp. It had been cut out of a bamboo grove by the stream and consisted of a very simple shelter: a bamboo platform raised two feet from the forest floor, with rough bamboo decking and a crudely thatched roof. The structure was no more

than eight foot by five, with a fireplace on the ground at one end.
It had been built the previous season and was now dilapidated
but usable. I tied my hammock between two nearby trees, as did
True Love. But Sunshine the nurse and the young porters crowded
onto the platform, those with hammocks slinging them as near to
the fireplace as they could.

I soaked the leech bites on my leg with potassium permanganate,
yellowing my skin. Sunshine took out her box of pills and gave
one to True Love, swallowing one herself. It was Vitamin B.

> 'What's wrong? I asked.
> 'I have tired eyes', said Sunshine.
> 'I have a sore spleen,' said True Love.

Sunshine had been gathering watergreens which she now served
with the rice. The boys caught fish which were tossed live onto
the fire and thrashed for a few seconds. We stuffed ourselves and
slumped. True Love said, from his hammock:

> 'I am thinking now of four years ago; I brought forty of my students
> to Betelwood for our KNU District Congress. All of us walking
> through the forest together, sleeping on plastic sheets, we had
> such a good time! We wanted to play music for the congress,
> so all the guitars and the drumkit went upriver by boat and
> were carried in secret round the Burmese positions. Then we
> could give a concert in Betelwood!'
> More quietly:
> 'Seven of those students have been killed now, at the Front Line.'

The next day we ran into traffic. An elephant plodded by us
on the narrow path, carrying the nurse from Betelwood hospital
back to Riverside. Further on, negotiating a steep hillside, we came
face to face with buffalo being driven eastwards, up from the coastal
plains of Burma and out to Thailand. The buffalo had never seen
a white, bearded face before. The leading animal stared and rolled
its eyes and stepped smartly off into the undergrowth. The herdsman
glared at me. In such a vast forest it seemed extraordinary to have
to step aside, to be crowded. But, in all that forest, it is effectively
the *only* track. You cannot get lost until you descend from the mountain to the patchwork of the valleys.

On day three, after mindless hours of trailing True Love, we
began to drop down through deciduous woods; easy going. And
then, with no warning, there were rice fields around us. True Love
examined them:

'Karen fields.'
'Good.'
'Our journey is over.'

We reached a fork in the track. A large tree in the angle was marked with several cuts and crosses. True Love looked at this, and nodded:

'This is a Karen map.'
'Ah. Which way do we go?'
'I don't know. I can't read it.'

We took the wrong turning and wasted another exhausting half-hour before reaching the village of Four Springs, entering across a high, fallen tree trunk over the river. My balance in this feat was not improved by my heavy rucksack. Like all foreigners, I was overladen. Great Lake taught me a rhyme on the subject:

Twee maw – mata hay.
Twee maw – kola hay.
Kola hay wee ta mer nuh leh.
Hay wee ta law suh law say.

Dog barks   who's coming?
Dog barks – it's the English!
What are the English carrying now?
Carrying junk in every pocket.

War has made of the Karen a nation of porters, lugging rice and bullets for the Burmese and schoolbooks between the villages. In the Western Valley, villagers were fascinated by my large alpine rucksack, and many offered to carry it. They carry from the forehead, I carry on the hip. I spent much time in adjusting the thick padded straps for small Karen connoisseurs.

Midway between Thailand and the sea, the Western Valley is the heartland of our district. More open and fertile than the valley at Riverside, it has been settled in a far more permanent manner. Houses and schools are large, solid hardwood with pretty fretworked verandahs and dark interior panelling. The villages are larger too; one hundred houses at Betelwood, with a church and school neatly thatched and tastefully tiered – not tin-roofed cement sheds as at Riverside. The betel, or areca, groves are old-established. The valley is sheltered on three sides by hills and by the KNLA on the fourth. Although the enemy is only a short day's walk from Betelwood, no one is moving, no one is retreating to Riverside. On the contrary, as other Karen territory has become less secure,

this is where the population often comes. To demonstrate their
determination to hold the valley, the District held its annual Congress in Betelwood in 1987. A unit of the Burmese Army made
an attempt to disrupt it, attacking from the southwest, but were
headed off a day's march short of the river.

The stereotype of the Karen as a shifting population interested
only in a self-sufficient swidden economy fades rapidly in the Western Valley. They grow swidden rice, of course, for their own use.
But they also tend expanses of areca groves, so extensive that there
is insufficient labour to harvest it all. When the harvest is due,
migrant labourers move into the valley, establishing settlements
at regular sites with their families, their shops, even their livestock.
These people are poor Burmese, employed by the Karen.

Trade comes and goes from the valley without much interruption.
On the trail out to the north – cut long ago and marked on old
maps – the trade route is straddled by both Karen and Burmese
checkpoints. For all their talk of *Four Cuts* throttling the Karen
economically, local Burmese Army commanders and civilian potentates are just as interested in rake-offs from the traffic as are the
Karen. Certain items are regarded more critically; petrol and
ammunition, food supplies and medicines are supposedly prevented
from reaching the Karen in the valley. This embargo, in Burma's
present economic prostration, has become rather notional. Drugs
are now so scarce in Burma that it is rapidly becoming cheaper
and easier for the Karen to bring them all the way over the hills
from Thailand.

And safer travelling, though Betelwood is deep into Burma and
a long way from Thai sanctuaries. In the twilight zones of the war,
Karen never know just how safe or threatened they are, whether
to stay, flee or move about freely. One day the Burmese will be
shooting at them, the next day taxing them, and the next resonantly
declaring all the peoples of Burma to be one nation. At Betelwood,
not a few of the people have had unpleasant experiences. A woman
that I met had just been released after nine days' detention, under
suspicion of smuggling drugs.

> 'But I am lucky', she said, 'I was carrying nothing and they let
> me go. They are holding a friend of mine. She was carrying
> medicines and they caught her, and now she is sent to prison
> at Moulmein.'
> 'Is it a very serious offence?'
> 'She was supporting the rebels', said True Love. 'That is treason.
> Burma has the same penalties for treason as other countries.'

Plate 18. The church at Betelwood, with school classes underneath.

The next house was high and open. It had a roof, it had floor joists at ten feet off the ground, and half a floor, but only one wall. White Moon, the owner, was a busy man: 'I'll finish it one day', he said.

True Love introduced me, saying respectfully: 'White Moon is our chief boatman. Some years ago he was imprisoned by the Burmese. He was just a civilian, but they accused him of being a KNLA captain. They hung him upside down and beat him so hard that for a while he was blinded. At last he falsely confessed to being a KNLA sergeant just to stop the beatings; he was in jail for two years. Now he wants his revenge and he is with the KNDO. His boat is on standby for skilled emergency work.'

For ten days we wandered about the valley. I asked to be taken to meet everyone from traditional healers to the local hospital committee, youth organisers, shop keepers and musicians, and True Love patiently escorted me. We went in the morning to a Karen Buddhist monastery with a three-tiered tin roof and a monk who fancied himself as a radio engineer, and in the afternoon to the house of a KNU Transport Officer whose house was adorned with a biblical quotation, in English, three-foot blue-painted wooden letters pinned to an end wall: 'As ye sow, so shall ye reap'. Whereas at Riverside I felt myself to be in the orbit of Bangkok, here we were definitely in Burma. In the shops we bought Burmese blankets for the cold nights, ate Burmese sweets paid for in Burmese currency, and walked past camps of Burmese nut-harvesters.

'We don't hate the Burmese people', said White Rock, in whose house we were sleeping. 'It is only their government and their army that oppress us. Some of the Burmese here are refugees too. They cannot stand the pressures that their own authorities put on them. You know, the KNU asks for a tax of just B.25 and one basket of rice from each household per year, but the Burmese government taxes their people almost to starvation. These poor people are our friends.'

In the same conversation, he and True Love attacked me for regarding the Karen civilians and soldiers as distinct. But the Burmese is a conscript army – civilians as short-service soldiers – and they shoot Karen farmers in the back, out in the fields. True Love said: 'When the Burmese Army was approaching this place last year, they forced a pregnant Karen woman to guide them through the forest. And then, when they had finished with her, they cut off her head.'

In the Western Valley a change came over True Love, as though he had only to be back in the heartland to throw off his painful nostalgia for Rangoon and his nervous anticipatory glances towards Thailand. Betelwood suggested to him what modern rural Karen society could be like – settled and prosperous, proud in its economic, educational and political self-determination. True Love thrilled to it.

And yet, for all that we were only hours from the enemy, the KNLA and the KNU seemed more out of place here than back at the relative safety of Riverside and the border. The Army camp, on the river bank near Four Springs, was a poor place, a clutch of thatched huts around a scruffy compound, at odds with the affluent solidity of the villages. Chickens roosted in the radio shack, dogs did the washing up. The most substantial structure was an open-work storage bin for yams.

> 'Who would you like to speak with?' said the young Sergeant-major.
> 'Well, I had hoped that we might stay with the Headman tonight', I said, 'but he's not at his house.'
> 'He's at his harvest now', said the soldiers. 'Stay with us here.'

So we did, tucking our hammocks into the crowded little house shared by Sharon the army nurse and the radio operator. They had caught an otter, and curried it for us that evening.

The next morning the Sergeant-major said,

> 'We shall send for this headman.'
> 'But not if he's harvesting . . .'
> 'Don't worry. We shall send a runner to the fields.'
> True Love smiled delicately: 'When the Army calls people, usually they come.'

But not the Headman of Four Springs. He ignored two runners, and by mid-afternoon we were all embarrassed; the Sergeant-major that the man had not appeared, and myself because they kept asking him to. We slept that night at the District Health Officer's home. The Headman finally came to talk, after supper. I asked,

> 'What's it like having the Army for neighbours?'
> 'Sometimes we have different priorities', said the Headman. 'But now is the time of revolution. What we are most interested in is being a village in our own right, administratively independent of Betelwood, deciding things for ourselves.'

Riverside, the Colonel, Edward, the Departmental hierarchs – they are a long way from the Western Valley.

What does it mean, to call the Karen 'hill people' or 'forest people'?
In the nineteenth century the labels seemed sensible enough. The
Karen were not only shy and retiring; they were at one with their
habitat, and regarded as such by both missionaries and their lowland neighbours. They were often referred to as a species of wildlife.
The Burmese called them 'wild cattle of the hills', and they spoke
of themselves as 'insects'. In 1894 a Thai prince, Narathrip,
remarked that they resembled birds or wild deer, so instinctive
was their enjoyment of the forest.[1] Today the KNU lays claim to
this reputation:

They (the Burmese) care about wildlife even less than about human rights,
which is to say not at all. Tiger and leopard skins and tortoiseshell products
have been dealt in openly. In contrast, even within the stresses of a frontier
war, the KNU has outlawed since 1978 the hunting of hornbills, elephants
and rhinoceros. Some of Asia's last examples of endangered species thrive
in our liberated zone ... (KNU press release, 26 June 1989).

The northern Thai language put the Karen into the some noun-
class as wild animals. The Thais admired the Karen as hunters
and trackers but were suspicious; the Karen were said to have a
fearsome jungle 'death magic'. Lunet de Lajonquière passed by
some gloomy forest gorges:

The Siamese ... are much afraid of this [the jungle] which is haunted
by evil spirits, and in which one may be struck down by terrible fevers.
Thus they leave it to the Kariengs ... [and] all those mountaineers whom
they strongly suspect of being sorcerers and who, at any rate, seem resistant
to these unhealthy vapours.[2]

On the long walk home over the hills, as I treated True Love
with quinine for his malaria, he told me that Karen relations with
the little people were not what they once had been: 'Before, it was
easy to meet spirits in the forest. But now you don't come across
them so much. We think it is because they are offended; people
use so much bad language in the forests these days.'

On occasion, the spirits do throw their weight behind the KNLA.
At the Four Springs camp they told me how a detachment at the
Front had been saved from destruction. The whole unit was fast
asleep. One soldier woke and thought he heard footsteps, but he
was so frightened that he didn't wake the others – he thought they
were surrounded by Burmese. In the morning the villagers told
them that the Burmese had almost attacked the camp but had met

a 'big detachment' of Karen troops, and had run away without a shot being fired – and, all around the KNLA campsite there were the marks of army boots in the mud.

The young men from the Delta could never lay claim to the same rapport with the forest spirits as the locals. True Love made no claim to be a forester; he was just someone who 'loved camping'. But it would be wrong to suggest that the revolutionary urban Karen are irredeemably out of place in the forest. They may not know the uses of every plant, but they cope and adapt remarkably well. If plastic flipflops, nylon T-shirts, short-wave radios and M16s appeared incongruous to me, that was only because I had never thought of that particular combination in a tropical rainforest before. They all work well enough.

On the second day of our walk home, they gave me a demonstration of contemporary forest competence. There were monkeys around us in the trees; we could hear, and occasionally see them. Travelling with us now were three young KNLA porters from Riverside. They asked True Love for a loan of his M16, and crept off the track. Ten minutes later we heard the shot and when they rejoined us, one of them was carrying a large black monkey with its side blown out and its reeking intestines gushing all over his clothes.

It was only midday and we had a long way yet to walk, but they asked if we could halt for the day, so that they could cook the monkey. It would take some hours. We agreed to stop.

At once, slick industry began. The three boys took the monkey, skinned, washed and butchered it. One of them then collected sufficient wood and stones to build three fires, and he put water on to boil. Another looked in his bag and found a small plastic box – salt, fishpaste, and twist of paper containing all the spices required for currying monkeys; he carried this at all times, together with a handful of shallots. He began to prepare the sauce. The third boy took his *parang* and went to the nearest bamboo grove, where he cut and fashioned two large drinking cups, a long trough for finger washing and two small spoons. One of these – an upright dipper for the juices – had a handle formed by slicing a long strip of the outer skin of the bamboo almost but not quite off, leaving it attached at the bottom end and doubling the free end back. The other spoon or scoop was formed by cutting the bamboo precisely at the node – that is, where the tube has an interior partition and a lateral shoot coming out at 45°. The shoot made the handle.

Both spoons worked fine. He then went off to gather large leaves as plates.

All these tasks were performed in silence; the boys knew exactly what they were doing. The monkey's head was scorched, trimmed and then tossed onto the fire to roast. The hands and feet, held in split lengths of bamboo, were propped up around the fire to toast, the triumphant marksman getting the brain as a delicacy, his assistants having the hands to nibble. Two hours later we feasted on rice and monkey curry.

The boys travelled light. In their small backpacks they each carried (apart from curry spices) the same equipment: a toothbrush and paste, a small bar of soap, a small towel; a clean pair of shorts, a spare T-shirt, and a sarong. One of them also had a torch, another a cigarette lighter – I had the pack of cigars. Before eating, they bathed wearing the sarong, then dressed again and dried the sarong by tying a knot in one end, then twirling it over the fire so that it filled out like a hot air balloon. The sarong served as a thin blanket. On its own it was quite inadequate against the bitter night but the three of them slept by the fire curled up in a heap together, like kittens.

The next day we descended the long mountain slope towards Riverside. I happened to be leading and moved down warily, the path being steep and covered with tree roots and other snags; it was all too easy to imagine being tripped and landing fifteen feet below face down on a bamboo shoot. But of a sudden, behind me came crashes, thumps and shrieks of laughter; the three boys, in flipflops, ran, jumped and skidded all the way to the bottom, delighted to be back with the videos and sophisticates of Riverside – where they were equally at home.

The forest never was the secluded fastness it has sometimes been made out to be, where the Karen lived secure in timeless isolation. Far from it. The old overland routes between the world's most ancient and powerful civilisations, India and China, lay through the territory of the hill tribes of Burma. Travellers went this way at least as early as 128 BC – and that is merely the first surviving record.[3] The Chinese especially were concerned to protect and develop these highways; garrisons and staging posts were built which had to be self-sufficient, growing their own rice, and toll gates were introduced very early. By the eighth century AD the system of levies and protection for trade caravans passing through the forest was well established, with people settling the high valleys around the main trails to take advantage of it. Thus, it was not refuge and seclusion that attracted people to the forested hills, but their opening up to communications.[4]

Trade has ebbed and flowed but has never let up. In the nineteenth century the Kachin to the north were reputedly making very large profits on the tolls. Lt Col MacMahon (1876, p. 276), relates that the British authorities had to deal with Karen who had for some time been making excessive toll demands and, when cattle traders had been slow to pay up, had pricked their beasts over precipices. They had finally overstepped the mark by mistreating two American Baptists, Alonzo Bunker and Dr Vinton. Realising that the Karen and the trade routes went together, the British tried to regulate matters by making the tolls a payment for roadmending – not something the Karen were overzealous about, then or since.

In general, the trade caravans carried finished luxuries – velvets, porcelain, brassware – from the north and east (China) to the south and west (Burma and India), taking raw materials – grain, opium, gemstones, dyes and aromatics – back with them. Today that pattern still holds, with televisions going from Thailand into Burma, and rubber, timber and opium coming out – and the hill-tribes still take their tolls. Certain items have reversed their direction of travel: in 1910, the British Consul at Chiang Mai, Reginald Le May (1926, pp. 99–102) wrote of cotton being taken into Thailand from Burma, and cattle returning. Now it is cheap nylons from Thailand that flood across into Burma and Burmese cattle that are bought by the Thais.

Thus, for as long as the Karen have been settled in the hills and the high river valleys, traders and trade goods have been passing among them. The part played by the Karen in the trade itself, apart from taking tolls, has usually been small. Many writers have concluded that they are 'naturally' poor traders. Although the Karen could provide the forest exotics that the outside world wanted, the traffic itself was always in the hands of others, especially Shan and Thais. Today Thais run shops well within Kawthoolei. The wholesalers supplying the shops are all Thai. The foremost of these, who ran a very profitable business from a large cement house at Headquarters, was finally expelled for expanding into a forbidden market – blue videos. When the honey and sesame seasons began, would-be Karen intermediaries like Vermilion often found that they'd been beaten to it by energetic Thais who had come into Kawthoolei and got to the producers first.

The tolls used to provide a nice source of income for individual communities along the border. Today, the State of Kawthoolei controls the border and the passes (those which the Burmese haven't now captured), and there is no possibility of local enterprise. The villages' foreign earnings have been sequestrated by the Revolution. So to raise any cash at all, the Karen have to find valuables in Burma to trade out to Thailand. Their demand for Thai luxury items being greater than that of the foresters, the Rangoon sophisticates now scour Burma for something to sell.

White Rock, the tall, slow-moving, flunked botany student turned revolutionary teacher, was only the most visible example. There was nothing rustic about White Rock. He'd been a pop singer in Burma, and many of his pleasures revolved around night-life in Bangkok.

'I am trying to make a modern person of myself', he said, 'and to do that I must visit Bangkok at least once a year.'

Part of the object was education, part dissolution and another part the purchase of luxuries, especially pop cassettes, for his home in Betelwood. But all these required money; as a revolutionary teacher, White Rock received no salary, only a rice-and-salt stipend.

So he was looking for 'opportunities'. Fate was never very kind to White Rock. His first throw for the big time came when a friend in Rangoon produced a large cut ruby and asked him to take it to Bangkok to sell, for half the proceeds. Making the long journey over the hills to Riverside, then out to Thailand and down the motorway to Bangkok, White Rock went straight to a jeweller to cash in his fortune, presenting his ruby. It was a fake, made of glass.

'They laughed at me', he said.

He didn't repeat this foray into the gems trade, but turned to cattle, both buffalo – 'the real basic coin of the far east' (Le May, 1926) – and cows. He could buy a cow on the Burmese coast for 2,000 *kyat* (*c.* £25) and resell it to Thais on the border for 3,000 *baht* (£75). But it didn't always come off. Fattened at the coast and unused to mountains and forests, the cows might sicken and die on the way. White Rock also bought two baby elks from a Burmese, a mating pair, and brought them over the hills. In theory they could together be worth B.5–6,000. But everything went wrong:

> 'It took me ten days – how long did it take you, three? – *ten* days to get over the mountains. I had to push them up! And then what happens? One of them, the male, catches a cold and dies. I get the female to the foot of the mountain and she

decides to stop moving. You know that last stretch between the mountain base-camp and the river, which should be one and a half hours' walk? That took two days.'

In addition to the elks, he'd brought a dried bear's gallbladder. I saw him again a week later.

'How did it go?'
'I was cheated. You can sell those things in Thailand for B.4–5,000 and I gave it to someone at Headquarters because he knew the Thai dealers. When he came back he'd only got enough to give me B.1,400 – but I found out that he'd actually made B.4,500.'

What he really needed all this money for was a Thai residence permit. In the meantime, he wanted the same thing as most of the revolutionary teachers – to get out of teaching and back into the Army, which meant lots of travelling around in the forest. More fun, and more 'opportunities'.

In one aspect of forest life, Karen supremacy went unchallenged for one hundred years or more, and that was forestry itself. Their partners in this were the British; the first British presence in Burma, a factory built at Bassein in 1757, was an agency for the purchase of teak. From the moment they took over Lower Burma in 1825, teak was their main economic interest, and control of the forests a source of conflict. The Karen were, from the outset, heavily involved as loggers and elephant drivers. When the British acted in a high-handed manner towards them, the Red Karen burnt down a teak forest in protest. The British treated them with more respect thereafter, but by 1850 there were already reports of serious forest depletion.[5] Teak increased in value so fast that in the late nineteenth century the British and Thai authorities agreed rules to prevent forest owners selling the same trees to more than one person at a time.

On both sides of the border, lowlanders who regarded the forests with a mixture of boredom, distaste and outright fear were content to let the Karen elephant men do the work. In fact, Captain Low (1837, p. 37) found that, in the early 1800s, they had no choice:

Few countries yield such a variety of useful woods as the three Tenasserim provinces . . . The Burmans used to force the Karen to fell a certain quantity yearly, without receiving any wages.

In many areas the Karen established a monopoly in forestry,

which the Burmese acknowledged by making a Karen, Hla Pe, the first Minister of Forests after Independence. But in March 1955, an experiment took place that changed everything: direct extraction of timber, by tractor and truck.

By the mid 1960s, several lumber companies had stopped using Karen elephants to haul logs to the rivers, but still needed them to get the trees to the roadside, from where the trucks would take over. Today they don't even bother with that; the bulldozers take the roads to the logs.

In our District, the once essential Karen have been cut out of forestry altogether. Every aspect of the operation – felling, hauling, sawmills, middle and senior management, and all the capital behind it – is in Thai hands. A few Karen military commanders are said to have a stake, to take cuts. The forest people have no part in it any more.

Quick returns on capital are all that matters. Typically, investors in tropical lumber operations – whether in S.E. Asia, Africa or the Americas – do not trust local political conditions to remain stable. They want the fastest possible returns, rapid stripping of the forest and then their machinery out fast. They can't wait for rain, rivers or elephants, and they have not the slightest interest in replanting the trees after they've gone. The KNU use their cut of the trade to buy rice and bullets, and plant nothing either. The forest fuels the war, but there will soon be nothing left worth fighting for. A casual glance around Riverside gives an impression of a forest landscape – but it would take a long second look to find a single hardwood tree standing of decent commercial size and quality.

As the forests on the eastern side of the river (towards Thailand) are progressively stripped, the astonishing network of roads appears to double in extent each month. In early 1988 a major physical and psychological barrier was passed: the Thais bridged the river and began extracting on the western side, deeper into Burma. When the Burmese finally get round to stopping them (probably by driving military vehicles down these same logging roads), the Thais will simply pull back over the border. By that stage, the Karen would probably do as well to go with them.

Apart from timber, the Karen once dominated the trade in forest exotics that went to Siam and beyond. In 1784 a Siamese trade mission left Bangkok for Beijing. With the exception of the gem-stones (rubies and sapphires), everything the envoys carried could have been provided by the Karen. These included elephants and ivory, rhino horn and ebony, peacock and kingfisher feathers, cardomons and sticlac (lacquer in its natural form, encrusted on twigs), gamboge (a gum-resin used as a purgative and also as a bright yellow dye), cutch (another resin used as a preservative in tanning and sailmaking), eaglewood (an aromatic formed by a disease affecting the heartwood of the tree *aquilaria agallocha*, also called 'sinking incense' and 'honey incense' because it sinks in water and smells like honey), sappanwood (a rich red dye), sandalwood, and others.[6]

But today that colourful and fragrant trade is gone. One by one these forest products have either fallen out of favour or have been superseded by synthetics. There's no demand for cutch, and the development of aniline dyes in Germany in the nineteenth century made the forest colours redundant. By the turn of the century, ICS surveyer G. P. Andrews could write that '... sappanwood, once the foremost product of the district, exists ... but is not now worked'.[7]

The Thais buy the occasional bundle of monitor lizards, or an anteater from the Karen, but with the forest so accessible they are increasingly going in on their own account. Why should they buy, when they can simply take? It is Thais who sling nets in the trees for songbirds, Thais who hire Edward's boat to search for eaglewood (still sold to the Middle East), Thais who seek out beautiful trees to take cross cuts to polish up for Bangkok table tops. All that Kawthoolei gets out of this is a 5 per cent toll and doubtless a kickback or two. The Karen word for trade – *ka* – is taken from the Thai, but not the activity itself.

The KNU do better out of cattle – less politically sensitive than timber. It was another British innovation. The colonial authorities started making loans to the foresters for livestock purchases back in 1883, 'in order to diminish the destruction of forests by the practice of *taungya* [swidden] cutting and to bring the influences of civilisation to bear upon the Karen people'.[8] The KNU now not only takes a toll on all cattle brought across the border by private traders; they have begun cattle ranching themselves, with two herds of some fifty animals each in our district. On this scale, the operation is clearly much less destructive than forestry. If they make a success and a profit from it, however, it is not difficult to imagine a repeat of the disasters of the Amazon where, in order to provide cheap beef for US hamburgers, great tracts of rainforest have been cleared, grazed for a few years and then left as useless scrub. When the tall trees are all gone from Kawthoolei, such ranching will be an appealing short-term money spinner for the Revolution. Now they have very little else. The other major natural resource, tin mining, has been cut away from under them.

Mining was never a favorite occupation of the Karen. Although the best mines were often within Karen territory, European mine managers in the 1890s could not persuade the Karen to work them and had to bring in Chinese labour. Over the border, the Thais didn't like doing it either, saying that it offended the soil deities. They eventually persuaded the Karen to work the tin, because the latter were recent immigrants and very hard up.

Kawthoolei has made a lot of money out of mines in the past, but the collapse of the international tin market in the early 1980s was, apart from its well-publicised effect on Malaysia, a cruel blow to Kawthoolei.

I walked to the mining villages with Bartholomew in February 1987 and again in July. These were official Health Department tours. The KNU Mines Department supposedly provides health care for the workers but in reality the nurse stayed down by the river at the small village named Football Field, a settlement of Mines Department families. To reach the mines area we had to climb a high, steep hill. We found ourselves to be skirting the top edge of a dramatically angled swidden field, newly burned. Bartholomew clicked his tongue and shook his head: 'Too many people up here now, you see? We would never have farmed slopes like that ten years ago.'

The mines were also at their best ten years ago. In 1975 there were some 400 houses in the area: now there are 200. All the mines are privately financed and owned; the KNU Mines Department buys the ore from the producers and resells it to Thailand.

In February many of the workings were shut down, there being a lack of water for the blasting jets. They told me things would be different when the rains came. They were; by July there was almost nobody working at all except a few elderly freelance panhandlers wading in the streams. The Mines Department supervisor had moved house, most of the open-cast pits were deserted and the workforce had vanished. I asked,

> 'Where did they all go?'
> 'Oh, I don't know. Home. They were not Karen, they were Mon.'

Bartholomew and I came to a mine owner's house. He was sitting at an outdoor table, shaving off a few whiskers with a fragment of mirror, no soap and an old safety razor. He said,

'Did you see the aeroplane? It came over here this morning, quite
    low.'
'Burmese?' asked Bartholomew. The mine owner replied with a
    proud display of English:
'Burmese. Fokker Friendship. Not friendly!'
'What was it doing?' I asked.
'Looking at the logging roads', said Bartholomew.
'Looking at the state of the mines. There's not much to see, is
    there? I'm getting out of mining.'

It simply didn't pay any more. A few years ago he could get
B.160 per kilo of tin ore from the KNU. Now it was costing him
B.60 to produce (mostly on diesel for the pumps), the KNU bought
for B.73 and resold to the Thais for B.92.

'For twelve or thirteen *baht* it's not worth the effort. So, I'm
going into cattle. I've been building up my herd for a few years
now. Beef cattle are worth B.50 a kilo, they cost very little to rear
and they carry themselves to the border. The only trouble is the
milk. They tell me that a B.10 tin of milk now costs K.35 in Burma,
and we import crates of it – but Karen just won't drink it fresh.'

The top end of the mining valley had been quite lively in February; there was enough water then to run one big jet that cut
the hillsides out from under swidden fields. Shops, traders, officials
and schools had all been busy. In June it was a ghost town. It
had the curious grim beauty of decayed mining districts that I know
from North Wales, the same abandoned workings, cold slag heaps,
collapsing water chutes, faded managerial mansions. But whereas
Tan y Grisau, stark solid basalt and slate, has even in its deserted
condition hardly changed in fifty years, here things were disappear-
ing every month. A house where in February I had been served
Mekhong whisky, *Fanta* and prawn crackers, in July had ceased to
exist, a riverbank having collapsed beneath it. There was a shop
building with heavy wooden elephant sledges and tackle parked
outside – but no stock in the shop, and no elephants. The KNDO
border guard was fast asleep and the army radio had been taken
away. Bamboo shacks were subsiding into the quick grass. The
valley was already reverting to forest of secondary scrub.

As the old-established resources of the forest fail, the Karen cling
to the belief that they can, at least, outmanoeuvre the Burmese
in jungle warfare. In 1827 Major Snodgrass (p. 21), wrote:

Roads, or anything deserving that name, are wholly unknown in the lower
provinces. Footpaths, indeed, lead through the woods in every direction,

but requiring great toil and labour to render them applicable to military purposes: they are impassable during the rains, and are only known and frequented by the Carian tribes . . .

Fifty years later, D. M. Smeaton (1887, p.139) added:

. . . the Karen is a dangerous fellow . . . from his perfect knowledge of woodcraft which enables him to live for months in the jungle without any supplies . . . He cooks his food in green bamboos, and will be off scouting for a month without giving his enemy a sign of his presence until he closes with him.

The urban newcomers, Delta revolutionaries like True Love and White Rock, are not this breed at all. They got lost almost as easily as I did. And yet they too loved the forests, even the boys from Rangoon. There was nothing insincere about their songs, nor about True Love's enjoyment of camping, and they are learning as fast as they can.

With every day, however, the forest is less of a resource and less of a refuge. Curiously, even with its high proportion of hillsmen, the KNLA seems to make remarkably little use of that stealthy acumen noted by Snodgrass and Smeaton. In my year with them they were, on two occasions, completely outplayed by the Burmese who got behind by cutting through Thailand. Instead of the high-mobility guerrilla tactics one might expect, the KNLA are now dug into positions in front of their bases in trenches which a television reporter described as resembling First World War Flanders.[9] Instead of creeping silently upon the enemy, when the KNLA attacks it prefers head-on assaults, all guns blazing and the little cow-horn trumpets shrilling.

True Love and sudden death 19

The Karen will never be your slaves.
When the very stones float on the water
they'll wave flags for Kawthoolei.
This is our land, which our forebears knew;
dead or alive, it will always be ours.
                    Recorded for me by Riverside teachers.

'What does "expendable" mean, Jo?' said True Love one afternoon. I asked him the context.

'It comes into *Rambo*, about soldiers being expendable. And there
was another film I remember seeing in Burma, about soldiers.'

John Ford's *They Were Expendable*, perhaps, which concludes
with Douglas MacArthur's defiant, 'I shall return!' I told True
Love what the word meant and he thought about it for a moment.

'Sometimes I worry about my commanding officers. Some are
very good, they love their men and we love them. But there
are some . . . I don't know. Maybe they don't really care about
their soldiers. Sometimes they ask us to take risks, and I cannot
always see the point.'

Silver's pregnancy was concentrating his mind.

'I came to Kawthoolei prepared to die for my people, but now
I am to have a family. Should I not think about that? Should
I not think about surviving, for their sakes? That is not cowar-
dice, I think. I know that Silver worries about this, too, when
there is talk of my going to the Front. Her family has been
forced to flee the Burmese once.'

'What's making you anxious just now?'

'The French. We hear talk that the French may come down here
to help train our soldiers. I will be involved, I know. Maybe
I will have to go to the Front as their interpreter. The Burmese
would love to catch these French.'

In January 1987, True Love escorted me up into the hills to
the mining villages. There was one in particular that he was keen
to visit. It was a largely Buddhist community.

'Why is that important?' I asked him.

'I wish to get to know our Buddhist people better. This is very important to me.'

So what had he been doing during his twenty-five years among the Buddhists of the Delta? It turned out that True Love had a more specific interest in this village:

'There is a small monastery here: shall we visit? I would like to speak with the monk.'

The monastery was no more than a very small thatched bamboo hut in which a saffron monk sat smoking cheroots and spitting into an enamelled bowl. He was, he said, a missionary. He had come from the north to stay among these villagers for a few months because they had no priest of their own and their faith needed to be supported. Then he would move on. In his early forties, alert and energetic, he said he would walk the length of Kawthoolei if he had to.

He and True Love questioned each other closely for half an hour, exchanging news. Then True Love asked if the monk would cast his fortune. As he asked, he looked at me with a laugh: 'What do you think of this? Do you like to have your fortune told?' When I grinned and shrugged, he said, 'I need a relationship with these people.'

The Monk drew some squares on a piece of paper, asked True Love a few questions about his age and so forth, and began making calculations. In a quarter of an hour, he came up with his prediction, as follows: for the next four years, from the ages of thirty-two to thirty-six, True Love would be frustrated and continually passed over for promotion, but after that things would improve. In the meantime he would be prone to gastric ulcers. He should be exceedingly careful if and when he got sent to the Front, and he should be wary of his commanding officers who might not always have his best interests at heart. In other words, faced with an anxious young junior officer in battledress, he focussed the obvious fears neatly.

'It's all just as I thought', said True Love.

But his fears were very well grounded. As the dry season campaigns continued, his friends were being killed. And not just soldiers, either.

In 1827 Dr John Crawfurd (1829, p. 422) was sent on an embassy from the Governor-General of India to the Burmese Court of Ava. He reported:

The conduct of the Burmans on their predatory excursions is cruel and ferocious to the last degree ... 'You see us here', said some of the Chiefs to Mr Judson, 'a mild people living under regular laws. Such is not the case when we invade foreign countries. We are then under no restraints, we give way to all our passions, we plunder and murder without compunction or control. Foreigners should beware how they provoke us when they know these things.'

In 1988 Amnesty International published a report on the treatment of the Karen and Kachin in Burma which showed that little had changed. It is full of accounts of the destruction and viciousness brought by Burmese soldiers to Karen villages – of people shot in the back as they unsuspectingly worked the fields, of daughters seeing their fathers buried and burnt alive, and young men having the flesh stripped off their shins with bamboo rollers to make them talk. If Amnesty should ever need any further evidence, many families in Riverside can supply it.

After one of our breakfasts at his house, Moses talked about fear:

'It's very frightening, to be Karen in Burma now. You dare not say anything, your friends are taken away in the night, never seen again. I know a man who was a simple, innocent Karen but he was arrested and held for ten years. When he was released, his family didn't know him. And when the soldiers come to Karen villages, even in Burmese territory, they burn the houses and force people to move away, they make no provision for them – or they make them carry army supplies with insufficient food for themselves. If the villagers obey, they starve. If they disobey or argue, they may be shot. So they have to just run away. And then what happens? The Burmese attack us, their operations fail and they are humiliated, and so they return to Burma and burn Karen villages, accuse the people of spying for the KNLA and punish them. It happens so often.'

As the KNLA retreats into the hills season by season, more Karen villages are exposed to the Burmese soldiers. The 4 or 5,000 KNLA troops face at least ten times that many regular Burmese Army. Hardly surprising, therefore, that everyone from Edward to the youngest of the *Boarders*, the Colonel, Vermilion, every father and mother in the village thought about the possibility that someday they could be overwhelmed.

True Love, watching Silver's pregnancy fill out, and at the same time hearing the Army talk of Burmese pressure and incursions into villages, became tense and thoughtful. The KNLA put out monthly battle reports detailing the number of Burmese soldiers killed in a plethora of skirmishes, but with no indication of Karen ground lost, or of the inability of the KNLA to keep the vast Burmese forces out of Karen lands. Working at the accounts each day at Headquarters, True Love knew better, and doubtless often wished that he didn't.

On the 5th of March 1987, the news was particularly bad. The Burmese had seized and wrecked the Karen base at Wali. The incident was major enough to be reported by the BBC and to cause the Thais to close the border. For a while the KNU system was virtually frozen, with neither officials nor civilians able to move. The response at Riverside was mixed; we still thought of ourselves as living in a backwater. The Colonel declared, 'We must be more vigiliant!' and ordered that security be tightened up. The only visible effect of this was that for a week or so they searched bags at the border, Colonel's orders. But as soon as travel was possible once more, the Colonel went off to Maw Daung in the south, everyone relaxed again and the checks stopped. No one in our District was too perturbed by the Wali attack. The KNLA had seen it coming, after all, and the civilians had been got out in time.

But in May there came a brutal shock. The Burmese out-manoeuvred the KNLA completely in our own northern Township, capturing many civilians in the process. Everyone had someone there that they knew. For the first time in years the fighting had seriously impinged on our territory. 'It is a lesson to us', said Moses – a lesson that vigilance didn't mean avoiding the Colonel's wrath but staying awake to keep the Burmese out of your own homes. And, just as uncomfortable, that the Thais would allow the enemy to attack through Thai territory if it suited them. It had been an almost exact repeat of the Wali attack, and the Karen had been caught out both times. Not long afterwards, the Burmese entered a Karen village and massacred the inhabitants. Enraged KNLA pursued the Burmese, trapping and killing forty-five of them, so I was told. But they couldn't stop the Burmese in the first instance.

True Love's attitude changed. He had by now got used to the prospect of fatherhood, but his patriotic anger needed a vent. A new tone of soldierly excitement came into his conversation. In June he said that he had been given to understand that this would be his last year as a teacher, then it was back to the Front.

'Now my Adjutant Officer gives me and the other NCOs a talk every day about what we must learn in order to be a good soldier and a good officer. He wants me to be promoted, he has told me!

Colonel Oliver has to recommend me to Headquarters for approval but he says there is no problem. I shall be a Second Lieutenant. I want to do this. Yes, I like teaching, but I want to be out in the villages fighting for my people, being with my people! I will serve at the Front for perhaps two or three years. I must be careful, you remember? Like the monk told me. Dan wants to go too, we all want to go now. You get perhaps one or two months' leave, especially during the quiet rainy season.'

Good, I thought, because you'll have a small child by then. However, nothing much seemed to happen. He continued to shuttle between the school and the Army offices up the hill.

It occurred to me that the situation was possibly *more* frightening if you lived at Riverside – with time and quiet to contemplate the macro-strategy and with no immediate enemy in front of you to limit your imagination – than it was for Front Line troops who had, at least, someone to shoot at. At Riverside, the most tangible evidence of the Burmese was overhead.

The Karen have, of course, no air force of their own, and are thus virtually defenceless against air raids. Admittedly, they held the Burmese air force in contempt. As Moses had observed at the seige of Insein in 1949, Burmese bombs never seemed to hurt very many people. Burmese pilots had a splendid reputation for incompetence, and Karen told me with relish of how a wing of six fighters had taken off, wandered into cloud and smacked into a mountain. The Burmese possessed few aircraft of any great destructive capacity. At Insein they'd been dropping home-made bombs from Dakota transports, and on 16 April 1987 the *Far Eastern Economic Review* reported that they were now using converted Swiss propeller-driven trainer aircraft as bombers. Nonetheless, their inability to respond distressed the Karen. The Colonel was unhappy, and at monthly intervals he would issue instructions that everyone should have an air-raid shelter. Privately, many people thought the idea stupid, saying that they'd prefer to run into the forest than to try and pack their family (let alone 300 schoolchildren) into a hole in the ground where a single bomb would kill them all. Great Lake dug his, had it inspected and then turned it into a latrine. The *Boarders*, with a bit more design flair, dug an elaborate zig-zag trench on the riverbank; when the rains came and filled it with water, they stood giggling at the thought that they'd drown before they were shot.

But no one dismissed the danger. Their ears were attuned to

aircraft. Long before I had noticed anything, they would know what was approaching and if it was threatening. High-flying jets were either Thai military or international passenger flights, and were therefore ignored. But the sound of a propeller meant Burmese, as did anything low or off the usual flight paths. Sometimes, as I sat on a verandah talking with a family or with the *Boarders* girls, they would of a sudden get up and rush outside to scan the sky, tracking the hostile plane, ready to run for cover. They made me nervous – as did William the headmaster when he painted the roof of his house black. 'Just against the rust', he assured me, and then added, 'and for camouflage'. Which made me painfully aware of how brilliantly my new tin sheets shone up out of the forest.

Just once they had reversed the tables, and that was at the very beginning of the war. On Karen National Day I took a photograph of Colonel Marvel and his entourage. Most of the faces in the group I knew well, but there was one stranger. I asked True Love: 'Oh, that is our hijacker. We think he is the first aircraft hijacker in the world.'

A true story: in 1949 a group of young Karen rebels had boarded a transport aircraft and forced the foreign pilot at gunpoint to fly to the rescue of a Karen contingent at Maymyo base. Ironically, the Commander-in-Chief of the Burmese air force at the outbreak of the rebellion was a Karen; he sensibly made himself scarce. The KNDO did capture some aircraft on the ground, but had no one to fly them – a consideration that hadn't stopped them paying large sums to the American con-man who offered to fix the crashed fighter for them (see p. 293).

Helicopters were a bigger worry. There came a report that the United States was to supply the Burmese with helicopters for spraying defoliant onto the poppy fields in the north. There are, obviously, other things that you can spray from helicopters.

Direct air attack was one concern; being watched from the air was another. As the mine-owner had said of the snooping Fokker Friendship: 'Not friendly'.

> 'And they help the spies', said Sam. 'A couple of years ago we caught some spies here at Riverside. Two Karen had come to join us from Burma, a man and a woman. He was a teacher and she was a nurse, so of course they were very welcome here. But they were traitors, they were reporting to the Burmese. The teacher had a diary full of suspicious writing and when we searched further we found a special radio that could speak to aircraft overhead.'

'What happened to them?' I asked, unnecessarily.
'Shot', said Sam.
'Criminals go before the Judge', said True Love, 'but for spies
and Fifth Columnists, sudden death!'

They saw spies everywhere, spies who would report to Rangoon
and spies who would assassinate their leaders. In January I noticed
more than the usual number of soldiers in the village.

'Are they planning another attack?' I asked True Love.
'No; at least, not that I know. But there has been a man around
the village whom we don't know and who has now disappeared.
He was asking a lot of questions about the Colonel's house
and Harvest Moon's house, and so we have posted guards.'

Shortly afterwards, Highlander told me his sad tale of the poor
Burmese miner who'd been mistakenly executed as a spy (see p.
108). At the same time, I was carrying out demographic and morbi-
dity surveys and discovering from True Love that some people suspected my motives:

'They think maybe you will reduce their rations, and that you
will give information about them to the enemy.'
I said that I thought that was daft; what could the Burmese possibly want with information about the incidence of miscarriages
in Karen women? But True Love put me in my place:
'Many of these people have seen their families hurt and have
fled their villages. They have a right to be suspicious.'

Of course; I instinctively mistrust and resent the decennial census
in Britain. In fact, even as we discussed the matter, there were
demonstrations and riots in West Germany against similar information gathering. I felt less sympathetic, however, when I heard
that Thomas, the Karen missionary, had started a rumour that
I was an informer.

In February they arrested three Burmese spies at Maw Daung.
It did nothing to halt the attack in March; still, the KNLA had
the satisfaction of repelling an assault so inept that the Burmese
commanders could obviously have used some information. The
trouble was that it seemed to make little difference to the Burmese
whether they were well prepared or not. With such superiority in
numbers and firepower, they came anyway.

After the Maw Daung attack, the Karen dithered; the retreating
Burmese column escaped without further loss. Trevor, the New
Zealand photojournalist, could not disguise his contempt for KNLA

tactics: 'What the hell do they think they're doing? Sitting waiting to be walked over? They've got to be out there taking the war to the enemy, blowing up their trains, raiding their bases. These Burmese troops are a load of amateurs; the Karen could easily put the frighteners on them if only they tried.'

From time to time they did try – at least, in other districts. In February, thirty KNLA commandos attacked a Burmese ammunition depot which had been brought rashly deep into Karen territory. They inflicted heavy casualties, and captured so much ammunition that they wildly claimed that it had taken 700 porters to carry off the loot. The cache was put on display at GHQ and a video made of it, which we all got to see soon afterwards. But our District remained in a 'defensive posture'.

I took Trevor to meet Colonel Oliver, the local KNLA Commander. When we arrived, he was upstairs, seated at an old pedal sewing machine and sewing knapsacks. When we left, with permission for Trevor to photograph the camp, the latter could not contain himself.

> 'For fuck's sake, what's the commanding officer doing sewing bags?! Why isn't he at the Front Line? How often does he go to the Front anyway?'
> 'Not so often', I said. 'When he can.'
> 'Well, then!' snorted Trevor.

I should have loaned him Marshall's 1922 (p. 157) description of Karen war parties:

The organiser of the foray did not go in person with his men, lest he be killed and thus unable to dispense the spoils, but remained at home to receive and reward the valiant fighters on their return with the booty.

True Love was defensive: 'Of course the Colonel goes to the Front. He is one of the best officers.' Nonetheless, True Love was growing despondent again. He was neither teaching full-time nor committed to the Army, neither settled in the classroom nor confronting his enemies. As the dry season drew to a close it was obvious that, as regards furthering the Revolution, one of its brighter young activists had achieved very little that year. He moped, he stopped singing. The guitar was never at his house but always at *Boys Boarders* where less thoughtful spirits banged away at it each evening. True Love spent time on his Thai grammar. His son was born in June. Relief at Silver and the boy's health was now coloured by worry: a larger household to protect.

Fear strained every family. At Bartholomew's house, James was of an age to serve. As he strutted on the football field with the other schoolboy trainees, bamboo rifle at the slope, Vermilion managed to laugh at the performance but not to hide her anxiety. Bartholomew could not reassure her, since he was less and less at home. As the Health Department threatened to collapse under the weight of its impossible responsibilities, he passed much of his time waiting for transport to take him from one patch-up to the next, to do what he could with a small box of pills. Increasingly it was Fragrance who ran the household and, as if she didn't have enough to think about in her teaching, her father was now proposing to take her into the Health and Welfare Department and turn her into a peripatetic nurse.

William's wife Bella wanted to go home. Ten years younger than her husband, she had placed all her trust in his calm and professional confidence when they had married down on the coast. Now she was the wife of the headmaster, in the public eye. Inevitably she seemed inexperienced and out of place in Education circles. She was homesick, like True Love, and in March she left Riverside to make her way downriver. She was going to meet her mother whom she had not seen for seven years. She would go as far as a village near the Front, and then send a message asking her mother to meet her there, just as True Love's family had attempted to do in reverse. Bella didn't dare go to her home village near Mergui; she'd be recognised as the woman who'd married a rebel, and almost certainly be betrayed by Burmese in the village.

In her absence, William had to run both the school and his family of small children. Day by day the demands got on top of him, the children were not cared for. For a while they went regularly to Ruth's house to be fed. Then William persuaded another young girl to come each day to manage the home. With their mother gone and their father working all day and much of the night, the sweet-natured children began to run wild.

For weeks there was no word from Bella. By the end of April, eyebrows were being raised. The young housekeeper did her best but the house was squalid. 'So what's new?' said the unkinder Gossips. 'Bella was useless, lazy and stupid. Did you see what happened when the children were sick? She didn't do a thing!'

True Love was more sympathetic: 'Bella is young and a little immature, perhaps. But she's frightened. She fears that she may never see her mother again, and I know exactly how she feels.'

In the meantime, William led the school in the daily oath of loyalty to the Revolution, and organised the military training of the schoolboys. By June, Bella had still not reappeared, but William was reluctant to talk about it, saying only, 'I know where she is. She is safe.' The Gossips began to wonder if she ever would come back; if not, who would be sorry? William, they thought, could do a lot better, and there were *some* grounds for divorce. Meanwhile, the young housekeeper moved in full-time, and could often be seen cheerfully toting the littlest boy about the village.

At the end of June we heard news. Bella was simply scared to return. 'She's terrified of the Burmese soldiers', said Edward. 'So her mother is coming here instead, to look after the children.' The war was threatening to stand the family on its head and destroy it. Then, in mid July, I was in Barterville with Great Lake and Bartholomew and there appeared Bella, nervous and shy. William, in his quiet way, was overjoyed at her return. The only problem for him was that, in her absence, he had been sorely in need of cash and had sold *her* pig to True Love for half the going rate.

The KNLA had begun to show its desperation, recruiting women and young boys. They were far from happy about allowing either but, as the Burmese showed no signs of retreating with the onset of the rains, it was clear that the balance between civilian and military life was shifting. They would protest that all Karen were one in the Revolution, that there was no divide between the people and their war. But creeping militarisation had begun to affect every aspect of Riverside life and the civilians didn't like it. Great Lake didn't like the big new Army-managed shop that threatened ordinary traders' business. Bartholomew didn't like the military stranglehold on 'his' hospital. Edward didn't want his teachers reverting to the Army. Moses had sleepless nights about his eldest son, a good Christian, now at the Front waiting to kill or be killed. Nobody liked the fact that most of the financial resources and, increasingly, the best of the human resources were going to shore up the fragile perimeter. I thought of the Colonel's speech at New Year, of his exhortations to his people to make greater progress in building the State. And I wondered what he could expect of them now.

We could not relax; the war was an ever stronger presence in District life. In July, they debated at Headquarters whether the District should be raised to full KNLA Brigade status. The enhanced war footing seemed to be called for, but might it not both alarm the people and attract even greater attention from the

Plate 19. 'The KNLA began to show its desperation, recruiting women and young boys.'

Burmese? As the rains failed to get into their full protective stride, there were fears of a new Burmese attack. True Love said, 'They may raid Maw Daung again, to finish what they started there. And we have intercepted radio signals which suggest that they're planning an assault against New Fields' – the township immediately to the south of Riverside, only a few hours away by river.

In July, an external development heightened the palpable

nervousness. The Burmese Minister of Defence made an official visit to Bangkok, the first such contact for some years. I was back in Thailand at the time, and the newspapers spoke often, but vaguely, of 'greater cooperation'. On my return to Kawthoolei, everyone wanted to know what was going on. I probably knew less than they did, but still they asked: 'What are they saying to each other? Maybe they will take joint action against us. What have you heard?' Well-used to having their backs against an accommodating Thai wall, they were now wondering if it was being dismantled behind them.

True Love, as usual, was being pushed around. The District audit, months overdue, hadn't been completed because the Forestry Department, having to adjust almost daily to changed political circumstances in Thailand, couldn't supply full data. So, one faction at Headquarters wanted True Love back with the accounts to try and get matters straightened out. His Adjutant Officer wanted him full-time as an interpreter for the military training now proposed by 'Captain Jock', the American. Colonel Marvel, having sacked Edward and appointed himself Education Officer, wanted True Love back teaching, and the Health Department were trying to have him appointed full-time guide and interpreter to visiting medical teams. Helpless in the middle, True Love stayed at home with his wife and little son, waiting for the world to sort itself out.

This, for me, was the saddest time in our relationship. I found it increasingly difficult to talk with him. Preoccupied and irritable, he had no taste for music. Our evenings of expedition planning were now ended; too many trips had been scrapped, and we had given up trying. I wanted to ask what he was thinking of for the future. How long could he stay? Might he consider taking his family away to safety? In what sort of health was his idealism and his faith in the Revolution? He knew what I wanted to ask, but we never talked about it. He probably didn't know the answers, and I didn't have the nerve to press the questions.

Shortly after I left Kawthoolei, the Burmese did attack New Fields. There were few casualties because, as usual, the Karen got wind of their approach and evacuated the villages. They couldn't prevent the incursion, however; homes were burnt, crops destroyed. The villagers camped on the riverbank upstream for months, not daring to return.

Some time later I received a letter from True Love:

I want to give up all government jobs and I want to be a farmer. But my boss won't allow me to quit my job because we have a big problem with manpower. I wish to be a simple man again.

I'm sure that you must have read about Burma in your local newspapers. The situation there is worse and worse. Students are killed by the government troops.

Hope to see you. With love,

True Love, Silver, Eddy our boy.

20 Portraits

> This is welding the Karen into a nation.
>
> Dr Vinton[1]

A dispute about time in Riverside: another visitor, sitting on the verandah of Ruth's house, looked at her watch and pronounced it to be 4:30 p.m. Ruth asked,

> 'Is that Thai time or Kawthoolei time?'
> 'It's Burma time', said the visitor.
> There was an awkward pause. Ruth was angry:
> 'If you call it that, you cannot love the Karen.'
> 'Still, that's what it is. In Thailand it's five o'clock.'

And that is what many of the watches in Riverside said: five o'clock. Officially, Kawthoolei is in the same time zone as Rangoon, but many people have their watches synchronised to Bangkok. Everyone makes their own choice.

Time to go. When I left, they held a prayer meeting at Bartholomew's. Moses gave a short speech; I was presented with full Karen dress, and put it on. True Love wandered in wearing battle fatigues, realised that there were formalities in progress, hurriedly went into a sideroom and borrowed a Karen shirt of Bartholomew's to dress himself properly. Fragrance had made me a garland of flowers. The *Boarders*, all in new uniform of white shirts and trim green dresses, performed a hymn composed for the occasion by Charlie. Great Lake did not attend.

The next morning I walked to the frontier with True Love, the neck of the 'bent guitar' projecting from my rucksack. There was a pickup passing through and I hitched a lift. Two hours later I was in a Thai city, booking into a hotel where each double bed had mirrors the full length alongside, split and angled in the middle so that my sex life would be multiplied therein. I had switched into a different morality, by taxi, and I have been trying to remember Kawthoolei accurately ever since.

The Karen: what makes someone a Karen? Surely we should be able to characterise a 'tribe' – but the Karen elude definition, side-step common notions of race, have no language, religion, dress, food, 'culture' in common among them. Anthropologists, attempting to identify the essence of Karen society, write essays with despairing titles such as, 'Do the Karen Really Exist?'[2] and, 'Who are the Karen, and If So, Why?'[3] These people can't even agree on their own name! Scholars sometimes suggest that it was the missionaries and bureaucrats who created the Karen, and point out that, if by chance the first contacts had been made from the Thai side, the people would be known today as the *Yang*, that being the usual name for them in Northern Thailand. They argue that it was nineteenth-century notions of race applied to Burma (so as to sort it out administratively) that crystallised the idea of separate tribal nations, and led to the contemporary confrontations.[4] Recently, Robert Taylor (1987, pp. 285–7), has suggested that post-war Karen leaders with ambitions for national importance within Burma played up this new-fangled ethnicity for their own ends, seeing that, in the post-colonial turmoil, a racial constituency would be more powerful than one based on, say, religion or geography.

Fine distinctions of Karen/not-Karen are scarcely a problem for the people themselves. It has been said that the one common distinguishing feature of the Karen is the conviction that they *are* Karen. The Burmese Army don't seem nearly as confused as the scholars either; they know a Karen when they kill one. What the Burmese cannot decide is whether they *want* to know. In their 1973 constitution, ethnicity was effectively declared redundant. At the same time, Karen still have to carry identity cards declaring their ethnic group. The Burmese wish simultaneously to absorb them and to discriminate against them, to dissolve and to define.

What about a Karen state? Do you exist, politically, if you are recognised by yourself alone – or even, as in Burma, by certain other non-existents? For a brief moment this was a practical issue for me. A legal document had been sent out to me from the UK, requiring my signature and that of a witness. I meant to ask the Colonel to oblige:

> *Name*: Colonel Marvel.
> *Occupation*: insurgent.

But I had a sudden, ignorant doubt. If no one acknowledges your legal existence, can you be a legal witness? I asked someone else to sign, and I now rather regret it. I'd have liked to have given Kawthoolei a little recognition in English law, however oblique. They, after all, had acknowledged me.

I carried no Burmese documents, but I did have travel papers given me by the Kawthoolei authorities. I doubt that these, or their absence, made any actual difference to my freedom of movement. Only the Thais and Burmese did that. Highlander wanted the KNLA to capture a port and the KNU to issue passports. Would a European immigration official allow anyone to pass on such a document? It would depend on their desire to offend, or not offend Burma. Or Thailand. They couldn't care less whether Kawthoolei really existed or not. Meanwhile, the KNU has recently been accused of plotting armed interference in Laos, in cahoots with the CIA.[5] What interest could they have in such a foray, other than a very familiar desire to give their regime more substance at home by having an effect abroad? Once again: reifying themselves in contradistinction to others?

Many Karen are convinced that they were, once before, a nation state. They believe that they had a king and a capital city. Songs and stories speak of it, with monarchs and princes and princesses, city walls and palaces. Moses told me that archaeological remains with traces of the ancient Karen script had been found near Prome, but that the Burmese government had halted the excavations, not wanting to find anything that gave substance to Karen nationhood in the past.

No one else seems much inclined to believe in the Karen past either. There is not one firm piece of evidence for a Karen city, say the historians. Just as there is little evidence for the ancient Karen script. Or for Karen un-Christianity. Karen historians demand of their sympathisers a constant act of faith. It's not that the facts contradict them; just that there are so few facts.

What I have to hold onto are my daily jottings in four black notebooks, and a thousand and one photographs. I don't 'believe in' the Karen. I have, rather, an image that swims in and out of focus in this sea of recorded moments. It is like the hologram of a bird on my credit card; it changes shape as I view it from different angles, but the precise sense in which it can be said to exist is difficult. No two people ever see it the same at any one moment.

Last time I was in Penang I was offered a fake student card and a fake press card in any name I wanted. I was very tempted.

I paid an agent to arrange for me another Thai tourist visa. This allowed me to stay in Burma. I carried a hospital ID card which I had made myself. The evidence of my presence was almost as suspect as that of Kawthoolei.

I lie naked on a bed in a gloomy old Bangkok brothel by the railway station. I am here simply because it is a cheap place to sleep. Four prostitutes sit on a bench outside my door and from time to time one of them taps and asks if I want a massage. Are any of them Karen? I don't think so, but my grounds for that are uncertain: reputation and prejudice, no more. Why should the stern morality of Kawthoolei apply here? Why shouldn't these women change as readily as I do? If I was to discover that one of the girls was a Karen, I think my perception of what 'Karen' means would be changed, just slightly. Bangkok is a dreadfully destructive place. Frankly, I don't want to risk investigating. One day out, and slipping. I turn up the fan, twist open my new bottle of *Mekhong* whisky, put a tape of Prokofiev piano concertos into my Walkman and blot them all out.

They are millenarians, forever generating warrior leaders, sects, 'White monks' and prophets, all persuading themselves that the Karen Kingdom is, once again, at hand. Animists talk of the coming of Y'wa, Baptists of the coming of Christ and the Buddhists of Arrimettaya, the Future Buddha.[6] Somebody is imminent, Toh Meh Pah is coming, something will happen. 'Remember the Israelites in Egypt, Jo. Forty years in the wilderness, and then the Promised Land. The same will happen for the Karen, when forty years have passed.'

Which it now has. Their Revolution began in 1948. I write this in October 1988, and the Burmese State is crumbling, the *ancien régime* tottering. Or is it? The Karen are rumoured to have offered the Rangoon students arms with which to topple the military dictators. There are 4,000 Burmese in KNLA camps, learning to shoot. Ne Win has resigned, the Burmese Army is in disarray, some units are said to have mutinied, while the Karen are reported to be in control of Pa-an. For the rebels, a respite, if nothing else.

I write in Scotland, in a hayloft 1,000 feet up in the Grampians. Seven months after leaving Kawthoolei, I have had an unpleasant bout of malaria, somewhat to the astonishment of my GP. It put me firmly back on a level with the Karen soldiers in the forest. It anchored the slipping image a little. I was almost grateful.

In 1880, Carl Bock (1884, p. 90), got himself into difficulties trying to draw a portrait of a Karen woman in a remote village:

I asked permission of the chief to sketch his wife, and he at once complied. Scarcely had I made the first outlines when she turned round to see how the sketch was progressing, and in order to get her back in the original position I touched her chin. Immediately she altered the expression of her face, got up, and hurried off into an interior apartment. I looked at the chief, whose face was full of passion, and who had difficulty in restraining his anger ... No one was allowed to touch a Karian woman ... [a] bribe acted like oil on the troubled waters.

An attempt to draw a second portrait of a young man, drew protests from the boy's mother: 'It is an evil spirit; my son will be ill!' Bock, 'unwilling to make an unconditional surrender', deceived the Karen by sketching a rapid duplicate and ostentatiously tearing it in half, preserving the original and thinking himself very smart.

I had, at least, no such difficulties. Now they want all the portraits that they can get. No revolution can go long without a few good icons. In any Karen home of substance there is a copy of a painting of a dark young man with humorous eyes and – most unusual in a Karen – a beard and drooping moustache. He looks far more Russian than Karen; he could easily be passed off as the young Dostoevsky. But, in a few prints, a little more of the portrait is reproduced, including some of the man's jacket, which is dark and heavy, with a large zip fastener, casually half-open. This is no Slav mystic; it is Ba U Gyi, founder of Free Kawthoolei. Only his quiet sense of humour looks Karen.

Kawthoolei is full of photographs. Stuck onto bamboo walls, photographs of F15 fighter aircraft, soft pornography, the Californian coastline at Big Sur, Burmese film stars, the Tower of London, anything. And calendars, calendars everywhere, packed with mugshots of the leadership, of the KNU, of the Revolution. There are even, in one or two houses, photographs of me.

And my walls in Scotland are thick with photographs of Karen. Each time I went to Penang I took a pocketful of films, sent the prints home and took a selection of the best back in for my friends. None of Bock's problems now; they loved them. I have 1,000 or

Plate 20. My neighbours posing: 'Now they want all the photographs they can get.'

more prints, slides too. I have tapes and books and my bent guitar. I stare at them.

Very occasionally there are letters. Greetings, remembrances, a little gossip. Henri Mouhot wrote in 1860 of the life-saving morale-boost that letters from home give to the lonely forest traveller. To me the reverse is now a lifeline, evidence that the sad and delightful Free State still exists. I can tell you a little recent news; the old Burmese miner, the *Pu Payor* who lived next to *Boarders*, has died, his corpse found cold in the river one morning. There have been more attacks, and villages on the river have been burnt by the Burmese. Fragrance has not yet been successful in finding a lover. Bartholomew has been sacked because he never wrote reports, and

Arthur has taken over Health and Welfare. The Colonel is almost permanently hospitalised in Bangkok. Great Lake has gone to Thailand, and True Love too has obtained Thai residence papers. I send him books, but I shan't go back. They might none of them be there.

Notes

PREFACE

1 Quoted in the preface to Hamilton. The author was Alleyne Ireland.

2 *Kaw* = 'Land', but *thoolei* (or *thu lay*) does not necessarily mean flower, for which the usual general term is *paw*. *Thoolei* is the name of a specific plant (I don't know its botanical title) with a large white flower like a lily, which is found in the area; the Karen are more interested in its edible root. I knew a woman called *Thoolei Paw*, which makes the point of distinction. Some Karen point out that *thoolei* can, depending on pronunciation of the tones, equally well mean 'black field' and that, given Karen slash-and-burn agriculture, 'Land of Blackened Fields' is very plausible. Yet another version is 'Land Purged of Evil' – a good name for a revolutionary state, said my informant.

In a conciliatory move, the Burmese government established the 'Karen State' in 1954, with Pa-an as its capital. At the time of the 1964 peace negotiations, the name was changed to the traditional Kaw-thoolei. Under the 1974 constitution, which limited the autonomy of the states, the name reverted to Karen State.

I A BRONZE DRUM

1 A traditional reward in Burma and Siam. The beneficiary could 'eat the country' in the sense of enjoying the revenues of a certain district. See, for example, Le May (1926) p. 209.

2 Pu Taw U's booklet is unfortunately not generally available. Renard, p. 127 mentions Karen drum making *c*. 1800 at Nwedaung, which was safely to the north of British control for another half century. Marshall (1922) p. 9 wrote that the Karen 'do not make them, but buy them from the more industrious Shan, who do not appear to set much store by them'. Le May (1926) p. 252 mentions other labourers in North Thailand saving up their wages to buy 'large Karen drums'.

3 Stern, T. and T. A. report the same feature of troupe organisation.

2 BOAR TUSK'S CHILDREN

1 Huc (1851) p. 170. Leach used such considerations to pour scorn on similar migration theories as applied to the Karen's neighbours, the

Kachin: 'It is intriguing to contemplate the discomfiture of a jungle-dwelling Kachin who reversed the journey and found himself on the edge of the Gobi Desert!' (p. 230, fn.). G. H. Luce (1986) once also a 'migrationist', later became more guarded, proffering only '... some faint picture of the ancient history of the Karen. Originally jungle hillmen, coming from the north along the ranges between the Salween and the Irrawaddy ...' (p. 28). Many modern writers still offer the migrations as established fact.

2 MacMahon, p. 349. Renard (chapter one) surveys the various theories. The Hun thesis was also proposed by British Chief Commissioner Albert Fytche in 1878.

3 The usual Sgaw term for the Karen is *pwakenyaw* meaning, approximately, 'the people'. Luce (1986) speculates that *kenyaw* is a much decayed form of something like 'karen' in Old Karen, which word was thus close to variants we know from Old Burmese and Thai such as *kariang*. Nonetheless, the modern term 'Karen' does not feature in their language, while the Thai/Burmese variants may have applied to quite different groups at different times. See also Lehman (p. 299).

4 Richardson (1981) p. 74. The first sentence is taken from the book's cover.

5 Dr Richardson (1869) quoted by Renard, p. 135.

6 Mrs Judson, quoted approvingly by MacMahon, p. 50.

7 *Burma Gazetteer*, Salween District (1910) p. 2.

8 By U Za, *c.* 1950. Quoted by Renard, p. 161.

9 Dr Vinton's letters are quoted at some length in Smeaton's introduction of 1887.

10 *Burma Gazetteer* Tharawaddy District (1910) by B. W. Perkins, p. 64.

11 Slim, p. 113.

12 Rhodes James, p. 115. The author is actually speaking of the Karen's neighbours, the Kachin, in this paragraph, but his own and other accounts all give equal praise to the Karen.

13 Morrison, pp. 165 ff.

14 Translation given by Lonsdale, back cover.

15 *ibid.*, p. 7.

16 See Tinker (1967), Cady and, continuing the story until 1989 more sympathetically to the Karen, Smith.

17 *Ibid.*

3 WHITE COLLAR FLOWERLAND

1 Renard, p. 184. The translations given by Renard are very literal renderings of the Thai which I have slightly simplified.

5 WATER CHILD, LAND CHILD

1 Karen saying quoted by Smeaton, p. 156.

2 Low (1836) p. 131.

3 Inappropriately, I'm afraid; trade here was mostly for cash, and supplied by Thai traders.

4 Orwell, *Burmese Days*. See also Campbell.

6 A SIMPLE MAN

1 The 'Kuang Chi', quoted by Luce (1937) pp. 240–1.
2 Marco Polo, *Travels*, chapter 41, 'Of the Province of Kardandan and the Vochang'. Everyman edition pp. 49 and 262.
3 Bock (1881) plate 6, 'Tattooed woman of Long Wai', and (1885) p. 170–4.
4 Seidenfaden, p. 119 suggests a link with 'a former solar cult' as well.
5 Quoted by Le May (1926) p. 30.
6 Phya Anuman Rajadhon, p. 284. This Thai scholar describes 'a test done on the tattooed man by throwing something hard at him, or striking him with a sharp instrument and if he comes out unscathed, it means that the ritual process is magically a success'.
7 Somphob L. (both), and Lewis, p. 98.

7 FIGHTING MEAN, FIGHTING CLEAN

1 The various theories are summarised by Seymour-Sewell.
2 Quoted in Scott O'Connor (1907) p. 378, sixteenth-century English translation.
3 Described by MacMahon, p. 372 and Low (1837) p. 315. I quote the nineteenth-century terminology. 'Nitrate of Lime' would today be calcium nitrate $Ca(NO_3)_2$. 'Carbonate of Potash' is potassium carbonate K_2CO_3. The desired end product, 'nitrate of potash' is potassium nitrate KNO_3. My thanks to Dr Harold Dixson for checking MacMahon's chemistry.
4 Marshall (1922) p. 97 and Morrison, pp. 53–5.

8 GREAT LAKE AND THE ELEPHANT MAN

1 P. Radley, 'A la rencontre des Karens', in *Sudestasie* 37 (1985) p. 39.
2 Tachard p. 172.
3 Lunet de Lajonquière (1904) pp. 172 and 188. My translation.
4 Tachard p. 172.
5 *Observer* magazine, 22 May 1988.
6 de la Loubère (1693) p. 92. Some eighty years later, and just nineteen years after Plassey, Edward Gibbon made a similar judgement: 'There is no surer proof of the military skill of the Romans, than their first surmounting the idle terror, and afterwards disdaining the dangerous use, of elephants in war.' *History of the Decline and Fall of the Roman Empire* (1776) chapter 5, note.
7 In Rangoon they do not seem to have heard about the international

campaigns to save the last of East Africa's elephants from extinction at the hands of ivory poachers. In 1989, the Burmese government announced that, amongst other worthy efforts to improve the balance of payments, Burma had exported £250,000 worth of ivory. The KNU issued an outraged press release condemning Burmese destruction of the environment generally and of elephants in particular. The bulletin concluded:

The Burmese Army uses guns to invade Karen territory and rob ivory. It sells the ivory to get dollars to buy more guns. It uses the guns to invade Karen territory to rob our timber. It sells the timber to buy more guns. The end results?

No more forest.
No more elephants.
No more Karen nation.
No more political opposition.
MANY more guns for the Burmese for more atrocities.
    (KNU Department of Foreign Affairs 26 June 1989)

8 Tachard p. 233.

9 BARTHOLOMEW'S BOARDERS

1 The 'orphan' theme underpins much of Renard's examination of earlier Karen relations with various protectors, Thai and British.

10 THE THREE SEASONS

1 The interpretation of calendar names is that given by Marshall (1922) p. 49. I could never get two Karen to agree on the meanings.
2 Dickinson *et al.*, p. 269 on the drongo (*dicruridae*) family in general.
3 Zinke, Sabhasri and Kunstadter, in Kunstadter (1978) chapter seven, describe such fires in technical terms. They measured in-draughts of up to 65 kph, temperatures of over 600°C and estimated the height of the smoke column at anything up to 20,000 feet.

INTERLUDE: FROM THE KOK RIVER

1 Bock (1884) p. 300.
2 Lunet de Lajonquière (1904) p. 200, my translation.
3 Renard chapter three.
4 *Ibid.*, p. 183.
5 Gandasena, pp. 78–9.
6 Kunstadter (1978) examines almost all aspects of swiddening in the region in great detail.
7 Cohen.
8 Winter, p. 5.
9 *Ibid.*, p. 6.

11 LAST OF THE LONGHOUSES

1 For the history of the pass, see Collis chapter nine and Scott O'Connor book 4, chapter 3.
2 Christie, p. 296. Other embassies and missions are described by Collis and Scott O'Connor.
3 Scott O'Connor p. 405.
4 *Burma Gazetteer*, Mergui District (1912) p. 36.
5 McCoy, p. 339.
6 True Love said that he believed that some of the Pa-O Karen still live in longhouses, but he didn't know where. Mika Rolley, in his booklet on the Pa-O, makes no mention of these.
7 Recorded by Major J. P. Anderson (1923).
8 *Burma Gazetteer*, Tharawaddy District, by B. W. Perkins (1920) p. 64.
9 Marshall (1922) p. 55.
10 *Ibid.*, p. 158.
11 Pastor Moses told me that before the Second World War the Bombay-Burmah Trading Company took some of its best Karen loggers to Borneo where they were delighted to meet these 'kindred'.
12 There is doubt as to how many Karen actually used longhouses, when and where. Evidence examined by Shigeru Ijima (in Keyes, p. 100) suggests that they were mostly built in times of danger: when, for instance, the Karen moved out of Burma looking for new land in areas of Northern Thailand where there was localised insecurity and a need for some sort of *kraal* such as the thorn-fenced longhouses. These people appear to have given up longhouse living later.

　'Cultural' interpretations of longhouse design, such as Lévi-Strauss' *société à maison*, throw light on the social role of the structure – but that doesn't dissolve the practical considerations. They go together. In Kawthoolei, 'defence' is simultaneously a cultural, a symbolic and a practical matter.
13 Winter, p. 5.
14 Renard, pp. 17 and 119.

12 A DELICATE BAMBOO TONGUE

1 Kindly found for me at SOAS by the late Professor Eugenie Henderson.
2 Bunker.
3 See Luce (1986) and the introduction to Roop.
4 See Wylie, D. Richardson chapter two and, for a more sceptical version of the ministry to the Lahu, McCoy, p. 302.
5 Wylie, p. 64.
6 *Ibid*, p. 58.
7 For the regional family of languages, see Matisoff (1986). Exactly how these languages are related has been much debated. Captain Low (1837) said that, 'the Karen dialect leans towards the Siamese'.

Academic opinions shift. Eugenie Henderson wrote: 'People used to classify Karen as Tibeto-Burman, along with Chin, Burmese, Kachin etc. However, some scholars have argued that the relationship is not as close as has sometimes been thought, and have proposed a separate "Karenic" branch of the Sino-Tibetan family.' (Personal communication.)

For comparison of the varieties of Karen, see Jones.

 8 McCoy, p. 302.
 9 This and the translation following are mine.
10 Saw Moo Troo's eight attributes of the true Karen are:

   1 The knowledge that there is God, the Divine Being,
   2 High moral and ethical standards,
   3 Honesty,
   4 Simple, quiet and peaceful living,
   5 Hospitality,
   6 Language,
   7 National costume,
   8 Aptitude for music.

11 There is a published translation into Sgaw Karen of a book called *Where There Is No Doctor*, by David Werner. This is a modern classic of self-help village health care, originally designed for Mexico, now available in a dozen languages and used in poor communities worldwide. On the face of it, the book would seem the answer to Bartholomew's prayers, and indeed he knew it well. Unfortunately, in spite of Werner's caution that it should be adapted to local needs, that had not been done. What we had was a word-for-word translation which included a chapter on the roots of ill health in poverty, caused in turn by inequitable land holding (which really doesn't apply to Kawthoolei), and sections on the treatment of Mexican exotics such as Gila Monster bite. The index had been left in English, as had the drugs information, which was well out of date. Bartholomew and the Karen found it difficult to use, and they didn't trust it. All in all, a sadly fluffed opportunity.

13 TRUE LOVE IN LOVE

 1 Aubric, J. (1969). *Siam: Kingdom of the Saffron Robe*. London.
 2 *Burma: The Fourth Anniversary*. Rangoon, Department of Information, (1952) p. 31, quoted by Tinker, p. 217.
 3 Low (1839) p. 229. Many writers note similar situations. See, for instance, references to exogamy in Keyes (1979). In one area, 46 per cent of Karen men were married to non-Karen.
 4 The British deserved this reputation, as Orwell illustrated in *Burmese Days*. In 1926, Le May wrote: '. . . it is not long since "Western men and Eastern morals" was one of the topics of the day. As a result of that agitation, the Government of Burma took drastic action and

laid it down that the only form of union that could be permitted between a white civil servant in that country and a Burmese lady, was marriage' (p. 59).

14 FERMENTED MONKEY FAECES

1 Lunet de Lajonquière (1904) p. 200. My translation.
2 The various estimations are reported in Kunstadter (1979) p. 120.
3 Lunet de Lajonquière (1904) p. 171. My translation.
4 In Sgaw Karen: *Ner aw may wee lee ah*. The same form is used in Burmese: *Hta-min" sa" pi" bi la"*.
5 E. P. Durrenberger.
6 *Burma Gazetteer*, Salween District (1910) by R. C. Rogers, p. 4.
7 Quoted by Renard, p. 101.
8 Quoted by MacMahon, p. 50.
9 *Burma Gazetteer*, Henzada District (1915) by W. S. Morrison, p. 46.
10 Published by the Medical Directorate, GHQ India, p. 38.

15 PERFECT HOSTS

1 At least, the cover of his book does.
2 Le May (1926) p. 141.
3 Mouhot (1864) chapter fourteen: 'Notwithstanding all my efforts to discover the traces of the probable migrations of the Jewish people through Siam and Cambodia, I have met with nothing satisfactory excepting a record of a judgement of Solomon ... preserved *verbatim* in one of the Cambodian sacred books ... Nevertheless ... I could not but be struck by the Hebrew character of many of the faces.' Vol. 2, p. 32.
4 'Colonel Marvel's Mission', by Andrew Drummond, *Observer*, 6 December 1987.
5 Kunstadter (1986) p. 156.
6 The Burmese have made their feelings on the matter quite clear: in 1950 an American mission doctor, Gordon Seagrave, who ran a hospital for the hill people at Namkham, was sentenced to five years' imprisonment for treating wounded Karen and Kachin. The incident, and the exploits of J. C. Tulloch *et al.* are described by Glass.
7 Kunstadter (1986) p. 156 reports that just after the Second World War a Lua tribesman tried to persuade his fellow villagers to build just such a forest landing strip, to receive aeroplanes from the land of spirits laden with food and gifts. Just as the Melanesian cargo cults were inspired by the Second World War military airdrops to remote islands, one wonders if Karen and other hilltribe attitudes to aircraft are not still a little coloured by tribesmen's experiences serving with the Chindits, who were almost entirely supplied by air, and by other drops to resistance groups in the hills.

8 Some Karen (and their supporters) like to imply that refusal of pass-ports is a modern form of oppression aimed specifically at the minorities by post-war Burmese governments. This is not so, as the following illustrates:

> A Burman, being the property of the King, can never quit the country without his especial permission, which is only granted for a limited time, and never to a woman on any pretence. *Encyclopaedia Britannica*, ninth edn Edinburgh (1876), 'Burmah', vol. 4, p. 554.

9 Submission by Saw Mae Plet Htoo to the UN Working Group on Indigenous Populations, Geneva, August 1987.
10 Luce (1937) p. 240.

17 TRUE LOVE AND WHITE ROCK

1 Scott, J. G., p. 31.
2 MacMahon, p. 77. The harmonium has often been blamed for the abandonment of indigenous instruments in other areas of British India.
3 I am quoting these lines from memory and, I'm afraid, inaccurately. I've tried to track down the Blackwood Brothers' volume *Radio Favorites* through British and North American libraries, but without success.

18 INSURGENTS IN A LANDSCAPE

1 Renard, p. 21.
2 Lunet de Lajonquière (1904) p. 176, my translation.
3 Hall, p. 23 and Hill, p. 123.
4 See Leach p. 28 for a discussion of settlement patterns around these routes through the hills.
5 Renard, p. 139.
6 The decline in the Karen forest economy is described in detail in Renard, chapter three
7 *Burma Gazetteer*, Mergui District (1912) p. 13.
8 *Burma Gazetteer*, Toungoo District (1913) by B. W. Swithinbank, p. 19.
9 *Burma's Forgotten War*, 20/20 Television (BBC Everyman series) 22 May 1988.

20 PORTRAITS

1 Quoted by Smeaton, p. 15.
2 By Peter Hinton.
3 By F. K. Lehman.
4 Kunstadter (1967) p. 103, and Lehman.
5 *Observer*, 21 August 1988.
6 Stern (1968a).

Bibliography

Amnesty International. 1988. *Burma: Extrajudicial Execution and Torture of Members of Ethnic Minorities* London

Anderson, Major J. P. 1923. 'Notes on the Karen in Siam'. *Journal of the Siam Society* (Bangkok) 17.2: 55–7

Bock, C. 1881. *The Head-Hunters of Borneo*. London, Sampson Low. Reprint: Singapore, Oxford University Press, 1985

    1884. *Temples and Elephants*. London, Sampson Low. Reprint: Bangkok, White Orchid Press 1985

Bunker, A. 1871. 'On a Karen Inscription Plate.' *Journal of the American Oriental Society* 10: 172–6

Burma Gazetteer. Published at intervals, by administrative district, throughout the latter period of British rule. Date and author given with each reference

Cady, J. 1958. *A History of Modern Burma*. Ithaca, New York, Cornell University Press.

Campbell, R. 1935 *Teak Wallah*. London, Hodder and Stoughton. Reprint: Singapore, Oxford University Press 1986

Christie, A. 1967 'The Sea-Locked Lands'. In Piggot, S. (ed.) *The Dawn of Civilisation*. London, Thames and Hudson, chapter ten

Coedès, G. 1962. *Les Peuples de la Peninsule Indochinoise*. Paris, Dunod. English translation, Berkeley, Calif., University of California Press 1966

Cohen, E. 1986 'Hill Tribe Tourism', In McKinnon, *Highlanders*, pp. 307–25

Collis, M. *Siamese White*. 1936. London, Faber and Faber. Reprint: Bangkok, DD Books 1986

Crawfurd, J. 1829. *Journal of an Embassy to the Court of Ava* second edn, 1834 2 vols. London, Henry Colburn

Dickinson, D. C., King, B., and Woodcock, M. 1975 *Birds of South-East Asia*. London, Collins

Durrenberger, E. P. 1986. 'The Economics of Sufficiency', in McKinnon, *Highlanders*, pp. 87–98

Gandasena, Nai C. 1925. 'The Red Karen'. *Journal of the Siam Society* (Bangkok) 17.2: 74–99. English translation by E. J. Walton

Gilmore, D. C. 1898. *A Grammar of the Sgaw Karen*. Rangoon

Glass, L. 1985. *The Changing of Kings: Memories of Burma 1934–49*. London, Peter Owen

Hall, D. G. E. 1981. *A History of South-East Asia*, fourth edn London, Macmillan

Hamilton, J. W. 1976. *Pwo Karen: at the Edge of Mountain and Plain*. St. Paul, Minn., West Publications

Handbook on Burma. 1968. Rangoon, Directorate of Information

Hill, A. M. 1986. 'The Yunnanese: Overland Chinese in Northern Thailand'. In McKinnon, *Highlanders*, pp. 23–34

Hinton, P. 1986. 'Do the Karen Really Exist?' In McKinnon, *Highlanders*, pp. 155–68

Htoo La E. 1955. *The Golden Book*. Rangoon, Karen Baptist Convention

Huc, R-E. 1851. *Souvenirs d'un voyage dans la Tartarie et le Thibet*. Paris. English translation by John Keay as *Lamas of the Western Heavens*. London, Folio Society 1982

Jones, R. B. 1961. *Karen Linguistic Studies*. Berkeley, Calif., University of California Press

Kan Gyi, Saya. 1915. *Introduction to the Study of Sgaw Karen*. Rangoon, American Baptist Mission Press

Keyes, C. F. (ed.) 1979. *Ethnic Adaptation and Identity*. Philadelphia, Institute for the Study of Human Issues (University of Pennsylvania)

Kunstadter, P. (ed.). 1967 *Southeast Asia Tribes, Minorities & Nations*, vol. 1, Princeton University Press

(ed.). 1978. *Farmers in the Forest*. Honolulu, East-West Centre (University of Hawaii)

1986. 'Animism, Buddhism and Christianity: Religion in the Life of Lua People of Pa-Pae, N.W. Thailand.' In McKinnon, *Highlanders*, pp. 135–54

Leach, E. R. 1954. *Political Systems of Highland Burma*. London, Bell (London School of Economics)

Lehman, F. K. 1979. 'Who are the Karen, and If So, Why?' In Keyes, *Ethnic Adaptation*, pp. 215–53

Le May, R. 1926. *An Asian Arcady*. Cambridge, Heffer. Reprint: Bangkok, White Lotus Books, 1986

Levi-Strauss, C. 1979. *La Voie des Masques*. Paris, Plon

Lewis, E and Lewis, P. 1984. *Peoples of the Golden Triangle*. London, Thames and Hudson

Lonsdale, M. No date. *The Karen Revolution in Burma*. Kawthoolei (Burma), KNU Publications

de la Loubère, S. 1693. *A New Historical Relation of the Kingdom of Siam*. English translation by 'A.P.' London, Tho. Horne. Reprint: Bangkok, White Lotus, 1986

Low, Capt. J. 'History of Tenasserim'. In *Journal of the Royal Asiatic Society* 2 (1835) 248–275, 3 (1836) 25–54, 4 (1837) 42–108, and 5 (1839) 141–164

Luce, G. H. 1937 'The ancient Pyu'. *Journal of the Burma Research Society* 27: 239–53

1959. 'Geography of Burma under the Pagan Dynasty'. *Journal of the*

Burma Research Society 42.1: 32–51

1986 *Phases of Pre-Pagan Burma*. Oxford University Press

Lunet de Lajonquière, Capt. E. 1904. *Le Siam et les Siamois*. Paris. Reprint: Bangkok, White Orchid, 1986

McCoy, A. W. 1973. *The Politics of Heroin in Southeast Asia*. New York, Harper and Row

McKinnon, J. and Wanat, B. (eds.). 1986. *Highlanders of Thailand*. Singapore, Oxford University Press

MacMahon, Lt Col A. R. 1876. *The Karens of the Golden Chersonese*. London, Harrison

Marshall, Rev. H. I. 1922. *The Karen Peoples of Burma: A Study in Anthropology and Ethnography*. Columbus, Ohio University Press

1945. *The Karens of Burma*. London, Burma Research Society pamphlet no. 8

Mason, F. 1861. *The Karen Apostle*. Boston, Gould and Lincoln

Matisoff, J. 1969. 'Lahu Bilingual Humour'. *Acta Linguistica Hafniensa* (Copenhagen) 12.2: 171–206

1986. 'Linguistic Diversity and Language Contact'. In McKinnon, *Highlanders*, pp. 56–86

Moo Troo, Saw. 1981. *Karens and Communism*. Kawthoolei (Burma), KNU Publications, (with Rolley, M.)

Morrison, I. 1947. *Grandfather Longlegs*. London, Faber and Faber

Mouhot, H. *Travels in Indo-China*, vols. 1 and 2. London, John Murray. Reprint (reissued as 1 vol.): Bangkok, White Lotus 1986

Orwell, G. 1934. *Burmese Days*. New York, Harper and Row

Phya Anuman Rajadhon, *Essays on Thai Folklore*. Bangkok, Duang Kamol, undated *c*. 1969

Preecha Chaturabhand. 1987. *People of the Hills*. Bangkok, Duang Kamol

Renard, R. D. 1980. 'Kariang: A History of Thai-Karen Relations'. unpublished PhD thesis, University of Hawaii

Rhodes James, R. 1980. *Chindit*. London, John Murray

Richardson, D. 1984. *Eternity in Their Hearts*. Revised edn, Ventura, Calif., Regal Books

Richardson, Dr 1869. 'Journal of 1836–7'. In *Papers relating to the route of Captain W. C. McCleod from Moulmein to the Frontier of China and to the Route of Dr Richardson on his Fourth Mission to the Shan Provinces of China*. India Office Compilation, London (House of Commons)

Rolley, M. 1980. *The Karens Fight For Peace*. Kawthoolei (Burma), KNU Publications (with Saw Moo Troo)

Pa-Oh People. (No place or date: perhaps Thailand, *c*. 1984.)

Roop, D. H. 1972 *Introduction to the Burmese Writing System*. New Haven, Yale University Press

Scott, J. G. 1916. 'The Red Karens'. *Journal of the Central Asian Society* 3: 27–39

Scott, J. G. and Hardiman, J. P. 1900–1. *Gazetteer of Upper Burma and the Shan States*. 5 vols. Rangoon, Superintendent of Government Printing

Scott O'Connor, V. C. 1907. *Mandalay and Other Cities of the Past in Burma.* London, Hutchinson. Reprint: Bangkok, White Lotus 1987

Seidenfaden, E. 1967. *The Thai Peoples.* Bangkok, The Siam Society

Seymour-Sewell, C. A. 1922. 'Notes on Some Old Siamese Guns.' *Journal of the Siam Society* (Bangkok) 15.1: 1–40

Slim, W. (Field-Marshal) 1956. *Defeat into Victory.* London, Cassell

Smeaton, D. M. 1887. *The Loyal Karens of Burma.* London, Kegan, Paul and Trench

Smith, M. 1990. *Burma: The Politics of Insurgency.* London, Zed Press

Snodgrass, Major J. J. 1827. *Narrative of the Burma War.* London, John Murray

Somphob Larchrojna, 1975. 'Karen Medicine'. Unpublished PhD thesis, University of Sydney

　1986. 'Pwo Karen, Spirits and Souls'. In McKinnon, *Highlanders,* pp. 169–72

Stern, T. 1968a, 'Ariya and the Golden Book: A Millenarian Buddhist sect among the Karen.' *Journal of Asian Studies* 27.2: 297–328

　1968b, 'Three Pwo Karen Scripts: A Study in Alphabet Formation.' *Anthropological Linguistics* 10: 1–39

　1971. And Stern, T. A. 'I Pluck My Harp: Musical Aculturation Among the Karen of Western Thailand.' *Ethnomusicology* 15.2: 186–219

Tachard, G. (SJ) 1686. *A Relation of the Voyage to Siam.* Paris. English translation, London 1688. Reprint: Bangkok, White Orchid 1981

Taylor, R. H. 1985. *Marxism and Resistance in Burma.* Columbus, Ohio University Press

　1987. *The State in Burma.* London, Charles Hurst

Tinker, H. 1957. *The Union of Burma.* London, Oxford University Press, fourth edn. 1967

Wade, J. 1883. *Anglo-Karen Dictionary.* Rangoon, Burma Baptist Convention. Reissue 1954

Winter, R. P. 1987. *The Karens of Burma: Thailand's Other Refugees.* Washington, United States Committee for Refugees

Wylie, M. 1859. *The Gospel in Burma.* London, W. H. Dalton

Index

Note: the following are Burmese or Karen titles and are not indexed: Bo, Naw, Pipi, Pu, Saw, Saya, Thera, U. Thus the former Burmese Secretary General of the United Nations is indexed as Thant, U.

K = Karen, throughout

Academy for the Development of National Groups, 234
Adultery, *see* kinship
Agriculture: buffaloes and cattle, 175, 181, 214, 340, 352, 355; crops, cash: betel, 163, 343, 344; honey, 165; kapok, 1, 165, 167, 173; sesame, 168; gardens, fruit and veg, 42, 70, 90, 149–50, 164–5, 170, 174, 177, 180; rice, (dry), 42–3, 161, 163, 185, 344; (wet), 181, 216, 233, 269; small stock, 57, 71, 80, 167; swidden ('taungya'), 38, 67, 72, 189–90, 214, 233, 355, 356; *see also* forests
Alaungpaya, King of Ava, 16, 198
Akha (people), 183, 185, 189
Albuquerque, Duke of, 197
Alcohol, 19, 21, 278–280; KNU attitude to, 278–80
American Baptist Mission, *see* Baptists
Amnesty International: on Burmese atrocities, 109, 361
Anderson, Major J. P.: on adultery, 260; on longhouses, 205 n 7
Andrews, G. P.: on 'pwenyet', 76; on decline of Tenasserim port, 198; on sappanwood, 355
Animists, 18, 43, 46, 47, 48, 72, 123, 184, 185, 287, 288, 322; as birth attendants, 98; and funerals, 327; and literacy, 223, 230, 231; and ritual foods, 273, 277; and schools, 142; as swidden farmers, 38; and tattooing, 91; and Y'wa, 375
Arakanese (people), xv, 28, 279
Areca, *see* agriculture (betel)
Arrimetaya (Ariya, Future Buddha)
Arthur, 39, 156, 241, 269, 378
Aung Mo, 108–9
Aung San, 25–6
Australians: mercenaries, 290, 291; *see also* missionaries

Ava, Kingdom of, 17, 92, 113, 197, 291
Ayutthia, 16, 112, 128, 197

Bamboo, 1, 162, 165; dance, 7, **8**, 10, 188; in forest, ii, 10, 66, 162, 165, 180, 338–9, 350; in story, 270–1; *uses of*: baskets, 39; buildings, 55–6, **56**, 71, 72–3, 85–6, 135–6, 141, 162; musical instruments, 135–8, 321; rafts, 24, 70, 191; scaffolding, 165, 180; stages, 9, 10, 328; traps, 121; weapons, 110; watch towers, 161
Bangkok, 5, 45, 50, 127, 157, 192, 197, 236, 256, 295, 300, 301, 302, 307, 335, 375
Bangkok Post, 192, 306
Baptists: American, xv, 13, 17, 18, 21, 141, 221, 225, 227, 351; on alcohol, 278–9; Bethany Church, 32, 47, 49, 61, 121, 148, 328; Bible translation, 222–3; conversions among K., 13, 17–18, 221–2, 285; influence of, 285–7; *K. Baptist History*, 21; on K. character, 18–19; on K. morals, 245; and language, 224–5, 239; and literacy, 222–3, 226; and literature, 226; music, 322–3; and Ne Win, 28; Pan-K. concept, 225–6; schools, 2, 32, 47–51, 141–2, 309–14; in Thailand, 285; *see also* Judson, A.
Bartholomew, 1, 2, 40, 62, **100**, 152, 331, 372; background, 83–5, 290; and Boarders, 147–8; character, 82–3, 96–7, 99–101; family of, 84–5, 179; family life of, 85–90, 164–5, 174, 177–8, 182, 246–7, 248, 271–5; as head of Health and Welfare, 40, 96–7, 156–7, 214, 356, 377; and language, xix, 83, 224, 237–8, 241–2; and medicine: K., 94, 96, 174; 'Western', 94, 95, 96; and refugees, 177, 208–9, 217, 286; and tattooing, 90, 91, 93–4
Bassein, 353
Bastion, 11–12, 228–31, 233, 261, 282, 284

Ba U Gyi, 26, 27, 84, 102, 203, 306; death of, 30, 290, 334; Four Principles of, 50; portrait of, 376
Beho, *see* agriculture (kapok)
Beijing, 354
Bengal, Bay of, 196, 198
Bengalis, 209, 211
Beryte, Bishop of, 197
Betel, *see* agriculture
Bible: translations, 222–3, 233; in K. verse, 226–7; and Golden Book, 231, 227–31
Birthing, 98; and 'Family Life', 99, 151; male midwives, 98, 152–3
Bismarck and Judith, 199–201, 215–16
Boarders, Boys, 38, 116–17, 145, 172, 252, 311, 323, 336, 361, 363, 366; Girls, 141, 142–5, 146–51, 155–60, **158**, 170–1, 173, 178, 244, 254, 267–8, 296, 309–10, 331, 364, 372; *see also* orphans
Boardman, G. and Mrs, 221–2, 231
Boar Tusk, *see* Toh Meh Pah
Bock, Carl: on tattoos, 90, 91; on guns, 113; on Mekok (river), 183; on portraits, 376
Bodawpaya, King of Ava, 279
Bowring treaty, 188
Bright Star, 184–5
British, xv, xix, 4, 6, 14, 17–18; East India Co, 16; Burma Corps, 22; in nineteenth century Burma, 17–18; Burma Rifles, 22, 30, 298; Burma Wars (nineteenth century), 17, 20–1, 22, 24, 112, 221; and cattle, 355; Chindits, 23; 340; and forestry, 25, 80, 353; Frontier Areas Commission of Enquiry, 25; and Burmese independence, 25–6; and K. Central Organisation, 25; and 'Kawthoolei', 24; colonial morals, 260, 384, ch 13 n 4; and 'orphans', 20, 146; and rice production, 266; and Saya San rebellion, 266; 'teak wallahs', 130; and tolls, 351; and village headmen, 43; *see also* World War Two
British Institute of Recorded Sound, xx
Buddhists, 18, 21, 46, 47, 72, 83, 142, 223, 246, 331, 360; and birthing, 98; conversion of, 222; education, 142, 223; as farmers, 38; monastic script, 231; old music, 327; refugees, 269
Bunker, A.: on old script, 220; K. translations, 226; K. mistreatment of, 351
Burma/Burmese, 13, 14, 16; airforce, 28, 48, 363–5; atrocities, 26, 106, 108, 293, 346, 360–1, 362; B. Communist Party, 25–6, 28, 156; *B. Days* (Orwell), 111–12; B./Siam wars, 112; B. Service of the BBC, 139, 241; B. wars in nineteenth century, (*see* under British); exports ivory, 381 ch 8 n 4; *Handbook on B.*, 15, 25–6;

B.Gazetteer, 22, 141, 205, 227, 275; immorality of, 256–7; Independence, 26; B. Indep. Army, 23; and K. dance, 9; and K. literacy, 142, 230; and K. racial cohesion, 234–5, 261; and K. rebellion, 28; military offensive against K., 73, 80, 163, 172, 181–2, 201, 218–19, 314–15, 361–71, 377; and missionaries, 222, 285–7; rebellion of (1988), 376; rice production, 263, 266; Saya San rebellion, 22; spies, 48, 218, 267, 364–5; *Sun* newspaper, 223; and tattooing, 90, 91; and teachers, 41, 310; and timber trade (Bombay-Burmah Trading Co, 39; Union of, 25, 298, 307; *see also* language, music
Bwe Karen, 15, 220, 232, 260

Cakraw, *see* Sgaw Karen
Cady J.: on K. rebellion, 285
Caltrops, *see* weapons
Cambodia (Kampuchea), 15, 16, 160, 187, 285
Campbell, R.: on forests, xvii
Cargo Cult, 290, 385 ch 15 n 7
Cattle ranching, 355, 356
Cekosi, *see* tattooing
Central Asian Society, 24, 278
Chai (broken taboo), 246
Chiang Mai, 186, 190, 191, 192, 241, 260, 351
Chiang Rai, 183
Chin (people), 90, 383 ch 12 n 7
China/Chinese, 14, 90, 105, 112, 350, 356
Chindits, *see* British
Christianity, 14, 18, 21, 46–7, 48, 142, 222, 223, 227, 232, 311; K. Christian Relief Committee, 202; *see also* Baptists, missionaries
Christie, A.: on bronze drums, 4; on Roman envoys, 197
Chulalongkorn, King of Siam, 37, 187, 188, 189
Churchill, W., 24
Cochin-China, 16
Coedès, G.: on bronze drums, 4; on migrants, 13; on position of women, 152; on language, 232
Collis, M.: on forests; xvii; on Maw Daung pass, 197
Common Prayer and Psalms, Book of, 222
Communications: by elephant, 31–2, 69, 131, 163, 267, 339, 342; Morse code, 223; radio, 203, 314, 369; railway, 196, 229; river, 78–81; roads: Burma–China Highway, 32, 229; logging, 32, 80–1, 354; trade caravans, 351, 354–5; telegraph, 30

Communism: Burmese C. Party, 28, 105–6;
    Communist Party of Thailand, 189, 198;
    and longhouses, 207; in rebellion, 26, 28;
    and swidden farming, 105; World Anti-
    Communist League, 294
Conti, Nicolo di: visits Mergui, Tenasserim,
    197
Courrèges-Clerq, P., 290
Courtship, see Kinship
Crawfurd, Dr. J., 360–1
Crossbows, see weapons

Dacoits, 22, 92, 116
Dances, traditional, 6–10
Dawina Hills, 28, 72, 120
Deirdre, Pipi, 41–2, 282
Delta Karen, 7, 23, 27, 29, 269, 275–6;
    educated Revolutionaries, 3, 43, 52, 54,
    120, 141, 215, 234, 254, 296, 349, 358;
    loose morals of, 256; Sgaw, 232; teachers,
    155, 298
Devourer of the Country, 22, 40–1, 304, 379,
    ch 1 n 1
Dictionary, Anglo-K., 223, 294
Drugs: narcotic, 106, 107, 189, 191–2,
    203–4, 218, 279; medicinal, 94–5, 96–7,
    344
Drums, bronze, 1, 4–6
Durand, Sir Mortimer: on 'insects of the
    hills', 18
Dyaks, 90, 206

Education, 141–2, 368; of boys, 116–17; of
    girls, 155–6; and language, 232, 234,
    235–6; and music, 330; schools, 330;
    teachers, 334; upgrading course, 311–14,
    323
Edward, 2, 32, 40, 52, 241, 282, 296–319;
    and Departmental conflict, 296, 316; and
    guns, 115–16, 303, 315; and language,
    235, 241, 302; on mercenaries, 290; and
    music, 332, 334; and nurse training,
    155–7
Ee U, Naw (and Ther Ner, Saw), 230
Elephants, 4, 25, 32, 38, 69, 80, 128–34, **129**,
    163, 176, 191, 267, 284, 339, 342, 353–4;
    in war, 130–1, 381 ch 8 n 3; ivory
    poaching, 381 ch 8 n 4; trappers, 132,
    135–6 (and musical instruments), 135,
    136–8

Far Eastern Economic Review, 363
Flowerland (Kawthoolei), xvi, 379 preface
    n 2
Food, 276–6, 280; family meals, 271–2; fish,
    280–1; imported, 275; lizards, 181, 277;

monkey, 276, 280; pork feasts, 273, **274**,
    314; prawns, 163, 168; rice, 263–4, 271–2;
    ritual and taboos, 273, 277; snakes, 276;
    wedding, 247–8, 250
Forests, xvi–xviii, 173, 175, 179, 350–5;
    decline of, 354–6, 357–8, 386 ch 18 n 6;
    exotic woods in, 188; fires, xvi, 167–9,
    170–1, 204, 382 ch 10 n 3; and K., 348,
    353; Thais in, 355; teak, xvi–xvii, 25, 353;
    'Teak Wallahs' 80, 130, 176, 205; warfare
    in, 340; see also agriculture (swidden)
Forestry Department, see Government
    Departments
'Four Cuts', see Ne Win
Frederick, Ceasar, 112
French: pre-nineteenth century influence,
    16–17, 128, 130; and Cambodian tribes,
    285; and KNLA, 359; medical teams, 32,
    48, 186, 288 (Médecins Sans Frontières),
    290–1; mercenaries, 262, 290, 292; and
    Royal Ordnance Factory (Ava), 113

Gandasena, Nai C.: on Karen, 188; on Red
    Karen marriage, 245
Germans, 183, 185
    Thai-German Hilltribe Development
    Project, 186
Gilmore, D. C.: *Grammar of the Sgaw Karen*,
    220
Gobi Desert 13, 379, ch 2 n 1
Golden Book 221, 228; myth and restoration
    of 'the Book', 228–31; verse compilation
    (Htoo La E), 228–9; vocabulary of 233,
    and Htoo La E, 240
Golden Horn (*Ta Nuh Tuh* – newssheet), 241
Golden Triangle, 183
Government Departments, Kawthoolei/
    KNU: Agriculture, 41; Education, 10,
    32–3, 36, 40, 47, 50, 103, 298, 300, 301,
    309, 314, 317, 332, 334; Finance, 40, 298,
    300, 316, 317; Forestry, 41, 130, 370;
    Health and Welfare, 32, 40, 70, 84, 96,
    98, 99, 101, 144, 151, 156, 240, 356, 357;
    Information (Organisation/Propaganda),
    40, 47, 61, 100, 156, 241; Mines, 356;
    Transport, 40–1, 240–1
Great Lake, 40, 118–124, 280; as boatman,
    60, 79, 124–5, 138–40, 175, 255, 256, 266,
    267, 378; makes gun, 113; and K., 120–1,
    122; and language, 130, 139–40, 234, 236,
    237; Lili, wife of, 119, 121–2, 124, 125–6,
    127, 134, 140; and lizard traps, 121; and
    maidens, 159, 171; and music, 138; and
    Red Star, 132, 134–8; and rhymes, 137,
    281, 343; and trading, 126–8, 175; and
    Yodoyamai Cordial, 118–19, 122, 123
Gurkhas, 340

Gunpowder, *see* weapons
Gyi, Bo, 317

Hall, D. G. E.: on elephants and rebels, 130
Hamilton, J. G.: and K. Music, 323
Harvest Moon, 2, 34, 218, 249, 254
Headquarters, District (KNU), 56; armoury
 at, 111–12; communications with, 203;
 debates at, 156, 297; military instructors
 from, 116; and Riverside, 31, 98;
 schoolchildren from, 58
Headquarters, Kawthoolei General (KNU),
 40, 44, 47, 54, 98, 124, 151, 215, 260, 292,
 334; Burmese munitions at, 366; and
 Education course, 312; and elephants,
 133; Health Department doctors at, 54,
 101, 128, 295; and Col Marvel, 309; and
 morality, 255; munitions at, 111–12; and
 recruitment of women (military), 153;
 (nursing), 157; teacher training, 310
Henderson, E., 383 ch 12 n 1
Health Unlimited, xiv
Highlander, 41, 54, 90, 297, 365; on
 ideology, 105–6; on judicial system, 107;
 on K. isolation, 294, 374; on morality,
 255, 260; on news and propaganda, 241;
 on opium and guns, 107–8
Hill trekking (tourism), 191, 284, 287
Hilltribes, xv, xviii, 18, 184–5; *see also* under
 tribal names: Karen, Lua, etc.
Hla Pe, 353–4
Hmong (people), 189
Htoo La E, *see* Golden Book
Huc, R-E.: on travel in Tibet, 13–14

Indian Civil Service (ICS), 205, 206–7
Insein, 26–7, 30, 307, 363
International Labour Organisation, 295
'Introduction to the Study of Sgaw Karen',
 see Kan Gyi
Ivory, 381, ch 8 n 4

Jakay, Bo, 27, 102
Janice and Two Shoes, 39, 45, 180, 210–11,
 216, 257
Japan, *see* World War Two
Java/nese, 206
Jones, R. B.: on k. language, 383 ch 12 n 7
Judson, Adonirum, 221–2, 231; College,
 142; Mrs, 221, (quoted on K.), 18; (on K.
 drunkenness), 278

Kachin (people), 28, 222, 233, 383 ch 12 n 7
Kalimantan, 206
Kan Gyi, Saya: 'Introduction to the Study
 of Sgaw Karen', 220, 224–6, 233, 235, 239
Kapok, *see* agriculture

Karen (*var.* Carian, Carianer, Cariani,
 Karian, Kariang, Karien, Karieng,
 Yang), 15, 16, 17, **19**, 184, 189, 191;
 anthem, 25; betrayal by British, 22, 25,
 30, 290; K. Baptist History, 21; and
 Burmese, 23, 27 234–5, 236–7, 261, 375;
 character of, 18, 102, 104, 188; 'Cattle of
 the hills', 17, 348; dances, 6–10; dress, 1,
 2, 38, 58, 87, 121, 123, 186, 248–9, 372;
 drunkenness, 18, 278; and 'flight'
 mythology, 14, 187; as farmers, *see*
 agriculture; forebears of, 230; and
 foreigners, 284–5, 286–9, 303; in forests,
 348, 353–6; gardens of, 42, 70, 90, 177;
 and gifts, 286–7; hospitality, 186, 272–3,
 282; humour, 237–9; hygiene, 36–7;
 isolation of, 294, 298; literacy, 220, 221,
 223, 246, 311; literature, *see* language,
 lyrics, Golden Book; as Lost Tribe of
 Israel, 14, 230–1, 285; and mining, *see* tin
 mining; morality, *see* kinship; national
 identity, 235, 254, 294–5, 373–4; New
 Year, 1–3, 10, 38, 84, 273; origins, 13–15,
 112; Hun thesis, 380 ch 2 n 4; and
 passports, 294, 386 ch 15 n 7; proper
 names, xvi; 'pwakenyaw', 120–1, 380 ch 2
 n 3; subgroups of *see also* Bwe, Delta, Pwo,
 Sgaw, Karenni; in Thailand, 7, 194–5,
 235; *see also* British, Burmese, Dress,
 Education, Food, Kawthoolei; Language,
 Moo Troo, Music, Stories, Villages,
 Women
Karen Central Organisation, 25
Karen Christian Relief Committee, 202
Karen Cultural Committee, 239
Karen National Association, 24, 234, 239
Karen National Defence Organisation
 (KNDO), 26, 83, 176, 212, 290, 307, 316,
 357, 364
Karen National Liberation Army (KNLA),
 2, 28–9, 204, 212–13, 344, **369**; brigade
 status, 368; camps of, 213–14, 347, 349;
 and elephants, 130, 132, 339; and forest
 spirits, 348–9; insignia, 3, 38, 187, 213; in
 jungle warfare, 357–8; and mercenaries,
 290, 293; nurses (military), 151; porters,
 349; recruits, 50, 116, 368; (women), 368;
 rice supplies, 265–6; and river, 79–80; and
 torture, 108; fight Burmese, 28, 166, 198,
 219, 314, 361–2, 365–6; in Western
 Valley, 347; *see also* weapons
Karen National Liberation Council, 308
Karen National Union (KNU), 25–26, 27,
 28, 105, 288, 315, 362; Bulletin, 215, 220,
 294; and Burmese rebels (1988), 375;
 calenders, 7, 88; declares K.
 Independence, 22; and diet, 277–8; and

education, 143; and health care provision, 97–8; and morality, *see* Kinship; recruitment, 53–4; and refugees, 208; and sabotage, 109; taxes, 346; and torture, 107–8; and trade (especially cattle and tin), 355, 356–7; and K. typeface, 242; and U Nu, 308; in Western Valley, 347; *see also* Government Departments, Kawthoolei, women

Karen New Words Committee, 239–40

Karenni (Kayah, Red Karen), 15, 21, 28, 245, 261, 278, 353

Kawthoolei, xviii–xix, 2, 24, 27, 142, 234, 266–7, 298, 333, 337, 374, 379 preface n 2; alcohol in, 279; Kawthoolei K. Baptist Convention, 47, 240; Boundary Commission on, 27; border tolls, 28–9, 80–1; *see also* trade; elephants in, 130–1, 133–4; flag of, 1, 6, 33; health care in, 97–8; literacy in, *see* education; Martyrs' Day, 38, 328; National Day, 364; national identity of, 232, 236, 254, 294–5, 299; organisation of State, 38–9; population of, 29; president of, 28, 44; Refugee Committee, 202; and refugees, 215, 217–8; subgroups in, 16, 230; traditional values in, 217, 303; war situation, xix, 28–9, 375

Kayah, *see* Karenni

Kemuh ('Chinese Karen'), 4

Keyes, C. F.: on exogamy, 261, 384 ch 13 n 3; on missions and rebellion, 285

Kinship: adultery, 258–61; courtship, 245–6, 252–3; endogamy, 261–2; and Burmese 261; exogamy, 262, 384, ch 13 n 4; homosexuality, 255–6; inheritance, 57; morality, 58, 217, 245–6, 255–6; polygamy, 257; pre-marital sex, 244; prostitution, 256; weddings, 246–51, **251**, 252, 253–4

Ko Tha Byu, 222

Kok River (Mekok), 183

Kra, Isthmus of, 196, 197, 198

Kunstadter, P.: (*et al.*) on forest fires, 382, ch 10 n 3; on swiddening, 382, interlude n 6; on K. rice consumption, 263; on conversions and medicine, 288; on race and confrontation, 373; on cargo cults, 385, ch 15 n 7

Ku Wah, 6, 7, 10, 54, 57, 118, 196, 243, 331–3, 336

Lahu (people), 4, 184, 185, 191 conversions among, 222, 227

Land mines, *see* weapons

Language, Burmese, 221, 222, 224, 234–5

Language, English, xix; in schools, 309, 311–14; KNU Bulletin, 185, 241

Language, Karen: 'Anglo-K. Dictionary', 223, 224; British attitude to, 224; and Burmese language, 234–5; 'Introduction to Study of Sgaw K.', *see* Kan Gyi; linguistic jokes, 237–9; literature, 226–31; 'lost writing' myth, 220–1; and nationality, 226, 234–7; New Words Committee, 239–40; origins of, 220–1, 383 ch 12 n 7; Pwo Karen, 38, 223, 231, 232, 234; Rangoon Karen, 234; script, 220, 221, 223, 231, 374; Sgaw Karen, 38, 141, 220, 221, 223, 224, 231, 232, 234; structure of, 237–40; in Tavoy, 232; typeface and printing, 223, 241–2; variants, 232; *see also* education, Golden Book, lyrics, stories

Language, Thai, 235; lack of, in Kawthoolei, 45, 235–6

Lao (people), 90

Laos, 16, 103, 189, 374

Leach, E. R.: on cultural differences, 233; on migration theories, 379, ch 2 n 1; on settlement patterns, 386 ch 18 n 4

Leke sect, 231

Le May, R.: on wildlife in forests, xvii; on missionaries and Thai K., 285; on trading, 351; on 'Devourer of the Country', 379 ch 1 n 1; on drums, 379 ch 1 n 2; on tattooing, 92; on white morals, 384 ch 13 n 4

Let Ya, 308

Levi-Strauss, C.: on longhouse culture, 383 ch 11 n 12

Lisu (people), 128

Longhouses, 205–7, 259, 383 ch 11 n 6 and 12; sawmill at Maw Daung, 207–8

Lonsdale, M.: on Karen State, 25; on Declaration of Independence of Burma, 26

Lost Tribes of Israel, *see* Karen

Lost Writing myths, *see* language

de la Loubère, S.: on elephants, 131

Low, Capt J.: on K. huts, 73; on captives in Siam, 109; on elephants, 133; on K. dress, 256; on racial purity, 261; on tortoise hunting, 276; on forestry, 353; on gunpowder, 381 ch 7 n 3; on K. dialects, 383 ch 12 n 7

Lua (people), 128

Luce, G. H.: on migrations, 379 ch 2 n 1; on name 'Karen', 379 ch 2 n 2; on tattooing, 90; on K. script, 221

Lunet de Lajonquière, Capt. E.: on hill K., 18; on Baptist convert, 21; on dirtiness of K., 37; on elephant transport, 129–30; on

Lunet de Lajonquière, Capt. E. (*contd.*)
K. in Siam, 187; on K. and Thai
language, 235; on eating habits, 263, 264;
on tourists, 287; on K. in forest, 348
Lyrics: *titles (traditional)*; Kwe Ke Baw
(mountain), 54, 322; 'Heirs of our
Costume', 118; 'Pwa Ter Moh (woman in
Thailand)', 137; 'Tuh Ploh Wah (split
loyalties)', 137; 'Do Puh Weh (Brothers
and Sisters)', 196, 322; 'War Song', 206;
'Y'wa is Eternal', 226; 'Y'wa formed the
World (The Fall)', 226; 'Repent our Sins',
226; 'White Sons of Y'wa', 226; 'Look out
to Sea', 227; 'Saw Ter Kwa (Lovers)',
243, 330; 'Little Girl!', 262; 'When the
Moon is Shining', 330; 'When the stones
float on water', 359; *titles (modern/
revolutionary)*; 'Our Flag', 6; 'Moulmein,
Tavoy', 27; 'O Blessed Land', 61; 'I Love
You, K. Girl', 63; 'Forward K. Soldiers',
117; 'The Mountain's Beauty (Come to
Us!)', 237; 'God Bless You', 326; 'going
to the Front', 329–30; 'Love and Duty',
240, 330, 334; 'Darkness to Light', 334;
'Kawthoolei, my Beloved Land', 338;
Misc.: 'The Lord's Chosen' (anthem), 25;
'One Man and a Dog', 314; 'The Royal
Telephone', 323; 'Scarborough Fair', 329;
'The Bold Fenian Men', 329, 337; 'Other
peoples have sweet water', 324; 'We Are
The People', 333

McCoy, A. W.: read by True Love, 63; on
U Nu rebellion, 198; on Lahu
conversions, 222, 227
MacMahon, Lt. Col. A. R.: on drums, 5, 6;
on K. origins, 380 ch 2 n 2; on K.
physique, 15; quotes Mrs. Judson, 18,
278; on K. gunpowder, 113, 381 ch 7 n 3;
on elephant decoration, 128; on K.
elephants, 130; on old K. script, 220; on
K. literacy, 223; on K. humour, 238; on
British colonial morals, 260; on K. eating
habits, 263; on K. and rice, 264; on edible
snakes, 276; on K. and foreigners, 284; on
harmoniums, 323, 386 ch 17 n 2; on trade
tolls, 351
Madras, 197
Mae Suai (river), 184, 186
Mahn Ba Zan, 44
Malacca (and Straits of), 196, 197
Malaria, 44, 99, 144, 149, 172, 176, 180, 181,
185, 198, 322, 348, 375
Malaysia, 176, 216, 356
Manerplaw, 124
Mao Zedong, 308
Marco Polo, 90, 112

Marijuana, *see* drugs
Marshall, Rev H. L.: describes K., 18; on
K. nicknames, xx; on K. villages, 70; on
'blowing magic', 95–6; on crossbows, 114;
on outcasts (orphans), 146; on K. seasons,
161; on K. longhouses, 205; quotes K. war
song, 206; on K. language, 232; on
arranged marriages, 245; on K.
transvestites, 256; on music of converts,
322; on measuring distance, 339; on K.
war parties, 366; on K. drums, 379 ch 1
n 2
Marvel, Colonel, 2, 40, 44, 100–1, 104, 161,
235, 288, 304–9, **305**, 317, 378; borrows
boat, 124–5; and Burmese attacks, 315,
362; and Edward, 315–18; on K.
Revolution Day, 304; at Maw Daung,
201–4, 362
Mason, F.: and Pwo K. script, 223, 231;
founds *Morning Star*, 223; and K.
language, 224; translates K. verse, 226–7;
pro-K., 242
Matisoff, J.: on bilingual jokes, 237; on
language structure, 239; on family of
languages, 383 ch 12 n 7
Maw Daung: Burmese attacks, 198, 219,
365, 369; militia at, 212–13, **213**, 218;
other rebels at, 209, 211, 216–17; Pass:
history of, 196–8; refugees at, 201–5,
207–11, 244, 316
Maymyo (air base), 364
Médecins Sans Frontières, *see* French
Medicine: traditional, 94, 95, 96, 174,
187–8, 341; (Thai), 94–5; 133
Western, 95–6, 180; (Burmese), 97,
288–9, (aid workers and), 286, 288–9
Mekok, *see* Kok
Mercenaries: pre-twentieth century, 289
in K. revolution, 106–7, 289–94
Mergui, 27, 214, 218; District, 76; port, 197,
198
Midwives, *see* birthing
Mining, *see* tin mining
Missionaries
Australian Pentecostalists, 282–4, **283**,
286–7, 312, 328; Gary (Word
International), 286; Sally (Californian),
286; Catholic (early), 17; and rebellion,
285; *see also* Baptists
Mon (people), 13, 20, 279, 356; in rebellion,
28, 209; and tattooing, 92; monks and
script, 221; and exogamy, 261
Months, K. calendar, 382 ch 10 n 1
Moo Troo, Saw: on K. dancing, 6–7; on K.
indentity, 11; on 'flight' of K., 14; on K.
and common ownership, 105, 265; on
moral values, 161, 217; eight attributes of

K., 232, 384 ch 12 n 10; on K. language, 239; on courtship, 245; on adultery, 259; on K. hospitality, 282; on K. music, 320
Morning Star (newspaper), 223
Morning Star, 40, 96, 98–9
Morrison, I: on K. and parachute cloth, 24; on recompense to K., 24
Morrison, W. S. (*Burma Gazetteer*): on crossbow darts, 114; on village schools, 141–2; on K. and alcohol, 278
Moses, Pastor, 40, 46, 103–4, **225**, 318, 330, 372; on British, 30; at Insein, 26–7; on tattooing, 92; on K. language, 239; performs weddings, 250, 254; on Burmese rice controls, 266; and fish paste, 281; and Australians, 284; on Burmese attacks, 314, 361, 362; on excavations at Prome, 374; on longhouse dwellers, 383 ch 11 n 11
Mouhot, H.: on 'Karians', 18; on 'Hebrews' in Indo-China, 385 ch 15 n 3; on letters from home, 377
Moulmein, 26, 27, 183, 257, 344
Music, Karen: concerts, *see* Riverside
    at deaths, 327–8
    decline of, 322–3
    instruments: drum (bronze), 1, 2, 3–6, 321; flute (bamboo) 321; harp (Jews) 135, 137–8, 321; harp (strung) 136–7, 321; horn, 1–2, 138, 321; mouth organ (bamboo) 321, 322; marching songs, 326–7; modern, 325–6, 333; Revolutionary, 334; role of sexes in, 332–3; in schools, 326, 328–9, 331–2; songs, *see* lyrics; traditional, 322, 329, 332; at weddings, 248–9
Music, Western: British military, 325, 326; Christian, 48, 224, 322–3, 324–6; Country and Western, 61, 323–5, 331; pop, 38, 327, 330–1; Revolutions, 320–1, 329–30; Victorian, 281
Muslims: in Kawthoolei, 211; Kawthoolei Muslim Liberation Front. 78
Mya, Gen Bo (KNLA), 44, 47, 316; and communists, 105; establishes KNLA, 28; enforces morality, 255, 260–1; loyalty of K. soldiers to, 287; President of Kawthoolei, 28; Seventh Day Adventist, 28; Wife, and Womens Organisation, 153
Myanmar, xx–xxi; *see also* Burma
Myawaddi, Battle of, 28, 30, 44, 84

National Democratic Front, 105
Narathrip, Prince: on K., 348
Nerini, Father, 17
Ne Win, 28, 29, 103, 198, 212, 234–5, 299, 308, 375; Four Cuts policy, 28, 51, 204, 288, 344

Nicaragua, 106, 115, 321, 330, 334
Nolan, Maj: on K. and music, 320
Nurses, 97–98, 99, 100, 145, 151, 155–7 military, 44, 99, 151
Nu, U, 198, 308
Nwedaung, drum making at, 379 ch 1 n 2

Observer 130–5, 288, 274 n 7
Oliver, Col (KNLA), 2, 314, 363, 366
Orphans, 144–5; in K. mythology, 13–14, 20, 146, 216; *see also* Boarders
Orwell, G.: on Baptist converts, 18; on 'teak wallahs', 80; on arms of rebels, 111–12, 114; on British morals, 384 ch 13 n 4

Pa-an, 379 preface n 2, 108, 233, 375
Pagan, 197, 221, 289
Palaw, 27
Pallava script, 221
Pa-o Karen, 15, 83, 383 ch 11 n 6
Papun, 23, 120, 233
Parachuap Khiri Khan, 197, 218, 219
Passports, 284, 386 ch 15 n 8
Payor, Pu, 149–51, 377
Po, Sir San Crombie: on a K. state, 24, 25
Preecha Chaturabhand: on K. temperament, 102; on K. and Thai language, 235; on happiness, 284; on K. spokesmen, 294–5; on K. insularity, 295
Prisoners, 40, 141; of war, 109; women, 260
Prome, 374
Pwo Karen, 15–16, 285
    see also language
Pyu (ancient people), 15, 221

Radley, P: on traps, 121
Rangoon, 12, 20, 142, 199, 256; Judson College, 142; Rangoon-K. language, 234; in rebellion, 27; rebels' provenance, xv, 12, 38, 46, 53, 54, 101, 141, 190, 199, 233; in Second Burma War, 20; University of, 24
Rebellion/revolution (of K. against govt. of Burma), xv, 5, 43, 57, 122, 125, 279, 355; and Christianity, 45–6, 285, 324; and courtship and marriage, 246, 252; and education, 116, 310–1; and health care, 97–8; history of, 25–8; jungle warfare, 357–8 guerrillas, 29, 107; language of, 232; organisation of K. state in, 43–4; rations, rice and salt, 267–9; K. Revolution Day, 304; river, role in, 78–81; situation in 1980s, xv, 29, 299, 371; war as source of stress, 367, 368–70; *see also* Burmese, mercenaries, weapons, women
Red Karen, *see* Karenni

Red Star, 132–8; and musical instruments, 135, 321

Refugees, 166, 199–202, 207–11; (Burmese) 217; camps on Burma-Thai border, 194–5; *see also* Maw Daung

Renard, R. D.: on drum making, 379 ch 1 n 2; on orphans, 146; on K. and forest trade, 188; on K. flight, 216; on decline of forests, 353, 386 ch 18 n 6

Rhodes James, R.: on Chindits and hilltribes, 23–4, 380 ch 2 n 12; in Burmese jungle, 340

Rice: and Burmese, 184, 265, 266; K. consumption of, 263–4; (for comfort), 339; decline in production of, 266; Planting Dance, 7; rations, 43, 267–9; and refugees, 208–9; in Revolution, 267, 269; *see also* agriculture

Richardson, Dr. David 18

Richardson, D. (evangelist): on Captain Symes' meeting with K., 17; on K. verse, 227

River, 65–9, 78–81, 166, 171–2, 175, 178–9, 180; *see also* communications, KNLA, wildlife, villages

Riverside, xviii, 5, 31, **33**, 38, 42–4, 177, 223, 317, 350, 361; and Burmese attacks, 361, 362–3; concerts at, 328; as 'new town', 38–9; KNU 'family lines' and hospital, 98; Great Lake critical of, 120; houses in, 33–6; orphans in, 145; prisoners in, 40; river at, 36–7; school at, 32, 38, 47–8, 309–10, 311–14, 331, 344; Thais in, 22, 44–6; video shows, 103; women at, 153

Rogers, R. C.: on K. and British, 20–1; on food and adultery, 273

Rolley, M.: on tattoos, 90; on 'Tiger of the Delta', 93

Ruth, 296–7, 301–3, 314, 317, 319; on drums, 5; on orphans, 145; and school roof, 174; and language, 233; on exogamy, 262

Salai, Saw, 95, 126

Salween River, 13, 27

Samroiyot (Three Hundred Peaks), 196

Sangkhlaburi, hospital at, 84

Saw Moo Troo, *see* Moo Troo, Saw

Saya Kan Gyi, *see* Kan Gyi, Saya

Saya San rebellion, 22; tattooing, in 92, 266

Schools, *see* education

Schwe Tun Kya ('Tiger of the Delta'), 93

Schwedagon pagoda, 20

Scott, J. G.: on White K., 18–19; on independent K. state, 24; on K. women and washing, 37; on K. and Y'wa, 227;

on K. and funerals, 245; on edogamy, 261; on converts and music, 322–3; on drunkenness, 278

Scott O'Connor, V. C.: on guns in Siam (quote), 112; on embassies, 383 ch 1 n 2; on Tenasserim, 198

Scripts, *see* language

Seagrave, G., 385 ch 15 n 6

Seagrim, Maj Hugh, 23, 24

Secret Services, 290; (CIA) 290, 292–3, 374

Seymour-Sewell, C. A.: on guns, 112 n 1

Siedenfaden, E.: on K. origins, 15; on tattooing, 381 ch 6 n 4

Selung (pirates), 197

Sesame, *see* agriculture

Seventh Day Adventists, 47, 260, 278, 288

Sgaw Karen (people), 15–16, 122, 232, 284; Cakraw, 15, 221; *see also* Karen, language

Shan (people), xv, 185, 186, 191; and food, 276–7; and slave trade, 21, 25; and tattooing, 90; trading, 351, (opium), 107; and drums, 379 ch 1 n 2

Shwebo, 16

Siam/Siamese; Burma, war with, 16, 112, 279; captives, treatment of, 109; and drums, 4–5; and elephants, 128–9, 131; firearms in, 112; Gulf of, 196; and K., 16, 22, 187, 216, 235, 348; and K. dialects, 383 ch 12 n 7; and mercenaries (seventeenth century), 289; and missionaries, 285; Siam Society (of Bangkok), 188–9; and tattooing, 90; Tenasserim (as Siamese port), 198; and trade 188, 196–7, 354–5 (slaves), 21; *see also* Thai/Thailand

Silver, *see* True Love

Silver Book (of education), 142, 221, 298

Singapore, 196, 197, 198; Army exercises, 176

Sittang River, 122, 124

Slave Trade, *see* trade

Slim, Gen W., 23 n 11, 24

Smeaton, D. M.: origins of K., 14; 'Loyal K.', 20; K. Christianity and education, 48; K. saying quoted by, 380 ch 5 n 1; on K. violence, 102; on Burmese fear of K., 142; on K. language, 224, 232; on longhouses, 205; on K. food, 276; on K. and missionaries, 285; on K. inferiority-complex and xenophobia, 295; on K. in jungle, 358

Smuggling, 79, 186; cattle, 198, 204; drugs, 344

Snodgrass, Maj J. J.: on K. in First Burma War, 20; on Karen houses, 31, 34; on tattooing of Burmese troops, 92; on K. character, 102; on 'Carians' and alcohol,

278; on 'Carians' and jungle warfare, 357–8
Somphob Larchrojna: on K. medicine, 94 n 7
Song, *see* Music, lyrics
Spies, *see* Burma
Stern, T. (and T.A.): on tattooing, 92; on K. scripts, 231; on K. song, 245, 329; (harp song), 245; on dance troupes, 379, ch 1 n 3, 331
Stories: Po Ghweh (orphan), 66; Horn and Harp, 138; Fire and Disobedience, 167–8; Art of Adultery (Ku Naw Lay and python), 257–9; Story about Storytelling (weevils), 264–5; Flesh and Famine (New Ler Ker), 270–1; Tokay (lizard), 121; Drongos, 166; Toh Ki Baw ('Yellow Parrot'), 244
Supreme National Congress (KNU), 43, 44
Suez canal, 188
Swidden (slash-and-burn); *see* agriculture
Swithinbank, B. W.: on imported food, 275
Symes, Capt. M.: investigates K., 17

Tachard, Father: on elephants, 128 n 2, 131 n 4
Ta Maik, Pu, 231
Tattooing, 90–4, 381 ch 6 n 4 and 6; (Cekosi) 92
Taw U, Pu: on drums, 4, 5
Taungya, *see* agriculture
Tavoy, 27, 47, 222, 242, 326; T-K. language, 233
Taylor, R.: on K. ethnicity, 373
Teak, *see* forests, trade commodities
Tenasserim: hills, 28; port, 197, 198; provinces, 253; river, 204, (Little T. River), 197
Thailand/Thais, xv, xvi, 194, 196, 267, 290–1, 183–6, 188–90, (hilltribes); border with Kawthoolei, 189, 362; and Burmese against K., 315, 362, 370; Communist Party of, 189, 198; immorality of, 256; and K., 7; (exodus), 187, 188–9, 194, 202–3, 235–6, 245, 294; (refugee camps), xix, 193–5; and marijuana, 204; and missions, 285; (publications for K. in), 241; in Riverside, 45; and tattooing, 90, 91; and timber, 58, 80, 130, 181, 354–4; (sawmills) 32, 44–6, 207; and weapons, 115; and women, 192–3; *see also* Language, Siam/Siamese
Than Byah, Thera: 'Karens and Their Progress', on language, 239
Thant, U, 199–200
Thatcher, M., 104, 106, 306

Thaton, 26, 83, 221
Three Pagodas Pass, 196, 198
Tibet, 13
Timber, *see* forests, trade commodities
Tinker, H.: on 'lesser languages', 234
Tin mining, 164, 180, 356, *see also* Govt. Depts
Toh Meh Pah (Boar Tusk): K. defence band, 23; orphans of, 13, 14, 20; patent medicine, 30; return of, 216, 229, 231, 295, 375; story of, 11–12, 120
Toungoo: Bishop of, 263; District of, 122; 'Old Man of', *see* Taw U, Pu
Trade: history of (slaves), 21, 25; (guns) 112, 196–8; routes, 344, 350–2; and teachers, 310; and Thais, 45, 164, 351; tolls and K., 351–2, 355
Trade commodities: pre-nineteenth century, 197, 354–5; armaments, 344; cattle, 166, 212, 351, 355; drugs, 344, (opium) 107, 351; honey, 74, 166, 351; ivory, 381 ch 8 n 4; lizards, 74, 166; luxuries, 351; songbirds, 74, 165–6; sesame, 351, 164, 166, 351; timber, 58, 80, 351; (forest exotics) 45; videos (blue), 351
Trevor, 111, 365–6; on mercenaries, 292
True Love, 42, 52–3, **56**, 256, 292, **335**, 359–61, 362, 365, 372, 375, 378; and Edward, 39; on homosexuality, 255–6; and house, 55–8; and language, xix, 232, 234, 236, 238–9, 280, 366; and music, 61, 68, 118, 196, 243, 326, 336; Revolutionary career, 53–4, 58–61, 319, 363, 366, 370–1; river journey with, 65–78; as teacher, 53, 60–1, 319, 347; to Western Valley with, 338–50; and wife Silver, 55, 61–2, 251, 301, 313, 361, 366
Tulloch, Lt. Col. J. C.: assists KNDO insurgents, 290
Two Shoes, *see* Janice

United Nations: and indigenous populations, 294, 295; High Commission for Refugees, 208
United States Committee for Refugees, 193

Vermilion, *see* Bartholomew, family of
Verse: Baptist reducing of, 226–7; K. verse forms, 228–30; rhymes, 137, 164, 281, 343; *see also* lyrics
Vietnam/ese, 4, 16, 90, 115, 176, 189
Videos, 10, 103; of K. war, 117; of K. attack on B. ammunition dump, 366; *Aladdin*, 216; *Battle of the Bulge*, 10; *Killing Fields*, 103; *Rambo*, 103; *Streets of Fire*, 313

Villages in Kawthoolei: autonomy and
headmen, 43, 122; (on river), 69, 70–3, 79;
(in Western Valley), 343; Barterville, 31,
44, 69, **74**, 74–5, 102, 164, 166, 175, 179,
224, 255, 368; Betelwood, 49, 164, 309,
326, 338, 343. 344, 345, 347; Black Turtle,
69, 148, 154, 163, 175, 176; Bombshell,
163, 175; Durianville, 69, 269, 290;
Football Field, 356; Four Springs, 347,
348; Gold Rock, 154; Lama, 47, 48, 124,
163, 182; Moha, 176; New Fields, 369,
370; Wali, 362; White Elephant, 30, 283;
White Ponds, 76, 163, 246, 310; White
Sand, 69
Villages, North Thailand: Ban Yang, 184;
Wawi, 184
Vinton, Dr.: on militant Christianity, 21–2,
47, 285, 372; on tattooing of dacoits, 92;
mistreated by K., 351

Wa (people), xv, 336
Wade, J.: translates Bible into K., 222–3;
compiles Anglo-K. Dictionary, 223, 224;
works on Sgaw script, 231; typeface
problem, 242
Wan Kha, 195, 261
Weapons: ammunition, 114; caltrops, 110;
capture of, 114–15; crossbows, 114;
firearms, 111–12; (history of), 112–13; (K.
manufacture of), 111, 113–14;
gunpowder, 113, 381 ch 7 n 3; landmines,
73, 110, 214
Wee Maw Leh, 230
Werner, D.: on self-help village health care,
384 ch 12 n 11
Western Valley, 301, 309, 330, 338, 346;
access to, 344; District Congress at, 344;
and teachers, 310–38; walk to, 338–50; see
also villages (Betelwood, Four Springs,
Gold Rock)
White younger brother, myth of, xv, 17;
(and Golden Book), 221, 222, 227, 230
White Karen, 18
White Moon: tortured by Burmese, 346
White Rock, 1, 32, 54,260; on Burmese, 346,

and pop music, 226–7, 328, 335–6; as
teacher, 310; trading, 352
Wildlife, xvii–xviii, 348, (on river) 67–8;
centipedes, 163, 172; deer, 134, 165;
drongos, 166, 169; eagles, 67, 75, 150;
hornbills, 67, 168; landcrabs, 179; leeches,
191, 339, 341–2; lizards, 42, 68, 121, 181,
277, 355; monkeys, 68, 349; otter, 294;
rats, 162, 164; scorpions, 110, 163, 179;
squirrels, 164, 169; snakes, 68, 110, 162,
175, 179, 215; termites, 107, 172; tigers,
198, 288; turtles, 68; wild pigs, 161, 170
William, 2, 41; on adultery, 259, song by,
117; on tattooing, 91, 94; as teacher, 41,
236, 317; tells astories, 41; and wife, Bella,
41, 367–8
Wingate, Gen. O., see British (Chindits)
Wingate, Sonny, see mercenaries
Winter, R. P.: on K. refugees, 193–4, 208
n 13
Women in Kawthoolei, 152; and education,
155; and Revolution, 152–3, 154, 155; as
song collectors, 232–3; see also Boarders,
Kinship, nurses
Women's Organisation (KNU), 152–5, 272;
on home cures, 96; and homosexuality,
255–6; magazine of, 241; Sal, 154–5
Word International, 286
World War One, 358
World War Two: British airborne forces
(Chindits), 385 ch 15 n 7; Burma Railway
museum, 37; Burma, 22–3; Burma Rifles,
22, 30; Force 136, 289–90; Japanese in,
22–4, 84, 122, 198, 232; K. in, 22–5;
tattooing in, 93
Wylie, M.: on conversions, 222 n 4; on
Prayer Book, 222 n 5; K. verse
translation, 226

Yang (Thai, 'Karen') : river, 13; people, 373
Yao (people), 128
Young, Maj.: killed with Ba U Gyi, 290
Young, W. M., and conversions, 222
Yunnan (Chinese): 131; (Galloping Haw),
184; and tattooing, 90
Y'wa, 226–7, 229, 230